Richard Johnson

The renowned history of the seven champions of Christendom....

Richard Johnson

The renowned history of the seven champions of Christendom....

ISBN/EAN: 9783741182310

Manufactured in Europe, USA, Canada, Australia, Japa

Cover: Foto ©Andreas Hilbeck / pixelio.de

Manufactured and distributed by brebook publishing software (www.brebook.com)

Richard Johnson

The renowned history of the seven champions of Christendom....

THE RENOWNED HISTORY

OF

THE SEVEN CHAMPIONS
OF CHRISTENDOM;
AND THEIR SONS.

THE THREE SONS OF ST GEORGE CONTENDING WITH THE DRAGON

CHAP X PART 2

THE RENOWNED HISTORY OF THE SEVEN CHAMPIONS OF CHRISTENDOM

THE THREE SONS OF ST GEORGE CONTENDING WITH THE DRAGON

CHAP X PART 2

THE RENOWNED HISTORY OF THE SEVEN CHAMPIONS OF CHRISTENDOM

HALIFAX
MILNER & SOWERBY
SIMPKIN MARSHALL & Cº LONDON

THE
RENOWNED HISTORY
OF
THE SEVEN CHAMPIONS
OF
CHRISTENDOM:

ST. GEORGE, of ENGLAND, | ST. ANDREW, of SCOTLAND,
ST. DENIS, of FRANCE, | ST. PATRICK, of IRELAND,
ST. JAMES, of SPAIN, | AND
ST. ANTHONY, of ITALY, | ST. DAVID, of WALES;

AND THEIR SONS.

HALIFAX:
MILNER AND SOWERBY.

1862.

PREFACE.

The origin of romances is doubtful, but it appears to be of very ancient standing. Fleury is of opinion they were not known until the twelfth century. Dom Rivet fixes their origin in the tenth century; but as they appear to have sprung from the east, it is probable they may be traced much higher. The Theagenes and Chariclea of Heliodorus, a bishop who lived in the fourth century, is undoubtedly a genuine romance; and perhaps the Golden Ass of Apuleius may be quoted as a yet earlier specimen of this composition.

France and Italy have exhibited the models from which the more modern romances have been constructed; and it appears to have been the idea of their authors, that nothing was too improbable or extravagant to be admitted in these narratives. In particular they seem to have considered extreme length of story as an essential qualification, and never conceived it possible to tire the patience of their readers. Against these prolix, and often indecent and absurd works, Cervantes employed his inimitable talent for ridicule, and may have been said to have driven romances into the libraries of the curious, where alone they are now to be found.

England has given but few specimens of original romances. The work now before the reader is one of the most popular; and has maintained its popularity, although in an abridged and mutilated state, for nearly two centuries. It is now reprinted from the genuine black-letter edition, and from the last London edition of 1755, which has been long out of print; while the public demand has been generally supplied by paltry abridgments in various cheap forms.

It was written, or compiled, in the reign of James the First, by one Richard Johnson, of whom we know little more than the name. Mr. Warton is of opinion that he availed himself of the most capital fictions in the old Arabian romance, and other sources of the same kind. The popular traditions of the Seven Champions were perhaps at that time easily collected; and it may be observed, that in apportioning to each knight his share of valour, he is strictly impartial, with a reserve only in favour of his country's patron, St. George. It is yet more to his credit, that while he appears acquainted with the principal adventures in the older romances, he has carefully avoided their indelicacies, and has given a moral turn to his incidents, however extravagant they may appear.

The style of the Seven Champions is, like that of the age in which it was published, uncouth and rugged; yet the epithets and imagery are generally well chosen, and the poetical attempts are sometimes successful. Who Johnson was, is not known; but it is evident that he was intimately conversant with the ancient mythology, and with those popular fictions of all countries, from which he borrowed largely to illustrate the adventures and decorate the triumphs of his knight.

It only remains to be mentioned, that the old black-letter editions proceed no farther than to the end of the Second Part. The Third, which contains the adventures of St. George's Sons, appears to have been added by a modern hand; and in point of invention and fancy is considerably inferior to what we conceive to have been the original production of Johnson.

We shall now reprint, what has been unaccountably omitted in the later editions, Mr. Johnson's Original Dedications to the First and Second Parts, and some lines prefixed by himself.

"TO ALL COURTEOUS READERS,

"RICHARD JOHNSON

"*Wisheth Encrease of Vertuous Knowledge.*

"GENTLE readers, in kindness accept of my labours, and be not like the chattering cranes: nor Momus' mates, that carp at everything. What the simple say, I care not: what the spightful speak, I pass not: only the censure of the conceited I stand unto; that is the mark I aym at: whose good likings if I obtain, I have won my race; if not, I faint in the first attempt, and so lose the quiet of my happy goal.

"Yours in kindness to command,
"R. J."

"THE AUTHOR'S MUSE UPON HISTORY.

"The famous facts, O Mars, deriv'd from thee,
  By weary pen, and painful Author's toyl,
Enrol'd we find such feats of chivalry,
  As hath been seldom seen in any soyl.

"Thy ensigns here we find in field displaid,
  The trophies of thy victories erected;
Such deeds of armes, as none could have assaid,
  But knights whose courage fear hath ne'er dejected.

"Such ladies saved, such monsters made to fall,
  Such gyants slain, such hellish furies queld:
That human forces, few or none at all,
  In such exploits their lives could safely shield.

"But vertue stirring up their noble minds,
  By valiant conquest to enlarge their fames,
Hath caused them such adventures forth to find,
  Which registreth their never-dying names:
Then Fortune, Time, and Fame agree in this,
That honour's gain the greatest glory is."

DEDICATION TO THE SECOND PART.

"TO THE RIGHT HONOURABLE, THE LORD WILLIAM HOWARD,

"RICHARD JOHNSON

"*Wisheth Encrease of all Prosperity.*

"As it hath, right honourable, of late pleased your most noble brother[*] in kindness to accept of this History, and to grace it with a favourable countenance; so I am now emboldened to dedicate the Second Part unto your honour; which I here humbly offer to your lordship's hands, not because I think it a gift worthy the receiver, but rather that it should be as it were a witness of the love and duty which I bear to your right noble house.

"And when it shall please you to bestow the reading of these discourses, my humble request is, that you would think I wish your honour as many happy days as there be letters contained in this history.

"Thus praying for your honour's chief happiness,

"I remain
"Your honour's in all dutiful love,
"to his poor power
"R. J."

[*] This dedication does not appear in the copy now before us.

"TO THE GENTLE READER.

"I have finished the Second Part of the Champions of Christendom, for thy delight; being thereto encouraged by the great acceptance of my First Part. I will not boast of eloquence nor invention, thereby to invite thy willingness to read: only thy courtesy must be my buckler against the carping malice of mocking jesters, that being worse able to do well, scoff commonly at that they cannot mend, censuring all things, doing nothing, but (monkey-like) make apish jests at anything they see in print: and nothing pleaseth them, except it savour of a scoffing and invective spirit. Well, what these say of me, I do not care; thy delight only is my desire. Accept it, and I am satisfied; reject it, and this shall be my penance, never again to come in print. But having better hope, I boldly lead thee to the mayn, for this doubtful flood of suspicion, where I rest. Walk on in the history, as in an over-grown and ill-husbanded garden; if among all the weeds thou findest one pleasing flower, I have my wish.

"RICHARD JOHNSON."

CONTENTS.

PART I.

CHAPTER I.

The strange and wonderful birth of St. George of England. The manner of his birth, and how he was afterwards stolen from his nurse, by Kalyb, the lady of the woods. Her love to him, and her gifts. He encloses her in a rock of stone, and redeems six Christian knights out of prison 1

CHAPTER II.

Kalyb's Lamentations in the Rock; her last Will and Testament; she is torn in pieces by Spirits; with other occurrences in the cave ... 7

CHAPTER III.

St. George slays the burning Dragon in Egypt, and redeems Sabra, the king's daughter, from death. Is betrayed by Almidor, the black king of Morocco, and sent to the Soldan of Persia; where he slew two lions, and remained seven years in prison 9

CHAPTER IV.

St. Denis, the champion of France, lives seven years in the shape of a hart; and proud Eglantine, the king of Thessaly's daughter, is transformed into a mulberry-tree; but recover their former shapes by means of St. Denis's horse 23

CHAPTER V.

How St. James, the champion of Spain, continued seven years dumb for the love of the fair Jewess, and how he should have been shot to death by the maidens of Jerusalem, with other things that happened in his travels 29

CHAPTER VI.

The terrible battle between St. Anthony, the champion of Italy, and the giant Blanderon; and afterwards of his strange entertainment in the giant's castle by a Thracian lady; and what happened to him in the same castle... 35

CHAPTER VII.

How St. Andrew, the champion of Scotland, travelled into a vale of walking spirits; and how he was set at liberty by a moving fire, after his journey into Thrace, where he recovered six ladies to their natural shapes that had lived seven years in the likeness of milk-white swans; with other accidents that befel that most noble champion 44

CHAPTER VIII.

How St. Patrick, the champion of Ireland, redeemed six Thracian ladies out of the hands of thirty bloody-minded Satyrs, and of their purposed travels in pursuit of the champion of Scotland 50

CHAPTER IX.

How St. David, the champion of Wales, slew the Count Palatine in the Tartarian court; and after, how he was sent to the enchanted garden of Ormandine, wherein by magic art he slept seven years 52

CHAPTER X.

How St. George escaped out of prison in Persia, and how he redeemed the champion of Wales from the enchantment; with the tragical tale of the Necromancer, Ormandine.. 56

CHAPTER XI.

How St. George arrived at Tripoli, in Barbary, where he stole away Sabra, the king of Egypt's daughter, from the Moorish king, and how she was known to be a pure virgin by means of a lion; and what happened to him in the same adventure 66

CHAPTER XII.

How the Seven Champions arrived in Greece at the Emperor's Nuptials, where they performed many noble achievements; and how, afterwards, open wars were proclaimed against Christendom by the discovery of many Knights; and how every champion departed into his country 74

CHAPTER XIII.

How the Seven Champions of Christendom arrived with all their troops in the Bay of Portugal. The number of the Christian armies; and how St. George made an oration to the soldiers 78

CHAPTER XIV.

Of the dissensions and discord that happened among the army of the Pagans in Hungary. The battle between the Christians and the Moors in Barbary; and how Almidor, the black king of Morocco, was scalded to death in a cauldron of boiling lead and brimstone... 83

CHAPTER XV.

How the Christians arrived in Egypt, and what happened to them there. The tragedy of the designing Earl of Coventry. How Sabra was bound to the stake to be burnt; and how St. George redeemed her.

CONTENTS. xi

PAGE

Lastly, how the Egyptian king cast himself from the top of a tower and broke his neck 89

CHAPTER XVI.

How St. George, in his journey towards Persia, arrived in a country inhabited only by Maids, where he achieved many strange and wonderful adventures; also of the massacre of seven Virgins in a wood; and how Sabra preserved herself from a terrible giant 103

CHAPTER XVII.

How St. George and his lady lost themselves in a wilderness, where she was delivered of three goodly boys. The Fairy Queen's prophecy upon the children's fortunes. Of St. George's return into Bohemia, where he christened his children: and of finding his father's grave, over which he built a stately tomb 117

CHAPTER XVIII.

How St. George with his lady arrived in Egypt; of their royal entertainment in the city of Grand Cairo; and also how Sabra was crowned Queen of Egypt.. 125

CHAPTER XIX.

The bloody battle between the Christians and Persians; and how the Necromancer, Osmand, raised up, by his magic art, an army of spirits to fight against the Christians; how the six champions were enchanted, and recovered by St. George; the misery and death of the conjuror, and how the Soldan brained himself against a marble pillar 127

PART II.

CHAPTER I.

How St. George's three sons were entertained in the famous city of London; and afterwards how their mother was slain in a wood with the brambles of a thorny brake. The blessings she gave her sons. St. George's lamentation over her bleeding body. And likewise of the journey the Seven Champions intended to Jerusalem, to visit the Sepulchre of Christ 138

CHAPTER II.

Of the strange gifts that St. George's sons offered at their mother's tomb, and what happened thereupon. How her ghost appeared to them, and counselled them to the pursuit of their father. Also how the king of England installed them with the honour of knighthood, and furnished them with the habiliments of war 143

CHAPTER III.

How St. George's sons, after they were knighted by the English king, travelled towards Barbary; and how they redeemed the Duke's daughter of Normandy from defilement, that was assailed in a wood by three tawny Moors 146

CHAPTER IV.

Of the adventures at the golden fountain in Damasco. How six of the Christian champions were taken prisoners by a mighty giant; and how, afterwards, they were delivered by St. George. And also how he redeemed fourteen Jews out of prison. With divers other strange incidents that happened 149

CHAPTER V.

Of the Champions' return to Jerusalem; and afterwards how they were almost famished in a wood; and how St. George obtained them food by his valour in a giant's house.. 157

CHAPTER VI.

What happened to the champions after they had found an image of fine crystal in the form of a murdered maiden; where St. George had a gold book given him, wherein was written the true tragedies of two Sisters. Likewise how the champions intended a speedy revenge upon the Knight of the Black Castle for the deaths of the two ladies 162

CHAPTER VII.

A wonderful and strange adventure that happened to St. George's sons, in the pursuit of their father, by finding certain drops of blood, with virgin's hair scattered in the field; and how they were informed of the injurious dealings of the Knight of the Black Castle against the Queen of Armenia 168

CHAPTER VIII.

Of the preparations that the Knight of the Black Castle made by Magic Art to withdraw his enemies; and how the Seven Champions entered the castle, where they were enchanted into a deep sleep so long as seven lamps burned; which could not be quenched but by the water of an enchanted fountain.. 176

CHAPTER IX.

How St. George's three sons, after their departure from the Queen of Armenia's sepulchre, in company of her daughter Rosana, met with a wild man, with whom there happened a strange adventure 186

CHAPTER X.

How St. George's three sons and Rosana entered the Black Castle: where they quenched the lamps, and awaked the Seven Champions of Christendom after they had slept seven days upon an enchanted bed 189

CHAPTER XI.

How, after the Christian knights were gone to bed in the Black Castle, St. George was awakened from his sleep in the dead time of the night, in a most fearful manner; and likewise how he found a knight lying upon a tomb that stood over a flaming fire 195

CHAPTER XII.

Of a tragical discourse pronounced by a lady in a tomb, and how her enchantment was finished by St. George 197

CHAPTER XIII.

How the Knight of the Black Castle, after conquest of the same by the Christian Champions, wandered up and down the world in great terror of conscience; and how he was found in a wood by his own daughter, in whose presence he desperately slew himself 202

CHAPTER XIV.

How the magician found Leoger's armour hanging upon a pine-tree, kept by Rosana the queen's daughter of Armenia, between whom happened a terrible battle; also of the desperate death of the lady 208

CHAPTER XV.

How the Seven Champions of Christendom restored the Babylonian king unto his kingdom; and how honourably they were received at Rome, where St. George fell in love with the Emperor's daughter 211

CHAPTER XVI.

Of the triumphs, tilts, and tournaments, that were solemnly held in Constantinople by the Grecian Emperor; and of the honourable adventures that were there achieved by the Seven Champions 219

CHAPTER XVII.

How a Knight with two heads tormented a beautiful Maiden, that had betrothed herself to the Emperor's son of Constantinople; and how she was rescued by St. George's Sons; and how they were brought by a strange adventure into the company of the Christian Champions 224

CHAPTER XVIII.

Of the praiseworthy death of St. Patrick; how he buried himself; and for what cause the Irishmen to this day, wear their red cross upon St. Patrick's day 233

CHAPTER XIX.

Of the honourable victory won by St. David in Wales; of his death, and the cause why leeks are by custom, worn on St. David's day, by Welshmen 235

CHAPTER XX.

How St. Denis was beheaded in his own country, and by a miracle shown at his death, the whole kingdom of France received the Christian Faith 237

CHAPTER XXI.

Of the infamous death the Spanish Champion was put to 239

CHAPTER XXII.

The honourable and worthy death of the Italian Champion 240

CHAPTER XXIII.

Of the Martyrdom of St. Andrew, the Scottish Champion 242

CHAPTER XXIV.

Of the adventure performed by St. George: how he received his death by the sting of a venomous Dragon.. 243

PART III.

CHAPTER I.

The great joy of the Infidels at the death of the Seven Champions. The Soldan of Persia's letter for the mustering up of an army; with the effects thereupon 245

CHAPTER II.

How St. George's three sons left England to seek adventures in Foreign Countries; how they arrived in Sicily, and killed a terrible monster, named Pongo; how Urania, the king of Sicily's daughter, fell in love with Sir Guy; with other things which happened................... 249

CHAPTER III.

How Sir Guy took his leave of the Princess Urania; the battle between the Sicilians and Thracians; the message of the Princess Mariana to the enchanted castle, and how Sir Alexander courted the Princess 259

CHAPTER IV.

The great battle between the three English Knights and the Sicilians on the one side, and the three Giants and Count Brandami on the other side; the finishing of an adventure of the Enchanted Castle; with the story of the wicked Sir Vuylen 263

CHAPTER V.

How Sir Guy conducted the army of Sicilians into their own country, and Sir Alexander that of the Thessalians; how, hearing of the great preparation of the Infidels, they returned into Christendom, to raise forces to withstand them.. 274

CHAPTER VI.

How the Christian army assembled together in Naples: the Oration of Sir Guy unto the soldiers; and how they marched against the Pagan army 277

CHAPTER VII.

How the Seven Champions, being raised from their graves, resolved to follow the Christian army; how by a tempest they were cast upon the coast of Thessaly. The great battle fought between the Thessalians. How afterwards they went to the Christian army, and of the great battle fought between the Christians and Pagans............ 281

CHAPTER VIII.

How Sir Turpin of France, Sir Predo of Spain, Sir Phelim of Ireland, and Sir Owen of the Mountains, arrived in Cyprus; how they put down the tyrant Isakius, and restored the rightful Prince Amadeus to the throne 290

CHAPTER IX.

The famous adventures of the two renowned Captains, Sir Orlando of Italy, and Sir Ewin of Scotland; how they redeemed the Duke of Candy's daughter from her enchantment, with other things that happened.. 297

CHAPTER X.

How the Seven Champions came to a land where the men for their sins were changed into the shape of beasts; and how by finishing the Adventure of the Golden Cave, they returned to their shapes again... 304

CHAPTER XI.

How St. George's three Sons were separated by a tempest; and how Sir Alexander met with the ship wherein the Seven Champions were. How he was married to the Princess Mariana, and crowned king of Thessaly. The tragical story of the Duke of Ursini, and death of the Seven Champions 310

CHAPTER XII.

What happened to St. George's eldest Son, Sir Guy, after he was parted from his two Brothers. The woful Story of Selindus; how he was deprived of his Barony by Euphemius, and restored again by the Valour of Sir Guy and Captain Bolus............... 318

CHAPTER XIII.

How Sir Guy arrived in Sicily, where he overcame the Rebels, which, after the King of Sicily's Death, had rebelled against the Queen Urania; how he was married to her, and was afterwards crowned King of Sicily............... 326

CHAPTER XIV.

How Sir David and his company were almost famished with hunger; how they came to the Isle of Fortuna, where Sir David slew a dragon, and delivered the Island of Ancona from enchantment ... 332

CHAPTER XV.

Sir David is married to Queen Rosetta, and overcomes the remains of the Pagan army. Sir Pandrasus, with his men, land in Ancona... 338

CHAPTER XVI.

The taking of the Horse-faced Tartar, as also of the Necromancer Orpin. The Relation of Sir Pandrasus, concerning his strange Adventures after his departure from the Seven Champions of Christendom 343

CHAPTER XVII.

How Sir Pandrasus, in his return homewards, came to an Island where Sir Phelim and Sir Owen had killed a great Giant, and taken his Castle, and what torments the Giant inflicted on his prisoners ... 351

CHAPTER XVIII.

How Sir Phelim and Sir Owen, with Sir Pandrasus, fought with the Giant Curlo, who came to be revenged for the death of his brother Briomart 356

CHAPTER XIX.

How Sir David sailed to the precious Fountain, and rescued Sir Wonder. How he put to death the tyrant Almantor, and settled again Pandion in his estate 359

CHAPTER XX.

How Sir Guy, Sir Alexander, Sir David, as also Sir Turpin of France, Sir Predo of Spain, Sir Orlando of Italy, Sir Ewin of Scotland, Sir Phelim of Ireland, and Sir Owen of Wales, met at great Jousts at Constantinople 364

THE SEVEN CHAMPIONS

OF

CHRISTENDOM.

PART I.

CHAPTER I.

The strange and wonderful birth of St. George of England. The manner of his birth, and how he was afterwards stolen from his nurse, by Kalyb, the lady of the woods. Her love to him, and her gifts. He encloses her in a rock of stone, and redeems six christian knights out of prison.

AFTER the angry gods had ruined the capital city of Phrygia, and turned king Priam's glorious buildings to a waste and desolate wilderness, duke Æneas, driven from his native habitation, with many of his distressed countrymen, wandered about the world, like pilgrims, to find some happy region, where they might erect the Palladium, or image of their subverted Troy: but before this object could be accomplished, Æneas ended his days in the confines of Italy, and left his son Ascanius to govern in his stead. Ascanius dying, left the sovereign power to Sylvius; from whom it descended to the noble and adventurous Brute, who, being the fourth in lineal descent from Æneas, first conquered this island of Britain, then inhabited with monsters, giants, and a kind of wild people, without any form of government. He had no sooner subdued these, but he established good and wholesome laws, and then first laid the foundation of New Troy, which he named Troynovant, but, in course of time, it came to be called London.

Thus began the island of Britain to flourish, not only in magnificent and sumptuous buildings, but in courageous and valiant knights, whose most noble and adventurous attempts in the truly heroic feats of chivalry, fame shall draw forth, and rescue from the dark and gloomy mansions of oblivion.

The land was now replenished with cities, and divided into shires or counties: dukedoms, earldoms, and lordships, were the rewards of merit, and noble services performed in martial fields, and not bestowed as bribes to enslave the state, or given to indulge the slothful pride or effeminacy of the favourers of their princes' lust.

The ancient city of Coventry gave birth to the first Christian hero of England, and the first who ever sought adventures in a foreign land; whose name is to this day held in high esteem through all parts of Europe, and whose bold and magnanimous deeds in arms gave him the title of "The valiant knight, St. George of England," whose golden garter is not only worn by nobles but by kings, and in memory of whose victories the kings of England fight under his banner. It is the history of this worthy champion of our native country, that, by the assistance of the heavenly muse, divine Calliope, I have undertaken to write.

For some time previous to the birth of the renowned champion, the princess, his mother had a terrible dream, which occurred several succesive nights. She dreamed that she had conceived a dragon, which should cause her death. The frequent repetition of this dream so powerfully affected her, that she took an opportunity to disclose it to her lord and husband, then lord high steward of England. She spoke to him in this manner:

"My honourable lord—You know I am by birth the daughter of a king, of England's king, and that I have been, for one-and-twenty years, your true and loyal wife, and yet, till now, had never any hope of having a child, whereby your name might survive when you shall be no more; therefore I conjure you, by the pleasure of your youth, and by the dear and natural love you bear the infant of which I am pregnant, that you will seek by some artful means, to unfold the mysterious indications of my dreams, which for thirty nights together have disturbed my soft slumbers; when methought I had conceived a dreadful dragon, that would cause its parent's death. Thus Hecuba, the beautious queen of Troy, when pregnant of Paris, dreamed that she had conceived a fire-brand; which indeed proved true; for this Paris having violated the paragon of Greece, and brought Helen into Troy, the Grecians, in revenge thereof, turned the towers of Ilium into flames of fire. Therefore, most dear and beloved lord, let us consult how to prevent the like danger, and my being mother of a viperous son."

These words struck such terror to his heart, that, for a time, he stood speechless; but having recovered his lost senses, he answered in this sort:

"My dearest and most beloved lady, what art and science

can perform, with all convenient speed shall be essayed; for never will I close my eyes till I have found some skilful person, who will undertake to unfold the mystic meaning of these terrific dreams."

This noble lord, leaving his dejected partner in company with other ladies, who came to comfort her in her melancholy condition, took his journey to the solitary walks of Kalyb, the wise lady of the woods, attended only by a single knight, who bore under his arm a white lamb, which they intended to offer as a sacrifice to the enchantress. Thus travelling, for the space of two days, they came to a thicket beset about with old withered and hollow trees, wherein they were entertained with such dismal croackings of the night raven, hissing of serpents, bellowing of bulls, and roaring of monsters, that it seemed to be rather the habitation of furies than a mortal dwelling; but here was the dark and dreary mansion of the enchantress Kalyb, lady of the woods, in the midst of which she took up her abode, in a lonely cave, which had a strong iron gate at its entrance, whereon there hung a brazen trumpet for those to sound, who wanted audience of the sorceress.

The lord and knight, first offering their lamb with all humility before the postern of the cave, then casting off all fear, blew the trumpet, the sound of which, with one blast, seemed to shake the foundation of the earth. After which, they heard a loud and hollow voice utter the following words:

"Sir knight, from whence thou cam'st return:
Thou hast a son most strangely born;
A champion bold, from thence shall spring,
Who'll practice many a wond'rous thing;
Return, therefore, make no delay,
For all is true that here I say."

This dark riddle, or rather mystic oracle, being thrice repeated in this order, so much amazed them, that they stood in doubt whether it were best to return, or sound the brazen trumpet a second time; but the lord high steward, being persuaded by the knight not to move the impatience of Kalyb, rested content with the answer she had given them, and, quitting the enchanted cave, made all the speed he could to his native habitation: but in the mean time his lady, being overpowered with the extreme pain and anguish she was suffering, was forced either to give up her own life, or destroy that of the infant, but she, regarding more the benefit of her country than her own safety, and for the preservation of her own offspring, most willingly consented to a surgical operation, that the infant's life might be saved.

Thus after a learned consultation of many of the most eminent surgeons, to try if there was any possibility of saving her, which being found impracticable, this noble and magnanimous lady was cast into a deep sleep, when the surgeons succeeded in delivering her of the child alive; but the mother's life was sacrificed under the operation. Nature, on his breast, had pictured the lively image of a dragon; upon his right hand a blood-red cross, and a golden garter on his left leg. He was named George, and three nurses were provided for him; one to give him suck, another to lull and rock him asleep, and the third to prepare his food. Not many days after his nativity, the fell enchantress Kalyb, being an utter enemy to all true nobility, by the help of charms and witchcraft, found means to steal away the infant from his careless nurses.

The lord high steward of England, at this time returning, how were his expectations frustrated! when, instead of the safe delivery of his lady, and the comfort of a son, he found the one in her cold grave, and the other carried he knew not whither. The news of these disasters for a while bereaved him of his senses, and he stood speechless, like weeping Niobe; but at last he broke forth into these bitter exclamations:

"O heavens! why cover ye not the earth with everlasting night? Why do these eyes accursed behold the sun? O that the waves of Œnipus would end my days; or yon high mountains crush me with their fall! Or, heavens! let me rove a wretched exile and forlorn, in solitary woods to make my moan; the senseless trees, the savage and untamed beasts, would grieve at miseries like mine. What monster has bereaved me of my child? What tyrant glutted with his blood? O that the winds would bring me tidings of him, though from the most distant quarters of the world, thither would I fly to see him; or were he hid beneath the ocean's deepest floods, thither would I dive to bring him forth; or if, like feathered fowls, he winged the liquid air, thither would I mount to catch him in my arms, and embrace him that never yet mine eyes beheld. But why do I rave, and vainly thus exclaim, when neither earth, or air, or seas, or any thing in earth, air, or seas, can bring me comfort?"

Thus complained he many months for the loss of his son, and sent messengers into every part of the land to make inquiry after him; but no man was fortunate enough to return with happy tidings. He, therefore, storing himself with gold and many precious jewels of an inestimable value, resolved to travel the world over, to find what he wanted, or to leave his bones in some remote region. So leaving his native country, he wandered from place to place, without success, till, through care and age, his locks were turned to silver grey, and his venerable beard became like down upon a thistle: till at length, quite wearied out with grief, and fruitless toil, he laid himself down close by the ruined walls of a decayed monastery in the kingdom of Bohemia, and there finished his inquiry and his life together. The common people of the country, coming to the knowledge of his name, by a jewel he wore in his bosom, caused it to be engraven on a marble stone, right over the place where he was buried. And there we will leave him to sleep in peace, and return to his son, still kept by Kalyb, the lady of the woods, in her enchanted cave.

And now twice seven times the sun had run his annual course, and passed through every sign of the zodiac, since Kalyb had first in keeping the noble St. George of England, whose mind many times thirsted after honourable adventures, and who many times attempted to set himself at liberty; but the fell enchantress, tendering him as the apple of her eye, appointed twelve sturdy Satyrs to attend his person, so that neither force nor policy could farther his intent. She kept him not to insult over as a slave, nor triumph in his wretchedness, but daily fed his fancy with all the delights that art or nature could afford; for she placed her whole felicity in him, and loved him for his beauty. But he, seeking glory from martial discipline and knightly achievements, utterly refused her proffered embraces, and highly disdained so wicked a creature. She, seeing how much he neglected her love, drawing him to a private part of the cave, began thus to court him to her arms:

"Thou knowest, divine youth, how eagerly I have sought thy love, and how I doat upon thy manly charms; yet thou, more cruel than the Lybian tiger, canst reject my sighs and tears. But now, my dear knight, if thou wilt make me happy in thy wished embrace, for thy sake I will show all the powers of my magic charms, move heaven, if thou dost request it, to rain down stones in showers upon thy enemies, I will convert the sun and moon to fire and blood, depopulate whole regions and lay the face of nature waste."

Our noble knight St. George, considering that love might blind the wisest, and guessing, by these fair promises, that he might find an opportunity to obtain his liberty, made her this answer:

"Most wise and learned Kalyb, thou wonder of the world, I will condescend to all thy heart desires upon these conditions—That I may be sole governor and protector of this enchanted cave, and that thou discoverest me to my birth, my name, and parentage."

She very willingly consented to these terms; and began to answer his demands as follows; "Thou art by birth," said she, "son to the lord Albert, high steward of England; and from thy birth to this day have I kept thee, as my own child, within these solitary woods." So taking him by the hand, she led him into a brazen castle, wherein remained prisoners six of the bravest knights of the whole world. "These," said she, "are six worthy champions of Christendom: the first is St. Denis of France, the second St. James of Spain, the third St. Anthony of Italy, the fourth St. Andrew of Scotland, the fifth St. Patrick of Ireland, the sixth St. David of Wales; and thou art born to be the seventh, thy name St. George of England, for so shalt thou be named in times to come."

Then leading him a little farther, she brought him to a magnificent building, where stood seven of the most beautiful steeds that ever eye beheld. "Six of these," said she, "belong to the six champions, and the seventh, whose name is Bayard, will I bestow on thee." Then she led him to another apartment, where hung the richest armour in the world; there choosing out the strongest corslet from her armoury, she with her own hands buckled it upon his breast, laced on his helmet, and dressed him in the armour: afterwards bringing forth a mighty falchion she likewise put it in his hand, and said to him; "Thou art now clothed in richer armour than Ninus the first monarch of the world. Thy steed is of such force and invincible power, that whilst thou art mounted on his back, no knight in the world shall be able to conquer thee. Thy armour is of the purest Lydian steel, that no battle-axe can bruise, nor any weapon can pierce. Thy sword, which is called Ascalon, was made by the Cyclops; it will hew in sunder the hardest flint, or cut the strongest steel; and in its pommel there lies such magic virtue, that neither treason, witchcraft, nor any other violence can be offered to thee as long as thou wearest it."

Thus the designing Kalyb was so blinded by the love she had for him, that she not only bestowed all the riches of her cave upon him, but gave him power and authority, by putting a silver wand in his hand, to work her own destruction. For coming by a huge rock of stone, he struck it with this enchanted wand, whereupon it immediately opened, and laid fully to his view a vast number of young infants, whom the enchantress had murdered by her witchcraft and sorceries. "This," said she, "is a place of horror, where nought is heard but shrieks and groans of dying men and babes; but if your ears can endure to hear, and eyes behold them, I will lead you that way." So the lady of the woods, boldly stepping in before, and little suspecting any danger from the secret policy of St. George, was deceived in her own practices; for no sooner had she entered the rock, but he struck the silver wand thereon, and it closed in an instant; and there confined her to bellow forth her lamentable complaints to senseless stones, without any hope of being released.

Thus this noble knight deceived the wicked enchantress Kalyb, and likewise set the other six champions at liberty, who rendered him all knightly courtesies, and gave him thanks for their safe delivery. So providing themselves with all things suiting their generous purposes, they took their journey from the enchanted grove. Their proceedings, fortunes, and heroical adventures, shall be shown in the following chapters.

CHAPTER II.

Kalyb's Lamentation in the Rock; her last Will and Testament; she is torn in pieces by Spirits; with other Occurrences in the Cave.

AFTER the departure of the seven worthy champions, Kalyb, finding herself close imprisoned in the rock, by the policy of the English knight, grew into such extreme passion, that she cursed the hour of her creation, and bitterly inveighed against all the horrid powers of her barbarous and bloody art. The earth she wearied with her cries, and even the flinty stones seemed to weep in pity of her anguish. The oaks were blasted round the enchanted rock, and hollow winds re-echoed murmurs to her hideous groans. "O miserable Kalyb," cried she, "cursed be thy destiny, for now thou art inclosed within a desolate and darksome den! where neither sun can lend thee comfort with his enlivening beams, nor the cool breath of air refresh thy parched and burning body; thou art thyself, by magic art, impaled and rooted to the centre of earth, who wert thyself the wonder of the times for magic. I, that by art have made my journey to the lowest depths of hell, where multitudes of black and ugly spirits have trembled at my charms; I, that have bound the Furies in my iron chains, and caused them to attend my pleasure through the wilds of Egypt, or where the tawny Moor inhabits, am now myself constrained to languish in eternal darkness. Woe to my soul! woe to my charms! and woe to all my magic spells! for they have bound me in this hollow rock. Let the sun grow pale, and the earth be covered with eternal darkness. Let the firmament be turned to pitch; roar hell! quake earth! swell seas! and all ye stars and planets burst from your spheres! Let all nature be convulsed and tortured with the misery of wretched Kalyb!"

Thus wiled she the hours, one while accusing fortune of tyranny, another blaming the falsehood and treachery of the English knight; sometimes tearing her curled locks, that, like wreathing snakes, hung dangling down her deformed neck; then, beating her breasts, and rending her garments, she thundered forth these terms of conjuration: "Come! come, ye princes of the elements, fire, air, earth, and water, come tear this rock in pieces; this rock that holds confined in adamantine chains the limbs and body of excruciated Kalyb. Appear, ye shadows of black Night; Magol, Cumoth, Helveza, Zontoma, come when I call." At which words the earth began to quake, and all the elemental spirits were obedient to her voice; some from the fire, in the resemblance of burning dragons, breathing flaming sulphur, from their nostrils; some from the water, in the shape of hideous and unwieldly fish; some from the air, the purest of the elements, like the shadows of human beings; and others from the gross earth, most ugly, black and dreadful to behold. Now when these legions of spirits had encompassed the wicked enchantress about, hell began to bellow forth such harsh and jarring sounds, that the enchanted rock was burst asunder with the very noise thereof, and then lost Kalyb's charms were gone for ever. The hundred years her magic was to last, were now completely finished; and the bond subscribed with her own precious blood, and sealed with her own hands, was brought in witness against her, by which she knew her life was at an end. Therefore in this most fearful manner she began to make her last will and testament:

"First, welcome," said she, "my sad executors. Welcome, my grave and everlasting tomb, which are prepared in the fiery lakes of Phlegeton. The winding-sheet, wherein is to be wrapped my foul body and condemned soul, is melted lead and boiling brimstone. No worms shall consume this horrid carcase, but it shall be tossed about with fiery forks, from place to place, and from one furnace to another. Therefore attend to Kalyb's woeful testament, and engrave the legacies she gives in rolls of brass upon the burning banks of Acheron.

"First, these eyes, that now be in too late to weep with hapless tears, I give unto the watery spirits, for they have ransacked all the treasures of the hidden deep to satisfy my insatiable desires; next I bequeath these hands, which did subscribe the bloody obligation of my perpetual banishment from joy, unto those spirits that hover in the air; my tongue, that did conspire against the majesty of heaven, I give to those spirits that have their being in the fire; my earthly heart I bequeath to those gross demons that dwell in the dark dungeons of the earth; and the rest of my condemned body to the torments due to my demerits."

The strange and dreadful testament was no sooner made, than all the spirits seized upon the enchantress, and tore her body into a thousand pieces, scattering her members among the four elements; some to the spirits of the air, some to the water, others to the fire and earth; and these carried them away with such terrible noises, that all nature seemed amazed, and all things within hearing of them died instantly away; birds, beasts, and even the reptile worms that crawled upon the ground; trees, which but just before were flourishing and green, were blasted all at once; and the grass faded away for want of that natural moisture, that the clouds denied to shed on so vile a place.

Thus, by the just judgment of heaven, was Kalyb punished for her wickedness, whom we leave to endless torments, and return to the seven worthy champions of Christendom, whose laudable adventures fame has enrolled in the records of eternity.

CHAPTER III.

St. George slays the burning Dragon in Egypt, and redeems Sabra, the king's daughter, from death. Is betrayed by Almidor, the black king of Morocco, and sent to the Soldan of Persia; where he slew two lions, and remained seven years in prison.

AFTER the seven champions departed from the enchanted cave of Kalyb, they made their abode in the city of Coventry, for the space of nine months; in which time they erected a sumptuous monument over the remains of St. George's mother. And at that time of the year when Flora had embroidered the green mantle of the spring, they armed themselves like knights-errant, and took their journey to seek for foreign adventures, accounting nothing more dishonourable than to spend their time in idleness, and not achieve something that might make their names memorable to posterity. So travelling thirty days without any adventures worth noticing; at length they came to a broad plain, where stood a brazen pillar, and where seven several ways met, which the worthy knights thought a proper place to take leave of each other, and every one went a contrary road; in which we will, for this time, likewise take leave of six, that we may accompany the fortunes of our English knight, who, after many months' travel, by sea and land, happily arrived within the territories of Egypt, which country was then greatly annoyed by a dangerous dragon. But before he had journeyed far in this kingdom, the silent night outspread her sable wings, and a still horror seemed to cover every part of nature. At length, he came to a poor old hermitage; wherein he purposed to seek some repose for himself and horse, till the rosy-fingered morning should again reluminate the vault of heaven, and light him on his destined course. But entering the cottage, he found an ancient hermit, bowing under the weight of age, and almost consumed with holy watching and religious tears, to whom he thus addressed himself:

"Father, may a traveller, for this night, crave shelter with you for himself and horse; or can you direct me to any town or village to which I may proceed on my journey with safety?"

The old man, starting at the sudden approach of St. George, made him this answer:

That he need not inquire of his country, for he knew it by his burgonet (for indeed thereon were engraved the arms of England). "But I sorrow," continued he, "for thy hard fortune, and that it is thy destiny to arrive in this our country of Egypt, wherein those alive are scarce sufficient to bury the dead; such cruel devastation is made through the land by a most terrible and dangerous dragon, now ranging up and down the country; the raging appetite of which must every day be appeased with the body of a pure virgin, whom he swalloweth down his envenomed throat: and the day on which this horrid sacrifice is omitted, he breathes such a pestiferous stench as occasions a mortal plague. And this having been practised for twenty-four years, there is not one true virgin left throughout all Egypt but the king's daughter; and she, to-morrow, is to be made an offering to the dragon, unless there can be any brave knight found who shall have courage enough to encounter with him, and kill him: and then, the king hath promised to give such knight his daughter, whose life he shall have saved, in marriage, with the crown of Egypt after his decease."

This royal reward so animated the English knight, that he vowed he would either redeem the king's daughter, or lose his own life in so glorious an enterprise. So taking his repose that night in the old man's hermitage, till the cheerful cock, the true messenger of day, gave him notice of the sun's uprise, which caused him to buckle on his armour, and harness his steed with all the strong caparisons of war, he took his journey, guided only by the old hermit, to the valley, where the king's daughter was to be offered up in sacrifice. When he approached within sight of the valley, he saw at a distance the most amiable and beautiful virgin that ever eyes beheld, arrayed in a pure white Arabian silk, led to the place of death, accompanied by many sage and modest matrons. The courage of the brave English knight was so stimulated by this melancholy scene, that he thought every minute a whole day till he could rescue her from the threatened danger, and save her from the insatiable jaws of the fiery dragon; so advancing towards the lady, he gave her hopes that her deliverance was at hand, and begged her to return to her father's court.

The noble knight, like a bold and daring hero, then entered the valley where the dragon had his abode, who no sooner had sight of him, but his leathern throat sent forth a sound more terrible than thunder. The size of this fell dragon was fearful to behold, for, from his shoulders to his tail, the length was fifty feet; the glittering scales upon his

"The knight nimbly recovering himself, gave the dragon such a thrust with his spear" &c.

body were as bright as silver, but harder than brass; his belly was of the colour of gold, and larger than a tun. Thus issued he from his hideous den, and so fiercely assailed the gallant champion with his burning wings, that at the first encounter he had almost felled him to the ground; but the knight, nimbly recovering himself, gave the dragon such a thrust with his spear, that it shivered in a thousand pieces! upon which, the furious dragon smote him so violently with his venomous tail, that then, indeed, he brought both man and horse to the ground, and sorely bruised two of St. George's ribs in the fall; but he, stepping backwards, chanced to get under an orange-tree, which had that rare virtue in it that no venomous creature durst come within the compass of its branches; and here the valiant knight rested himself, till he had recovered his former strength. But he no sooner felt his spirits revived, than, with an eager courage, he smote the burning dragon under his yellow burnished belly, with his trusty sword Ascalon; and from the wound there came such an abundance of black venom, that it spouted on the armour of the knight, which, by the mere force of the poison, burst in two, and he himself fell on the ground, where he lay for some time nearly lifeless, but had rolled himself under the orange-tree; in which place the dragon had not power to offer him any farther violence. The fruit of this tree was of that excellence, that whoever tasted it was immediately cured of all manner of wounds and diseases.

Now, it was the noble champion's good fortune to recover himself a little by the pure effluvia of the tree, and then he chanced to espy an orange which had lately dropped from it, by tasting of which he was so refreshed that in a short time he was as sound as when he began the encounter. Then he kneeled down and made his humble supplication, that heaven would send him such strength and agility of body as might enable him to slay the fell monster; which being done, with a bold and courageous heart, he smote the dragon under the wing, where it was tender and without scale, whereby his good sword Ascalon, with an easy passage, went to the very hilt, through the dragon's liver and heart; from whence there issued such an abundance of reeking gore, as turned all the grass in the valley to a crimson hue; and the ground, which was before parched up by the burning breath of the dragon, was now drenched in the moisture that proceeded from his venomous bowels, the loss of which forced him to yield his vital spirit to the champion's conquering sword.

The noble knight St. George of England, having performed this, first paid due honour to the Almighty for his victory; and then with his sword cut off the dragon's head, and fixed it on a truncheon made of that spear which, at the beginning of the battle, shivered in pieces against the dragon's scaly back. During this long and dangerous combat, his trusty steed lay, as it were, in a swoon, without any motion; but the English champion now squeezing the juice of one of the oranges in his mouth, the virtue of it immediately expelled the venom of the poison, and recovered his former strength. There was then in the Egyptian court, and had been for some time, Almidor, the black king of Morocco, who had long sought the love of Sabra, the king's daughter; but by no policy, means, or manhood, could he accomplish what his heart desired. And now having less hope than ever, by the successful combat of St. George with the dragon, he resolved to try the utmost power of art, and treacherously despoil the victor of his laurels, which he falsely designed to crown his temples with, and thereby obtain the grace of the lady, who loathed his company, and more detested his person than the crocodile of the Nile. But, even as the wolf barks in vain against the moon, so shall this fantastical and cowardly Almidor attempt to seize in vain the glory won by the English knight; although he had hired, by gifts and promises, twelve Egyptian knights to beset the valley where St. George slew the burning dragon, who were to bereave him, by force, of the spoils of his conquest. Thus, when the magnanimous champion came riding in triumph, from the valley, expecting to have been received as a conqueror, with drums and trumpets, or to have heard the bells throughout the kingdom ringing with the joyful peals of victory, and every street illuminated with bonfires and blazing tapers; contrary to his expectation, he was met with troops of armed knights, not to conduct him in triumph to the Egyptian court, but, by insidious baseness and treachery, to bereave him of his life, and the glory he had that day so nobly acquired by his invincible arms: for, no sooner had he passed the entrance of the valley, but he saw the Egyptian knights brandishing their weapons, and dividing themselves, to intercept him in his journey to the court. So, tying his horse to a tree, he resolved to try his fortune on foot, there being twelve to one; yet did St. George, at the first onset, so valiantly behave himself with his trusty sword Ascalon, that, at one stroke, he slew three of the Egyptian knights, and before the golden chariot of the sun had gone another hour in its diurnal course, some he had dismembered of their heads and limbs, and some had he cut in two, and not one was left alive to carry home the news of their defeat.

Almidor, the black king, stood the whole time of the battle on the top of a mountain, to behold the success of his hired champions, but when he saw the dismal catastrophe of these

mercenary knights, and how the good fortune of the English
champion had carried the honour of the day, he cursed his
destiny, and accused blind chance of cruelty in thus disappointing the hopes of his treacherous enterprise: but having a heart
full fraught with malice and envy, he secretly vowed to
himself that he would pratice some other treachery to bring
St. George to destruction. So running before to the court of
king Ptolemy, and, without relating what had happened to
the twelve Egyptian knights, he cried out, "Victoria, Victoria,
the enemy of Egypt is slain!" Upon which Ptolemy ordered
every street of the city of Memphis to be hung with rich
arras and embroidered tapestry, and likewise provided a
sumptuous chariot of massive gold, the wheels and other timber work whereof were of the purest ebony, the covering
rich silk embossed with gold; this, with an hundred of the
noblest peers of Egypt, attired in crimson velvet, mounted on
milk-white coursers, richly caparisoned, attended the arrival
of St. George, who was conducted in the most solemn manner into the city, all the largest as well as sweetest instruments of music both going before and following after the
resplendent chariot in which he was drawn to the court of
king Ptolemy; where he surrendered up the trophies of his
conquest into the hands of the beauteous Sabra, who was
so delighted with the noble person and princely presence of
the English knight, that for a time, she was scarce able to
speak; but having recovered herself, she took him by the
hand, and led him to a rich pavillion, where she unarmed him,
and with the most precious balsam anointed his wounds, and
with fine linen cloths wiped off the blood; after which she
conducted him to a rich repast, furnished with all manner of
delicate meats, where the king her father was present, who
inquired of his country, parentage, and name. After the
banquet was over, he installed him with the honour of
knighthood, and put upon his feet a pair of golden spurs.
But the lovely princess, his daughter, could feast on nothing
but the hopes of the champion's love; and, having attended
him to his night's repose, she sat near his bed, and striking
the melodious strings of her lute, lulled him to rest with the
sweetest harmony that ever was heard. No sooner had the
blushing morn displayed her beauties in the east, and gilded
with her radiant beams the mountain tops, but Sabra repaired to the English champion's lodgings; and, at his first
uprising, presented him with a diamond of inestimable value,
which she prayed him to wear on his finger, not only as an
ornament, but as it was endued with many most excellent
and occult virtues. The next who entered the room was Almidor, the treacherous black king of Morocco, having a bowl of
Greek wine in his hand, which he offered to the noble cham-

pion St. George of England; but when he stretched forth his arm to accept the same, the diamond, which fair Sabra had made him a present of, waxed pale, and from his nose fell just three drops of blood, which the king's daughter observing, suspected some secret poison to be infused in the wine; whereupon she shrieked out so loudly, and so suddenly, that it alarmed the whole court, and carried her suspicions to the ears of her father; but so great was his love for the black king, that he would not give credit to any thing that could be suggested against him.

Thus was Almidor a second time prevented in his evil designs, which made him more enraged than a chased boar; yet, resolving the third should pay for all, he impatiently expected another opportunity to put his hellish purposes in execution.

St. George remained many days in the Egyptian court, sometimes revelling among the gentlemen, and dancing and sporting among the ladies, at other times in tilts, tournaments, and other noble and heroic exercises; and all that time was the breast of the beauteous Sabra inflamed with the most ardent love for him, of which the treacherous Almidor had intelligence by many secret practices, and many times his own ears were witnesses to their discourses. One evening in particular, after the glorious sun was set in Thetis's lap, it was his fortune to wander near a garden wall, to taste the cooling air, where the two lovers, without seeing him, were seated in a bower of jessamine, and after much talk, he heard the love-sick Sabra thus complain:

"My soul's delight, my noble George of England, dearer than all the world beside, why art thou more obdurate than the flint, since all my falling tears can never mollify thy heart? Nor all the sighs, the many thousand sighs, I have sent as messengers of my true love, were ever yet requited with a smile. Refuse not her, my dear-loved lord of England, refuse not her, that, for thy sake, would leave her parents, country, and inheritance, although that inheritance be the crown of Egypt, and would follow thee as a pilgrim through the wide world. The sun shall sooner lose its splendor, the pale moon drop from her orb, the sea forget to ebb and flow, and all things change the course ordained by nature, than Sabra, heiress of Egypt, prove inconstant to St. George of England; let, then, the priests of Hymen knit the gordian knot, the knot of wedlock, which death alone has power to untie."

These words so fired the champion's heart, that he was almost entangled in the snares of love; he, who before had never given way to any passion but the love of arms. Yet, to try her patience a little more, he made her this answer:

"Lady of Egypt, art thou not content that I have risked my own life to preserve yours, but you would have me also sacrifice my honour, give over the chase of dazzling glory, lay all my warlike trophies in a woman's lap, and change my truncheon for a distaff.—No! Sabra; George of England is a knight, born in a country where true chivalry is nourished, and hath sworn to see the world, as far as the lamp of heaven can lend him light, before he is fettered in the chains of wedlock. Therefore think no more of one that is a stranger, a wanderer from place to place, but cast your eyes on one more worthy of your own high rank. Why do you decline the suit of Almidor, who is a king, and would think no task too arduous to obtain your love?"

At which words, she instantly replied: "The fell king of Morocco is more bloody-minded than a serpent, but thou art as gentle as a lamb; his tongue more ominous than the screeching night-owl, but thine sweeter than the morning-lark; his touch more odious than the biting snake, but thine more pleasant than the curling vine. What if thou art a stranger to our land, thou art more precious to my heart, and more delightful to my eyes, than crowns and diadems."

"But stay," replied the Christian champion, "I am a Christian, madam; thou a Pagan. I honour God in heaven; you, shadows earthly of a vile imposter here below. Therefore, if you would obtain my love, you must forsake your Mahomet, and be baptised into the Christian faith." "With all my soul," replied the Egyptian lady; "I will forsake my country's gods, and for thy love become a Christian." And thereupon she broke a ring, and gave him one half as a pledge of her love, and kept the other half herself; and so, for that time, went out of the garden.

The treacherous Almidor, who had listened during all this discourse, was galled to the very heart to hear how much his mistress despised him and his proffered love; but was now resolved to strike a bold stroke with the king her father, to separate her from his too successful rival; and accordingly hastened away to the Egyptian king, and prostrating himself before him, he spoke in the following manner:

"Know, great monarch of the east, that I am come to unfold a secret which nearly concerns the welfare of your country. It was my chance this evening, when the sun had withdrawn his radiant beams, to seek the cool refreshing air close by your private garden wall, where, being myself unseen, I overheard a deep concerted plan of treason, laid between your daughter and the English knight; for she hath given him a solemn pledge of love, and with that pledge a promise to forsake the faith of Egypt, sets the great prophet at defiance, and will embrace the Christian doctrine. Nay, she forsakes not only Mahomet, but her father, and her native land, to wander with this stranger knight, who, for being so highly honoured in your court, thus robs you of your daughter."

"Now, by our holy prophet," replied the king, "this damned Christian shall not reap the harvest of our daughter's love, for he shall lose his head, though not in our court, where we have heaped such honours on him. But Almidor, be secret, and I'll acquaint you with my purpose: I will send him to my kinsman, the soldan of Persia; from whom he shall never more return to Egypt, except his ghost bring tidings of his fate in that country." And to answer this pupose they contrived between them the following letter:

"*To the soldan of Persia.*

"I Ptolemy, king of Egypt, and the eastern territories, send greeting to thee, the mighty soldan of Persia, great emperor of the provinces of the larger Asia. I make this my request, trusting to the league of friendship between us, that thou put the bearer hereof, thy slave, to death; for he is an utter enemy to all Asia and Africa, and a proud contemner of our religion. Therefore fail not hereof, as thou tenderest our mutual friendship. So we bid thee farewell,
"Thy kinsman,
"PTOLEMY, king of Egypt."

As soon as this letter was signed and sealed with the great seal of Egypt, St. George was sent on an embassy with the bloody sentence of his own destruction; and was sworn, by the honour of knighthood, to deliver it safe; leaving behind him, as a pledge of his fidelity, his good steed, and trusty sword Ascalon, in the keeping of Ptolemy, taking with him only one of that king's horses, for his easy travelling.

Thus was the innocent lamb betrayed by the subtle fox, and sent to the hunger-starved lion's den; not being suffered to give the least notice to the fair Sabra of his sudden departure, but travelled day and night through many a solitary and dismal wilderness, without any adventure worth notice; only hearing the sad cry of the night-raven croaking in his ear, and the fearful sound of screeching owls from the blasted oak, and such like ominous messengers of ill-boding fortune, which foretold some direful accident at hand. Yet no fear could daunt his noble mind, nor danger hinder his intended journey, and so at length he arrived within sight of the soldan's palace, which looked more like Paradise than any earthly habitation. For as history reports, the walls and towers of the palace were of the purest marble; the windows crystal, set in work of carved silver enamelled with oriental pearl: the outward walls, the gates and pillars, were of brass; and the building gilt with gold. About the palace was a river of great depth and breadth, over which stood a bridge erected on arches adorned with images, and carvings in alto and basso relievo; under these arches were hung a hundred silver bells, so that no creature could pass into the palace, but they gave warning to the soldan's guard. At the end of the bridge was built a tower of alabaster, on the top of which stood an eagle of gold, with eyes of such precious stones, that all the palace glittered with the splendor of them.

On the day that St. George entered the soldan's court, there was a solemn procession in honour of the false prophet Mahomet, with which the English champion was so moved, that he tore down their ensigns and streamers, and trampled them under his feet: whereupon the infidels present fled to the soldan for succour, and showed him how a strange knight had despised their Mahomet, and trod their banners in the dust. Whereupon he sent an hundred of his armed knights to know the cause of the sudden uproar, and to bring the Christian champion bound before his majesty: but he entertained these Persian knights with such a bloody banquet, that some of their heads were tumbled in the dirty streets, and the channels overflowed with streams of their blood; the pavement before the palace was almost covered with slaughtered men, and the walls were besprinkled with purple gore. So victoriously he behaved himself, that ere the sun declined in the west, he had brought to the ground most part of the soldan's knights, and forced the rest, like frighted sheep, to fly to their soldan for aid, who then remained in his palace with a guard of a thousand men; but at the report of this unexpected tumult, he furnished his soldiers with all the proper habiliments of war, and came marching from his palace with such a mighty force, as if he had apprehended all the powers of Christendom had been coming to invade the territories of Asia. But such was the invincible courage of St. George, that he encountered with them all, and made such a massacre in the soldan's court, that the whole area was covered, and the gates stopped up with heaps of slaughtered Persians. At last the alarm-bell was rung, and the beacons set on fire; upon which the populace rose in arms, and came flocking about the English champion like swarms of bees: whereat, through his long fatigue, and the multitude of his enemies, his undaunted courage was forced to yield, and his restless arm, wearied with the fight, constrained to let his weapon fall to the ground. And thus he, whose fortitude had sent thousands to wander on the banks of Acheron, stood now obedient to the mercy of his enemies, who, with their brandished weapons and sharp-edged falchions, environed him about.

"Now, bloody-minded monster," said the soldan, "what countryman soe'er thou art, Jew, Pagan, or misbelieving Christian, look for a sentence of severe punishment for every drop of blood thy unhappy hand hath here shed: first, thy skin shall be flayed from off thy flesh alive; next, thy flesh shall be torn with red-hot pincers from thy bones; and lastly, thy limbs parted from each other by wild horses." This bloody sentence being pronounced by the soldan, St. George answered in the following manner:

"Great potentate of Asia, I crave the liberty and law of arms, whereto all the kings of the earth are by oath for ever bound. First, in my native country my descent is of royal blood, and therefore I challenge a combat: secondly, I am an Ambassador from the mighty Ptolemy, king of Egypt; therefore is my person sacred: lastly, the laws of Asia, and indeed all nations, grant me a safe conduct back; and Ptolemy is answerable for every thing I have done."

Thereupon he delivered the letter, sealed with the great seal of Egypt, which was no sooner broke open and read, but the soldan's eyes sparkled with fire, and upon his brow sat the image of wrath and indignation.

"By the report of Ptolemy," said the soldan, "thou art a great contemner of our holy prophet, and his laws; therefore his pleasure is, that you be put to death. Which, by Mahomet, I swear shall be fulfilled."

And upon this he gave him up to the safe custody of an hundred of his guards, till the time of execution, which was ordered to be in thirty days. Hereupon they disrobed him of his rich apparel, and clothed him in base and servile weeds: his arms, that were lately employed in supporting the mighty target, and wielding the weighty battle-axe, were now strongly fettered up in iron bolts; and those hands, which were wont to be garnished with steel gauntlets, were bound with hempen cords, till the purple blood started from his finger's ends; and being thus despoiled of all knightly dignity, he was conveyed to a dark dungeon, where the light of heaven was never seen, nor the glorious sun could send one gladdening ray, to show a difference betwixt day and night. All his comfort was to reckon up the number of the Persians he had slain; and sometimes his restless thoughts were pondering on ungrateful Ptolemy; sometimes running on the charms of lovely Sabra, distracted with reflecting how she would take his sudden departure. He then sketched out her picture on the wall, and to the senseless form would often thus complain:

"O cruel destiny! Why am I punished in this sort? Have I conspired against the majesty of heaven, that it has hurled such vengeance on my head? O! shall I never regain my former liberty, that I may be revenged on those who have imprisoned me? Frown, angry heavens, on these bloodyminded infidels, these daring rebels against the truth of thy divinity; these professed enemies of Christ. And may the plagues of Pharaoh light upon their country, and the miseries of Œdipus upon their princes. Let them be witnesses of their daughters' misery, and behold their cities flaming like the burning battlements of Troy."

Thus lamented he the loss of his liberty, accursing the day of his birth, and the hour of his creation, wishing it might be never numbered in the year, but be accounted ominous to all future ages. His sighs exceeded the number of sands on the sea-shore, and his tears the water bubbles on its surface.

Thus sorrow was his companion, and despair his chief solicitor, till Hyperion's golden car had rested thirty times in the purple palace of Thetis; which was the precise time allotted by the soldan of Persia for him to live; so expecting every minute to entertain the wished-for messenger of death, he heard afar off the terrible roaring of two lions, that for the space of four days had been restrained from food and natural sustenance, that with the more eagerness and fury they might satiate their hunger-starved bowels with the body of the thrice-renowned English champion. The cry of these lions so terrified his mind, that the hair of his head grew stiff; and on his brows were large drops of sweat, and in his soul such fire and rage, that with violence he broke his chains asunder, then rent the amber-coloured tresses from his head, with which he wrapped his arms, preparing for the assault of the lions, which he imagined were designed to be the executioners of the soldan's sentence upon him, as indeed they were; and at that instant the guards, who brought them, let them out of their cage upon him. But such was his invincible fortitude, and so politic was he in his defence, that when the starved lions came running on him with open jaws, he courageously thrust his sinewed arms, that were covered with the hair of his head, into their throats, whereby they were presently choked, and then he pulled out their hearts.

This spectacle the soldan's guards beheld, and were so amazed with fear, that they ran in all haste to the palace to acquaint the soldan with what had happened, who commanded every part of the court to be strongly guarded with armed soldiers, supposing the English knight rather some monster, ascended from the infernal regions, than one of the human species. And such terror seized the soldan, when he heard that he had killed the two lions, after having slaughtered two thousand Persians with his own hands; and having likewise intelligence of his having destroyed the burning dragon of Egypt, that he caused the dungeon, wherein he was kept, to be doubly fortified with iron bars, lest, by force or stratagem, the champion should recover his liberty, and thereby endanger the whole kingdom of Persia. Here, for the term of seven winters, he remained in the greatest want and distress, feeding upon rats and mice and creeping worms, which he caught in the dungeon, not tasting, in that whole time, of any bread but what was made of bran, and drinking only channel water, which was daily served him through the iron gates. Here we will now leave St. George, languishing under want and oppression, and return to Egypt, where we left Sabra, the champion's betrothed lady, lamenting the absence of him whom she loved dearer than all the world besides.

Sabra, the fairest virgin that ever mortal eye beheld, in whom nature had shown the utmost perfection; her body was straighter than the stately cedar, and the tincture of her skin surpassed the beauty of the Paphian queen; but one was bending with her weight of woes, and the other tarnished with the brackish tears that daily trickled down the roses of her cheeks, whereupon sat the image of discontent, and she herself seemed a mirror of patient sorrow. All company was loathsome to her sight; she shunned even the fellowship of those ladies, who were once her most intimate companions, and betook herself only to a solitary cabinet, where, with her needle, she passed the time, and having wrought the figures of many a bleeding heart, she bathed them with the lukewarm tears that fell from the conduit of her eyes; then, with her auburn locks, that hung in wanton ringlets down her ivory neck, she dried them up; and thinking on the plighted promises of her dear-loved knight, fell into these sad complainings:

"O Love!" said she, "more sharp than keenest razors, with what inequality dost thou torment my wounded heart, not linking my dear lord's in like affections with it. O Venus! whom both gods and men obey, if thou art absolute in thy power, command my wandering lord to return, or let my soul be wafted to his sweet bosom, where my bleeding heart already is enshrined. But, foolish fondling that I am! he hath rejected me, and even shuns my father's court, where he was honoured and esteemed, to wander through the world to seek another's love. No, no, it cannot be; he is more constant, his mind more noble than to forget his plighted vows; and much I fear some treachery has bereft me of him, some stony prison keeps him from me, for only chains and fetters could thus long withhold him from my arms. If so, sweet Morpheus, god of golden dreams, reveal to me my lover's abode, show me in sleep the shadow of his lovely form, give me to know the reason of his sudden departure, and of his long and painful absence."

After this exclamation, she closed her radiant eyes in sleep, when presently the very image, as she thought, of her dear-loved knight, St. George, appeared; not as he was wont, in shining arms, and with his burgonet of glittering steel, nor mounted on his stately steed, decked with a crimson plume or spangled feather, but in overworn and simple attire, with pale looks and emaciated body, like a ghost new risen from the hollow grave, breathing, as it were these sad and woful expressions:

> Sabra, I am betrayed for love of thee,
> And lodg'd in cave as dark as night;
> From whence I never more, ah woe is me!
> Shall have the pleasure of thy beauteous sight:
> Remain thou true and constant for my sake,
> That of my absence none may 'vantage make.
>
> Let tyrants know, if ever I obtain
> What now is lost by treason's faithless guile,
> False Egypt's scourge I ever will remain,
> And turn to streaming blood Morocco's soil.
> That hateful prince of Barbary shall rue,
> The fell revenge that is his treason's due.
>
> The Persian towers shall smoke with ardent fire,
> And lofty Babylon be tumbled down:
> The cross of Christendom shall then aspire,
> To wear the proud Egyptian triple crown,
> Jerusalem and Judah shall behold
> The fall of kings by Christian champions bold.
>
> Thou maid of Egypt, still continue chaste,
> A tiger seeks thy virgin's name to spill,
> Whilst George of England is in prison plac'd,
> Thou shalt be forc'd to wed against thy will:
> But after this shall happen mighty things,
> For forth from thee shall spring three wond'rous kings.

This strange and woful speech was no sooner ended, but she awoke from her sleep, and presently reached out her ivory arms, thinking to embrace him, but met with nothing but empty air, which caused her to renew her former complaints.

"Oh! wherefore died I not in this my troublesome dream," said the sorrowful lady, "that my ghost might have haunted those inhuman monsters who have thus betrayed the bravest champion that the eye of heaven or the sons of earth have e'er beheld? For his sake will I exclaim against the ingratitude of Egypt, and, like the wretched Philomel, fill every corner of the land with echoes of his wrong. My woes are greater, and by far exceed the sorrows of Dido queen of Carthage, mourning for Æneas."

With such-like plaintive words wiled she the time away, till twelve months were fully finished: at last her father, understanding what ardent affection she bore to the English champion, spoke to her in this manner:

"Daughter, I charge thee, on the obedience and duty which thou owest to me, both as thy father and thy king, to banish from thy thoughts all fond affection for the wandering knight; whom thou hast made unworthily the object of thy love, for he hath neither home nor habitation. Thou seest he has forsaken thee, and in his travels is wedded to another. Therefore, as you value my love, or dread my displeasure, I charge thee again to think of him no more; but cast your eyes on the black king of Morocco, who is deserving of thee, and whose nuptials with thee I intend to celebrate in Egypt shortly, with all the honours due to my own and his high rank."

Having said these words, he departed, without waiting for an answer; by which fair Sabra knew, he was not to be thwarted in his will. Therefore she poured forth these sad words:

"O unkind father! to cross the affection of thy child, and thus force love where there is no liking: yet shall my mind continue true to my dear-loved lord; although my body be forced against nature to obey, and Almidor have the honour of my marriage-bed, yet shall English George only have my heart, and my purity, if ever he return to Egypt."

Hereupon she pulled forth a chain of gold, and wrapped it seven times about her alabaster neck. "This," said she, "hath been seven days steeped in tiger's blood, and seven nights in dragon's milk, whereby it hath obtained such excellent virtue, that so long as I wear it about my neck, I shall remain pure: though I should be forced to the state of marriage, and lie seven years in the bed of wedlock, yet, by the virtue of this chain, shall I still continue a true virgin."

These words were no sooner ended, but Almidor entered her sorrowful chamber, and presented her with a weddinggarment, which was of the purest Median silk, embossed with pearl and glittering gold, perfumed with sweet Syrian powders; it was of the colour of the lily, when Flora had bedecked the fields in May with nature's ornaments; glorious and costly were her vestures, and so stately were the nuptial rites solemnized, that Egypt admired the grandeur of her wedding, which for seven days was held in the court of Ptolemy, and then moved to Tripoli, the chief city in Barbary, where Almidor's forced bride was crowned queen of Morocco; at which coronation the conduits ran with Greek wines, and the streets of Tripoli were beautified with pageants and delightful shows. The court resounded such melodious harmony, as though Apollo with his silver harp had descended from the heavens: such tilts and tournaments were performed betwixt the Egyptian knights, and the knights of Barbary, that they exceeded the nuptials of Hecuba the beauteous queen of Troy. Which honourable proceedings we leave for this time to their own contentments, some masking, some dancing, some revelling, some tilting, some banquetting. Leave we also the champion of England, St. George, mourning in the dungeon in Persia, as related before, and return to the other six champions of

Christendom, who departed from the brazen pillar, every one his several way, whose knightly and noble adventures, if the Muses grant me their assistance, I will most amply discover, to the honour of Christendom.

CHAPTER IV

St. Denis, the champion of France, lives seven years in the shape of an hart: and proud Eglantine, the king of Thessaly's daughter, is transformed into a mulberry-tree; but recover their former shapes by means of St. Denis's horse.

COMMENCING with the long and weary travels St. Denis, the champion of France, endured, after his departure from the other six champions at the brazen pillar, as related in the beginning of the former chapter, from which he wandered through many a desolate grove and wilderness, without any adventure worth noting, till he arrived upon the borders of Thessaly (being a land, as then, inhabited only with wild beasts); wherein he endured such a scarcity of victuals, that he was forced, for the space of seven years, to feed upon the herbs of the field, and the fruits of trees, till the hairs of his head were like eagles' feathers, and the nails of his fingers like bird's claws: his drink the dew of heaven, which he licked from the flowers in meadows; his attire, the bay leaves and broad docks, that grew in the wood; his shoes, the bark of trees, in which he travelled through many a thorny brake. But at last, as it was his fortune, or cruel destiny (being overpressed with the extremity of hunger), to taste and feed upon the berries of an enchanted mulberry-tree, whereby he lost the lively form and image of his human substance, and was transformed into the shape and likeness of a wild hart; which strange and sudden transformation this noble champion little mistrusted, till he espied his misshapen form in a clear fountain, which nature had made in a cool and shady valley; but when he beheld the shadow of his deformed body, and how his head, lately honoured with a burgonet of steel, was now disgraced with a pair of Sylvan horns! his countenance, which was the index of his noble mind, now covered with the likeness of a brute; and his body, which was erect, tall, smooth, and fair, now bending to the earth on four feet, and clothed in a rough hairy hide of a dusky brown colour; having his reason still left, he ran again to the mulberry-tree, supposing the berries he had eaten to be the cause of his transformation, and there laying himself upon the bare ground, he thus began to complain:

"What magic charms, or what bewitching spells," said he, "are contained in this cursed tree, poisonous fruit hath confounded my future fortunes, and reduced me to this miserable condition! O thou celestial Ruler of the world! O merciful Power of heaven! look down with pity on my hapless state; incline thine ears to listen to my woes: I, who was late a man, am now an horned beast; a soldier, once my country's champion, now a timorous deer, the prey of dogs; my glittering armour changed into a hairy hide, and my brave array now vile as common earth: henceforth, instead of princely palaces, these shady woods must be my sole retreat, wherein my bed of down must be a heap of sun-dried moss; my sweet delighting music, blustering winds, that with tempestuous gusts make the whole wilderness tremble; the company I am obliged henceforth to keep, must be the sylvan Satyrs, Driades, and airy Nymphs who never appear to human eyes, but at twilight, or the midnight moon; the stars that beautify the crystal vault, and wide expanse of heaven, shall hereafter serve as torches to light me to my woful bed; the scowling clouds shall be my canopy; and my clock, to give me notice how time runs stealing on, the dismal sounds of hissing snakes or croaking toads!"

Thus described he his own misery, till the bitter tears of wretchedness gushed out in such abundance from the conduits of his eyes, and his heavy sighs so violently forced their passage from his bleeding breast, that they even seemed to constrain the savage bears and merciless tigers to relent in pity of his moan, and like harmless lambs to sit bleating in the woods, to hear his mournful exclamations.

Long and many days continued this champion of France in the shape of an hart, in greater misery than the unfortunate English champion in Persia, not knowing how to recover his former shape, and human substance. But one day, as he lamented the loss of his natural form, under the branches of that enchanted mulberry-tree, which was the cause of his transformation, he heard a most grievous and terrible groan, which he supposed to portend that something extraordinary was to ensue: upon which, suspending his sorrows for a time, he heard an hollow voice breathe from the trunk of the mulberry-tree the following words:

The voice in the mulberry-tree.

Cease to lament, thou famous man of France,
With gentle ears come listen to my moan,
In former time it was my fatal chance
To be the proudest maid that e'er was known;
By birth I was the daughter of a king,
Though now a breathless tree, and senseless thing.

My pride was such that heav'n confounded me,
A goddess in my own conceit I was:
What nature lent, too base I thought to be,
But deem'd myself all others to surpass,

And therefore nectar and ambrosia sweet,
The food of heav'n, for me I counted meet.

My pride despis'd the finest bread of wheat,
And purer food I daily sought to find;
Refined gold was boil'd still in my meat,
Such self-conceit my senses all did blind;
For which the gods above transformed me,
From human substance to this senseless tree.

Seven years in shape of hart thou must remain,
And then the purple rose, by heav'n's decree,
Shall bring thee to thy former shape again,
And end at last thy woful misery:
When this is done, be sure you cut in twain
This fatal tree wherein I do remain.

After he had heard these words from the mulberry-tree, he was so much amazed at the strangeness thereof, that he for some moments was deprived of speech; and the thoughts of his long-appointed punishment bereaved him of his understanding: but at last, recovering his senses, though not his human form, he bitterly complained of his misfortunes.

"Oh! unhappy creature," said the distressed champion, "more miserable than Progne in her transformation, and more unfortunate than Acteon, whose perfect picture I am made! His misery continued but a short time; for his own dogs, the same day, tore him into a thousand pieces, and buried his transformed carcass in their hungry bowels: but mine is appointed by the angry destinies, till seven times the summer's sun shall yearly replenish his radiant brightness, and seven times the winter's rain shall wash me with the showers of heaven."

Such were the complaints of the transformed knight of France, sometimes remembering his former fortunes, how he had spent his days in the honour of his country; at other times thinking upon the place of his nativity, renowned France, the nurse and mother of his youth; and again treading with his foot (for hands he had none) in sandy ground, the print of the words which he had heard from the mulberry-tree, and many times numbering the minutes of his tedious punishment with the flowers of the field. Ten thousand sighs he daily breathed from his breast, and still, when the sable mantle of the dark and gloomy night had overspread the azure firmament, and drawn her curtains before the brighter windows of the heavens, all creatures took their sweet repose, and closed their eyes in sleep, but him; and when all things else were silent but the murmuring brooks and rills, the distressed champion made their music is only comfort. The queen of night was many hundred times a witness to his lamentations. The wandering owl, that ventures not abroad but in the dark, sat hooting o'er his head; and the sad, but sweetly complaining Philomel, with mournful melody, joined in the chorus of his sighs. But during the whole term of his seven years' misery, his trusty steed never once forsook him, but with all love and diligence attended on him day and night, never straying from his side; and if extreme heat in summer, or pinching cold in winter, grew troublesome to him, his horse would shelter and defend him.

At last, when the term of seven years was fully expired, when he was to recover his former substance, and human shape, his good horse, which he regarded as the apple of his eye, clambered a high and steep mountain, which nature had beautified with all kind of fragrant flowers, as odoriferous as the gardens of the Hesperides; from whence he pulled a branch of purple roses, and brought them betwixt his teeth to his distressed master, being still in the same disorder and discontent, under the mulberry-tree. The champion of France no sooner beheld this, but he remembered that by a purple rose he should recover his former shape, and so joyfully received the roses from his trusty steed; then casting his eyes up to the celestial throne of heaven, he conveyed these consecrated flowers into his empty stomach.

After which he laid himself down upon the bosom of his mother earth, where he fell into such a sound sleep, that all his senses and vital spirits ceased to perform their usual offices for the space of four-and-twenty hours, in which time the windows and doors of heaven were opened, from whence descended such a shower of rain, that it washed away his hairy coat and beast-like shape; his horned head and long visage were turned again into a lively countenance; and all the rest of his members, both arms, legs, hands, feet, fingers, toes, with all the rest of nature's gifts, received their former shape.

But when the good champion awoke from his sleep, and perceived the wonderful workmanship of heaven, in transforming him to his human likeness, he first gave honour to almighty God; next, blessed the ground whereon he had lived so long in misery; then beholding his armour, which lay near him, quite stained, and almost spoiled with rust; his burgonet and keen-edged cutlass besmeared over with dirt: then lastly, pondering in his mind the faithful service his trusty steed had done him, during the time of his calamity, whose sable-coloured mane hung frizzling down his brawny neck, which before was wont to be platted curiously with artificial knots, and his forehead, which was always beautified with a tawny plume of feathers, now disfigured with overgrown hair, the good champion, St. Denis of France, was so grieved, that he stroked down his jetty back till the hair of his body lay as smooth as Arabian silk; then pulled he out his trusty falchion, which, in so many fierce assaults, and dangerous combats, had been bathed in the blood of his enemies, and by the long continuance of time lying idle, was now almost consumed with cankered rust; but by his labour and great industry, he recovered its former beauty and brightness again.

Thus both his sword and horse, his martial furniture, and all other habiliments of war, being brought to their first and proper qualities, the noble champion resolved to pursue his intended adventure in cutting down the mulberry-tree: so taking his sword, which was of the purest Spanish steel, made such a stroke at the root thereof, that at one blow he cut it quite asunder, from whence immediately flashed such a mighty flame of fire, that the mane was burnt from his horse's neck, and also the hair of his own head would have been fired had not his helmet preserved him; and no sooner was the flame extinguished, but there ascended from the hollow tree a lovely virgin (in shape like Daphne, which Apollo turned into a bay-tree), fairer than Pygmalion's ivory image, or the northern snow; her eyes more clear than the icy mountains, her cheeks like roses dipped in milk, her lips more lovely than the Turkish rubies, her alabaster teeth like Indian pearls, her neck seemed an ivory tower, her dainty breasts a garden where milk-white doves sat and sung, the rest of nature's lineaments a stain to Juno, Pallas, or Venus; at whose dazzling beauty, this valiant and undaunted champion more admired, than at her wonderful transformation; for his eyes were ravished with such exceeding pleasure, that his tongue could remain no longer silent, but was forced to unfold the secrets of his heart, and in these terms began to utter his mind:

"Thou most divine and singular ornament of nature!" said he, "fairer than the feathers of the Sylvan swan that swims upon Meander's crystal streams, and far more beautiful than Aurora's morning countenance, to thee, the fairest of all fairs, most humbly and truly to thy beauty do I here submit my affections. Also I swear, by the honour of my knighthood, and by the love of my country of France (which vow I will not violate for all the treasures of rich America, or the golden mines of Higher India), whether thou art an angel descended from heaven, or a fury ascended from the vast dominions of Proserpine; whether thou art some fairy or Sylvan nymph, which inhabits the fatal wood, or else an earthly creature, for thy sins transformed into this mulberry tree; I am not competent to judge. Therefore, sweet saint, to whom my heart must pay its due devotion, unfold to me thy birth, parentage, and name, that I may the bolder presume upon thy courtesies." At which demand, this new-born virgin, with a shamefaced look, modest gesture, sober grace, and blushing countenance, began thus to reply:

"Sir Knight, by whom my life, my love, and fortunes are to be commanded, and by whom my human shape and natural form is recovered; first know, you magnanimous champion, that I am by birth the king of Thessaly's daughter, and my name was called for my beauty, proud Eglantine: for which contemptuous pride, I was transformed into this mulberry-tree, in which green substance I have continued fourteen years. As for my love thou hast deserved it before all knights in the world, and to thee do I plight that true promise before the Omnipotent Judge of all things. And before that sacred promise shall be infringed, the sun shall cease to shine by day, the moon by night, and all the planets forsake their natural order."

At which words the champion gave her the courtesies of his country, and sealed her promises with a loving kiss.

The beautiful Eglantine was clothed in a garment of green rushes, intermixed with such a variety of flowers, that it surpassed, for workmanship, the Indian maidens' curious webs; her curling locks of hair continued still of the colour of the mulberry-tree, and made her appear like Flora in her greatest royalty, when the fields were decked with nature's tapestry.

She now washed her lily hands and rose-coloured face in the dew of heaven, which she gathered from a bed of violets. Thus, in green vestments, she began, in company of her true love, the valiant knight of France, to take her journey to her father's court; where, after some few days' travel, they arrived safe, and were welcomed according to their wishes with the most honourable entertainments. The king of Thessaly no sooner beheld his daughter, of whose strange transformation he was ignorant, but he fell into a swoon through exceeding joy. but coming to his senses, he embraced her, and proffered such courtesy to the stranger knight, that St. Denis accounted him the mirror of all courtesy, and the pattern of true nobility.

After the champion was unarmed, his stiff and wearied limbs were bathed in new milk and white wine, he was conveyed to a sweet-smelling fire made of juniper, and the fair Eglantine, conducted by the maids of honour to a private chamber, where she was disrobed of her Sylvan attire, and apparelled in long robes of purple silk. In which court of Thessaly we will leave our champion of France with his lady, and go forward in the discourse of the other champions, discovering what adventures happened to them during the seven years.

CHAPTER V.

How St. James, the champion of Spain, continued seven years dumb for the love of the fair Jew, and how he should have been shot to death by the maidens of Jerusalem, with other things which happened in his travels.

Now must my muse speak of St. James of Spain, the third champion, and what happened unto him in his seven years' travels through many a strange country by sea and land, where his honourable acts were so dangerous and full of wonder, that I want skill to express, and art to describe. Also I am forced, for brevity sake, to pass over his dangerous battle with the burning drake, upon the flaming mount in Sicily, which terrible combat continued for the space of seven days and seven nights. Likewise I omit his travels in Cappadocia, through a wilderness of monsters, with his passage over the Red Sea, where his ship was devoured with worms, his mariners drowned, and himself, his horse, and furniture, safely brought to land by the sea-nymphs and mermaids: where after his long travels, past perils, and dangerous tempests, among the stormy billows of the raging seas, he arrived in the unhappy dominions of Judah; unhappy by reason of the long and troublesome misery he endured for the love of a fair Jew. For coming to the beautiful city of Jerusalem (being in that age the wonder of the world, for brave buildings, princely palaces, and wonderful temples), he so admired the glorious situation thereof (being the richest place that ever his eyes beheld), that he stood before the walls of Jerusalem, one while gazing upon her golden gates, glittering against the sun's bright countenance; another while beholding her stately pinnacles, whose lofty peeping tops seemed to touch the clouds; another while wondering at her towers of jasper, jet, and ebony, her strong and fortified walls, three times double about the city, glittering spires of the temple of Sion, built in the fashion and similitude of the pyramids, the ancient monuments of Greece, whose battlements were covered with steel, the walls burnished with silver, the ground paved with tin. Thus, as this noble and famous knight at arms stood beholding the situation of Jerusalem, there suddenly thundered such a peal of ordnance within the city, that it seemed, in his amazement, to shake the veil of heaven, and to move the deep foundations of the fastened earth; whereat his horse gave such a sudden start, that he leaped ten feet from the place whereon he stood. After this, he heard the sound of drums, and the cheerful echoes of brazen trumpets, by which the valiant champion expected some honourable pastime, or some great tournament to be at hand; which indeed so fell out: for no sooner did he cast his eyes towards the east side of the city, but he beheld a troop of well-appointed horse come marching through the gates; after them twelve armed knights mounted on twelve warlike coursers, bearing in their hands twelve blood-red streamers, whereon was wrought in silk the picture of Adonis wounded by a boar; after them, the king drawn in a chariot by Spanish mares. The king's guards were a hundred naked Moors, with Turkish bows and darts, feathered with ravens' wings; after them marched Celestine, the king of Jerusalem's fair daughter, mounted on a tame unicorn. In her hand a javelin of silver, and armed with a breast-plate of gold, artificially wrought like the scales of a porcupine; her guard were one hundred Amazonian dames clad in green silk: after them followed a number of esquires and gentlemen, some upon Barbary steeds, some upon Arabian palfreys, and some on foot, in pace more nimble than the tripping deer, and more swift than the wildest hart upon the mountains of Thessaly.

Thus Nebuzaradan, great king of Jerusalem (for so he was called), solemnly hunted in the wilderness of Judah, being a country very much annoyed with wild beasts, as the lion, the leopard, the boar, and such like; in which exercise the king appointed, as it was proclaimed by his chief herald at arms (which he heard repeated by the shepherds in the fields), that whosoever slew the first wild beast in the forest, should have in reward a corslet of steel so richly engraven, that it should be worth a thousand shekels of silver. Of which honourable enterprise when the champion heard, and with what liberal bounty the adventurous knight would be rewarded, his heart was fraught with invincible courage, thirsting after glorious attempts, not only for hope of gain, but for the desire of honour, at which his illustrious and undaunted mind aimed, to emblazon his deeds in the memorable records of fame, and to shine as a crystal mirror to all future times. So closing down his beaver, and locking on his furniture, he scoured over the plains before the hunters of Jerusalem, in pace more swift than the winged winds, till he approached an old unfrequented forest, wherein he espied a huge and mighty wild boar, lying before his mossy den, gnawing upon the mangled joints of some passenger, which he had murdered as he travelled through the forest.

This boar was of wonderful length and bigness, and so terrible to behold, that at the first he almost daunted the courage of the Spanish knight: for his monstrous head seemed ugly and deformed, his eyes sparkled like a fiery furnace, his tusks more sharp than pikes of steel, and from his nostrils fumed such a violent breath, that it seemed like a tempestuous whirlwind; his bristles were more hard than seven times melted brass, and his tail more loathsome than a wreath of snakes. Near whom when St. James approached, and beheld how he drank the blood of human creatures, and devoured their flesh, he blew his silver horn, which hung at the pommel of his saddle, in a scarf of green silk; whereat the furious monster turned himself, and very fiercely assailed the noble champion, who most nimbly leaped from his horse, and with his spear struck such a violent blow upon the breast of the boar, that it shivered into twenty pieces; then drawing his falchion from his side, he gave a second stroke, but all in vain, for he struck as it were upon a rock of stone, or a pillar of iron, not hurting the boar: but at last, with staring eyes and open jaws, the greedy monster assailed the champion, intending to swallow him alive; but the nimble knight trusting more to policy than fortitude, so skipped from place to place, till on a sudden he thrust his keen-edged battle-axe down his throat, and split his heart asunder. Which being accomplished to his own desire, he cut off the boar's head, and so presented the honour of the combat to the king of Jerusalem, who, with his mighty train of knights, just now entered the forest; who having graciously received the gift, and bountifully fulfilled his promises, demanded the champion's country, his religion, and the place of his nativity. But no sooner had he intelligence that he was a Christian knight, and born in the territories of Spain, but presently his kindness changed to a great fury, and by these words he expressed his anger to the Christian champion:

"Knowest thou not, bold knight," said the king of Jerusalem, " that it is the law of Judah to harbour no uncircumcised man, but either to banish him out of the land, or end his days by some untimely death? Thou art a Christian, and therefore shalt die: not all thy country's treasures, the wealthy Spanish mines, nor if all the Alps which divide the countries of Italy and Spain, were turned to hills of burnished gold, and made my lawful heritage, should redeem thy life. Yet for the honour thou hast done in Judah, I grant thee this favour by the law of arms, to choose thy death, else hadst thou suffered most grievous torment." This severe judgment so amazed the champion, that desperately he would have killed himself with his own sword, but that he thought it more honourable to his country to die in the defence of Christendom. So, like a true, noble knight, fearing not the threats of the Jews, he gave the sentence of his own death. First he requested to be bound to a pine tree, with his breast laid open naked against the sun; then to have an hour's respite to make his supplication to his Creator, and afterwards to be shot to death by a true virgin.

Which words were no sooner pronounced, but they disarmed

him of his furniture, bound him to a pine-tree, and laid his breast open, ready to receive the bloody stroke of some unrelenting maiden: but such pity, meekness, mercy, and kind lenity lodged in the heart of every maiden, that none would take in hand, or be the bloody executioner of so brave a knight. At last the tyrannous Nebuzaradan gave strict commandment, upon pain of death, that lots should be cast betwixt the maids of Judah that were there present, and to whom the lot fell, she should be the fatal executioner of the condemned Christian. But by chance the lot fell to Celestine the king's daughter, being the fairest maid then living in Jerusalem, in whose heart no such deed of cruelty could be harboured. Instead of death's fatal instrument, she shot towards his breast a deep-strained sigh, the true messenger of love, and afterwards to heaven she thus made her humble supplication:

"Thou great Commander of celestial moving powers, convert the cruel motions of my father's mind into a spring of pitiful tears, that they may wash away the blood of this innocent knight from the habitation of his stained purple soul. O Judah and Jerusalem, within whose bosoms live a wilderness of tigers, degenerate from nature's kind, more cruel than the hungry cannibals, and more obdurate than untamed lions! What merciless tiger can lacerate that breast, where lives the image of true nobility, the very pattern of knighthood, and the map of a noble mind? No, no, before my hand shall be stained with Christians' blood, I will, like Scylla, against all nature, sell my country's safety, or, like Medea, wander with the golden fleece to unknown nations."

In such manner complained the beauteous Celestine, the king's daughter of Jerusalem, till her sighs stopped the passage of her speech, and her tears stained the natural beauty of her rosy cheeks; her hair, which glittered like to golden wires, she besmeared in dust, and disrobed herself of her costly garments; and then, with a train of her Amazonian ladies, went to the king her father, where, after a long suit, she not only obtained his life, but liberty; yet therewithal his perpetual banishment from Jerusalem, and from all the borders of Judah: the want of whose sight more grieved her heart than the loss of her own life. So this noble and praiseworthy Celestine returned to the Christian champion, who expected every minute to be put to death: but he was agreeably disappointed, for the good lady, after she had sealed two or three kisses upon his pale lips, cut the bands that bound his body to the tree into many pieces; and then, with a flood of tears, she thus revealed her mind:

"Most noble knight, and true champion of Christendom, thy life and liberty I have gained, but therewith thy banishment from Judah, which is a heavy sorrow to my soul; for

in thy bosom have I built my happiness, and in thy heart I
account the paradise of my true love: thy first sight and lovely
countenance did delight me; for when these eyes beheld thee
mounted on thy princely palfrey, my heart burned in affection
towards thee. Therefore, dear knight, in reward of my love,
be thou my champion, and for my sake wear this ring, with
this motto engraven in it, '*Ardeo Affectione.*' And so giving
him a ring from her finger, and therewithal a kiss from her
mouth, she departed with a sorrowful sigh, in company of
her father and the rest of his honourable train, back to the
city of Jerusalem, being as then near the setting of the sun.
But now St. James, the champion of Spain, having escaped
the danger of death, and at full liberty to depart from that
unhappy nation, he fell into many cogitations, one while
thinking upon the true love of Celestine (whose name as yet
he was ignorant of), another while upon the cruelty of her
father; then intending to depart into his own country, but
looking back to the towers of Jerusalem, his mind suddenly
altered, for thither he purposed to go, hoping to have sight of
his lady and mistress, and to live in some disguised sort in
her presence, and be his love's true champion against all comers.
So gathering certain black berries from the trees, he coloured
his body all over like a Blackmoor; but yet considering that
his country speech would discover him, intended likewise to
continue dumb all the time of his residence in Jerusalem.

So when all things were arranged according to his desire, he
took his journey to the city, where with signs he declared his
intent, which was, to be entertained in the court, and to spend
his time in the service of the king. Whose countenance when
the king beheld, which seemed of the natural colour of the
Moors, he little mistrusted him to be the Christian champion,
whom before he greatly envied, but accounted him one of the
bravest Indian knights that ever his eye beheld; therefore he
installed him with the honour of knighthood, and appointed
him to be one of his guard, and likewise his daughter's only
champion. Thus when St. James of Spain saw himself invested
in that honourable place, his soul was filled with such exceeding joy, that he thought no pleasure comparable to his, no place
of Elysium but the court of Jerusalem, and no goddess so divine as his beloved Celestine.

Long continued he dumb, casting forth many a loving sigh
in the presence of his lady and mistress, not knowing how to
reveal the secrets of his mind.

So upon a time there arrived in the court of Nebuzaradan,
the king of Arabia, with the admiral of Babylon, both presuming
upon the love of Celestine, and craving her in the way of
marriage; but she exempted all their advances from her chaste

mind, only building her thoughts upon the Spanish knight, who she supposed to be in his own country.

At witnessing the melancholy of the princess Celestine, her importunate suitors, the king of Arabia and the admiral of Babylon marvelled: and therefore intended upon an evening to present her with some rare devised mask. So choosing out fit consorts for their courtly pastimes, of which number the king of Arabia was chief and first leader of the train, the great admiral of Babylon was the second, and her own champion, St. James, the third, who was called by the name of " Dumb Knight," in this manner the mask was performed:

First began a most excellent concert of music, after them the aforesaid maskers in cloth of gold, and most curiously embroidered, and danced about the hall: at the end whereof the king of Arabia presented Celestine with a costly sword, at the hilt whereof hung a silver glove, and upon the point was erected a golden crown. Then the music sounded another course, of which the admiral of Babylon was leader; who presented her with a vesture of pure silk of the colour of the rainbow, brought in by Diana, Venus, and Juno. Which being done, the music sounded the third time; in which course St. James, though unknown, was the leader of the dance, who at the end thereof presented Celestine with a garland of sweet flowers, which was brought in by three Graces, and put upon her head. Afterwards the Christian champion, intending to discover himself unto his lady and mistress, took her by the hand, and led her a stately Morisco dance; which was no sooner finished, but he offered her the diamond ring which she gave him at his departure in the woods, which she presently knew by the motto, and shortly after was made acquainted with his dumbness, his counterfeit colour, his changing of nature, and the great danger he put himself to for her sake; which caused her with all the speed she could possibly make, to break off the company, and to retire into a chamber which she had close by, where the same evening she had a long conference with her faithful lover and adventurous champion. And to conclude, they made an agreement betwixt them, and the same night, unknown to any in the court, she bade Jerusalem adieu, and by the light of Cynthia's glittering beams, stole from her father's palace, where in company of none but St. James, she took her journey towards the country of Spain. But this noble knight by policy prevented all ensuing dangers, for he shod his horse backwards, whereby, when they were missed in the court, they might be followed the contrary way.

By this means escaped the two lovers from the fury of the Jews, and arrived safely in Spain, in the city of Seville, wherein the brave champion St. James was born; where now we leave them for a time to their own contented minds. Also passing over the disturbances in Jerusalem for the loss of Celestine, the vain pursuits of adventurous knights, the preparing of fresh horses to follow them, the frantic passions of the king for his daughter, the melancholy moans of the admiral of Babylon for his mistress, and the woful lamentation of the Arabian king for his lady and love; we will return to the adventures of the other Christian champions.

CHAPTER VI.

The terrible battle between St. Anthony, the champion of Italy, and the giant Blanderon; and afterwards of his strange entertainment in the giant's castle by a Thracian lady, and what happened to him in the same castle.

AT that time of the year when the earth was newly decked with the summer's livery, the noble champion St. Anthony of Italy arrived in Thrace, where he spent his seven years' travels to the honour of his country, the glory of God, and to his own lasting memory. For after he had wandered through woods and wildernesses, by hills and dales, by caves and dens, and other unknown passages, he arrived at last upon the top of a high mountain, whereon stood a wonderful strong castle, which was kept by the most mighty giant under the cope of heaven, whose puissant force all Thrace could not overcome, nor once attempt to withstand, but with the danger of their whole country. The giant's name was Blanderon, his castle of the purest marble stone, his gates of brass, and over the principal gate were engraven the following verses:

> Within this castle lives the scourge of kings,
> A furious giant, whose unconquer'd pow'r
> The Thracian monarch in subjection brings,
> And keeps his daughters pris'ners in his tow'r;
> Seven damsels fair this monstrous giant keeps,
> That sing him music while he nightly sleeps.
>
> His bars of steel a thousand knights have felt,
> Which for these virgins' sake have lost their lives;
> For all the champions bold that with him dealt,
> This most inhuman giant still survives:
> Let simple passengers take heed betime,
> When up this mountain they intend to climb.
>
> But knights of worth, and men of noble mind,
> If any chance to travel by this tow'r,
> That for these maidens' sake will be so kind,
> To try their strength against the giant's pow'r,
> Shall have a vrgin's pray'r both day and night,
> To prosper them with good successful fight.

After he had read what was written over the gate, a desire of fame so encouraged him, and the thirst of honour so emboldened his valiant mind, that he vowed either to redeem these ladies from their servitude, or die with honour by the fury of the giant. So going to the castle gate, he struck so vehemently thereon, with the pommel of his sword, that it sounded like a thunder-clap. Whereat Blanderon suddenly started up, being fast asleep by a fountain-side, and came pacing forth to the gate, with an oak-tree upon his shoulder; who, at the sight of the Italian Champion, so lightly flourished it about his head, as though it had been a little battle-axe, and with these words gave the noble champion entertainment:

"What fury hath incensed thy overboldened mind, thus to adventure thy feeble force against the violence of my strong arm? I tell thee, hadst thou the strength of Hercules, who bore the mountain Atlas on his shoulders, or the policy of Ulysses, by which the city of Troy was ruined, or the might of Xerxes, whose multitudes drank up the rivers as they passed; yet all too feeble, weak, and impotent, to encounter with the mighty giant Blanderon; thy force I esteem as a blast of wind, and thy strokes as a few drops of water. Therefore betake thee to thy weapon, which I compare to a bulrush, for on this ground will I measure out thy grave, and after that will hurl thy feeble palfrey, with one of my hands headlong down this steep mountain."

Thus boasted the vain-glorious giant upon his own strength. During which time, the valiant champion had alighted from his horse where, after he had made his humble supplication to heaven for his good speed, and committed his fortune to the imperial queen of destiny, he approached within the giant's reach, who with his great oak so nimbly bestirred himself with such vehement blows, that they seemed to shake the earth, and to rattle the wall of the castle like thunder-claps; and, had not the politic knight continually skipped from the fury of his blows, he would have been soon killed, for every stroke the giant gave the root of his oak entered at the least two or three inches into the ground. But such was the wisdom and policy of the worthy champion not to encounter the force of his weapon, till the giant grew breathless, and not able, through his long labour, to lift the oak above his head; and likewise the heat of the sun was so intolerable (by reason of the extreme height of the mountain, and the mighty weight of his iron coat), that the sweat of the giant's brows ran into his eyes, and by reason he was so extreme fat, he grew so blind, that he could not see to combat with him any longer; and, as far as the knight could perceive, would have retired or run back again into his castle, but that the Italian champion with a bold courage assailed the giant so fiercely, that he was forced to let his oak fall, and stand gasping for breath; which when this noble knight beheld, with a fresh energy he redoubled his blows so courageously, that they fell on the giant's armour like a storm of winter's hail, whereby at last Blanderon was compelled to ask the champion mercy, and to crave at his hands some respite of breathing; but his demand was in vain, for the valiant knight supposed now or never to obtain the honour of the day; and therefore rested not his weary arm, but redoubled blow after blow, till the giant, for want of breath, and through the anguish of his deep-gashed wounds, was forced to give the world farewell, and to yield the riches of his castle to the most renowned conqueror, St. Anthony, the champion of Italy. But by the time this long and dangerous encounter was finished, and the giant Blanderon's head was severed from his body, the sun sat mounted on the highest part of the elements, which caused the day to be extremely hot and sultry: and the champion's armour so scalded him, that he was constrained to unbrace his corslet, to lay aside his burgonet, and to cast his body upon the cold earth, to mitigate his extreme heat. But such was the unnatural coolness of the earth, the vapours of it struck presently to his heart, from the effects of which he swooned away, and his body lay without sense or moving; where, at the mercy of pale death, he lay senseless for the space of an hour.

During this time fair Rosalinde (one of the daughters of the Thracian king, being at this time in the castle) by chance looked over the walls, and espied the body of the giant headless, under whose subjection she had continued in great servitude for the time of seven months, likewise beside him a knight unarmed as she thought, panting for breath, which the lady judged to be the knight that had slain the giant Blanderon, and the man by whom her delivery should be recovered; she presently descended the walls of the castle, and ran with all speed to the adventurous champion, whom she supposed dead. But yet being nothing discouraged of his recovery, feeling as yet warm blood in every member, retired back with all speed to the castle, and fetched a box of precious balm, which the giant was wont to pour into his wounds after his encounter with any knight. With this balm the courteous lady chafed every part of the breathless champion's body, one while washing his stiff limbs with her salt tears, which like pearls fell from her eyes, another while drying them with the tresses of her golden hair, which hung dangling in the wind; then chafing his lifeless body again with a balm of a contrary nature; but yet no sign of life could she see in the senseless knight, which caused her to despair of his recovery. Thereupon, like a loving, meek, and kind lady, considering he had lost his life for her sake, she intended to bear him company in death, and with her own hands to finish her days, and die upon his breast, as Thisbe died upon the breast of her true Pyramis. Therefore, as the swan sings awhile before her death, so this sorrowful lady warbled forth this swan-like song over the body of the noble champion:

> Muses, come mourn with doleful melody,
>   Kind Sylvan nymphs, that sit in rosy bow'rs,
> With brackish tears come mix your harmony,
>   To wail with me both minutes, days, and hours;
>   A heavy, sad, and swan-like song sing I,
>   To ease my heart awhile before I die.
>
> Dead is the knight for whom I live and die,
>   Dead is the knight which for my sake is slain;
> Dead is the knight for whom my careful cry,
>   With wounded soul, for ever shall complain.
>   A heavy, sad, and swan-like song sing I, &c.
>
> I'll lay my breast upon a silver stream,
>   And swim in Elysium's lily fields;
> There, in ambrosia fields, I'll write a theme,
>   Of all the woful sighs my sorrow yields.
>   A heavy, sad, and swan-like song sing I, &c.
>
> Farewell, fair woods, where sing the nightingales;
>   Farewell, fair fields, where feed the light-foot deer;
> Farewell, you groves, you hills, and flow'ry dales;
>   But fare you ill, the cause of all my woes.
>   A heavy, sad, and swan-like song sing I, &c.
>
> Ring out my grief, you hollow caves of stone,
>   Both birds, and beasts, with all things on the ground;
> You senseless trees, be assistant to my moan,
>   That up to heav'n my sorrows may resound.
>   A heavy, sad, and swan-like song sing I, &c.
>
> Let all the towns of Thrace ring out my knell,
>   And write in leaves of brass what I have said;
> That after ages may remember well,
>   How Rosalinde liv'd and died a maid.
>   A heavy, sad, and swan-like song sing I, &c.

She had no sooner ended, but this desperate lady unsheathed the champion's sword, which was besprinkled with the giant's blood, and being at the very point to execute her intended tragedy, with the sharp-edged weapon directly against her breast, she heard the distressed knight give a terrible groan; whereat she stopped her remorseless hand, and with more discretion tendered her own safety. For by this time the balm wherewith she anointed his body, by wonderful operation, recovered the champion, insomuch, that after some few gasps and deadly sighs, he raised up his stiff limbs from the cold earth, where, like one cast into a trance, for a time he gazed up and down the mountain, but at last, having recovered his lost senses, espied the Thracian damsel standing by, not able to speak one word, her joy so abounded: but after some time he revealed to her the manner of his dangerous encounter, and successful victory; and she the cause of his recovery, and her intended tragedy. Where, after many kind salutations, she courteously took him by the hand, and led him into the castle, where for that night she lodged his weary limbs in an easy bed stuffed with turtle feathers, and softest thistle down.

The noble-minded knight slept soundly after his dangerous battle, till golden Phœbus bade him good-morrow. Then rising out of his bed, he attired himself, not in his wonted habiliments of war, but in purple garments, and intended to overview the rarities of the castle: but the lady Rosalinde was busied in preparing delicacies for his repast, where, after he had refreshed himself with a dainty banquet, he, by the advice of Rosalinde, stripped the giant from his iron furniture, and left his naked body upon a craggy rock, to be devoured by hungry ravens, after which, the Thracian princess discovered all the castle to the adventurous champion. First she led him to a leaden tower, where hung a hundred well-approved corslets, with other martial furniture, which were the spoils of such knights as he had violently slain. After that, she brought him to a stable, wherein stood a hundred pampered steeds, which daily fed upon human flesh; against it was placed the giant's own lodging: his bed was of iron, corded with mighty bars of steel; the tester, or covering, of carved brass; the curtains were of leaves of gold; and the rest of a strange and wonderful substance, of the colour of the element. After this, she led him to a broad pond of water, more clear than quicksilver, the streams whereof lay continually as smooth as crystal, whereon swam six milk-white swans, with crowns of gold about their necks.

"Oh here," said the Thracian lady, "begins the cause of all my grief!" At which words a shower of pearly tears ran from her eyes, that for a time they stayed the liberty of her tongue. But having discharged her heart from a few sorrowful sighs, she began in this manner to tell her previous fortunes:

"These six milk-white swans, most honourable knight, you behold swimming in this river," said the lady Rosalinde, "are my natural sisters, both by birth and blood, and all daughters to the king of Thrace, being now governor of this unhappy country; and the beginning of our imprisonment began in this unfortunate manner:

"The king, my father, ordered a solemn hunting to be held through the land, in which honourable pastime myself, in company of my six sisters, was present. So in the middle of our sports, when the lords and barons of Thrace were in chase after a mighty she-lion, the heavens suddenly began to lour, the firmaments were overcast, and a general darkness overspread the face of the whole earth: then presently arose such a storm of lightning and thunder, as though heaven and earth had met together; by which our lordly troop of knights and barons were separated one from another, and we poor ladies forced to seek for shelter under the bottom of this high mountain; where, when this cruel giant Blanderon espied us, as he walked upon his battlements, he suddenly descended the mountain, and fetched us all under his arm up into the castle, where ever since we have lived in great servitude; and for the wonderful transformation of my six sisters thus, it came to pass as followeth:

"Upon a time the giant, being overcharged with wine, grew enamoured with our beauties, and desired much to enjoy the pleasure of our persons; our excellent gifts of nature so inflamed his mind with desire, that he would have forced us every one to satisfy his sinful pleasures; he took my six sisters, one by one, into his lodging, thinking to overcome them, but their earnest prayers so prevailed in the sight of God, that he preserved them pure by a most strange and wonderful miracle, and turned their comely bodies into the shape of milk-white swans, in the same form as here you see them swimming. So when this monstrous giant saw his intent crossed, and how there was none left behind to supply his want, but my unfortunate self, he restrained himself, not violating my honour with any stain of infamy, but kept me ever since a most pure maiden, only compelling me with sweet inspiring music to cause him to sleep.

"Thus have you heard, most noble knight, the true disclosure of my unhappy fortunes, and the wonderful transformation of my six sisters, whose loss to this day is greatly lamented throughout all Thrace." And there the princess made an end of her tragical discourse, not being able to utter the rest for weeping. Whereat the knight, being oppressed with great sorrow, embraced her about her slender waist, and thus kindly began to comfort her:

"Most dear and kind lady, within whose countenance I see how virtue is enthroned, and in whose mind lives true magnanimity, let these words suffice to comfort thy sorrowful thoughts. First, think that the heavens are most beneficial unto thee, in preserving thy honour from the giant's insatiate desires; secondly, for thy delivery by my means from the slavish servitude; thirdly and lastly, that thou, remaining in thy natural shape and likeness, may live to be the means of thy sisters' transformation; therefore dry up these crystal-pearled tears, and bid thy long-continued sorrows adieu, for grief is companion with despair, a procurer of a miserable death."

Thus the woful Thracian lady was comforted by the noble Christian champion; where, after a few kind greetings, they intended to travel to her father's court, there to relate what had happened to her sisters in the castle, likewise the giant's confusion, and her own safe delivery, by the illustrious prowess of the Christian knight. So, taking the keys of the castle, which were of a wonderful weight, they locked up the gates, and paced hand in hand down the steep mountain, till they approached the Thracian court, which was distant from the castle about ten miles: but by the time they had a sight of the palace, the night approached, which discontented the weary travellers; but at last, coming to her father's gates, they heard a solemn sound of bells ringing the funeral knell of some noble person; the cause of which they demanded of the porter; who in this manner expressed the truth of the matter to them:

"Fair lady and most renowned knight," said the porter, "for so you seem both, by your speeches and honourable demands, the cause of this ringing is for the loss of the king's seven daughters, the number of which bells are seven, called after the names of the seven princesses, which never yet have ceased their doleful melody since the departure of the unhappy ladies, nor ever must until news be heard of their safe return."

"Then now their tasks are ended," said the noble-minded Rosalinde, "for we bring news of the seven princesses' abode." At which words the porter, being filled with joy, in all haste ran to the steeple, and caused the bells to cease, whereat the king of Thrace, hearing the bells cease their wonted sound, suddenly started up from his princely seat, and like a man amazed, ran to the palace-gate, where he found his daughter Rosalinde in company with a strange knight. Which when he beheld, his joy was so great that he swooned on his daughter's bosom; but being recovered to his former state, he brought them up into his princely hall, where their reception was so honourable in the eyes of the whole court, as almost baffles description; but the courtiers' joy was presently dashed with Rosalinde's tragical discourse; for the good old king, when he heard of his daughters' transformation, and how they lived in the shape of milk-white swans, rent his locks of silver hair, which time had dyed with the pledge of wisdom; his rich embroidered garments he tore in many pieces, and clad his aged limbs in a dismal, black, and sable mantle; also he commanded that his knights and adventurous champions, instead of glittering armour, should wear the weeds of death, more black in hue than winter's darkest nights; and all the courtly ladies and gallant Thracian maidens, instead of silken vestments, he commanded to wear heavy, sad, and melancholy ornaments, and even as unto a solemn funeral, to attend him to the giant's castle, and there obsequiously to offer up unto the angry destinies many a bitter sigh and tear, in remembrance of his transformed daughters; which decree of the sorrowful Thracian king was performed with all convenient speed; for the next morning, no sooner had the sun poured his beams into the king's bedchamber, but he apparelled himself in mourning garments, and in the company of his melancholy train set forward on his woful pilgrimage. But here we must not forget the princely-minded champion of Italy, nor the noble-minded Rosalinde, who, at the king's departure towards the castle, craved leave to stay behind, and not so suddenly to begin new travels; wherefore the king condescended, considering their late journey the evening before. So taking the castle keys from the champion, he bade his palace adieu, and committed his fortune to his sorrowful journey; where we leave him in a world of discontented passions, and awhile discourse of what happened to the Christian champion and his beloved lady. For by the time the sun had thrice measured the world with his restless steeds, and thrice his sister Luna wandered to the west, the noble Italian knight grew weary of his long-continued rest, and desired rather to abide in a court that entertained the doleful murmuring of tragedies, than where the joyful sound of drums and trumpets should be heard; therefore he took Rosalinde by the hand, being then weeping for want of her father, to whom the noble knight in this manner expressed his intention:

"My most devoted lady and mistress," said the champion, "a second Dido for thy love, a stain to Venus for thy beauty, Penelope's compare for constancy, and for chastity the wonder of all maids; the faithful love that hitherto I have found since my arrival, for ever shall be shrined in my heart, and before all ladies under the cope of heaven thou shalt live and die my love's true goddess; and for thy sake I'll stand as champion against all knights in the world; but to impair the honour of my knighthood, and to live like a carpet-dancer in the lap of ladies, I will not; though I can tune a lute in a prince's chamber, I can sound a fierce alarm in the field. Honour calls me forth, dear Rosalinde, and fame intends to buckle on my armour, which now lies rusting in the idle courts of Thrace. Therefore I am constrained (though most unwillingly) to leave the enchanting sight of thy beauty, and commit my fortune to a longer travel; but I protest, wheresoever I come, or in what region soever I be harboured, there will I maintain, to the loss of my life, that both thy love, constancy, beauty, and chastity, surpasseth all dames alive; and with this promise, my most divine Rosalinde, I bid thee farewell." But before the honourable-minded champion could finish what he proposed to utter, the lady, being wounded inwardly with extreme grief, not able to remain silent any longer, but with the tears falling from her eyes, broke off his speech in this manner:

"Sir Knight," said she, "by whom my liberty hath been obtained, the name of lady and mistress, wherewith you entitle me, is too high and proud a name; but rather call me hand-maid; for on thy noble person will I evermore attend. It is not Thrace can harbour me when thou art absent; and before I do forsake thy company and kind fellowship, heaven shall be no heaven, the sea no sea, nor the earth no earth; but if thou provest unconstant, these tender hands of mine shall never be unclasped, but hang on thy horse's bridle, till my body, like Theseus's son, be dashed asunder against hard flinty stones: therefore forsake me not, dear knight of Christendom. If ever Camina proved true to her Sinatus, or Alstone to her lover, Rosalinde will be as true to thee." So with this plighted promise she caught him fast about the neck, from whence she would not unclose her hands till he had vowed, by the honour of true chivalry, to make her his sole companion, and only partner of his travels.

They being both agreed, she was most trimly attired like a page in green sarsenet, her hair bound up most tastefully with a silk artificially wrought braid, with curious knots, that she might travel without suspicion or blemish of honour; her rapier was a Turkish blade, and her poniard of the finest fashion, which she wore at her back tied with an orange tawny-coloured scarf, beautified with tassels of silk; her buskins of the smoothest kid-skins, her spurs of the purest Lydian steel: in which, when the noble and beautiful lady was attired, she seemed in stature like the god of love, when he sat dandled upon Dido's lap, or rather Ganimede, Love's minion, or Adonis, when Venus showed her white skin to entrap his eyes to her unchaste desires. But to be brief, all things being in readiness for their departure, this famous worthy knight mounted on his eager steed, and Rosalinde on her gentle palfrey, in pace more easy than the winged winds, or a tiny boat floating upon crystal streams, they both bade adieu to the country of Thrace, and committed their journey to the queen of chance; therefore smile, heavens, and guide them with a most happy star, until they arrive where their souls do most desire. The bravest and boldest knight that ever poised a lance, and the loveliest lady that ever eye beheld.

The future career of our travellers we must leave for a season, and speak of the Thracian mourners, who by this time had watered the earth with abundance of their briny tears, and made the elements true witnesses of their sad lamentations, as related in the next chapter.

CHAPTER VII.

How St Andrew, the champion of Scotland, travelled into a vale of walking spirits; and how he was set at liberty by a moving fire, after his journey into Thrace, where he recovered the six ladies to their natural shapes that had lived seven years in the likeness of milk-white swans; with other accidents that befell the most noble champion.

Now of the honourable adventures of St. Andrew, the famous champion of Scotland, must I discourse, whose seven years' travels were as strange as any of the other champions. For after he had departed from the brazen pillar, as related in the beginning of the history, he travelled through many strange and unknown nations, beyond the circuit of the sun, where but one time in the year he shows his bright beams, but continual darkness overspreads the whole country, and there lives a kind of people that have heads like dogs, that in extremity of hunger do devour one another, from which people this noble champion was strangely delivered; where after he had wandered certain days, neither seeing the gladsome brightness of the sun, nor the comfortable countenance of the moon, but only guided by the planets of the elements, he happened to come to a vale of walking spirits, which he supposed to be the very dungeon of burning Acheron; there he heard the blowing of unseen fires, boiling of furnaces, rattling of armour, trampling of horses, jingling of chains, lumbering of iron, roaring of spirits, and such-like horrid noises, that it made the Scottish champion almost at his wit's end. But yet, having an undaunted courage, exempting all fear, he humbly made his supplication to heaven, that God would deliver him from that place of terror; and so presently, as the champion kneeled down upon the barren ground (whereon grew neither herb, flower, grass, nor any other green thing), he beheld a certain flame of fire walking up and down before him, at which he stood for a time amazed, whether it were best to go forward, or to stand still; but remembering himself how he had read in former times of a moving fire, called *Ignis Fatuus*, the fire of destiny; by some, *Will with the Whisp*, or *Jack with the Lantern;* and likewise, by some simple country people, *The Fair Maid of Ireland*, which commonly used to lead wandering travellers out of their ways; the like imaginations entered into the champion's mind. So encouraging himself with fresh courage, and cheering up his dull senses, lately oppressed with extreme fear, he directly followed the moving fire, which so quickly went before him, that by the time the guider of the night had climbed twelve degrees in the zodiac, he was safely delivered from the vale of walking spirits, by direction of the moving fire.

Now began the sun to dance about the firmament, which he had not seen in many months before; whereat he very much rejoiced, being long covered before with darkness at every step he trod; his way now was as pleasurable as though he walked in a garden bedecked with all kinds of fragrant flowers.

At last, without any further molestation, he arrived within the territories of Thrace, a country, as remarked in the former chapter, adorned with the beauty of many fair woods and forests, through which he travelled with small rest, and less sleep, till he came to the foot of the mountain, whereupon stood the castle wherein the woful king of Thrace, in company with his sorrowful subjects, still lamented the unhappy destinies of his six daughters turned into swans, having crowns of gold about their necks. When the valiant champion St. Andrew beheld the lofty situation of the castle, and the invincible strength it seemed to be of, he expected some strange adventure to befall him in the castle, so preparing his sword in readiness, and buckling close his armour, which was a coat of silver mail, for lightness in travel, he climbed the mountain, whereupon he espied the giant lying upon a craggy rock, with his limbs and members all rent and torn, by the fury of the hunger-starved fowls; which loathsome spectacle was no little wonder to the worthy champion, considering the mighty stature and bigness of the giant. Here, leaving his putrified body to the winds, he approached the gates; where, after he had read the superscription over the same, without any interruption entered the castle, whence he expected a fierce encounter by some knight that should have defended the same; but all things were contrary to his imagination; for after he had found many a strange novelty and hidden secret closed in the same, he chanced at last to come where the Thracians duly observed their ceremonious mournings, which were daily performed in this order: first, upon Sundays, which in that country is the first day in the week, all the Thracians attired themselves after the manner of Bacchus's priests, and burned perfumed incense, with sweet Arabian frankincense, upon a religious shrine, which they offered to the sun as chief governor of that day, thinking thereby to appease the angry deities, and to recover the unhappy ladies to their former shapes; upon Mondays, clad in garments after the manner of Sylvans, a colour like to the waves of the sea, they offered up their tears to the moon, being the guider and mistress of that day; upon Tuesdays, like soldiers, trailing their banners in the dust, and drums sounding sad and doleful melody, in sign of discontent, they committed their proceedings to the pleasure of Mars, being ruler and guider of that day; upon Wednesdays, like scholars, unto Mercury; upon Thursdays, like potentates, to Love; upon Fridays, like lovers, with sweet-sounding music to Venus; and upon Saturdays, like manual professors, to the angry and discontended Saturn.

Thus the woful Thracian king, and his sorrowful subjects, consumed seven months away, one while accusing Fortune of despite, another while the Heavens of injustice; the one for his chlidren's transformations, the other for their long-lamented punishments. But at last, when the Scottish champion heard what bitter moan the Thracians made about the river, he demanded the cause, and to what purpose they observed such ceremonies, contemning the majesty of Jehovah, and only worshipping outward and vain gods. To whom the king, after a few sad tears, strained from the conduits of his aged eyes, replied in this manner:

"Most noble knight, for so you seem by your gesture and other outward appearance, if you desire to know the cause of our continual griefs, prepare your ears to hear a tragical and woful tale, whereat methinks I see the elements begin to mourn, and cover their azured countenance with sable clouds. These milk-white swans you see, whose necks are beautified with golden crowns, are my six natural daughters, transformed into this swan-like substance, by the appointment of the gods; for recently this castle was kept by a cruel giant, named Blanderon, who by violence would have dishonoured their persons, but the heavens, to preserve their chastities, prevented his wicked desires, and transformed their beautiful bodies to these milk-white swans. And now seven years the cheerful spring hath renewed the earth with her summer's livery, and seven times the nipping winter frosts have bereaved the trees of leaf and bud, since first my daughters lost their human shapes; seven summers have they swam upon this crystal stream, where, instead of rich attire, and embroidered vestments, their smooth silver-coloured feathers adorn their comely bodies; princely palaces, wherein they were wont, like tripping sea-nymphs, to dance their measures up and down are now exchanged into cold streams of water; wherein their chiefest melody is the murmuring of cold liquid bubbles, and their joyful pleasure to hear the harmony of humming bees, which some poets call the Muses' birds.

"Thus have you heard (most worthy knight) the woful tragedy of my daughters, for whose sakes I will spend the remnant of my days heavily, complaining of their long-appointed punishments, about the banks of this unhappy river." Which sad discourse was no sooner ended, but the Scottish knight thus replied, to the comfort and great rejoicing of the company:

"Most noble king, your heavy and dolorous discourse hath

constrained my heart to a wonderful passion, and compelled my very soul to mourn your daughters' miseries: but yet a greater grief and deeper sorrow than that hath taken possession of my breast, whereof my eyes have been witnesses, and my ears unhappy hearers of your misbelief; I mean your unchristian faith: for I have seen, since my first arrival into this same castle, your profane and vain worship of strange and false gods, as of Phœbus, Luna, Mars, Mercury, and suchlike poetical names, which the majesty of high Jehovah utterly contemns. But, magnificent governor of Thrace, if you seek to recover your daughters by humble prayer, and to obtain your soul's content by true tears, you must abandon all such vain ceremonies, and with true humility believe in the Christian's God, which is the God of wonders, and chief commander of the rolling elements, in whose quarrel this unconquered arm and this undaunted heart of mine shall fight: and now, be it known to thee, great king of Thrace, that I am a Christian champion, by birth a knight of Scotland, bearing my country's arms upon my breast (for indeed thereon he bore a silver cross, set in blue silk); and therefore, in the honour of Christendom, I challenge forth the proudest knight at arms, against whom I will maintain that our God is the true God, and the rest fantastical and vain ceremonies."

This sudden and unexpected challenge so daunted the Thracian champions, that they stood amazed for a time, gazing upon one another like men dropt from the clouds: but at last, consulting together how the challenge of the strange knight was to the dishonour of their country, and utter scandal of all knightly dignity, they with a general consent craved leave of the king that the challenge might be taken, who as willingly condescended as they demanded.

So both time and place was appointed, which was the morning following, by the king's commandment upon a large and plain meadow, close by the river side, whereon the six swans were swimming; whereupon, after the Christian champion had cast down his steel gauntlet, and the Thracian knights accepted thereof, every one departed for that night, the challenger to the east side of the castle to his lodging, and the defendants to the west, where they slept quietly till the next morning, who, by the break of day, were awakened by a herald of arms. But all the preceeding night our Scottish champion never enjoyed one moment of sleep, but busied himself in trimming his horse, buckling on his armour, lacing on his burgonet, and making prayers to the divine majesty of God, for his conquest and victory, till the morning's beauty chased away the darkness of the night: and no sooner were the windows of the day full opened, but the valiant champion of Christendom entered the lists, where the king, in company of the Thracian lords, was present to behold the combat; and so after St. Andrew had twice or thrice walked his horse up and down the lists, bravely flourishing his lance, at the top whereof hung a pendant of gold, whose motto was thus written in silver letters—" This day a martyr or a conqueror ;" then entered a knight in exceeding bright armour, mounted upon a courser as white as the northern snow, whose caparison was of the colour of the elements; betwixt whom was a fierce encounter, but the Thracian had the foil, and with disgrace departed the list. Then secondly entered another knight in armour, varnished with green varnish, his steed of the colour of an iron grey; who likewise had the repulse by the worthy Christian. Thirdly entered a knight in a black corslet, mounted upon a big-boned palfrey, covered with a veil of sable silk; in his hand he bore a lance nailed round about with plates of steel; which knight among the Thracians was accounted the strongest in the world, except it were those giants that descended from a monstrous lineage; but he no sooner encountered this hardy champion, but his lance shivered asunder, and flew so violently into the air, that it much amazed the beholders; then he alighted from his steed, and so valiantly bestirred himself with his keen falchion, that the fiery sparks flew as thick from this noble champion's steel helmet, as from an iron anvil: but the combat endured not very long, before the most hardy Scottish knight espied an advantage wherein he might show his matchless fortitude; whereupon he struck such a mighty blow upon the Thracian's burgonet, that it cleaved his head just down to his shoulders; whereat the king suddenly started from his seat, and with a wrathful countenance threatened the champion's death in this manner:

"Proud Christian," said the king, "thou shalt repent this death, and curse the time that ever thou came to Thrace; his blood we will revenge upon thy head, and reward thy present cruelty with a sudden death:" and so, in company of a hundred armed knights, he encompassed the Scottish champion, intending by multitudes to murder him. But when the valiant knight St. Andrew saw how he was oppressed by treachery, and environed with mighty troops, he called to heaven for succour, and animated himself by these words of encouragement— "Now for the honour of Christendom, this day a martyr or a conqueror;" and therewithal he so valiantly behaved himself with his battle-axe, that he made lanes of murdered men, and felled them down by multitudes, like as the harvest-men do mow down ears of ripened corn, whereby they fell before his face like leaves from trees, when the summer's pride declines her glory. So at last, after much bloodshed, the Thracian king was compelled to yield to the Scottish champion's mercy, who swore him, for the safety of his life, to forsake his profane religion, and become a Christian, whose true living God the Thracian king vowed for evermore to worship, and thereupon he kissed the champion's sword.

This conversion of the pagan king so pleased the majesty of God, that he presently gave an end to his daughters' punishments, and turned the ladies to their former shapes. But when the king beheld their smooth feathers, which were as white as lilies, exchanged to natural fairness, and that their black bills and slender necks were converted to their first created beauty, he bade adieu to his grief and long continued sorrows, protesting ever after to continue a true Christian for the Scottish champion's sake, by whose pious aspirations his daughters obtained their former features. So taking the Christian knight, in company of the six ladies, to an excellent rich chamber, prepared with all things according to their wishes, where first the Christian knight was unarmed, then his wounds washed with white wine, new milk, and rose water, and so, after some dainty repast, conveyed to his night's repose. The ladies being the most joyful creatures under heaven, never entertained one thought of sleep, passing the night in their father's company, till the morning messengers bade them good morrow.

Thus all things being prepared in readiness, they departed from the castle, in a triumphant manner, marching back to the Thracian palace, with streaming banners in the wind, drums and trumpets sounding joyful melody, and with sweet inspiring music, which caused the air to resound with harmony. But no sooner had they entered the palace, which was in distance from the giant's castle about ten miles, but their triumphs were turned to exceeding sorrow, for Rosalinde, with the champion of Italy, as related before, were departed the court; which unexpected news so daunted the whole company, but especially the king, that the triumphs for that time were deferred, and messengers were despatched in pursuit of the adventurous Italian and lovely Rosalinde.

Likewise when St. Andrew of Scotland had intelligence, how it was one of those knights which was imprisoned with him under the wicked enchantress Kalyb, as related in the beginning of the history, his heart thirsted for his most honourable company, and his eyes seldom closed quietly, nor took any rest, until he had likewise departed in pursuit of his sworn friend, which he did the next night following, without making any one acquainted with his intent. Also when the six ladies understood the secret departure of the Scottish champion, whom they loved dearer than any knight in the world, they stored themselves with sufficient treasure, and by stealth took their journey from their father's palace, intending either to find out the victorious and approved knight of Scotland, or to end their lives in some foreign region.

The rumour of the departure of the princesses no sooner came to the king's ears, but he determined to set off on his travels, either to obtain the sight of his daughters again, or to make his tomb beyond the circuit of the sun : so attiring himself in homely russet, like a pilgrim, with an ebony staff in his hand, tipped with silver, he took his journey all unknown from his palace. Whose sudden and secret departure struck such an extreme intolerable heaviness in the court, that the palace-gates were sealed up with sable mourning cloth, the Thracian lords, exempted all pleasure, and like flocks of sheep strayed up and down without shepherds, and ladies and courtly gentlemen sat sighing in their private chambers; where we leave them for this time, and speak of the success of the other champions.

CHAPTER. VIII.

How St. Patrick, the Champion of Ireland, redeemed the six Thracian ladies out of the hands of thirty bloody-minded Satyrs, and of their purposed travels in pursuit of the champion of Scotland.

AND now of that valiant knight at arms, St. Patrick, the champion of Ireland, must I speak, whose adventurous incidents were so nobly performed, that if my pen were made of steel, I should wear it out to declare his prowess and worthy adventures. When he departed from the brazen pillar, from the other champions, the heavens smiled with a kind aspect, and sent him such a star to be his guide, that it led him to no courtly pleasures, nor to vain delights, but to the throne of Fame, where Honour sat installed upon a seat of gold. Thither travelled the warlike champion of Ireland, whose illustrious battles the northern isles have chronicled in leaves of brass. Therefore, Ireland, be proud, for from thy bowels did spring a champion, whose powess made the enemies of Christ to tremble, and watered the earth with streams of Pagans' blood; witness whereof the Isle of Rhodes, the key and strength of Christendom, was recovered from the Turks by his martial and invincible prowess; where his dangerous battles, fierce encounters, bloody skirmishes, and long assaults, would serve to fill a huge volume; all which I pass over, and wholly discourse of things appertaining to his history. For after the wars of Rhodes were fully ended, St. Patrick, (accounting idle ease the nurse of cowardice) bade Rhodes farewell, being then strongly fortified with Christian soldiers; and took his journey through many an unknown country, where at last it pleased the queen of chance to direct his steps into a solitary wilderness, inhabited only by wild Satyrs, and a people of vicious qualities, giving their wicked minds only to murder, lust, and rapine; wherein the noble champion travelled up and down many a weary step, not knowing how to satisfy his hunger, but by his own industry in killing venison, and

pressing out the blood between two flat stones, and daily roasting it by the sun: his lodging was in the hollow trunk of a blasted tree, which nightly preserved him from the dropping showers of heaven; his chief companions were sweet resounding echoes, which commonly re-answered the champion's words.

In this manner lived St. Patrick, the Irish knight, in the woods, not knowing how to set himself at liberty, but wandering up and down, as it were, in a maze wrought by the curious workmanship of some excellent gardener. It was his chance at last to come into a dismal shady thicket, beset about with baleful misletoe, a place of horror, wherein he heard the cries of some distressed ladies, whose bitter lamentations seemed to pierce the clouds, and to crave succour at the hands of God, which unexpected circumstance not a little daunted the Irish knight, so that it caused him to prepare his weapon in readiness against some sudden encounter; so crouching himself under the root of an old withered oak (which had not flourished with green leaves for many a year), he espied afar off a crew of bloody-minded Satyrs hauling by the hair of the head six unhappy ladies through many a thorny brake and briar; which woful spectacle forced such a terror in the heart of the Irish knight, that he presently rushed out for the rescue of the ladies, to redeem them from the fury of the merciless Satyrs, which were in number about thirty, every one having a club upon his neck, which they had made of the roots of young oaks and pine trees; yet this adventurous champion, being nothing discouraged, but with a bold and resolute mind, attacked the sturdiest Satyr, whose armour of defence was made of a bull's-hide, which he had dried so hard against the sun, that the champion's battle-axe fell powerless; after which the fell Satyrs encompassed the Christian knight round about, and so mightily oppressed him with downright blows, that had he not by good fortune, leaped under the boughs of a spreading tree, his life would have been forced to give the world farewell. But such was his nimbleness and active policy, that ere long he sheathed his sharp-pointed falchion in one of the Satyr's breasts; which woful sight caused all the rest to fly from his presence, and left the six ladies to the pleasure and disposition of the most noble and courageous Christian champion; who after he had sufficiently breathed, and cooled himself in the chill air (being almost breathless, through the long encounter, and bloody skirmish), he demanded the cause of the ladies' travels, and by what means they happened to be in the hands of those merciless Satyrs, who cruelly and tyrannically attempted the ruin and destruction of their immaculate virtue. To which courteous demand, one of the ladies, after a deep-fetched sigh or two (being strained from the bottom of her sorrowful heart), in the behalf of herself and the other distressed ladies, replied in this manner:

"Know, brave-minded knight, that we are the unfortunate daughters of the king of Thrace, whose lives have been unhappy ever since our births; for first we did endure a long imprisonment under the hands of a cruel giant, and afterwards, heaven, to preserve our virtue from the wicked desire of the said giant, transformed us into the shape of swans, in which likeness we remained seven years, but at last were recovered by a worthy Christian knight, named St. Andrew, the champion of Scotland; after whom we have travelled many a weary step, never assailed by any violence, until it was our unlucky fate to arrive in this unhappy wilderness, where your eyes have been true witnesses of our misfortunes."

This sad discourse was no sooner finished, but the worthy champion thus began to comfort the distressed ladies:

"The Christian champion for whom you have taken this weary travel," said the Irish champion, "is my approved friend, for whose company and wished-for sight I will go more weary miles than there are trees in this vast wilderness: therefore, most excellent ladies, true ornaments of beauty, be sad companions in my travels; for I will never cease till I have found our honourable friend, the champion of Scotland, or some of those brave knights, whom I have not seen these seven summers."

These words so contented the sorrowful ladies, that without any exception they agreed, and with as much willingness consented as the champion requested. So after they had rested themselves from their weariness, and cured their wounds, which was done by the secret virtues of certain herbs growing in the woods, they took their journey afresh under the conduct of this worthy champion, St. Patrick; where, after some days' travel, they observed a sight of a broad beaten way, where committing their fortunes to Providence, and setting their faces towards the east, they merrily journeyed together. To their future fortunes we will leave them, and speak of the seventh Christian champion, whose adventurous exploits, and knightly honours deserve a golden pen, dipped in ink of true fame, to discourse at large.

CHAPTER IX.

How St. David, the Champion of Wales, slew the Count Palatine in the Tartarian court; and after, how he was sent to the enchanted garden of Ormandine, wherein by magic art he slept seven years.

ST. DAVID, the most noble champion of Wales, after his departure from the brazen pillar, whereat the other champions of Christendom divided themselves severally to seek their foreign adventures, he achieved many memorable things, as well in Christendom, as in those nations that acknowledged no true God; which for this time I omit, and only discourse of what happened unto him among the Tartars; for he chanced to be in the emperor of Tartary's court (a place very much honoured with valorous knights, highly graced with a train of beautiful ladies), when the emperor upon a time ordained a solemn joust and tournament to be holden in honour of his birth-day. To this tournament resorted, at the time appointed (from all the borders of Tartary) the best and the hardiest knights there remaining. In which honourable and princely exercise, the noble knight, St. David, was appointed champion for the emperor, who was mounted upon a Morocco steed, adorned with a rich caparison, wrought by the curious work of Indian women, upon whose shield was set a golden griffin rampant in a field of blue.

Against the Welsh champion came the Count Palatine, son and heir-apparent to the emperor of Tartary, brought in by twelve knights, richly furnished with the habiliments of honour, who paced three times about the lists before the emperor and many ladies that were present, to behold the honourable tournament; which being done, the twelve knights departed the lists, and the Count Palatine prepared himself to encounter with the Christian knight (being appointed chief champion for the day), who likewise prepared himself, and at the trumpet's sound, by the herald's appointment, they rushed so fearfully against each other, that the ground seemed to shake under them, and the skies to resound with the echoes of their mighty strokes.

At the second race of the champions, St. David had the worst, and was constrained, through the great strength of the Count Palatine, to lean backward, almost beside his saddle, whereat the trumpets began to sound in sign of victory. But yet the valiant Christian, nothing dismayed, with courage ran the third time against the Count Palatine, and by the violence of his strength, he overthrew both horse and man, whereby the count's body was so extremely bruised with the fall of his horse, that his heart's blood issued forth from his mouth, and his vital spirit passed from the mansion of his breast, so that he was forced to bid the world farewell.

This fatal overthrow of the Count Palatine abashed the whole company, but especially the Tartar emperor, who having no more sons but him, caused the lists to be broken up, the knights to be unarmed, and the slain count to be brought, by four esquires, into his palace; where, after the armour was loosed from the body, and the Christian knight received in honour of his victory, the woful emperor bathed his son's body with tears, which dropped like crystal pearls upon the congealed blood, and after many sad sighs he breathed forth this woful lamentation:

"Now are my triumphs turned into everlasting woes, from a pleasant pastime to a direful and bloody tragedy. O most unkind fortune, never constant, but changeable! why is my life deferred to see the downfall of my dear son, the noble Count Palatine? Why rends not this accursed earth whereon I stand, and presently swallow up my body into her hungry bowels? Is this the use of Christians, for true honour to repay dishonour? Could not base blood serve to stain his deadly hands withal, but the royal blood of my dear son, in whose revenge the face of the heavens is stained with blood, and cries for vengeance to the majesty of mighty Jove. The dreadful furies, the direful daughters of dark night, and all the baleful company of burning Acheron, whose loins shall be girt with serpents, and hair be hanged with wreaths of snakes, shall haunt, pursue, and follow that cursed Christian champion, that hath bereaved my country Tartary of so precious a jewel as my dear son the Count Palatine was, whose magnanimous prowess did surpass all the knights of our realm."

Thus sorrowed the woful emperor for the death of his noble son; sometimes making the echoes of his lamentations pierce the elements; another while forcing his bitter curses to sink to the deep foundations of Acheron; one while intending to be revenged on St. David, the Christian champion; then presently his intent was crossed with a contrary imagining, thinking it was against the law of arms, and a great dishonour to his country, by violence to oppress a strange knight, whose actions had ever been guided by true honour: but yet at last this firm resolution entered his mind.

There was adjoining, upon the borders of Tartary, an enchanted garden, kept by magic art, from whence never any returned that attempted to enter; the governor of which garden was a notable and famous necromancer, named Ormandine, to which magician the Tartarian emperor intended to send the adventurous champion St. David, thereby to revenge the Count Palatine's death. So the emperor, after some days were passed, and the obsequies of his son performed, caused the Christian knight to be brought into his presence, to whom he committed this heavy task, and weary labour.

"Proud knight," said the angry emperor, " thou knowest since thy arrival in our territories, how highly I have honoured thee, not only in granting thee liberty to live, but making thee my chief companion, which high honour thou hast repaid with great ingratitude, and blemished true nobility, in being the cause of my dear son's death; for which unhappy deed thou rightly hast deserved death; but yet know, accursed Christian, that mercy harboureth in princely minds, and where honour sits enthroned, there justice is not too severe: although thou hast deserved death, yet if thou wilt venture to the enchanted garden, and bring hither the magician's head, I grant thee not only life, but likewise the crown of Tartary after my decease, because I see thou hast a mind furnished with all princely thoughts, and adorned with true magnanimity."

This heavy task and strange adventure not a little pleased the noble champion of Wales, whose mind ever thirsted after worthy adventures; and so, after some considerate thought, he replied in this manner:

"Most high and magnificent emperor, were this task, which you enjoin on me, as wonderful as the labours of Hercules, or as fearful as the enterprise which Jason made for the golden fleece, yet would I attempt to finish it, and return with triumph to Tartary, as the Macedonian monarch did to Babylon, when he had conquered part of the wide world." Which words were no sooner ended, but the emperor bound him by his oath of knighthood, and by the love he bore to his native country, never to follow any other adventure, till he had performed his promise, which was to bring the magician Ormandine's head into Tartary: whereupon the emperor departed from the noble knight St. David, hoping never to see him return, but rather to hear of his utter confusion, or everlasting imprisonment.

Thus the valiant Christian champion, being bound to his promise, within three days prepared all necessaries in readiness for his departure, and so travelled westward, till he approached within sight of the enchanted garden, the situation whereof somewhat daunted his valiant courage, for it was encompassed with a hedge of withered thorns and briars, which seemed continually to burn; upon the top thereof sat a number of strange and deformed things, some in the likeness of nightowls, which wondered at the presence of St. David; some in the shape of Progne's transformation, foretelling his unfortunate success; and some like ravens, that with their harsh throats sounded forth hateful knells of woful tragedies. The element, which covered the enchanted garden, seemed to be overspread with misty clouds, from whence continually shot flames of fire, as though the skies had been filled with blazing comets; which fearful spectacle, as it seemed the very pattern of hell, struck such a terror into the champion's heart, that twice he was in the mind to return without performing the adventure, but for his oath and honour of knighthood, which he had pawned for the accomplishment thereof. So laying his body on the cold earth, he made his humble petition to God, that his mind might never be oppressed with cowardice, nor his heart daunted with faint fears, till he had performed what the Tartar emperor had bound him to; the champion rose from the ground, and with cheerful looks beheld the elements, which seemed in his conceit to smile at the enterprise, and to foreshow a lucky termination.

So the noble knight St. David, with a valiant courage, went to the garden gate, by which stood a rock of stone, overspread with moss: in which rock by magic art was enclosed a sword, nothing outwardly appearing but the hilt, which was the richest, in his judgment, that ever his eyes beheld for the steelwork was engraven very curiously, beset with jaspers and sapphire-stones; the pommel was in the fashion of a globe, of the purest silver that the mines of rich America brought forth. About the pommel was engraven with letters of gold the following lines:

> My magic spells remain most firmly bound,
>   The world's strange wonder unknown by any one,
> 'Till that a knight within the north be found,
>   To pull this sword from out this rock of stone:
> Then ends my charms, my magic arts and all,
> By whose strong hand wise Ormandine must fall.

These lines drove such a conceited imagination into the champion's mind, that he supposed himself the northern knight by whom the necromancer should be conquered; therefore, without any further delay, he put his hand into the hilt of the rich sword, thinking presently to pull it out from the enchanted rock of Ormandine: but no sooner did he attempt that vain enterprise, but his senses were overtaken with a sudden and heavy sleep, whereby he was forced to let go his hold, and to fall flat upon the ground, where his faculties were drowned in a real slumber, that it was as much impossible to recover himself from sleep, as to pull the sun out of the firmament. The necromancer, by his magic skill, had intelligence of the champion's unfortunate success, who sent from the enchanted garden four spirits, in the similitude and likeness of four beautiful damsels, which wrapped the drowsy champion in a sheet of fine Arabian silk, and conveyed him into a cave, directly placed in the middle of the garden, where they laid him upon a bed, which was softer than the down of culvers: where those beautiful ladies, through the heart of the wicked Ormandine, continually kept him sleeping for the term of seven years.

Thus was St. David's adventure crossed with a bad success; whose day's travels was turned into a night's repose, whose night's repose was made a heavy sleep, which endured until seven years were finished: where we will leave the Welsh champion to the mercy of the necromancer, Ormandine, and return to the most noble and magnanimous champion St. George, where we left him imprisoned in the soldan's court.

CHAPTER X.

How St. George escaped out of prison in Persia, and how he redeemed the Champion of Wales from his enchantment, with the tragical tale of the Necromancer, Ormandine.

Now seven times had frosty-bearded Winter covered both herbs and flowers with snow, and hung the trees with crystal icicles, since the unfortunate St. George beheld the cheerful light of heaven, but lived obscure in a dismal dungeon, by the soldan of Persia's command, as chronicled before in a former part of this history. His unhappy fortune so discontented his restless thoughts, that a thousand times a year he wished an end of his life, and a thousand times he cursed the day of his creation.

But at last, when seven years were ended, it was the champion's lucky fortune to find in a secret corner of the dungeon, a certain iron instrument, which time had almost consumed with rust, where, with long labour, he digged himself a passage through the ground, till he ascended just in the middle of the soldan's court, which was at that time of the night when all things were silent. The heavens he then beheld beautified with stars, and bright Cynthia, whose glittering beams he had not seen in many hundred nights before, seemed to smile at his safe delivery, and to stay her wandering course, till he most happily found means to get without the compass of the Persian court, where danger could no longer attend him, nor the strong gates of the city hinder his flight, which he determined to attempt as soon as possible. But yet the noble knight, being as fearful as the bird newly escaped from the fowler's net, gazed about, and listened where he might hear the voice of people: at last he heard the grooms of the soldan's stable, getting ready horses against the next morning for some noble achievement. Whereupon the heroic champion St. George, taking the iron instrument, wherewith he redeemed himself out of prison, he burst open the doors, where he slew all the grooms in the soldan's stable; which being done, he took the strongest palfrey, and the richest furniture, with other necessities appertaining to a knight at arms, and so rode in great comfort to one of the city gates, where he saluted the porter in this manner:

"Porter, open the gates, for St. George of England is escaped, and hath murdered the grooms, in whose pursuit the city is in arms." Which words the simple Persian believed for truth, and so with all speed opened the gates; whereat the champion of England departed, and left the soldan in his dead sleep, little mistrusting his sudden escape.

By the time the dawn of morning had begun to break, and the sun's bright countenance appeared on the mountain tops, St. George had rode twenty miles from the Persian court; and before his departure was known in the soldan's palace, the English champion had recovered the sight of Greece, past all danger of the Persian knights that followed him with a swift pursuit.

But by this time the extremity of hunger so sharply tormented him, that he could travel no further, and was constrained to sustain himself with certain wild chestnuts instead of bread, and sour oranges instead of drink, and such poor food as grew by the way as he travelled, where the necessity and want of victuals compelled the noble knight to breathe forth this pitiful complaint :

"Oh hunger! hunger!" said the champion, "sharper than the stroke of death, thou art the extremest punishment that ever man endured. If I were now king of Armenia, and chief potentate of Asia, yet would I give my diadem, my sceptre, with all my provinces, for one piece of brown bread. O that this earth would be so kind, as to open her bowels and cast up some food, to suffice my want; or that the air might be choked with mists, whereby feathered fowl for want of breath might fall, and yield me some succour in this my famished state; but oh! now I see both heaven and earth, hills and dales, skies and seas, fish and fowl, birds and beasts, and all things under the cope of heaven, conspire my utter overthrow; better had it been that I had ended my days in Persia, than here to be famished in the broad world, where all things by nature's appointment are ordained for man's use. Now, instead of courtly delicacies, I am forced to eat the fruit of trees—and instead of Greek wines, I am compelled to quench my thirst with morning dew, which nightly falls upon the blades of grass."

Thus complained St. George, till glittering Phœbus had mounted the horizon, and drawn the misty vapours from the ground, whereby he might behold the face of the country, and which way to travel most safely. And as he looked, he espied directly before his face a tower standing upon a chalky cliff, distant from him about three miles, whither the champion intended to go, not to seek adventures, but to rest himself after his weary journey, and get such victuals as therein he could find to suffice his want.

The way he found so plain, and the journey so easy, that in half an hour he approached before the said tower; where upon the wall stood a most beautiful woman, attired after the manner of a distressed lady, and her looks heavy, like the queen of Troy, when she beheld her palace on fire. The valiant knight St. George, after he had alighted from his horse, gave her this courteous salutation :

"Lady, for so you seem by your outward appearance, if ever you pitied a traveller, or granted succour to a Christian knight, give to me one meal's meat, for I am now almost famished."

To whom the lady, after a sad frown or two, answered in this order : "Sir knight, I advise thee with all speed to depart, for here thou gettest but a cold dinner : my lord is a mighty giant, and believeth in Mahomet; and if he once do but understand that thou art a Christian knight, not all the gold of Higher India, nor the riches of wealthy Babylon, can preserve thy life." "Now, by the honour of my knighthood," replied St. George, "assisted by the God that Christendom adores, were thy lord stronger than mighty Hercules that bore mountains on his back, here will I either obtain my dinner, or die by his accursed hand."

These words so abashed the lady, that she went with all speed from the tower, and told the giant, how a Christian knight remained at the gate, who had sworn to suffice his hunger in despite of his will. Whereat the furious giant suddenly started up, being as then in a sound sleep, for it was the middle of the day, who took a bar of iron in his hand, and came down to the tower-gate. His stature was in height five yards, his head bristled like a boar, a foot there was between each brow, his eyes hollow, his mouth wide, his lips were like to flaps of steel, in all his proportion more like a fiend than a man. This deformed monster so daunted the courage of St. George, that he prepared himself for death, not through fear of the monstrous giant, but for hunger and feebleness of body. But here God provided for him, and so restored to him his decayed strength, that he endured battle until the closing up of the evening, by which time the giant grew almost blind, through the sweat that ran down from his monstrous brows; whereat St. George got the advantage, and wounded the giant so cruelly under the short-ribs, that he was compelled to fall to the ground, and to give an end to his life.

After which happy event, St. George first gave the honour of his victory unto God, in whose power all his fortune consisted. Then he entered the tower, whereat the lady presented him with all manner of delicacies and pure wines; but the English knight, suspecting treachery to be hidden in her proffered courtesy, caused her to taste of every dish, likewise of the wine, lest some violent poison should be therein mixed: finding all things pure and wholesome, as nature required, he sufficed his hunger, rested his weary body, and refreshed his horse.

After a short stay, he left the tower in keeping of the lady, and committed his fortune to fresh travels; where his revived spirits never entertained longer rest, but to the refreshing of himself and his horse: so travelled he through part of Greece, the confines of Phrygia, and into the borders of Tartary, within whose territorries he had not long journeyed, but he approached within sight of the enchanted garden of Ormandine, where St. David the champion of Wales had so long slept by magic art. But no sooner did he behold the wonderful situation thereof, but he espied Ormandine's sword enclosed in the enchanted rock; where, after he had read the superscription written about the pommel, he attempted to pull it out by strength; and he no sooner put his hand upon the hilt, but he drew it forth with much ease, as though it had been hung by a thread of untwisted silk: but when he beheld the glittering brightness of the blade, and the wonderful richness of the pommel, he accounted the prize of more worth than the armour of Achilles, which caused Ajax to run mad, and much richer than Medea's golden fleece. But by the time St. George had circumspectly looked into every secret of the sword, he heard a strange and dismal voice thunder in the skies, a terrible and mighty lumbering in the earth, whereat both hills and mountains shook, rocks removed, and oaks were rent in pieces. After this, the gates of the enchanted garden flew open; and immediately came forth Ormandine the magician, with his hair starting on his head, his eyes sparkling, his cheeks blushing, his hands quivering, his legs trembling, and all the rest of his body distempered, as though legions of spirits had compassed him about: he came directly to the worthy English knight, who remained still by the enchanted rock, from whence he had pulled the magician's sword: he took the most valiant and magnanimous champion St. George of England by his steel gauntlet, and with great humility kissed it; then proffering him the courtesy due unto strangers, which was performed very graciously, he afterwards conducted him into the enchanted garden, to the cave where the champion of Wales was kept sleeping by four virgins singing delightful songs, and after setting him a chair of ebony, Ormandine thus began to relate most wonderful things:

"Renowned knight at arms," said the necromancer, "Fame's worthiest champion, whose strange adventures all Christendom in time to come shall applaud; be silent till I have told my tale, for never after this must my tongue speak again. The knight which thou seest here wrapt in this sheet of gold, is a Christian champion, as thou art, sprung from the ancient seed of Trojan warriors, who likewise attempted to draw this enchanted sword, but my magic spells so prevailed, that he was intercepted in the enterprise, and forced ever since to remain sleeping in this cave. But now the hour is almost come for his recovery, which by thee must be accomplished. Thou art that adventurous champion whose invincible hand must put an end to my detested life, and send my fleeting soul to draw the fatal chariot on the banks of burning Acheron; for my time was limited to remain no longer in this enchanted garden, than till from the north should come a knight that should pull this sword from the enchanted rock, which thou happily hast now performed; therefore I know my time is short, and my hour of destiny at hand. What I report, write in brazen lines, for the time will come when this discourse shall highly benefit thee. Take heed thou observe three things : first, That thou take to wife a pure maid ; next, That thou erect a monument over thy father's grave ; and lastly, That thou continue a professed enemy to the foes of Christ Jesus, bearing arms in the honour and praise of thy country. These things being truly and justly observed, thou shalt attain such honour, that all the kingdoms of Christendom shall admire thy dignity. What I speak is upon no vain imagination, sprung from a frantic brain, put pronounced by the mystical and deep art of necromancy."

These words were no sooner ended, but the most honourable fortunate champion of England requested the magician to describe his past fortunes, and by what means he came to be governor of the enchanted garden.

"To discourse of my own life," replied Ormandine, "will breed a new sorrow in my heart, the remembrance of which will rend my very soul. But yet, most noble knight, to fulfil thy request, I will force my tongue to declare what my heart denies to utter ; therefore prepare thine ear to entertain the most woful tale that ever tongue delivered."

And so, after St. George had sat a while silent, expecting the disclosure, the magician spake as follows:

Woful and Tragical Discourse pronounced by the Necromancer Ormandine, of the Misery of his Children.

"I was formerly king of Scythia, my name Ormandine ; graced in my youth with two fair daughters, whom nature had not only made beautiful, but replenished them with all gifts that art could devise. The elder, whose name was Castria, was the fairest maid that ever Scythia brought forth ; among the number of knights that were ensnared with her love, there was one Floridon, son to the king of Armenia, equal to her in all the ornaments of nature ; a lovelier couple never trod on earth, or graced any prince's court in the whole world.

"This Floridon pretended to be deeply in love with Castria ; but the kind of love he bore towards her was not the pure love of an honourable mind, but merely based upon passion and guilty desire. Suffice it to say, that one night Floridon, by the connivance and assistance of her chambermaid, entered Castria's bed-room, and forcibly accomplished his wicked purpose ; and before many days expired, her shame began to appear, and the deceived lady was constrained to reveal her mind to Floridon ; who in the mean time had betrothed himself to my younger daughter, whose name was Marcilla, no less beautiful than her elder sister ; but when this unconstant Floridon perceived that the unhappy Castria upbraided him with many ignominious words, forswearing himself ever to have committed any such infamous deed, protesting that he ever scorned to sink in woman's hands, and counted chamber-love a deadly sting, and a deep infection to the honour of his knigthhood.

"These unkind speeches drove Castria into such extreme passion of mind, that she, with shameful looks and blushing cheeks, after this manner revealed her sorrows unto him:

"'What! knows not Floridon,' quoth the lady, 'her whom his base passion hath stained with dishonour? Is there not sufficient evidence in my altered appearance to convince any one that I have been basely betrayed? You are the cause of that which stains my father's ancient house, and sets a shame-faced blush upon my cheeks, always when I behold the company of chaste virgins. Dear Floridon, cover my shame with marriage rites, that I be not accounted a by-word to the world, nor that this my unborn babe, in time to come, be termed a base-born child. Remember what plighted promises, what vows and protestations, passed betwixt us; remember the place and time of my dishonour, and be not like furious tigers, that repay love with despite.'

"At which words Floridon, with a wrathful countenance, replied in these words:

"'Shameless creature, with what brazen face darest thou out-brave me thus: I tell thee, Castria, my love was ever yet to follow arms, to hear the sound of drums, to ride upon a nimble steed, and not to trace a carpet dance, like Priam's son, before the amorous eyes of Menelaus' wife. Therefore begone, thou stain to women; go, sing thy harsh melody in the company of night birds, for I tell thee the day will blush to cover thy monstrous shame.'

"This reproachful speech was no sooner ended, but Floridon departed her presence, not leaving behind him so much as one kind look. Whereat the distressed lady, being oppressed with intolerable grief, sunk down, not able to speak for a time, but at last, recovering her senses, she began anew to complain.

"'I that was wont,' quoth she, 'to walk with troops of maids, must now abandon and utterly forsake all company, and seek some cave, wherein I may sit for evermore and bewail myself: if I return to my father, he will refuse me; if to my friends, they will be ashamed of me; if to strangers, they will scorn me; if to my Floridon, oh! he denieth me, and accounts my sight as ominous as the baleful crocodile's. O unconstant Floridon! thou didst promise to shadow this fault with marriage; but now vows, I see, are vain. Thou hast forsaken me, and tied thy faith unto my sister Marcilla, who must enjoy thy love, because she continues chaste, without any spot of dishonour.'

"Thus complained the woful Castria, roving up and down

the court of Scythia, for five months. At the end of which time, the appointed marriage of Floridon and Marcilla drew nigh, and the princes and potentates of Scythia were all present to see Hymen's holy rites; in which honourable assemblies, none were more busy than Castria to beautify her sister's wedding. The ceremonies being no sooner performed, and the day spent in pleasures, fitting the honour of so great and mighty a train, but Castria requested that the custom of the country might be observed, which was this: that the first night of every maiden's marriage, a known virgin should lie with the bride, which honourable task was committed to Castria; who provided against the hour appointed a silver bodkin, and hid it secretly in the tresses of her hair, wherewith she intended to prosecute her revenge. The bride's lodging-chamber was appointed far from the hearing of any one, lest the noise of people should hinder her quiet sleep.

"But at last, when the hour of her wishes approached, that the bride should take leave of her ladies and maidens that attended her to her chamber, the new-married Floridon, in company of many Scythian knights, committed Marcilla to her quiet rest, little mistrusting the bloody purpose of her sister's mind.

"But now, behold how every thing fell out according to her desires. The ladies and gentlemen were no sooner departed, and silence taken possession of the whole court, but Castria locked the chamber door, and secretly conveyed the keys under the bed's head, not perceived by the betrayed Marcilla; who, poor lady, after some speeches, departed to bed; wherein she was no sooner laid, but a heavy sleep over-mastered her senses, whereby her tongue was forced to bid her sister good-night, who then sat discontented by her bed-side, watching the time wherein she might conveniently act the bloody tragedy: upon a court cupboard stood two burning tapers, that gave light to the whole chamber, which in her conceit seemed to burn blue. After this, she took her silver bodkin, that before she had secretly hidden in her hair, and came to her new-married sister, being then overcome with a heavy slumber, and with her bodkin pierced her tender breast; who immediately, at the stroke thereof, started from her sleep, and gave such a pitiful shriek, that it would have awakened the whole court, but that the chamber stood far from the hearing of company, except her bloody-minded sister, whose hand was ready to re-double her fury with a second stroke.

"But when Marcilla beheld the sheets and ornaments of her bed stained, and from her breast run streams of crimson blood, she breathed forth this sad exclamation against the cruelty of Castria:

"'O sister,' quoth she, 'hath nature harboured in thy breast a bloody mind? What fury hath incensed thee thus to commit this tragedy? In what have I deserved this, or wherein hath my tongue offended thee? What cause hath been the occasion that thy remorseless hand against nature hath converted my joyful nuptials to a woful funeral?' 'This is the cause,' replied Castria, 'that I have been basely betrayed by the man to whom thou hast been this day married; and to revenge myself upon him, I have bathed my hands in thy blood.'

"Which words being no sooner finished, but she violently pierced her own breast, whereby the two sisters' blood were equally mingled together.

"Now when the morning sun had chased away the dark night, Floridon, who little expected the tragedy of the two sisters, repaired to the chamber-door, with a concert of skilful musicians, where the inspiring harmony sounded to the walls, and Floridon's morning salutations were spent in vain: he burst open the door, where being no sooner entered, but he found the two ladies weltering in their own gore. Which woful spectacle presently so bereaved him of his wits, that, like a frantic man, he raged up and down, and in this manner bitterly complained:

"'Oh, immortal powers! open the wrathful gates of heaven, and in your justice punish me, for my inconstant love hath murdered two of the bravest ladies that ever nature framed. Revive, sweet dames of Scythia, and hear me speak, that am the vilest wretch that ever spoke with a tongue: if ghost may here be given for ghost, dear ladies, take my life and live; or if my heart might dwell within your breasts, this hand shall equally divide it.'

"Which woful lamentation being no sooner breathed from his sorrowful breast, but he finished his days by the stroke of that same destructive bodkin that was the bloody instrument of the two sisters' death; which he found still remaining in the remorseless hand of Castria.

"Thus have you heard, most worthy knight, the true tragedy of three of the best personages that ever nature framed. But now, with diligent ears, listen unto the unfortunate discourse of my own misery, which in this unhappy manner fell out: for no sooner came the flying news of the murdered princesses to my ears, but I grew into such a discontented passion, that I secluded myself from the company of all people, and sat for seven months in a solitary state of mind, lamenting the loss of my children, like weeping Niobe, which was the most sorrowful lady that ever lived.

"During this time, the report of Floridon's unhappy tragedy was bruited to his father's ears, being the sole king of

Armenia; whose grief so exceeded the bounds of reason, that with all convenient speed he gathered the greatest strength Armenia could make, and in revenge for his son's murder, entered my territories, and with his well-approved warriors subdued my provinces, slaughtered my soldiers, conquered my captains, slew my common subjects, burnt my cities, and left my country villages desolate; where, when I beheld my country overspread with famine, fire, and sword, three intestine plagues, wherewith heaven scourgeth the sins of the wicked, I was forced, for the safeguard of my life, to forsake my native habitation and kingly government, and submit my fortune, (like a banished exile) to wander in unknown places, where Care was my chief companion, and Discontent my only solicer. At last it was my destiny to arrive in this unhappy place, which I supposed to be the walks of Despair; where I had not remained many days in my melancholy position, but methought the many jaws of deep Avernus opened, from whence ascended a most fearful fiend, that enticed me to bequeath my fortune to his disposing, and he would defend me from the fury of the whole world. To which I presently condescended, upon some assurance; then presently he placed before my face this enchanted sword, so surely closed in stone, that it should never be pulled out, but by the hands of a Christian knight, and till that task was performed, I should live exempt from all danger, although all the kingdoms of the earth assailed me; which task (most adventurous champion) thou hast now performed, whereby I know the hour of my confusion is at hand."

This discourse pronounced by the necromancer Ormandine, was no sooner finished, but the worthy champion St. George heard such fearful sounds in the skies, such a shaking of the earth that he expected some strange event to follow. Then casting his eyes aside, he saw the enchanted garden vanish, and the champion of Wales to awake from his long sleep, wherein he had remained seven years; who like one risen from a swoon, for a time stood speechless, not able to utter one word, till he beheld the noble champion of England, stedfastly gazing upon the necromancer; who, at the vanishing of the enchantment, presently gave a terrible groan and died.

The two champions, after many courteous embracings and kind greetings, revealed to each other the strange adventures they had passed. St. David told how he was bound by the oath of knighthood to perform the adventure of Ormandine: whereupon St. George presently delivered the enchanted sword, with the necromancer's head, into the hands of St. David, which he presently severed from his body. But here must my weary muse leave St. David travelling with Ormandine's head to the emperor of Tartary, and speak of the following adventures that happened to St. George, after his departure from the enchanted garden.

CHAPTER XI.

How St. George arrived at Tripoli, in Barbary, where he stole away Sabra, the king's daughter of Egypt, from the Moorish king; and how she was known to be a pure virgin by the means of a lion: and what happened to him in the same adventure.

ST. GEORGE, after the recovery of St. David, as set forth in the former chapter, hastened his journey towards Christendom, whose pleasant banks he long desired to behold, and thought every day a year, till his eyes enjoyed a sweet sight of his native country of England, upon whose chalky cliffs he had not rode for many a weary summer's day. Therefore committing his journey to a fortunate success, he travelled through many a dangerous country, where the people were not only of a bloody disposition, given to all manner of wickedness, but the soil greatly annoyed with wild beasts.

Thus in extreme danger travelled the noble champion St. George, till he arrived in the territories of Barbary, in which country he purposed for a time to remain, and to seek for some noble achievement, whereby his fame might be increased; and being encouraged with this princely cogitation, the noble champion of England climbed to the top of a huge mountain; where he unlocked his beaver, which before had not been lifted up for many a day, and beheld the wide and spacious country, how it was beautified with lofty pines, and adorned with many goodly palaces. But amongst the number of the towers and cities which the English champion beheld, there was one which seemed to exceed the rest both in situation and handsome buildings, which he supposed to be the chiefest city in all the country, and the place where the king usually kept his court: to which St. George intended to travel, not to furnish himself with any needful thing, but to accomplish some honourable adventure, whereby his worthy deeds might be engraven in the records of fame. So after he had descended from the top of the steep mountain, and had travelled into a low valley about two or three miles, he approached an old and almost ruinous hermitage, overgrown with moss and other weeds; before the entry of this hermitage sat an ancient father upon a round stone, taking the heat of the warm sun, which cast such a comfortable brightness upon the hermit's face, that his white beard seemed to glitter like silver, and his head to exceed the whiteness of the northern icicles; to whom, after St. George had given the due reverence that belonged unto age, he demanded the name of the country, and the city he travelled to, and under what king the country was governed. To whom the courteous hermit thus replied:

"Most noble knight, for so I guess you are, by your furniture and outward appearance, you are now in the confines of Barbary, the city opposite before your eyes is called Tripoli, remaining under the government of Almidor, the black king of Morocco, in which city he now keepeth his court, attended on by as many gallant knights as any king under the cope of heaven."

At these words the noble champion of England suddenly started, as though he had intelligence of some baleful news, which deeply discontented his princely mind: his heart was presently incensed with a speedy revenge, and his mind so extremely thirsted after Almidor's overthrow, that he could scarce answer again to the hermit's words. But bridling his fury, the angry champion spake in this manner:

"Grave father, through the treachery of that accursed king, I endured seven years' imprisonment in Persia, where I suffered both hunger, cold, and extreme misery. But if I had my good sword Ascalon, and my trusty palfrey, which I left in the Egyptian court, where remains my betrothed love, the king of Egypt's daughter, I would be avenged on the head of Almidor, were his guard more strong than the army of Xerxes, whose multitudes drank the rivers dry."

"Why," said the hermit, "Sabra, the king of Egypt's daughter, is queen of Barbary; and since her nuptials were solemnly performed in Tripoli, seven summers have fully passed."

"Now by the honour of my country, England, the place of my nativity," said St. George, "as I am a Christian knight, these eyes of mine shall never close until I have obtained a sight of the sweet princess, for whose sake I have endured such long imprisonment. Therefore, dear father, be thus kind to a traveller, as to exchange thy clothing for this my rich furniture and steed, which I brought from the soldan of Persia, for in the habit of a palmer I may enjoy the happiness of seeing her without suspicion; therefore courteously deliver me thy hermit's gown, and I will give, with my horse and armour, this box of costly jewels." Which when the grave hermit beheld, he humbly thanked the noble champion, and so with all the speed they could possibly make, exchanged apparel, and in this manner he departed.

The palmer being glad, repaired to his hermitage with St. George's furniture; and St. George in the palmer's apparel departed to the city of Tripoli, who no sooner came to the sumptuous buildings of the court, but he espied a hundred poor palmers kneeling at the gate, to whom St. George spake after this manner:

"My dear brethren," said the champion, "for what intent remain you here, or what expect you from this honourable court?"

At which the queen let fall from her eyes such a shower of pearly tears, and sent such numbers of strained sighs from her grieved heart, that her sorrow seemed to exceed that of the queen of Carthage, when she had for ever lost the sight of her beloved lord. But the brave-minded champion purposed no longer to continue secret, but with his discovery to convert her sorrowful moans to smiling joy. And so casting off his palmer's weed, acknowledged himself to the queen, and therewithal showed the half ring whereon was engraven this motto, "*Ardeo Affectione.*" Which ring in former time (as related before) they had very equally divided betwixt them, to be kept in remembrance of their plighted faith.

This unexpected sight highly pleased the beauteous Sabra, and her joy so exceeded the bounds of reason, that she could not speak one word, but was constrained through the height of her pleasure to breathe a sad sigh or two into the champion's bosom, who like a true ennobled knight, entertained her with a loving kiss; and these two lovers now fully discoursed to each other of the secrets of their souls. Sabra told him how she continued for his love a pure virgin, through the secret virtue of a golden chain steeped in tiger's blood, which she wore seven times double about her ivory neck, and then took him by the hand, and led him into her husband's stables, where stood his approved palfrey, which no sooner espied the return of his master, but he was more proud of his presence than Bucephalus of the Macedonia monarch, when he most joyfully returned in triumph from any victorious conquest.

"Now is the time," said the lovely princess Sabra, "that thou mayest seal up the quittance of our former loves; therefore, with all convenient speed take thy approved palfrey, and thy trusty sword Ascalon, which I will presently deliver into thy hands, and with all celerity convey me from this unhappy country: for the king my husband, with all his adventurous knights, are now out hunting, whose absence will further our flight; but if you stay till his return, it is not a hundred of the hardiest knights in the world can bear me from this accursed palace."

At which words St. George, having a mind graced with all excellent virtues, replied in this manner:

"Thou knowest, my divine lady, that for thy love I would endure as many dangers as Jason suffered in the isle Calchos, so I might at last be sure of thy purity. But how is it possible thou canst remain a pure maid, when thou hast been a crowned queen these seven years, and every night hast entertained a king in thy bed.

"If thou findest me not a true virgin," quoth she, "in all that thou canst say or do, send me back hither again unto my foe, whose bed I count more loathsome than a den of snakes, and his sight more ominous than the crocodile's. As for the Morocco crown, which by force of friends was set upon my head, I wish it might be turned into a blaze of quenchless fire, so it might not endanger my body. And for the name of queen, I account it a vain title; for I had rather be an English lady, than the greatest empress in the world."

At which assertions St. George willingly condescended, and with all speed purposed to go into England. So losing no time, Sabra furnished herself with sufficient treasure, and obtained the good will of a eunuch, that was appointed for her guard in the king's absence, to accompany them in their travel and to serve as a trusty guide, if occasion required.

So these three worthy personages committed their travels to the guidance of Fortune, who preserved them from the dangers of pursuing enemies, which at the king's return from hunting followed immediately to every port and haven that divided the kingdom of Barbary from the confines of Christendom. But kind Destiny so guided their steps that they travelled another way, contrary to their expectations; for when they looked to arrive upon the territories of Europe, they were cast upon the fruitful banks of Greece: in which country we must tell what happened to the three travellers.

And now, Melpomene, thou tragic sister of the Muses, report what unlucky crosses happened to these three travellers in the confines of Greece, and how their good fortune was unluckily turned into misery and woe: for when they had journeyed about three or four leagues, over many a lofty hill, they came nigh unto a vast wilderness, through which the way seemed so long, and the sun so exceedingly overclouded, that Sabra, what for weariness in travel, and the extreme heat of the day, was constrained to rest under the shelter of a mighty oak, whose branches were very thickly covered with foliage. Here she had not long remained, but her heart began to faint for hunger, and her colour, that was but a little before as blooming as any lady's in the world, began to change for want of a little drink; whereat, the famous champion St. George, half dead with grief, comforted her as well as he could, after this manner:

"Faint not, my dear lady," said he, "here is that good sword that once preserved thee from the burning dragon, and before thou shalt die for want of sustenance, it shall make way to every corner of the wilderness; where I will either kill some venison to refresh thy hungry stomach, or make my tomb in the bowels of some monstrous beast. Therefore abide thou here under this tree, in company of thy faithful eunuch till I return either with the flesh of some wild deer, or else of some flying bird, to refresh thy spirits for further travel."

Thus he left his beloved lady with the eunuch in the woods, and travelled up and down the wilderness, till he espied a herd of fat deer, from which company he singled out the fairest, and like a tripping satyr coursed her to death : then with a keen-edged sword cut out the goodliest haunch of venison that ever hunter's eye beheld; which gift he supposed would be most welcome to his beloved lady. But mark what happened in his absence to the two weary travellers under the tree : for after St. George departed, they had not long sat discoursing, one while of their long journey, another while of their safe delivery from the Moorish king, spending the stealing time away with many an ancient story, but there appeared out of a thicket two huge and monstrous lions, which came directly pacing towards the two travellers. Which fearful spectacle when Sabra beheld, having a heart overcharged with the extreme fear of death, wholly committed her soul into the hands of God, and her body, almost famished for food, to suffice the hunger of the two furious lions, who by the appointment of heaven, offered not so much as to lay their wrathful paws upon the smallest part of her garment, but with eager mood assailed the eunuch, tore him in pieces, and each swallowed the entire portions of the mangled body ; then with their teeth lately imbrued in blood they rent the eunuch's steed into shreds : which being done, they came to the lady, who sat quaking half dead with fear, and, like two lambs, couched their heads upon her lap, where with her hand she stroked down their bristled hairs, not daring scarcely to breathe, till a heavy sleep had over-mastered their furious senses, by which time the princely-minded champion St. George returned with a piece of venison upon the point of his sword : who at that unexpected sight stood in amaze, whether it was best to fly for safeguard of his life, or to venture his fortune against the furious lions. But at last the love of his lady encouraged him to such courage when he beheld her quaking before the dismal gates of death : so laying down his venison, he sheathed his falchion in the bowels of one of the lions. Sabra keeping the other sleeping in her lap till his prosperous hand had likewise dispatched him ; which adventure being performed, he first thanked heaven for victory, and then in this kind manner saluted his lady.

"Now, Sabra," said he, " I have by this sufficiently proved thy purity : for it is the nature of a lion, be he ever so furious, not to harm the unspotted virgin, but humbly to lay his bristled head upon a maiden's lap. Therefore, divine paragon, thou art the world's chief wonder for love and chastity, whose honoured virtues shall ring as far as Phœbus sends his lights, and whose constancy I will maintain in every land where I

...they came to the lady who sat quaking half dead with fear, and like two lambs couched their heads upon her lap.

come, to be the truest under the circuit of the sun." At which words he cast his eyes aside, and beheld the bloody spectacle of the eunuch's tragedy, which by Sabra was wofully disclosed to the grief of St. George, whose sad sighs served for a doleful knell to bewail his untimely death : but having a noble mind, not subject to vain sorrow, where all hope of life is past, he ceased his grief, and prepared the venison in readiness for his lady's repast, which he dressed in this manner. He had in his pocket a firelock, wherewith he struck fire, and kindled it with sun-burnt moss, and increased the flame with other drywood which he gathered in the wilderness: against this fire they roasted the venison, and sufficed themselves to their own contentment. After which joyful repast, these two princely persons set forward on their wonted travels, whereby the happy guide of heaven so conducted their steps, that before many days passed, they arrived in the Grecian court, even upon that day when the marriage of the emperor should be solemnly held: which nuptials, in former times, had been published in every nation in the world, as well in Europe, as Africa and Asia. At which honourable marriage the bravest knights then living on earth were present; for golden Fame had spread the report thereof to the ears of the seven champion: in Thessaly, to St. Denis, the champion of France, there remaining with his beauteous Eglantine; into Seville, to St. James, the champion of Spain, where he remained with his lovely Celestine; to St. Anthony, the champion of Italy, then travelling into the borders of Scythia, with his lady Rosalinde; likewise to St. Andrew, the champion of Scotland; to St. Patrick, the champion of Ireland; and to St. David, the champion of Wales.

But now Fame and smiling Fortune consented to make their knightly achievements to shine in the eyes of the whole world, therefore by the conduct of heaven they severally arrived in the Grecian emperor's court.

CHAPTER XII.

How the Seven Champions arrived in Greece at the Emperor's Nuptials, where they performed many noble achievements; and how, afterwards, open Wars were proclaimed against Christendom by the discovery of many Knights; and how every Champion departed into his country.

To enumerate the number of knights that assembled in the Grecian court together, were a labour too tedious, requiring the pen of Homer: therefore will I omit the honourable train of knights and ladies that did attend them to the church; their costly garments and glittering ornaments, exceeding the royalty of Hecuba, the beauteous queen of Troy. And also I pass over the sumptuous banquets and delicious cheer that celebrated the emperor's nuptials, with the stately mask and courtly dances performed by many noble personages, and chiefly discourse of the knightly achievements of the seven champions of Christendom, whose magnanimous encounters deserve a golden pen to relate. For after some few days the emperor proclaimed a solemn jousting to be held for the space of seven days, in honour of his marriage, and appointed for his chief champions the seven Christian knights.

Against the day appointed the tournaments were to begin, the emperor caused a large frame of timberwork to be erected, whereon the empress and her ladies might stand, for the better view of the tilters, and at pleasure behold the champions' encounters; likewise in the compass of the lists were pitched seven tents of seven several colours, wherein the seven champions might remain till the sounds of the silver trumpets summoned them to appear.

Thus, every thing prepared in readiness fitting so great an event, the princes and ladies placed on their seats, the emperor with his new-married empress seated on their lofty thrones strongly guarded with an hundred armed knights, the king's heralds solemnly proclaimed the tournaments, which in this manner began: The first day St. Denis of France was appointed chief champion against all comers, and he was called by the title of the Golden Knight, who at the sound of the trumpet entered the lists. His tent was of the colour of the marigold; upon the top an artificial sun flamed, that seemed to beautify the whole assembly; his horse, an iron-grey graced with a spangled plume of feathers: before him rode a page in purple silk, bearing upon his crest three golden flower-de-luces, which did signify his arms. Thus in this royal manner entered St. Denis the lists; where after he had paced twice or thrice up and down, to the open view of the whole company, he prepared himself in readiness to begin the tournament; against whom ran many Grecian knights, which were foiled by the French champion, to the wonderful admiration of all beholders; but, to be brief, he so worthily behaved himself, and with such fortitude, that the emperor applauded him for the bravest knight in the world.

Thus in great royalty, to the exceeding pleasure of the emperor, was the first day spent till the dark evening caused the knights to break off company, and repair to their night's repose. And the next morning, no sooner did Phœbus show his splendid brightness, but the chief of heralds, under the emperor, with a noise of trumpets, awaked the champions from their silent sleep, who with all speed prepared for the second day's exercise. The chief champion appointed for that day, was the victorious knight St. James of Spain; who after the emperor and empress had seated themselves with a stately train of beautiful ladies, entered the lists upon a Spanish jennet: directly over-against the emperor's throne, his tent was pitched, which was of the colour of quick-silver, wherein was pourtrayed many fine devices; before the tent attended four esquires, bearing four several escutcheons in their hands, whereon were curiously painted the four elements; likewise he had the title of the silver knight; who behaved himself no less worthy of all princely commendations than the French champion the day before.

The third day St. Anthony of Italy was chief challenger in the tournament, whose tent was of the colour of the skies, his steed furnished with costly habiliments, his armour after the manner of Barbary, his shield plated round about with steel, whereon was painted a golden eagle, in a field of blue, which signified the ancient arms of Rome; likewise he had the title of the azure knight, whose matchless chivalry for that day, won the prize from all the Grecian knights.

The fourth day, by the emperor's appointment, the worthy knight St. Andrew of Scotland obtained the honour to be chief challenger for the tournament: his tent was framed in the manner of a ship swimming upon the waves of the sea, environed about with dolphins, tritons, and many strange-contrived mermaids; upon the top stood the picture of Neptune, the god of the seas, bearing in his hand a streamer, whereon was wrought, in crimson silk, a corner cross, which seemed to be his country arms: he was called the red knight, because his horse was covered with a bloody veil: his worthy achievements obtained such favour in the emperor's eyes, that he threw him his silver gauntlet, which was prized at a thousand portagues; where, after his noble encounters, he enjoyed a sweet repose.

The fifth day St. Patrick of Ireland, as chief champion, entered the lists upon an Irish steed, covered with a veil of green, attended by six Sylvan knights, every one bearing upon his shoulder a blooming tree: his tent resembling a summer's bower, at the entry whereof stood the picture of Flora, beautified with a wreath of sweet-smelling roses, ; he was named the green knight; whose worthy prowess so daunted the defendants, that before the tournament began, they gave him the honour of the day.

Upon the sixth day the heroical and noble-minded champion of Wales entered the lists upon a Tartar palfrey, covered with a veil of black, to signify that a black and tragical day should befal those Grecian knights that durst prove his fortitude: his tent was pitched in the manner and form of a castle, in the west side of the lists; before the entry whereof hung a golden shield, whereon was lively pourtrayed a silver griffin rampant upon a golden helmet, which signified the ancient arms of Britain. His princely achievements not only obtained due commendations at the emperor's hands, but of the whole assembly of the Grecian ladies, wherewith they applauded him to be the most noble knight that ever shivered lance, and the most fortunate champion that ever entered into the Grecian court.

Upon the seventh and last day of the honourable tournaments, the famous and valiant knight at arms St. George of England, as chief challenger, entered the lists upon a sable-coloured steed, betrapped with bars of burnished gold, his forehead beautified with a gorgeous plume of purple feathers, from whence hung many pendants of gold; his armour of the purest Lydian steel, nailed fast together with silver plates; his helmet engraved very curiously, be-set with Indian pearl, and jasper stones; before his breastplate hung a silver tablet in a damask scarf, whereon was pictured a lion rampant in a bloody field, bearing three golden crowns upon his head: before his tent stood an ivory chariot, guarded by twelve coal-black negroes; wherein his beloved lady and mistress, Sabra, sat enthroned upon a silver globe, to behold the heroical encounters of her most noble and magnanimous champion St. George of England: his tent was as white as the swan's feathers, glittering against the sun, supported by four elephants, framed of the purest brass; about his helmet he tied a wreath of virgin's hair, where hung his lady's glove, which he wore to maintain her excellent gifts of nature to exceed all ladies on the earth. These costly habiliments ravished the beholders with such unspeakable pleasure, that they stood gazing at his furniture, not able to withdraw their eyes from so heavenly a sight. But when they beheld his victorious encounter against the Grecian knights, they supposed him to be the invincible tamer of that seven-headed monster that climbed to the elements, offering to pull Jupiter from his throne. His steed never gave encounter with any knight, but he tumbled horse and man to the ground, where they lay for a time bereft of sense. The tournaments lasted for that day from the sun's rising till the dusky evening-star appeared; in which time he conquered five hundred of the hardiest knights then living in Asia, and shivered a thousand lances, to the wonderful admiration of the beholders.

Thus were the seven days brought to an end by the seven worthy champions of Christendom, in reward of whose noble achievements, the Grecian emperor, being a man that highly favoured knightly proceedings, gave them a golden tree with seven branches to be divided equally amongst them. Which honourable prize they conveyed to St. George's pavilion, where, in dividing the branches, the seven champions discovered themselves to each other, and by what good fortune they arrived in the Grecian court, whose long-wished-for sight so rejoiced their hearts, that they all accounted that happy day of meeting the most joyful day that ever they beheld. But now, after the tournaments were fully ended, and the knights rested themselves some few days, recovering their wonted agility of body, they fell to a new exercise of pleasure, not appearing in glittering armour before the tilt, nor following the loud-sounding drums and silver trumpets, but spending the time in courtly dances amongst their beloved ladies and mistresses, in more royalty than the Phrygian knights when they presented the paragon of Asia with an enchanted mask. There wanted no inspiring music to delight their ears, no pleasant sonnets to ravish their senses, nor no curious dances to please their eyes. Sabra, she was the mistress of the revels, who graced the whole court with her excellent beauty, which seemed to exceed the rest of the ladies in fairness, as far as the moon surpasseth her attending stars on a frosty night; and when she danced, she seemed like Thetis tripping on the silver sands, with whom the sun did fall in love: and if she chanced to smile, the cloudy elements would weep, and drop down heavenly dew, as though they mourned for love. There likewise remained in the court the six Thracian virgins, that in former time lived in the shape of swans, which were as beautiful ladies as ever eye beheld; also many other ladies attended the empress, in whose company the seven champions daily delighted; sometimes discoursing of amorous conceits, other times delighting themselves with sweet-sounding music; then spending the day in banqueting, revelling, dancing, and such-like pastimes, not once injuring their true betrothed ladies. But their courtly pleasures continued not long; for they were suddenly dashed with certain news of open war proclaimed against all Christendom: which fell out contrary to the expectation of the Christian knights. There arrived in the Grecian emperor's palace a hundred heralds, of a hundred several provinces, which proclaimed utter defiance to all Christian kingdoms by these words:

" We, the high and mighty emperors of Asia and Africa, great commanders both of lands and seas, proclaim, by general consent of all the eastern potentates, utter ruin and destruction to the kingdoms of Christendom, and to all those nations where any Christian knights are harboured: first, the soldan of Persia, in revenge of a bloody slaughter done in his palace, by an English champion; Ptolemy, the Egyptian king, in revenge of his daughter violently taken away by the same knight; Almidor, the black king of Morocco, in revenge of his queen, likewise taken away by the said English champion; the great governor of Thessaly, in revenge of his daughters, taken away by a French knight; the king of Jerusalem, in revenge of his daughter, taken away by a Spanish knight; the Tartar emperor, in revenge of his son, Count Palatine, slain by the unhappy hand of the champion of Wales; the Thracian monarch, in revenge of his vain travel after his seven daughters, now in keeping of certain Christian knights: in revenge of which injuries, all kingdoms from the further parts of Prester John's dominions to the borders of the Red Sea, have set down their hands and seals to be aiders in this bloody war."

This proclamation was no sooner ended, but the Grecian emperor gave speedy commandment to muster up the greatest strength that Greece could afford, to join with the Pagans, to the utter ruin and confusion of Christendom; which bloody edict, or rather inhuman judgment, pronounced by the accursed infidels compelled the Christian champions to a speedy departure, and every one to hasten to his own country, there to provide for the Pagans' entertainment. So, after due consideration, the champions departed, in company of their betrothed ladies, who chose rather to live in their husbands' bosoms, than with their misbelieving parents. Where after some few days they arrived in the spacious bay of Portugal, in which haven they vowed, by the honour of true knighthood, to meet again within six months ensuing, there to join all their Christian armies into one legion. Upon which plighted resolution, the worthy champions departed one from another: St. George into England, St. Denis into France, St. James into Spain, St. Anthony into Italy, St. Andrew into Scotland, St. Patrick into Ireland, St. David into Wales. Whose pleasant banks they had not beheld in many years before, where their entertainments were as honourable as their hearts desired.

CHAPTER XIII.

How the Seven Champions of Christendom arrived with all their Troops in the Bay of Portugal. The Number of the Christian Armies. And how St. George made an Oration to the Soldiers.

AFTER the seven champions of Christendom arrived in their native countries, and by true reports had spread abroad to every prince's ear the bloody resolutions of the Pagans, and how the provinces of Africa and Asia had mustered up their forces to the invasion of Europe; all Christian kings then, at the entreaty of the champions, appointed mighty armies of well-approved soldiers, both by sea and land, to intercept the infidels' wicked intention. Likewise, by the whole consent of Christendom, the noble and fortunate champion of England, St. George, was appointed chief general and principal leader of the armies, and the other six champions were elected for his council, and chief assistants in all attempts that appertained either to the benefit of Christendom, or the furtherance of their fortunate proceedings.

This war so fired the hearts of many youthful gentlemen, and so encouraged the minds of every common soldier, that some mortgaged their lands, and at their own charges furnished themselves: some sold their patrimonies to serve in these honourable wars; and others forsook parents, kindred, wife, children, friends, and acquaintance, and without constraint or pressing, offered themselves to follow so noble a general as the renowned champion of England, and to spend their blood in the just quarrel of their native country.

To be brief, one might behold the streets of every town and city throughout all the dominions of Europe, thronged with troops of soldiers which thirsted after nothing but fame and honour. Then the joyful sound of thundering drums, and the echoes of silver trumpets summoning them to arms; that followed with as much willingness as the Grecians followed Agamemnon to the woful overthrow of Troy. For by the time the champions had arranged their several households, the forward captains taken their courtly pastimes, and the willing soldiers bade adieu to their friends and acquaintance, the spring had covered the earth with a new livery; which was the appointed time the Christian armies should meet in Portugal, there to join their several troops into one legion: which appointment caused the champions to bid adieu to their native countries, and with all speed to buckle on their furnitures, to hoist up sails, where after a short time the wind, with a calm and prosperous gale, cast them happily into the bay of Portugal.

The first that arrived in that spacious haven, was the noble champion St. George, with one hundred thousand courageous English soldiers, whose forwardness betokened a fortunate success, and their willing minds a joyful victory. His army set in battle array, seemed to surpass the number of the Macedonian soldiers, wherewith worthy Alexander conquered the eastern world; his horsemen, being in number twenty thousand, were armed all in black corslets; their lances bound about with plates of steel, their steeds covered with mail, three times doubled; their colours were the sanguine cross, supported by a golden lion: his sturdy bow-men, whose conquering grey goose wing in former times hath terrified the circled earth, being in number likewise twenty thousand, clad all in red medallions, with caps of the same colour, bearing thereon likewise a sanguine cross, being the true badge of honour of England; their bows of the strongest yew, and their arrows of the soundest ash, with forked heads of steel, and their feathers bound on with green wax and twisted silk: his musketeers being in number ten thousand, their muskets of the widest bore, with firelocks, wrought by curious workmanship, yet of such wonderful lightness, that they required no rest at all to ease their arms : his light troops were likewise ten thousand of the smaller limbed men, but yet of as courageous minds as the tallest soldiers in his army : his pikemen to guard the waving ensigns, thirty thousand, clad all with glittering bright armour ; likewise followed ten thousand labouring pioneers, if occasioned served, to undermine any tower or castle, to intrench forts or sconces, or to make a passage through hills and mountains, as worthy Hannibal did, when he made a way for his soldiers through the lofty Alps, that divide the countries of Italy and Spain.

The next arrival in the bay of Portugal, was the princely-minded champion, St. David of Wales, with an army of fifty thousand, true-born Britons, furnished with all habiliments of war for so noble and valiant a service, to the high renown of his country, and true honour of his progeny : their armour in richness nothing inferior to the Englishmen ; their colours were a golden cross, supported by a silver griffin ; which escutcheon signified the ancient arms of Wales : for no sooner had St. George a sight of the valiant Britons, but he caused his musketeers presently to entertain them with a volley, to express their joyful welcome to shore. But no sooner were the skies cleared from the smoke of the volley, and that St. George might at pleasure discern the noble and magnanimous champion of Wales, who then rode upon a milk-white steed, in silver armour, guarded with a train of knights in purple vestures, but he greeted St. David with kind courtesies, and accompanied him to the English tent, which was erected close by the port side, where for that night these two champions remained, spending the time with unspeakable pleasure : and so upon the next day after, St. David departed to his tent, which he had caused to be pitched a quarter of a league from the English army.

The next that arrived on the fruitful banks of Portugal, was St. Patrick, the noble champion of Ireland, with an army likewise of fifty thousand, attired after a strange and wonderful manner : their furniture were of the skins of wild beasts, but yet more unpierceable than the strongest armour. They bore in their hands mighty darts, tipped at the end with pointed steel, which the courageous and valiant Irish soldiers, by the agility of their arms, could throw a full flight shot, and with forcible strength would strike three or four inches into an oak.

These hardy soldiers no sooner arrived on the shore, but the English musketeers gave them a princely entertainment, and presently conducted the noble-minded St. Patrick to the English tent, where the three champions of England, Wales, and Ireland, passed away the time with exceeding great benefit, laying down reasons how to pitch their camps to the most disadvantage of the misbelieving enemy, and setting perfect directions which way they were best to march, and such-like devices, for their own safety, and the benefit of Christendom.

The next that landed on the banks of Portugal, was St. Andrew, the worthy champion of Scotland, with threescore thousand of well approved soldiers: his horsemen, the old adventurous Galloways, clad in quilted jackets, with lances of the Turkish fashion, thick and short, bearing upon their beavers the arms of Scotland, which was a corner cross, supported by a naked virgin: his pikemen, the bold and hardy men of Orcady, which continually live upon freezing mountains, the icy rock, and the snowy valleys: his sharp-shooters, the light-footed Pallidonians, that on occasion can climb the highest hill, and for nimbleness in running outdo the swift-footed stag. These bold adventurous Scottish men in all forwardness, deserved as much honour at the English champion's hands as any other nation before; therefore he commanded his sharp-shooters, on their first entry on land, to give them a noble entertainment, which they performed most faithfully, and also conducted St. Andrew to the English tent, where, after he had given St. George the courtesy of his country, departed to his tent, which was distant from the English tent a mile.

The next that arrived was St. Anthony, the champion of Italy, with a band of fourscore thousand brave Italian soldiers, mounted on warlike coursers; every horseman attended by a naked negro, bearing in his hand a streamer of watchet silk, with the arms of Italy thereon set in gold; every footman furnished with approved furniture in as stately a manner as the Englishmen; who at their landing received as royal an entertainment as the other nations, and likewise St. Anthony was as highly honoured by the English champion, as any of the other Christian knights.

The next that arrived was St. Denis, the victorious champion of France, with a band of fourscore thousand. After him marched dukes of twelve several dukedoms, then under the government of the French king, every one at his own proper cost and charges maintained two thousand soldiers in these Christian wars: their entertainments were as glorious as the rest.

The last of the Christian champions that arrived upon the fruitful banks of Portugal, was the magnanimous knight St. James of Spain, with a band likewise of fourscore thousand; with him he brought from the Spanish mines ten tons of refined

G

gold, only to maintain soldiers in the defence of Christendom; who no sooner landed his troops, but the six champions gave him the honourable welcome of a soldier, and ordained a solemn banquet for the general armies, whose numbers nearly amounted to five hundred thousand; the whole legions they united into one camp royal, and afterwards placed their wings in squadrons battle-wise, chiefly by the direction of St. George, being then general-in-chief, by the consent of the Christian kings; who, after he had reviewed the Christian armies, his countenance seemed to prognosticate a triumphant victory, and to foretell a fatal overthrow to the misbelieving potentates: therefore, to encourage his princely followers to persevere in their wonted willingness, pronounced this princely oration:

"You men of Europe, and my country-men, whose conquering fortunes never yet have feared the enemies of Christ, you see we have forsook our native lands, and committed our destinies to the chance of war, not to fight in any unjust quarrel, but in the true cause of Israel's Anointed; not against nature, to climb to the heavens, as Nimrod and the giants proffered in former time, but to prevent the invasion of Christendom, the ruin of Europe, and the intended overthrow of all Christian provinces. The bloody-minded infidels have mustered up legions, in numbers like blades of grass that grow upon the flourishing downs of Italy, or the stars of heaven in the coldest winter's night, protesting to fill our countries with seas of blood, scatter our streets with mangled limbs, and convert our glorious cities into flames of quenchless fire; therefore, dear countrymen, live not to see our Christian virgins dishonoured by violence, nor dragged along our streets, like guiltless lambs to a bloody slaughter: nor to see our harmless babes, with bruised brains dashed against hard flinty stones; nor to see our feeble age, whose hair resembles silver, lie bleeding on the marble pavement; but, like true Christian soldiers, fight in the quarrel of your countries. What though the Pagans be in number ten to one, yet heaven, I know, will fight for Christendom, and cast them down before our faces, like drops of April showers. Be not dismayed to see them in serried ranks, nor fear not when as you behold the streamers hovering in the waving wind, when as their steeled pikes, like to a thorny forest, will overspread whole countries: thousands of them I know will have no heart to fight, but fly with cowardly fear, like flocks of sheep before the greedy wolf. I am the leader of your noble minds, that never fought in vain, nor ever entered battle but returned with conquest. Then every one with me build upon this princely resolution: 'For Christendom we fight; for Christendom we live and die.'"

This soldier-like oration was no sooner finished, but the

whole army, with a general voice, cried, "To arms, to arms, with victorious George of England!" which noble resolution of the soldiers so rejoiced the English champion, and likewise encouraged the other Christian knights with such a forwardness of mind, that they gave speedy commandment to remove their tents, and to march with easy journies towards Tripoli in Barbary, where Almidor, the black king of Morocco, had residence; in which travel we must leave for a while the Christian army, and speak of the innumerable troops of Pagan knights that arrived in the kingdom of Hungary, and how they fell at variance in the election of a general: which civil mutiny caused much effusion of blood, to the great hurt both of Africa and Asia, as here followeth.

CHAPTER XIV.

Of the Dissension and Discord that happened amongst the Army of the Pagans in Hungary. The Battle between the Christians and the Moors in Barbary; and how Almidor, the black King of Morocco, was scalded to Death in a Cauldron of boiling Lead and Brimstone.

THE ireful Pagans, after they had levied their martial forces both by sea and land, repaired to their general place of meeting, there to form plans for the utter ruin of Christendom: for no sooner had winter withdrawn his chill frost from the earth, and Flora taken possession of his place, but the kingdom of Hungary suffered excessive penury, through the numberless armies of accursed infidels, this being their appointed place of meeting: for though Hungary, of all other countries, then was the richest and most plentiful in victuals to maintain a camp of men, yet was it mightily oppressed, and greatly burthened with multitudes, not only with want of necessaries to relieve soldiers, but with the extreme cruelty of those bloody-minded miscreants, who through a civil discord which happened amongst them, about the election of a general, converted their union into a most inhuman slaughter, and their triumphant victory into a dismal bloody tragedy: for no sooner arrived their legions upon the plains of Algernos, being in length and breadth one-and-twenty leagues, but the king of Hungary caused their muster-rolls to be publicly read, and justly numbered, in the hearing of the Pagan knights, which in this manner was proclaimed through the camp.

First, Be it known unto all nations that fight in the quarrels of Africa and Asia, under the conduct of our three great gods Mahomet, Tarmagant, and Apollo, what invincible forces are now arrived in this renowned kingdom of Hungary, a land honoured through the world, not only for arms, but curious buildings, and plentified with all manner of riches.

Second, We have from the emperor of Constantinople, two

hundred thousand. From the emperor of Greece, two hundred and fifty thousand. From the emperor of Tartary, an hundred threescore and three thousand. From the soldan of Persia, two hundred thousand. From the king of Jerusalem, four hundred thousand. Of Moors, one hundred and twenty thousand. Of coal-black Negroes, one hundred and forty thousand. Of Arabians, one hundred and sixty thousand. Of Babylonians, one hundred and thirty thousand and odd. Of Armenians, one hundred and fifty thousand. Of Macedonians, two hundred and ten thousand. Of Syracusians, fifteen thousand six hundred. Of Hungarians, three hundred and six thousand. Of Sicilians, seven thousand three hundred. Of Scythians, one hundred and five thousand. Of Parthians, ten thousand three hundred. Of Phrygians, seven thousand three hundred. Of Ethiopians, sixty thousand. Of Thracians, fourscore thousand. Likewise from the provinces of Prester John, three thousand of unconquered knights, with many other petty dominions and dukedoms, whose number we omit for this time, lest we should seem over-tedious.

But to conclude, such a camp of armed soldiers arrived in Hungary, as might in one month have destroyed Christendom, had not God defended them from those barbarous nations, and by his invincible power, had foiled the Pagans in their own practices : for no sooner had the heralds proclaimed through the camp what a number of nations joined in arms together, but the soldiers fell at dissension one with another, about the election of a general : some vowed to follow none but the king of Jerusalem, some Ptolemy the Egyptian king ; and some the soldan of Persia ; either to persevere in their own wills, or to lose their lives in the same quarrel.

Thus in this manner parts were taken on all sides, not only by the meaner sort, but by leaders and commanders of bands ; whereby the kings and potentates were forced to commit their wills to their soldiers' pleasure. This civil broil so discouraged the whole army, that many withdrew their forces and presently marched homewards, namely the king of Morocco, and his tawny Moors, and coal-black Negroes : likewise the soldan of Persia, Ptolemy the Egyptian king, the king of Arabia and Jerusalem ; every one departed to their own countries, cursing the time they attempted first so vain an enterprise. The rest, not minding to put up with abuses, fell from brawling boasts to downright blows ; which continued without ceasing for the space of three days, in which encounters the murdered infidels, like scattered corn, overspread the fields of Hungary : the fruitful valleys lay drowned in purple gore ; the fields of corn consumed with flames of fire ; their towns and cities ruined with wasting war ; wherein the fathers were sad witnesses of their children's slaughter, and the sons beheld their parents' reverend hairs, more white than pure silver, besmeared with clotted blood.

In the meanwhile the seven worthy champions of Christendom had entered Barbary, before Almidor the black king of Morocco, with his scattered troops of Moors and Negroes, returned from Hungary, and by fire and sword had wasted many of their chiefest towns and forts, whereby the country was much weakened, and the people compelled to sue for mercy at the champions' hands, who bearing true Christian minds, vouchsafed to grant mercy to those that yielded their lives to the pleasure of the Christian knights: but when St. George had intelligence of Almidor's approach with his weakened troops, he presently prepared his soldiers in readiness to give the Moors a bloody banquet, which was the next morning by break of day performed, to the high honour of Christendom: but the night before, the Moors knowing the country better than the Christians, got the advantage both of wind and sun; whereat St. George being something dismayed, but yet not discouraged, emboldened his soldiers with many heroical speeches, proffering them frankly the enemy's spoils, and so with the sun's uprising commenced the battle, where the Moors fell before the Christians' swords as ears of corn before the reapers' sickles.

During this conflict, the seven champions still in fore-front of the battle, so adventurously behaved themselves, that they slew more negroes than a hundred of the bravest knights in the Christian armies. At last, Fortune intending to make St. George's prowess to shine brighter than the rest, singled out the Morocco king, betwixt whom and the English champion was a long and dangerous fight: but St. George so courageously behaved himself with his trusty sword, that Almidor was constrained to yield to his mercy. The army of the Moors, seeing their king taken prisoner, presently would have fled; but that the Christians, being the lighter of foot, overtook them, and made the greatest slaughter of them that ever happened in Barbary.

Thus after the battle ended, and the joyful shout of victory sounded throughout the Christian army, the soldiers furnished themselves with the enemy's spoils, and marched, by St. George's directions, to the city of Tripoli, being then almost unpeopled through the late slaughter which was there made: in which city, after they had rested some days, and refreshed themselves with wholesome food, the English champion, out of revenge for his former proffered injuries by the Morocco king, gave the following severe sentence of death.

First, He commanded a brazen cauldron to be filled with boiling metal: then Almidor to be brought to the place of death by twelve of the noblest peers in Barbary, therein to be consumed, which was performed within seven days following. The brazen cauldron was erected by the appointment of St. George, directly in the middle of the chief market-place, under which a very hot fire continually burned for the space of eight-and-forty hours.

Now all things being thus prepared in readiness, and the Christian champions present to behold the woful spectacle, the condemned Moorish king came to the place of execution in a shirt of fine Indian silk, his hands pinioned together with a chain of gold, and his face covered with a damask scarf, his attendants and chief conductors twelve Moorish peers, clad in sable gowns of taffety, carrying before him the wheel of Fortune, with a picture of a monarch vaunting, with this motto on his breast, "I will be king in spite of Fortune:" upon the top of the wheel the picture or perfect image of a deposed potentate, falling with his head downwards, with this motto on his breast, "I have been king while it pleased Fortune:" which plainly signified the chances of war, and of inconstant destiny. His guard was a hundred Christian soldiers, holding Fortune in disdain: after them attended a hundred of Morocco virgins in black ornaments, their hair bound up with silver wires, and covered with veils of black silk, signifying the sorrow of their country for the loss of their sovereign. In this mournful manner came the unfortunate Almidor to the boiling cauldron; which when he came near, his heart waxed cold, and his tongue was devoid of utterance for a time; at last he broke forth into these earnest protestations, proffering more for his life than the whole kingdom of Barbary could perform.

"Most highly and invincible champion of Christendom (quoth he), let my life be ransomed, and thou shalt yearly receive ten tons of tried gold, five hundred webs of woven silk, an hundred ships of spices and refined sugar shall be yearly paid thee by our Barbary merchants; an hundred waggons likewise laden with pearl and jasper stones, which by our cunning lapidists shall be yearly seated and brought thee home to England, to make that blessed country the richest within the dominions of Europe; likewise I will deliver up my diadem with all my princely dignities, and in company of the Morocco lords, like bridled horses, draw thee daily in a silver chariot up and down the circled earth, till death give an end to our live's pilgrimage; therefore, most admired knight at arms, let these salt tears, that trickle from the channels of my eyes, obtain one grant of comfort at thy hands, for on my bended knees I beg for life, that never before this time did kneel to mortal man."

Thou speakest in vain (replied St. George): not the treasures hidden in the deepest seas, nor all the golden mines of rich America, shall redeem thy life: thou knowest, accursed villain, thy wicked practices in thy court, where thou proceeded wrongfully to bereave me of my life; through thy treachery I endured a long imprisonment in Persia, where for seven years I drank foul channel water, and sufficed my hunger with bread of bran meal: my food was the loathsome flesh of rats and mice, and my resting-place a dismal dungeon, where neither sun nor the cheerful light of heaven lent me comfort during my long-continued misery: for which inhuman dealing, and proffered injuries, the heavens enforce me to a speedy revenge, which in this manner shall be accomplished.

"Thou seest the torment prepared for thy death, this brazen cauldron filled with boiled lead and brimstone, wherein thy accursed body shall be speedily cast, and boiled till thy detested limbs be consumed to a watery substance in this sparkling liquid: therefore prepare thyself to entertain the violent stroke of death, and willingly bid all thy kingly dignities farewell: but yet I let thee understand, that mercy harbours in a Christian's heart, and where mercy dwells, their faults are forgiven upon some humble penitence: though thy trespasses deserve no pity, but severe punishment, yet upon these considerations I will grant thee liberty of life.

"First, That thou wilt forsake thy gods Tarmagant and Apollo, which are the vain imaginations of men; and believe in our true and ever-living God, under whose banner we Christians have taken in hand this long war. Secondly, Thou shalt give commandment that all thy barbarous nations be christened, in the faith of Christ. Thirdly and lastly, That thy three kingdoms of Barbary, Morocco, and India, swear true allegiance to all Christian kings, and never to bear arms, but in the true quarrel of Christ and his anointed nations. These things duly observed, thy life shall be preserved, and thy liberty obtained, otherwise look for no mercy, but a speedy and most terrible death."

These words more displeased the unbelieving king of Morocco, than the sentence of his condemnation, whereupon in these brief speeches he spoke out his valorous resolution:

"Great potentate of Europe, by whose fortune sits fettered in the chains of power, my golden diadem and regal sceptre, by constraint I must deliver them up. But before I will forsake my country's gods, I will endure a hundred deaths; and before my conscience be turned to a new faith, the earth shall be no earth, the sea no sea, the heaven no heaven. Thinkest thou now, proud Christian, by thy threatened torments, to make me forget my Creator, and believe in thy God, the supposed king of the Jews, and basely born under an ox's stall? No, no, accursed Christians, you offspring of Cain, you generation of Ishmael, you seed of vipers, and accursed through the world, look for a speedy shower of vengeance to rain from heaven upon your wicked nations. Your bloody practices have pierced the battlements of Jove, and your tyrannies broken open the gates of mighty Mahomet, who has provided whips of burning wire to scourge you for your cruelties, proffered to and against his blessed worshippers. Now with this deadly curse I bid you all farewell: The plagues of Egypt light upon your kingdom, the curse of Cain upon your children, the famine of Jerusalem upon your friends, and the misery of Œdipus upon yourselves."

This wicked resolution and baleful curse, was no sooner ended by the desperate-minded Almidor, but the impatience of St. George was so highly moved that he gave present command to the appointed executioners to cast him into the boiling cauldron; which immediately they performed, to the terror of all the beholders. To see this woful spectacle, the battlements of the temple were so thronged with people, the houses covered with women and children, and the streets filled with armed soldiers, that it was a wonder to behold. Amongst this multitude, there were some particular persons, that at the sight of Almidor's death, fell down and broke their necks; but the general number, as well of Pagans as of Christians, cried with cheerful voices, "Honour and victory follow St. George of England, for he hath redeemed Barbary from a miserable servitude." Which joyful hearing so delighted the seven champions of Christendom, that they caused their conduits to run with wines, the streets to be beautified with bonfires, and a sumptuous banquet to be proclaimed throughout the city, which continued for the space of seven days, in more magnificent royalty than the banquet of Babylon, when the Macedonian monarch returned from the world's conquest.

The champions' generosity procured such faithful love in the hearts of the Morocco peers, that with a general consent they chose St. George for their lawful king; where, after they had invested him in the princely seat of the Morocco potentate, they set the crown upon his head, and afterwards presented him with an imperial robe, which the kings of Barbary usually wore upon their coronation-day; and the whole of the nobles promised to forsake their profane religion, and be christened in the faith of Christ.

This promised conversion of the infidels more highly delighted the English champion, than to have the whole world's honour at command: for it was the chiefest point of his knightly oath to advance the faith of Christ, and to enlarge the bounds of Christendom. After his coronation was so solemnly performed, the other six champions conducted him to a princely palace, where he took true allegiance before the Morocco lords, by plighted oaths to be true to his crown. After this, he established the Christian laws, to the benefit of the whole country: then he commanded all the ceremonious rites of Mahomet to be trodden under foot, and the true gospel of Christ to be preached: likewise he caused all that did remain in Barbary to be christened into the new faith. But these observances continued but for a time, as here-after shall be discovered at large. For fame, not intending to let the worthy champions long remain in the idle bowers of peace, summoned them to persevere in noble achievements, and to muster up anew their soldiers, whose armour-cankered case was almost stained with rust: therefore St. George committed the government of the country to four of the principal peers of Morocco, and marched towards the country of Egypt, where lived treacherous Ptolemy, the father of his beloved lady, Sabra, whom he had left in the kingdom of England. In their journey and happy arrival in Egypt we will leave the seven champions for a time, and speak of the faithless infidels in Barbary, after the departure of the Christians, whose former honours they slightly regarded: for no sooner had St. George, with his martial troops, bidden their country adieu, but the faithless Moors reconciled themselves to their former gods, and purposed a speedy revenge for the death of Almidor, against all Christians that remained within the limits of that heathen nation: for there were many soldiers wounded in the late battle, likewise a number oppressed with sickness, which the Christian champions had left behind for their better recoveries, upon whom the barbarous Moors committed their first tyranny; for they caused the distressed soldiers to be drawn upon sledges to the outermost parts of the city, and there put them into a large and old monastery, which they presently set on fire, and most inhumanly burned the Christian soldiers, and afterwards converted the place into a loathsome desert: many women and helpless children they dragged up and down the streets, till their brains were dashed against the stones, and the blood had covered the earth with a purple hue. Many other cruelties were committed by the wicked infidels against the distressed Christians, which we will pass over, and proceed to discourse of the Christian champions' transactions, who by this time were arrived in the kingdom of Egypt.

CHAPTER XV.

How the Christians arrived in Egypt, and what happened to them there. The tragedy of the designing Earl of Coventry. How Sabra was bound to a stake to be burnt: and how St. George redeemed her. Lastly, how the Egyptian King cast himself from the top of a tower and broke his neck.

THE champions of Christendom no sooner arrived in the territories of Egypt, where they expected to adventure their lives upon the chance of war, but all things fell out contrary to their expectations; they found the gates of every village and town unpeopled; for the people at the report of the Christians' arrival, secretly hid their treasure in the caves of the earth, in deep wells and such like obscure places, and a general fear and extreme terror assailed the Egyptians, the peers of the land as well as the simple country people: many fled into woods and wildernesses, and closely hid themselves in hollow trees; many digged cavities in the ground, where they thought to remain in safety; and many fled to high mountains, where they a long time lived in great extremity, feeding upon the grass of the ground. So greatly the Egyptians feared the army of the Christians, that they expected nothing but the ruin of their country, with the loss of their own lives, and the murder of their wives and children.

But to come to the Christian champions, who, finding the country destitute of people, suspected some deep policy of the Egyptians, thinking that they were lying in ambush to murder the warlike forces of the Christians; therefore St. George gave command through the whole camp, that not a man, upon pain of death, should break his rank, but march advisedly, with their weapons ready prest to encounter battle, as though the enemies had directly placed themselves opposite against them: which special charge the Christian soldiers observed, looking neither after the wealth of cities nor the spoil of villages, but circumspectly marched, according to their leaders' directions, along the country of Egypt, till they approached the sight of king Ptolemy's court: which when the noble champion of England beheld, in this manner encouraged he his followers:

"Behold (said he), you invincible captains of Christendom, yonder are those cursed towers where wicked Ptolemy keeps his court: those battlements, I say, were they as strongly built as the great pyramids, yet should they be subverted and laid as level with the ground, as the city of Carthage; there hath that accursed Ptolemy his residence, that for preserving his daughter from the burning dragon, treacherously sent me into Persia, where, for seven years I lived in great extremity in a dismal dungeon, where the sun never gave me light, nor the company of people comfort; in revenge whereof my heart shall never rest in quiet, till I see the buildings of his palace set on fire, and converted into a place of desolation, like to the glorious city in Phrygia, now overspread with stinking weeds and loathsome puddles; therefore let all Christian soldiers, that fight under the banner of Christendom, and all that love George of England, your chosen general, draw forth your warlike weapons, and like the angry Greeks overturn those glittering battlements; leave not one stone upon another, but lay it as level with the ground, as the harvest reapers do fields of ripened corn; let your wrathful furies fall upon this tower, like drops of April showers or like storms of winter's hail, that it may be published throughout the whole world what just vengeance did light upon the pride of Egypt: leave not (I say), as you love your general, when you have subverted the palace, spare not one man alive, no not a sucking babe, but let them suffer vengeance, for the wickedness of their king: this is my decree, brave knights of Christendom, therefore march forwards: heaven and fortune be your good speed."

At which words the soldiers gave a general shout, in sign of their willing minds. Then began the silken streamers to float in the air, the drums cheerfully to sound forward, the silver trumpets recorded echoes of victory; the barbed steeds grew proud of this attempt, and would stand upon no ground, but leaped and danced with as much courage, as did Bucephalus, the horse of the Macedonian Alexander always before any notable victory; yea, every thing gave an evident sign of good success, as well senseless things as living creatures.

With this resolution marched the Christians, purposing the utter confusion of the Egyptians, and the woful ruin and destruction of Ptolemy's sumptuous palace. But when the soldiers approached the gates, there came pacing out thereat the Egyptian king, with all the chiefest of his nobles, attired in black and mournful ornaments, bearing in their hands olive-branches: next came the bravest soldiers in Egypt, bearing in their hands broken weapons, shivered lances, and torn banners: likewise followed thousands of women and children, with cypress wreaths about their heads, and in their hands olive-branches, crying for mercy to the Christians, that they should not utterly destroy their declining country, but show mercy to unhappy Egypt. This unexpected sight, or rather admirable wonder, caused St. George to sound a halt, and give commandment through the Christian army, to withhold their former vow of vengeance from the Egyptians, till he understood what they required: which charge being given, and duly observed, St George with the other six champions came together, and admitted the Egyptian king with his nobles to their presence, who in this manner began to speak for his country.

"You unconquered knights of Christendom, whose worthy victories and noble achievements the whole world admires, let him that never kneeled to any man till now, and in former times disdained to humble himself to any potentate on earth; let him, I say, the most unfortunate wretch alive, crave mercy, not for myself, but for my country; my peoples' blood will be required at my hands: our murdered infants will call to heaven for revenge, and our slaughtered widows sink down to hell for revenge: so will the vengeance of heaven light upon my soul, and the curse of hell upon my head.

"Renowned champion of England, under whose custody my dear daughter is kept, even for the love of her, be merciful to Egypt. The former wrongs I proffered thee, when I sent thee, like a guiltless lamb, into Persia, were contrary to my will; for I was incensed by the flattery of that accursed Moorish king; may his soul for ever be scourged with whips of wire, and plagued with the punishment of Tantalus in hell. If my life will serve for a just revenge, here is my naked breast, let my heart's blood stain some Christian's sword, that you may bear the bloody witness of my death into Christendom, or let me be torn into a thousand pieces by mad untamed steeds, as was Hippolytus, son of Theseus, in his charmed chariot.

"Most mighty controllers of the world, command the dearest things in Egypt, they are at your pleasures. We will forsake our gods, and believe in that God which you commonly adore, for he is the true and living God, ours false and hateful in the sight of heaven."

This penitent lamentation of the Egyptian king caused the Christian champions to relent, but especially St. George, who having a heart filled with a well-spring of pity, not only granted mercy to the whole country, but vouchsafed Ptolemy liberty of life, upon condition that he would perform what he had promised; which was, to forsake his false gods, and believe in our true God, Christ Jesus.

This kindness of St. George filled the mind of Ptolemy with joy; and the whole land, both peers and people, more rejoiced at the friendship of the Christians, than if they had been made lords of the western part of the world. The news of this happy union was spread in all parts of Egypt; whereby the people, that before had for fear fled into the woods and wildernesses, dens and caves, hills and mountains, returned joyfully to their own dwellings, and caused bonfires to be made in every city, town, and village; the bells of Egypt rang day and night, for the space of a week; every place was seen banqueting, dancing, and masking; sorrow was banished, wars forgotten, and peace proclaimed.

The king at his own charge ordained a sumptuous and costly banquet for the Christian champions, wherein for bounty it exceeded that which the Trojans made, when Paris returned from Greece with the conquest of Menelaus' queen. The banqueting-house was built with cypress wood, covered with pure adamantine stone; so that neither steel nor iron could come therein, but it was presently drawn to the top of the roof. As for the variety of services which graced the banquet, it were too tedious to repeat; but to be brief, what both the land and sea could afford, was there present. The servitors that attended the champions at the banquet, were attired in damask vestments, wrought with the purest silk the Indian virgins spun upon their silver wheels: at every course the servitors brought in a number of Egyptian lady musicians who on their ivory lutes strained forth such admired harmony, that it surpassed Orion's music, which, when he was cast into the sea, caused the dolphins to bring him safe to the shore; or the sweetness of Orpheus' silver harp, which made both stones and trees to dance; or the melody of Apollo's inspiring music, when he descended to these lower parts for the love of Daphne. These pleasures so delighted the Christian champions, that they forgot the sound of warlike drums, which were wont to call them forth to bloody battles. But these delights continued but a short time, for there arrived a knight from England, that brought such unexpected news to St. George, as changed his joy into extreme sorrow; for after this manner begun the messenger to tell his woful tale:

"Fair England's champion," said he, "instead of arms, get swallow's wings, and fly to England, if ever thou wilt see thy beloved lady, for she is judged to be burned at a stake for murdering the earl of Coventry; whose base desires would have stained her honour with infamy, and made her the scorn of virtuous women: yet this mercy is granted by the king of England, that if within twelve months a champion can be found, that for her sake will venture his life; if it be his fortune to overcome the challenger of her death, she shall live: but if it be his fatal destiny to be conquered, then must she suffer the heavy judgment before pronounced; therefore, as you love the life of your chaste and beloved lady, haste into England; delay no time, for delay is dangerous, and her life in hazard to be lost."

This ill news struck such a terror to St. George's heart, likewise to the Egyptian king her father, that for a time they stood gazing at one another as though they had been bereaved of their wits, not able to speak one word; but at last St. George recovered from his consternation, and breathed forth this sorrowful lamentation:

"O England! O unkind England! have I adventured my life in thy defence, and for thy defence have stood in the field of Mars, buckled on my armour in many a parching summer's day, and many a freezing winter's night, when thy sons have taken their quiet sleep on beds of down; and wilt thou repay me with this discourtesy, to adjudge Sabra's spotless body to consuming fire? whose blood, if it be spilt before I come, I vow never to draw my trusty sword in England's quarrel more, nor ever account myself her champion; but I will wander over unknown countries, obscurely from the sight of any Christian eye. Is it possible that England will be so ungrateful to her friend? Can that renowned country harbour such a base monster, who has sought to dishonour her, within whose heart the fountain of virtue springs? or can that noble city, the nurse and mother of my life, entertain so vile a homicide, that will offer violence to her, whose chastity and true honour hath caused tameless lions to sleep in her lap?"

In this sorrowful manner spoke St. George the champion, until the Egyptian king, whose sorrow being as great as his, put him from his complaints, and requested the English knight to tell the true nature of Sabra's proffered violence, and how she murdered the earl of Coventry; to whom, after a bitter sigh or two, the messenger replied, in this manner:

"Most noble princes and potentates of the earth, prepare your ears to listen to the most woful tale that ever English knight disclosed, and your eyes to weep seas of briny tears. I would I had no tongue to tell it, nor heart to remember it; but seeing I am compelled, through the love and duty I owe the noble champions of Christendom, to express it, then thus it was.

"It was the fortune, nay I may say, unhappy destiny of your beloved lady, upon an evening, when the sun had almost lodged in the west, to walk without the walls of Coventry, to take the pleasures of the sweet fields and flourishing meadows, which Flora had beautified in summer's livery; but as she walked up and down, sometimes taking pleasure to hear the warbling birds how they strained their silver notes; other times taking delight to see how nature had covered both hills and dales with sundry sorts of flowers, then walking to see the crystal running rivers, the murmuring music of whose streams exceeded the rest for pleasure; but she (kind lady) delighting herself by the river side, a sudden and strange alteration troubled her mind; for the chain of gold that she did wear about her neck presently changed colour, from a yellow burnished brightness, to a dim paleness: her rings fell from her fingers, and from her nose fell drops of blood, whereat her heart began to throb, her ears to glow, and every joint to tremble with fear. This strange accident caused her speedily to hasten homewards: but by the way she met the earl of Coventry, walking at that time to take the pleasure of the evening air, with such a train of worthy gentlemen, as though he had been the greatest peer in England: whose sight when she beheld afar off, her heart began to be uneasy, thinking that fortune had allotted those gentlemen to proffer her some injury; so that upon her cheeks fear had set a vermilion dye, whereby her beauty grew admirable; which when the earl beheld, he was enamoured therewith, and deemed her the most beautiful creature that ever nature framed. Their meeting was silent; she showed the humility of a virtuous lady, and he the courtesy of a kind gentleman: she departed homewards, and he into the fields; she thinking all danger past, but he planning in his mind her utter ruin and downfall. For the dart of love had shot from her beauteous cheeks into his heart, not true love, but base passion; so that nothing might quench his desire, but the completion of his wishes: such extreme desire bewitched his mind, that he caused his servants every one to depart: and then, like a discontented man, he wandered up and down the fields, beating in his mind a thousand sundry ways to obtain his wishes: for without he enjoyed her love, he was likely to live in endless languishment.

"At length he departed home, where sending for his steward, he ordered him to provide a sumptuous and costly banquet, to entertain all the principal ladies in Coventry; the ladies accordingly repaired to his entertainment, at the time and hour appointed. The banquet was brought in by the earl's servants, and placed upon the table by the earl himself; who, after many welcomes given, began thus to move the ladies to delight:

"'I think my house most highly honoured,' said he, 'that you have vouchsafed to grace it with your presence, for methinks you beautify my hall, as the twinkling stars beautify the veil of heaven: but amongst the number you have a Cynthia, a glittering silver moon, that for brightness exceedeth all the rest; for she is fairer than the queen of Cyprus, lovelier than Dido, and of more majesty than the queen of love.'

"This commendation caused a general smile amongst the ladies, and made them look one upon another, thinking whom it could be. Many other court-like discourses pronounced the earl to move the ladies' delight, till the banquet was ended, which being finished, there came in certain gentlemen, by the earl's appointment, with most excellent music; some others that danced most curiously, with as much majesty as Paris in the Grecian court. At last the earl requested one of them to choose out his beloved mistress, and lead her in some graceful minuet: likewise requesting that none should be offended what lady soever he did affect to grace with that courtly pastime: at which request all of them were silent, and silence is commonly a sign of consent; therefore he emboldened himself the more to make his desires known to the beholders. Then with exceeding courtesy, and great humility, he kissed the beauteous hand of Sabra, who, with a blushing countenance and bashful look, accepted his courtesy, and like a kind lady disdained not to dance with him. So when the musicians strained forth their inspiring melody, the designing earl led her a course about the hall, and she followed with as much grace as if the queen of pleasure had been present to behold their courtly delights; and so when the first course was ended, he found a fit opportunity to unfold his secret love, and reveal unto the lady the desire of his mind, which he did in the following manner:

"'Most divine and peerless paragon!' said he, 'thou only wonder of the world for beauty and excellent ornaments of nature! know that thy twinkling eyes, that shine more bright than the light of heaven, have pierced my heart, and those thy crimson cheeks have wounded me with love; therefore, except thou grant me kind comfort, I am like to spend the remnant of my life in sorrow, care, and discontent. I blush to speak what I desire, because I have settled my love where it is unlawful, in a bosom where kings may sleep and surfeit with delight, thy breast I mean, most divine mistress, for there my heart is kept prisoner; beauty is the keeper, and love the key, my ransom is a constant mind. I admit that thy lord and husband is alive, yet hath he most unkindly left thee to spend thy young years in widowhood: he is inconstant, like Æneas, and thou more hapless than Dido. He marches up and down the world in glittering armour, and never doth intend to return: he abandoneth thy presence, and lieth sporting in strange ladies' laps; therefore, dear Sabra, live not to continue in singleness, for age will overtake thee too soon, and convert thy beauty to wrinkled frowns.'

"To which words, Sabra would have presently made answer, but that the music called them to dance, the second course; which being ended, she replied in this manner:

"'Most noble lord,' said she, 'for our bounteous banquet and courteous entertainment, I give thee the humble thanks of a poor lady; but for your suit and unlawful desire, I do detest them as much as the sight of a crocodile, and flattering glosses I esteem as much as doth the ocean of a drizzling shower of rain; your syren songs shall never entice me to listen to your fond requests; but I will, like Ulysses, stop my ears, and bury all your flattering enticements in the lake of forgetfulness. Think you that I will stain my marriage bed with the least spot of infamy, or that I will suffer one thought of wrong, for all the treasures of the wealthy seas? Surely the gorgeous sun shall lose his light by day, and the silver moon by night, the skies shall fall, the earth shall sink, and every thing shall change its kind and nature, before I will falsify my faith, or prove disloyal to my beloved George. Attempt no more, my noble lord, to batter the fortress of my good name with your flattery, nor seek to stain my honour with your base desires. What if my lord and husband prove disloyal, and choose out other loves, in foreign lands? yet will I prove as Penelope to her Ulysses; and if it be his pleasure never to return, but spend his days among strange ladies, yet will I live in single solitariness, like to the turtle dove when she hath lost her mate, abandoning all company; or as the mournful swan, that swims upon Meander's silver streams, where she records her dying tunes to raging billows; so will I spend away my lingering days in grief, and die.'

"'Why, my dear mistress, have you a heart more hard than flint, that the tears of my true love can never mollify? Can you behold him plead for grace that hath been sued by many worthy dames? I am a man, and can command countries, yet can I not command thy stubborn heart. Divine Sabra, if thou wilt grant me thy love, and yield to my desire, I will have thee clad in silken robes, and damask vestures, embossed with Indian pearls, and rich refined gold, perfumed with camphire, biss, and sweet Syrian perfumes; by day a hundred virgins shall attend thy person; by night a hundred eunuchs, with their strained instruments, shall bring thy senses into a golden slumber: all this, my dear, divine, and dainty mistress is at thy command, and more, so that I may enjoy thy love and favour: which if I have not, I will discontentedly end my life in woods and desert places, tigers and untamed beasts being my chief companions.'

"These vain promises caused the beauteous Sabra to blush with bashfulness, and to give him this sharp answer:

"'Think you, my lord, with promises to obtain the precious gem, which I will not lose for Europe's treasury? Henceforth be silent in that enterprise, and never after this attempt to effect my dishonour, which if you do, I vow by heaven, to make it known to every one within the city, and to fill all places with the rumour of thy base passion: this I am resolved to do, and so farewell.'

"Thus departed Sabra, with a sad countenance, whereby the rest of the ladies suspected the earl had attempted her dishonour by secret conference, but they all assuredly knew that she was as far from yielding to his desires, as is the aged man to be young again, or as the azure firmament to be a place for sylvan swains to inhabit. In such-like imaginations they passed away the day till the dark night caused them to break off company. The earl smothered his grief under a smiling countenance, till the ladies were every one departed, whom he courteously caused his servants to conduct homewards with torch-lights, because it began to be very dark. After their departure, he accursed his own fortune, and like a lion wanting food, raged up and down his chamber, filling every corner with bitter exclamations, rending his garments from his neck, tearing his hair, beating his breast, and using all the violence he could against himself.

H

"In this manner spent he away the night, suffering no sleep to recruit his wearied body. His melancholy and extreme passion so discontented his mind, that he purposed to put an end to his sorrows by some untimely death: so when the morning appeared, he repaired to an orchard, where Sabra once a day walked to take the air. The place was very melancholy, and far from the noise of people; where, after he had spent some certain time in exclaiming against the unkindness of Sabra, he pulled his poniard from his side, and prepared his breast to receive the stroke of death; but before the intended tragedy, with his dagger he engraved these following verses upon the bark of a walnut-tree.

> " ' O heart more hard than bloody tigers fell!
> O ears more deaf than senseless troubled seas!
> O cruel foe! thy rigour doth excell:
> For thee I die, thy anger to appease:
> But time will come, when thou shalt find me slain,
> Then thy repentance will increase thy pain.
>
> " ' I here engrave my will and testament,
> That my sad grief thou may'st behold and see,
> How that my woful heart is torn and rent,
> And gor'd with bloody blade, for love of thee;
> Whom thou disdain'st, as now the end doth try,
> That thus distress'd doth suffer me to die.
>
> " ' Oh God of love, if so there any be,
> And you of love that feel the deadly pain,
> Oh, Sabra, thou that thus afflictest me,
> Hear these words, which from my heart I strain:
> Ere that my corpse be quite bereav'd of breath,
> Here I'll declare the cause of this my death.
>
> " ' Ye mountain nymphs, which in the deserts reign,
> Leave off your chase for savage beasts awhile,
> Prepare to see a heart opprest with pain,
> Address your ears to hear my doleful style:
> No strength nor heart can work me any weal,
> Since she's unkind, and tyrant-like doth deal.
>
> " ' Ye fairy nymphs, of lovers much ador'd,
> And gracious damsels, which, in evenings fair,
> Your closets leave, with heavenly beauty stor'd,
> And on your shoulders spread your golden hair;
> Record with me that Sabra is unkind,
> Within whose breast remains a double mind.
>
> " ' Ye savage bears, in caves and dens that lie,
> Remain in peace, if you my sorrows hear;
> And be not moved at my misery,
> Though too extreme my passions do appear:
> England farewell, and Coventry adieu,
> But, Sabra, heaven above still prosper you.'

"These verses being no sooner finished, and engraved about the bark of the walnut-tree, but with a wrathful countenance he lifted up his hand, intending to strike the poniard up to the hilt into his breast; but at the same instant he beheld

Sabra entering the orchard to take her wonted walks of pleasure, whose sight hindered his purpose, and caused other horrid intentions to enter into his mind. The Furies did incense him to a wicked deed, which my trembling tongue falters to report: for after she had walked to the farthest side of the orchard, he ran unto her with his dagger drawn, and catching her about the slender waist, thus frightfully threatened her:

"'Now, stubborn dame,' quoth he, 'will I obtain my long-desired purpose, and revenge by violence thy former proud denials. First, I will wrap this dagger in thy locks of hair, and nail it fast into the ground: then will I overcome thee by force and violence, and triumph in the conquest of thy chastity: which being done, I will cut thy tongue out of thy mouth, because thou shalt not reveal nor disclose who is thy undoer: likewise, with this poniard will I chop off both thy hands, whereby thou shalt never write with pen thy stain of honour, nor in sampler record thy disgrace. Therefore, except thou wilt yield to quench my desired love, I will by force and violence inflict those vowed punishments upon thy delicate body. Be not too resolute in denials; for if thou art, the gorgeous sun shall not glide the compass of an hour, before I obtain my long-desired purpose.'

"And thereupon he stepped to the orchard door, and with all expedition locked it, and put the key in his pocket; then returned he, like an hunger-starved wolf, to seize upon the silly lamb: or like the chased boar, when he is wounded with the hunter's lance, he came running to the helpless lady, intending to accomplish her foul dishonour; but she, thinking herself bereft of all hope of aid and succour, fell into a deep swoon, being unable to move for the space of an hour: but at last, recovering from her stupor, she began in this pitiful manner to defend her assailed chastity from the wicked earl, who stood over her with his bloody dagger, threatening most cruelly her destrucion.

"'My lord of Coventry,' said she, with weeping tears, and kneeling upon the ground, 'is virtue banished from your breast? Have you a mind more tyrannous than the tigers in Hycola, that nothing may suffice to satisfy your base desires but the stain of mine honour and the conquest of my chastity? If it be my beauty that hath enticed you, I am content to have it converted to a loathsome leprosy, whereby to make me odious in your eyes; if it be my rich and costly garments that make me beautiful, and so entangle you, henceforth I will attire my body in poor and simple array, and for evermore dwell in dreary caves and humble cottages, so that I may preserve my chastity unspotted. If none of these may suffice to abate your tyrannous intent, but that your base passion will make me time's wonder, and a pointing-stock, and scorn of virtuous ladies, then will the heavens revenge my wrongs, to whom I will incessantly make my petitions: the birds in the air, after their kind, will evermore exclaim against your wickedness: the sylvan beasts that abide in woods and deserts, will breathe forth clamours of your wickedness: the creeping worms, that live within the crevices of the earth, will give dumb signs and tokens of your wickedness: the running rivers will murmur at your wickedness: the woods and trees, herbs and flowers, with every senseless thing, will sound some motions of your wickedness. Return, return, my noble lord, unto your former virtues; banish such fond desires out of your mind; stain not the honour of your house with such black scandals and disgrace: bear this in mind before you do attempt so vile a sin: What became of Helen's dishonour, but the destruction of renowned Troy? What of Roman Lucreti's defilement, but the banishment of Tarquin? And what of Progne's foul deflourment by her sister's husband, the cruel king of Thrace, but the bloody banquet of his young son Itys, whose tender body they served to his table, baked in a pie!'

"At these remarks the ireful earl wrapped his hands within her locks of hair, which was covered with a costly caul of gold, and, in this manner presently replied unto her:

"'Why tellest thou me of poets' tales; of Progne's defilement, and Tereus's bloody banquet? Thy dishonour shall be an induction to thy death, which, if thou yield not willingly, I will obtain by force and violence: therefore prepare thyself, either to receive the sentence pronounced, or yield thy body to my pleasure.'

"This resolution of the earl added grief upon grief, and heaped mountains of sorrow upon her soul. Twice did the hapless lady cast her eyes to heaven, in hopes the gods would pity her distress, and twice unto the earth, wishing the ground might open and devour her, and so deliver her from the fury of the wicked earl: but at last, when she saw that neither tears, prayers, nor wishes, could prevail, she gave an outward sign of consenting upon some conditions, under colour to devise a present means to preserve her chastity, and deliver herself from his base attempt. 'There is no condition,' said the earl, 'but I would yield unto, so thou wilt grant my desire, and make me chief commander of thy love.'

"'First, my lord,' quoth she, 'shall you suffer me to sit some certain hours upon this bed of violets, and bewail the loss of my good name, which shortly shall be yielded up to your pleasure; then shall you lie and dally in my lap, thereby to make my affections, yet freezing cold, to flame with burning brands of love; that being done, you shall receive that which shall put an end to your desires.'

"Those words caused the earl to convert his furious wrath to smiling joy, and casting down his dagger, he gave her a courteous kiss, which she in his conceit graciously accepted. Then caused he Sabra to sit down upon a bed of violets, beset about with divers sorts of flowers, whose lap he made his pillow, whereupon he laid his head, intending, as he thought, to increase desire: but women in extremity have the quickest wits; so Sabra busied herself by all means possible, either now or never to remove the cause of her deep distress, by producing his death, and so quit herself from her importunate suitor. One while she told him pleasant tales of love, in hopes to bring his senses to a slumber, the better to accomplish her desires; she then played and sported with his hair, that hung dangling below his shoulders like two threads of silk: but at last, when neither tales, discourses, nor dallying pastime with his hair, could bring him asleep, she strained forth the organs of her voice, and over his head sung this woful ditty:

> "'Thou god of sleep and golden dreams, appear,
>   That brings all things to peace and quiet rest;
> Close up the glasses of his eyes so clear,
>   Thereby to make my fortune ever blest:
> His eyes, his heart, his senses, and his mind,
> In peaceful sleep let them some comfort find.
>
> "'Sing sweet, you pretty birds in tops of trees,
>   With warbling tunes and many a pleasant note;
> Till your sweet music close his watchful eyes,
>   That on my love with vain desires doth dote:
> Sleep on, my dear, sleep on, my love's delight,
> And let this sleep be thy eternal night.
>
> "'You gentle bees, the Muses' lovely birds,
>   Come aid my doleful tunes with silver sound,
> Till your inspiring melody records
>   Such heavenly music that may quite confound
> Both wit and sense, and tire his eyes with sleep,
> That on my lap in sweet content I keep.
>
> "'You silver streams, which murmuring music make,
>   And fill each dale with pleasant harmony,
> Whereat the floating fish must pleasure take,
>   To hear your sweet recording melody,
> Assist my tunes his slumb'ring eyes to close,
> That on my lap now takes a sweet repose.
>
> "'Let whispering winds in every senseless tree,
>   A solemn, sad, and doleful music sing:
> From hills and dales, and from each mountain high,
>   Let some inspiring sound or echo ring,
> That he may never wake from sleep again,
> Which sought my marriage-bed with wrong to stain.'

"This delightful song rocked his senses to such a soothing slumber, that he slept as soundly upon her lap as on the softest bed of down; whereby she found a fit opportunity to deliver her undefiled body from his base desires. So taking the poniard in her hand, which he had cast a little aside, and gazing thereon with an ireful look, she made this sad complaint:

"'Grant, you immortal powers of heaven,' said she, 'that of these two extremes I choose the best; either must I yield my body to be dishonoured by his unchaste desires, or stain my hands with the trickling streams of his heart's blood. If I yield unto the first I shall be then accounted a vicious female: but if I commit the last, I shall be guilty of a wilful murder, and for the same the law will adjudge me a shameful death. What, shall I fear to die, or lose my virtue, and renown? No, my heart shall be as tyrannous as Danaus' daughters, that slew their fifty husbands in a night: or as Medea's cruelty, which scattered her brother's bloody joints upon the sea-shore, thereby to hinder the swift pursuit of her father, when Jason got the golden fleece from Colchos' isle. Therefore, stand still, you glittering lamps of heaven, stay, wandering time, and let him sleep eternally.'

"These words were no sooner ended, but with a wrathful and pale countenance, she sheathed the poniard up to the hilt in his breast, whereat he started, and would have gotten upon his feet, but the streams of blood so violently gushed from his wound, that he sunk immediately to the earth, and his soul was forced to give the world a doleful adieu.

"When Sabra beheld the bed of violets stained with blood, and every flower converted to a crimson colour, she sighed grievously: but when she saw her garments sprinkled with her enemy's blood, she ran speedily unto a flowing fountain, that stood on the farther side of the orchard, and began to wash the blood out of her clothes; but the more she washed, the more it increased.

"This wonderful accident so amazed the sorrowful lady, that she began anew to complain: 'Oh that my hand had been struck lame by some unlucky planet, when first it attempted the deed! Whither shall I fly to shroud me from the company of virtuous women, which will for evermore shun me as a detested murderer? If I should go into some foreign country, there heaven will cast down vengeance for my guilt; if I should hide myself in woods and solitary wildernesses, yet would the winds discover me; or if I should go live in caves, or dark dens within the deep foundations of the earth, yet will his ghost pursue me there, and haunt me day and night; so that in no place a murderer can live in rest, such discontented thoughts shall still oppress his mind.' After she had breathed forth this sorrowful lamentation to the air, she tore her blood-stained garment from her back, and cast it into the fountain.

"Thus being disrobed of her outer garments, she turned to the slaughtered earl, whose face she found covered with moss, which added more grief unto her soul, for she greatly feared her murder was descried; but in this matter her fear was groundless; for the robin-redbreast, and other birds, according to a mysterious instinct possessed by them, had carried moss in their beaks, and placed it over the face of the corpse. By this time the day began to shut up his bright windows, and sable night entered to take possession of the earth, yet durst not the woful distressed Sabra make her way homewards, lest she should be descried without her upper garment.

"During this time, there was a general search made for the earl by his servants, for they greatly suspected some danger had befallen him, considering that they heard him the night before so wofully complain in his chamber. At last, with torch-lights, they came to the orchard gate, which they presently burst open; wherein they had no sooner entered, but they found their murdered master lying by a bed of violets, covered with moss; likewise searching to find out the murderer, at last they espied Sabra in her bare petticoat, her hands and face besprinkled with blood, and her countenance as pale as ashes; by which signs they suspected her to be the bloody bereaver of their lord and master's life; therefore, because she descended from a noble lineage, they brought her the same night before the king, who then kept his court in the city of Coventry, and he immediately upon the confession of the murder, gave this severe judgment against her:

"'First, to be conveyed to prison, there to remain for the term of twelve months, and at the end thereof to be burned like a most wicked offender: yet because she was the daughter to a king, and a loyal lady to so noble a knight, his majesty in mercy granted her this favour, that if she could get any knight at arms, before the time was expired, that would be her champion, and by combat redeem her from the fire, she should live, otherwise, if her champion was vanquished, then to suffer the former punishment.'

"Thus have you heard the disclosure of all things which happened till my departure from England, where I left her in prison, and since that time five months are fully expired: therefore, most renowned champion, as you love the life of your lady, and wish her delivery, make no delay, but with all speed post into England, for I greatly fear before you arrive the time will be finished, and Sabra suffer death for want of a champion to defend her cause."

This doleful discourse drove St. George, with the other knights and champions, to such an excitement of mind, that every one departed to their lodging chambers with dumb signs of sorrow, being not able to speak one word; where for that night they lamented the misfortune of so virtuous a lady. The Egyptian king her father abandoned the sight of all company, and none could come within the hearing of his lamentation: then raged he up and down, accusing heaven of injustice, condemning the earth of iniquity, and accursing man for such an execrable crime ; one time wishing that his daughter's birth-day had been her burial-day ; another time that some unlucky planet would descend from the firmament, and fall upon his miserable head. Being in this extreme passion, he never hoped to see his daughter's countenance again; and so about midnight he cast himself headlong from the top of the tower, and broke his neck.

No sooner was the night vanished, and bright Phœbus entered the zodiac of heaven, but his bruised body, lifeless and senseless, was found by his servants lying in the palaceyard, all beaten in pieces against the ground. The woful news of this self-willed murder they told to certain Egyptian knights, who took his scattered limbs, and carried them to St. George's chamber, whom they found arming himself for his departure towards England ; but at this dismal spectacle the violence of his grief rose to such a pitch, that it had almost cost him his life, had not the Egyptian knights given him many comfortable speeches ; and by the consent of many dukes, earls, lords, and barons, with many other of the late king's privy-council, they elected him the true succeeding king of Egypt, by the marriage of Ptolemy's daughter; which royal offer St. George refused not, but took upon him the government of the whole country ; so that for a short time his journey towards England was stayed, and upon the third day following, his coronation was appointed, which they solemnly performed, to the high honour of all the Christian champions : for the Egyptian peers caused St. George to be apparelled in royal vestures like a king : he had on a suit of flaming green, like an emerald, and a mantle of scarlet, very richly furred, and wrought curiously with gold. Then the other six champions led him up to the king's throne, and set him in a chair of ebony, which had pommels of silver, that stood upon an alabaster elephant; then came three of the greatest lords in Egypt, and set a crown of gold upon his head ; then followed the knights, with a sceptre and a naked sword, to signify that he was chief governor of the realm, and lord of all that appertained to the crown of Egypt. This being performed in a most sumptuous manner, the trumpets with other instruments began to sound, whereat the general company with joyful voices cried altogether, 'Long live St. George, true champion for England, and king of Egypt.' Then was he conducted to the royal palace, where for ten days he remained among his lords and knights, spending the time in great joy and pleasure ; which being finished, his lady's distress constrained him to a sudden departure : therefore he left the guiding of his land to twelve Egyptian lords, binding them all by oath to deliver it at his return; likewise charging them to inter the body of Ptolemy in a sumptuous tomb, befitting the body of so royal a potentate: he also appointed the six champions to raise their tents, and muster up anew their soldiers, and with all speed march into Persia, and there, by dint of bloody war, revenge his former injuries upon the accursed soldan.

This charge been given, the next morning by break of day he buckled on his armour, mounted on his swift footed-steed, and bade his friends in Egypt for a season adieu; and so, in company of the knight that brought him that unlucky news, he took his journey with all speed towards England; in which travel we will leave him for a time; also passing over the speedy provision made by the Christian champions in Egypt, for the invasion of Persia, and return to sorrowful Sabra, being in prison, waiting each minute to receive the final stroke of impartial death: for now had the rolling planets brought the year's journey to an end; yet Sabra had no intelligence of any champion that would defend her cause; therefore she prepared her delicate body to receive the execution of the sentence. The time being come, she was brought to the place of execution, whither she went as willingly, and with as much joy, as ever she went before time unto her marriage: she had made humble submission to the world, and unfeignedly committed her soul to God. She being at the stake, where the king was present with many thousands to behold this woful tragedy, the death's-man stripping off her garment, which was of black sarsenet, and in her snowwhite robe bound her with an iron chain unto the stake; then placed they round about her body pitch, turpentine, and gunpowder, thereby to make her death the more easy, and her pain the shorter; which being done, the king caused the herald to summon in the challenger, who at the sound of the trumpet came prancing in upon a roan-coloured steed, without any kind of mark, and dressed with rich trappings of gold, and precious stones of great price. The champion was called the baron of Chester, a bolder and hardier knight they thought lived not then upon the face of the whole earth; he so advanced himself up and down, as though he had been able to encounter with an hundred knights. Then the king caused the herald to summon in the defence, if there were any to defend her cause; both drums and trumpets sounded three several times up and down the fields; betwixt every rest a full quarter of an hour, but yet no defender did appear, therefore the king commanded the executioner to set the stake on fire.

At which words Sabra began to grow pale as ashes, and her joints to tremble like two aspen leaves; her tongue that before continued silent began to record a swan-like dying tale, and in this manner she uttered the passion of her heart.

"Be witness, Heaven, and all you bright celestial angels; be witness sun and moon, all true beholders of the fact; be witness, thou clear firmament, and all the world be witness of my innocence; the blood I shed, was for the safeguard of my honour and unspotted chastity. Great God of heaven, if the prayers of my unstained heart may move thy mighty majesty, or my true innocence prevail with thy immortal powers, command that either my lord may come to be my champion, or the beholder of my death. But if my hands were stained with the blood of some wicked enterprise, then Heaven take present vengeance upon me, or else by some noble champion save my body alive."

At which instant, she heard the sound of a shrill trumpet, the which St. George caused to be sounded (for then he was near); which caused the execution awhile to be deferred. At last, they beheld afar off a stately banner waving in the air, which a squire carried before St. George; when they espied near unto the banner a most valiant armed knight, mounted upon a coal-black palfrey, with a warlike lance standing in his rest: by whose sudden approach they knew him to be the same champion that would defend the distressed lady's life. Then the king commanded the drums and trumpets to sound; whereat the people gave a general shout, and the poor lady, half dead with fear, began to revive, and her blushing cheeks to be as beautiful as red roses dipped in milk, or as blood mingled with snow. But when St. George approached the sight of his constant lady, whom he found chained to a stake, encompassed with many instruments of death, his heart was so filled with grief, that he almost fell beside his horse: yet remembering wherefore he came, he recalled his courage, and intended to try his fortune in the combat, before he would discover himself unto his lady. And when the trumpets sounded the encounter, the two knights set spurs to their horses and made them run so fiercely, that at the first attack they shivered both their lances to their hands, then rushed together so vigorously with their bodies and helmets, that they fell down both to the earth; but St. George nimbly leaped upon his feet without any hurt, but the baron of Chester lay still with his head downward, casting from his mouth abundance of blood, for he was mightily bruised with the fall; but when he revived from his swoon, he took his shield, drawing out a mighty falchion, and with wrathful countenance ran at St. George. "Now, proud knight," quoth he, "I swear by all the saints of heaven, to revenge my blood, which thou hast shed;" and therewithal he struck so violently upon St. George's shield, that it cleaved quite asunder. Then began he to wax angry, and took his sword in great wrath, and gave the baron of Chester such a stroke, that he cut away arms and shoulder, and all the flesh of his side to the bare ribs, and likewise cut his leg almost asunder in the thickest place of his thigh; then fell the baron of Chester to the ground, and breathed his last.

The whole company admired and applauded St. George as the most fortunate knight in the world: then the king delivered Sabra with his own hands to St. George, who most courteously received her, and, like a courteous knight, cast a scarlet mantle over her body, which a lady standing by bestowed upon him; yet he caring not to discover himself, set her upon his portly steed, and with his own hands led him by the bridal reins. So great was the joy throughout the city, that the bells rang without ceasing that whole day together: the citizens, through every place St. George had to pass, did hang forth at their windows, and on their walls, cloth of gold and silk, with rich carpets; cushion coverings of green velvet lay abroad in every window: the clergy, in copes of gold and silk, met them in solemn procession; the ladies and beautiful damsels strewed every street wherein he passed with roses and most pleasent flowers, and crowned him with a wreath of green bays, in sign of his triumphant victory and conquest.

In this manner went he to the king's palace, not known by any who he was, but that he was a knight of a strange country; yet Sabra, many times as they passed along, desired to see his face, and know his name, as he had adventured so far for her sake, and that for her delivery he had vanquished the bravest knight in England. Yet for all her persuasions, he kept himself undiscovered, till a troop of ladies, in company of Sabra, got him into a chamber richly hung with arras cloth, and there unlaced his beaver; whose countenance when she beheld, and saw that it was her lord and husband, which had redeemed her from death, she fell into a deep swoon for joy; but St. George sprinkled a little cold water on her face, and revived her presently. After this he gave her many a kind and loving kiss, calling her the most true and the most loyal lady that ever nature framed, who to the very death would not lose one jot of her unspotted honour. Likewise she accounted him the truest knight and loyalest husband that ever gracious Hymen linked in bands of marriage with any woman. But when the king had notice that it was St. George, his country's champion, which achieved that noble conquest, in vanquishing the baron of Chester, he was overwhelmed with such joy, that he came running in all haste to the chamber, and most kindly embraced him: and after he was unarmed, and his wounds washed with white wine and new milk, the king conducted him with his lady to his banqueting-house, where they feasted for that evening, and afterwards kept open court to all comers so long as St. George continued there, which was for the space of one month: at the end whereof, he took his lady and one page with him, and bade England adieu, and then travelled towards Persia, to the other Christian champions, whose dangerous journey, and strange adventure, you may read in this chapter following.

CHAPTER XVI.

How St. George, in his Journey towards Persia, arrived in a Country inhabited only by Maids, where he achieved many strange and wonderful Adventures; also of the massacre of seven Virgins in a Wood; and how Sabra preserved herself from a terrible Giant.

AFTER St. George, with his virtuous lady, departed from England, and had travelled through many countries, taking their direct course towards Egypt and the confines of Persia, where the other six champions remained with the warlike legions; at last they arrived in the country of the Amazonians, a land inhabited by none but women; in which region St. George achieved many brave and princely adventures, which are most wonderful to relate, as will be found in this chapter: for travelling up and down the country, they found every town and city desolate of people, yet very sumptuously built, the earth likewise untilled, the pastures uncherished, and every field overgrown with weeds, whereby he deemed that some strange accident had befallen the country, either by war, or by the mortality of some grievous plague, for they could neither set eye on man, woman, nor child, whereby they were forced to feed upon roots; and instead of beautiful palaces, they were constrained to lie on broad pastures, upon the banks of moss; and instead of curtains of silk, they had black and dark clouds to cover them.

In this extremity they travelled up and down for thirty days; but at last it was their happy fortunes to arrive before a rich pavilion, situated and standing in the open fields, which seemed to be the most glorious sight that ever they beheld, for it was wrought of the richest works in the world; all of green and crimson satin, bordered with gold and azure; the posts that bore it up were of ivory, the cords of green silk, and on the top thereof there stood an eagle of gold, and at the two corners two green silver griffins shining against the sun, which seemed in richness to exceed the monument of Mausolus, being one of the world's twelve wonders. They had not remained there long, admiring the beauty of the workmanship, but at the entry of the pavilion there appeared a maiden queen, crowned with an imperial diadem, who was the fairest creature that ever he saw. On her attended Amazonian dames, bearing in their hands silver bows of the Turkish fashion, and at their backs hung quivers full of golden arrows;

upon their heads they wore silver coronets, beset with pearls, and precious stones; their attire comely and gallant, their faces fair and gentle to behold, their foreheads plain and white, the ringlets of their hair like burnished gold; their brows small and proper, somewhat drawing to a brown colour; their visages plain, neither too long nor too round, but coloured like roses mixed with lilies; their noses long and strait, their ruddy cheeks somewhat smiling, their eyes lovely, and all the rest of their parts and lineaments by nature framed most excellent, which had made them in beauty without comparison. The queen herself was clothed in a gown of green, straitly girt unto her body with a lace of gold, so that somewhat of her round and lily-white breast might be seen, which became her wonderfully well: beside all this, she had on a crimson kirtle, lined with violet-coloured velvet, and her wide sleeves were likewise of green silk, embroidered with flowers of gold, and with rich pearls. When St. George had sufficiently beheld the beauty of this maiden queen, he alighted from his horse, and humbled himself unto her excellency; and then courteously began to speak to her after this manner:

"Most divine and fair of all fairs, queen of sweet beauty," said he, "let a travelling knight obtain this favour at your hands, that both himself and his lady, whom you behold here wearied with travel, may take our rest within your pavilion for a night: for we have wandered up and down this country many a day, neither seeing man to give us lodging, nor finding food to cherish us, which made us wonder that so brave a country, and so beautified with nature's ornaments as this is, should be left desolate of people, the cause whereof is strange, I know, and full of wonder."

This question being courteously demanded by St. George, caused the Amazonian queen as kindly to reply:

"Sir knight," quoth she, "what favour my pavilion may afford, be assured of; but the remembrance of my country's desolation, which you speak of, gives me cause of sorrow in my soul, and makes me sigh when I remember it; but because you are a knight of a strange land, I will report it, though unto my grief. About twelve years since it was a necromancer's chance to arrive within this country, his name is Osmond, the most cunning artist this day living upon the earth, for he can at his call raise all the spirits out of hell, and with his charms make heaven to rain continually showers of blood: my beauty at that instant tempted him to love, and drowned his senses so in desire, that he assailed, by all persuasions that either wit or art could devise, to win me to his will; but I having vowed myself to Diana's chastity, to live in singleness among these Amazonian maids, contemned his love, despised his person, and accounted his persuasions as ominous as snakes; for which he wrought the destruction of this my realm and kingdom; for by his magic art and wicked charms, he raised from the earth a mighty tower, the mortar whereof he mingled with virgin's blood, wherein are such enchantments wrought, that the light of the sun and the brightness of the skies was quenched, and the earth blasted with a terrible vapour and black mist that ascended from the tower, whereby a general darkness overspread our land, the compass of twenty-four leagues, so this country is clean wasted and destroyed, and my people fled out thereof. This tower is haunted day and night with ghastly fiends; and at his departure into Persia, where he now by enchantment aids the soldan in his wars against the Christians, he left the guarding of the same to a mighty and terrible giant, for shape the ugliest monster that ever eye beheld, or ever ear heard tell of, for he is thirty feet in height; his head three times larger than the head of an ox; his eyes bigger than two pewter dishes, and his teeth standing out of his mouth more than a foot, wherewith he will break iron and steel; his arms big and long without any measure, and his body as black as any coal, and as hard as brass; also of such a strength, that he is able to carry away at once three knights armed; and he never eateth any other meat, but raw flesh of mankind; he is so light and swift, that a horse cannot run from him, and oftentimes he hath been assailed with great troops of armed men, but all of them could never do him any harm, neither with sword, spear, cross-bows, nor any other weapon.

"Thus have you heard, most noble and courteous knight, the true discourse of my utter ruin, and the vengeance showered upon my country by this wicked necromancer: for which I have remained ever since in this pavilion amongst my maidens, where we pray both day and night, that some unhappy fortune or terrible vengeance may fall upon this wicked conjurer."

"Now as I am a true English knight," replied St. George, "no sooner shall the morning sun appear, but I will take my journey to that enchanted tower, in which I will enter in spite of the giant, and break the enchantment, or make my grave within the monster's bowels; which if I happily perform, then will I travel into Persia, and fetter up the most wicked necromancer, and like a bloodhound lead him up and down the world in chains."

"Most dangerous is the adventure," quoth the Amazonian queen, "from whence as yet did never knight return; but if you be so resolute and noble-minded as to attempt the enterprise, then happy be your fortune, and know, brave knight, that this tower lieth westward from hence about thirteen miles,"

And thereupon she took him by the hand, and caused Sabra likewise to alight from her palfrey, and led them both into her pavilion, where they were feasted most royally, and for that night slept securely. But when the morning sun began to glitter, in all haste St. George arose, and armed himself; and after he had taken his leave of the queen, and given her thanks for his courteous entertainment, he also took his leave of Sabra, whom he left in company of the queen's maidens till his return with conquest, and so rode forth till it was noon, and then he entered into a deep valley, and he rode lower and lower. It was then a fair day, and the sun shined clear; but by the time he had ridden ten miles and a half, he had lost both the light and the sun, and also the sight of heaven, for it was there as dark as night, and more dismal than the deepest dungeon.

At last he found a mighty river, with streams as black as pitch, and the banks were so high, that the water could scarce be seen running underneath, and it was so full of serpents, that none could enter among them that ever returned back with life: about his head flew monstrous birds and divers griffins, who were able to bear away an armed knight, horse and all, and were in as great multitudes as though they had been starlings; also there were flies as big as nuts, and as black as pitch, which stung him and his horse so grievously, that there issued down such streams of blood, that it changed his horse from a sable to a crimson colour; likewise the griffins struck at St. George with their talons so furiously, that had he not defended himself with his shield, which covered his whole body, he had been pierced to the heart.

In this dangerous manner he rode on, till he came to the gates of the enchanted tower, whereat the giant sat in his iron coat, upon a block, with a mace of steel in his hand, who at the first sight of St. George, beat his teeth so mightily together, that they rang like the stroke of an anvil, and he ran raging like a fiend of hell, thinking to have taken the champion's horse and all in his long teeth, that were as sharp as steel, and to have borne them presently into the tower: but when St. George perceived his mouth open, he took his sword, and thrust it therein so far, that it made the giant to roar so loud, that the elements seemed to thunder, and the earth to tremble, his mouth smoked like a fiery furnace, and his eyes rolled in his head like brands of flaming fire; the wound was so great, and the blood issued so fast from the giant's mouth, that his courage began to fail, and against his will he was forced to yield to the champion's mercy, and to beg for life; to which St. George agreed, but upon conditions that the giant would discover all the secrets of the tower, and ever after be sworn his true servant, and attend on him with all diligence: to which the giant swore by his own soul never to leave him in extremity, and to answer him truly all questions whatsoever. Then St. George demanded the cause of the darkness, and how it might be ended. To which the giant answered in this manner.

"There was in the country, about twelve years since, a cunning necromancer, that by enchantment built this tower, which you now behold, and therein caused a terrible fire to spring from the earth, that cast such a smoke over the whole land, whereby the people that were wont to dwell therein are fled and famished for hunger: also this enchanter by his art made the river that you have passed, which did never man before this time without death: also, within the tower, near unto the fire, there stands a fair and pleasant fountain, to which if any knight be able to attain and cast the water thereof into the fire, then shall the darkness ever after cease, and the enchantment end, for which cause I have been bound to guard and keep the tower from the achievement of any knight."

Then when the giant had ended his discourse, St. George commanded him to remain at the gate, for he would put an end to the enchantment, and deliver the country from so grievous a plague. Then went he close by the windows of the tower, which were sixteen yards in length and breadth, till he came to a little wicket, through which he must needs enter: yet was it set as thick with pieces of steel as the prickles of an urchin's skin, to the intent that no knight should approach near unto the door, nor once attempt to enter into the tower; yet with great danger he opened the wicket, whereout came such abundance of smoke, that the darkness of the country doubled, so that neither torch nor candle would burn in that place; yet nevertheless St. George entered, and went downwards upon stairs, where he could see nothing, but yet felt so many great blows upon his burgonet, that he was constrained to kneel upon his knees, and with his shield to defend himself, or else he had been bruised to pieces. At last he came to the bottom, and there he found a great vault, where he felt so terrible a heat that he sweat exceedingly; and as he felt about him, he perceived that he approached near the fire; and going a little further, he spied out the fountain, whereat he greatly rejoiced: and so he took his shield, and bore therein as much water as he could, and cast it into the fire. In conclusion, he laboured so long, that the fire was entirely quenched: then began the skies to receive their perfect lightness, and the golden sun to shine most clearly about him, when he plainly perceived that there stood upon the stairs many great images of brass, holding in their hands mighty maces of steel, which had done him much trouble at his coming down; but then their power was ended, the fire quenched, and the enchantment finished.

Thus when St. George, through his invincible fortitude, had performed this dangerous adventure, he grew weary, what with heat and sweating, and the mighty blows he received from the brazen images, that he returned again to the wicket, whereat the deformed giant still remained; who, when he beheld the champion returned both safe and sound, he fell upon his knees before him, and said:

"Sir knight, you are most welcome, and happily returned, for you are the flower of Christendom, and the bravest champion of the world. Command my service, duty, and obedience; for whilst I live, I do profess, by the burning banks of Acheron, never to follow any other knight but you, and hereupon I kiss your golden spur, which is the noble badge of knighthood."

This humble submission of the giant caused the champion to rejoice, not for his overthrow, but that he had gotten so mighty a servant; then unlaced he his helmet, and lay down after his weary encounter, where, after he had sufficiently rested himself, he took his journey, in company of the giant, to the Amazonian queen, where he left his lady in company of her virgins, who like a kind, modest, and virtuous wife, during all the time of her husband's absence, continually prayed to the immortal powers of heaven, for his fortunate success and happy return, otherwise, resolving to herself, if the lowering destinies should cross his intent, and unluckily end his days before the adventure was accomplished, then to spend the remainder of her life among those happy virgins. But on the sudden, before the queen and her virgins were aware, St. George arrived before the pavilion, dutifully attended by the giant, who bore upon his shoulder the body of a tall oak, by which the queen knew that his prowess had redeemed her country from darkness, and delivered her from her sorrow, care, and trouble: so in company of her maids, very gorgeously attired, she conducted the champion to a bower of roses, intermingled with creeping vines, the which in his absence they planted for his lady's delight. There found he Sabra at her devotions, like to a solitary widow, clad in mourning habiliments; but when she beheld her lord return in safety, she banished her grief, and in haste ran unto him, and in his bosom shielded herself.

To relate how the Amazonian queen feasted them, and in what manner she and her maids devised pastime for their entertainments, were too tedious here, but when night gave an end to their pleasures, and sleep summoned all things to a quiet silence, the queen brought them to a very sumptuous lodging, where stood a bed framed with ebony-wood, overhung with many pendants of gold, the bed was stuffed with down of turtle-doves, the sheets of Median silk, thereon lay a rich quilt wrought with cotton, covered with damask, and stitched with threads of gold. But all this while the giant never entered the pavilion, but slept as soundly at the root of a pine-tree, as St. George did in his embroidered bed, for he knew not what pleasures belonged thereunto, nor never before that time beheld any woman's face. At last the Night withdrew her black curtains, and gave the Morning leave to appear, whose pleasant light caused St. George to forsake his bed, and to walk some few miles to view the country; in which journey he took such exceeding pleasure, that he thought it the goodliest realm that ever he saw, for he perceived well how it was full of worldly wealth.

At last, he climbed up to the top of a high mountain, being about two miles from the queen's pavilion, where he stood and beheld many stately towns and towers, high and mighty castles, many large woods and meadows, and many pleasant rivers; and about the towns, fair vines, goodly pastures, and fields. At last, he beheld the city of Argenia shining against the sun, the place where the queen in former time was wont to keep her court; which city was environed with deep ditches, the wall strongly built, and more than five hundred towers made of lime and stone; also he saw many fair churches covered with lead; having tops and spires of gold, shining most gorgeously; with weather-cocks of silver, glittering against the sun. Also he saw the burgesses' houses stand like palaces, closed with high and strong walls, barred with chains of iron from house to house, whereat in his heart he praised much the nobleness and richness of the city, and said to himself, that it might well be called Argenia, for it seemed to be of argent, that is as much as to say, of silver.

During the time of the champion's walk, which continued from the break of day to the closing of the evening, happened an awful tragedy, near unto the queen's pavilion, committed by the monstrous giant, whom St. George brought from the enchanted tower: for that same morning, when the sun had mounted some few degrees unto the firmament, seven of the queen's virgins, in Sabra's company, walked into a pleasant thicket of trees, adjoining to her pavilion, not only to take the pleasure of the morning air, but to hear the chirping melody of the birds; in which thicket or grove, under a pine-tree, this giant lodged the past night: but no sooner came these beautiful ladies under the branches of the tree, but the giant cast his eyes upon them, whose rare perfections so fired the base passions of this huge monster, that he formed in his mind the horrid project of gaining possession of their persons, and indulging himself in wantonly overcoming their virtue. With this intention, he rushed upon them, and with his mighty arms he clutched seven of them within his grasp; Sabra slipping on one side, escaped for the moment falling into his power. But the giant, while he held in his arms the seven virgins, found he had more than he could manage; for, while one was tearing at his hair, which hung down his back, another was piercing his belly with a silver bodkin, which she carried about her; and in like manner was each engaged in some way torturing the enraged monster. At length, however, the giant grew so infuriated, that he dashed one of the maidens on the ground with such force, that her brains were scattered:—and his fury continuing, he served each of the virgins in the same way. Sabra, in the meanwhile retaining her presence of mind, with a composition which she carried about her, so disfigured her lovely countenance, that the giant, when he looked on her, turned away, and left her unharmed. But now the enormity of his crime began to harass the mind of the cruel monster; and when he reflected on the kindness of St. George in sparing his life, he was driven to desperation, and in a paroxysm of despair he rushed furiously against a oak-tree, and dashed his brains out on the spot. And now to relate the situation of Sabra must be our task: she wandered up and down the thicket many a weary step, until the sun began to set, and the dark night drew on, which caused her thus to complain:—

"Oh you immortal powers of heaven! and you celestial planets, being the true guiders of the firmament, open your bright celestial gates, and send some fatal planet, or some burning thunder-bolt, to rid me from the vale of misery, for I will never more return to my lord; since I am thus deformed, and made an ugly creature, my loathsome face will prove a corrosive to his heart, and my body a torment to his soul. My sight will be unpleasant, my company hated, my presence loathed, and every one will shun my sight, as from a crocodile; therefore I will remain within this grove, till heaven either bring me to my former beauty, or end my languishing misery; yet witness, heaven, of my loyalty unto my lord, and in what extremity I have maintained my chastity; in remembrance of my true love, here will I leave this chain of gold for my beloved lord to find, that he may know for his sake I have endured a world of woe."

At which speeches she took her chain, which was doubled twenty times about her neck, and left it lying besmeared in the blood of those virgins whom the giant had slain, and so betook herself to a solitary life, intending never to come in the sight of men, but to spend her days wandering in the woods; where we will likewise leave her for a time, and speak of St. George, who by this time was returned to the queen's pavilion, where he missed his lady, and had intelligence that she, in the company of seven other ladies, walked in the morning into a pleasant grove to hear the melody of birds, and since that time no news had been heard of them; for as then it grew towards night, which caused St. George greatly to mistrust that some mischance had befallen his lady. Then he demanded what was become of the giant: but answer was made, that he was never seen nor heard of since morning; which caused him greatly to suspect the giant's treachery, and how by his means the ladies were prevented of their purposed pleasures.

Therefore in all haste, like a frantic man, he ran into the thicket, filling every corner with clamours, and resounding echoes of her name, and calling for Sabra, through every bramble brush: but there he could neither hear the voice of Sabra, nor the answer of any other lady, but the woful echoes of his exclamations, which rattled through the leaves of the trees. Then began he to wax somewhat melancholy and passionate, passing the time away till bright Cynthia mounted on the hemisphere, by whose glittering beams he saw the ground besprinkled with purple gore; and found the chain that Sabra was wont to wear about her neck, besmeared in blood. He bitterly complained against his own fortune and his lady's hapless destiny, for he supposed then that the giant had murdered her.

"O discontented sight," said he, "here lies the blood of my beloved lady, the truest woman that ever knight enjoyed. That body, which for excellency deserved a monument of gold, more rich than the tomb of Angelica, I fear lies buried in the bowels of that monstrous giant, whose life unhappily I granted. But, fond fool that I am, why do I talk in vain? It will not recompence her murdered soul, the which methinks I hear how it calls for revenge in every corner of the grove. It was I that left her carelessly within the danger of the giant, whom I little mistrusted, therefore I will meet her in the Elysium shades, and crave remission for my committed trespass, for on this oak I will abridge my life, as did the worthy knight Melmeropolion for the love of Sillara."

Which lamentation being no sooner ended, but he took the chain of gold, and fastened one end to the arm of a great oak, and the other end to his neck, intending presently to strangle himself; but heaven prevented his desperate intent after a strange manner: for under the same tree the brained giant lay, not yet fully dead, who in this manner spake to St. George:

"O stay thy hand, most noble and invincible knight, the world's chief wonder for admirable chivalry, and let my dying soul convert thee from so wicked a deed. Seven virgins in this thicket have I destroyed, and buried all their bodies in my accursed bowels; but before I could destroy the eighth, in a strange manner her bright beauty was changed into a loathsome leprosy, whereby I detested her sight, and left her undefiled, but by her sad complaints, I since have understood, how that she is your lady and love, and to this hour she hath her residence within this thicket." And thereupon, with a doleful groan, which seemed to shake the ground, he bade adieu to the world.

Then St. George, being glad to hear such tidings, reverted from his desperate intent, and searched up and down the grove, till he had found Sabra, where she sat sorrowing under the branches of a mulberry-tree; between whom was a sad greeting: and as they walked back to the queen's pavilion, she discoursed to him the truth of his bloody stratagem; where she remained till the Amazonian queen had cured her leprosy by the secret virtue of her skill; of whom, after they had taken leave, and given her thanks for her kind courtesies, St. George with his lady took their journey towards Persia.

CHAPTER. XVII.

How St. George and his lady lost themselves in a wilderness, where she was delivered of three goodly boys. The Fairy Queen's prophecy upon the children's fortune. Of St. George's return into Bohemia, where he christened his children: and of finding his father's grave, over which he built a stately tomb.

ST. GEORGE having achieved the adventure of the enchanted tower, and Sabra the fury of the wicked giant, they took their journey towards Persia, where the Christian champions lay encamped before the soldan's great city of Belgor, a place most strongly fortified with spirits and other ghastly illusions, by the enchantment of Osmand, who was related before, in the last chapter, to be the rarest necromancer in the world. But as the English champion with his lady travelled thitherward, they passed into a desert and mighty wilderness, overgrown with lofty pines, cedar-trees, and many huge and mighty oaks, the spreading branches whereof seemed to withhold the light of heaven from their untrodden passage; the tops of such a height, as to reach into the elements : the inhabitants were sylvan satyrs, fairies, and other wood nymphs, which by day sported up and down the forest, and by night attended the pleasures of Proserpine the fairy queen. The music of silver-sounding birds, so cheerfully resounded through the woods, and the whistling wind made such melody amongst the leaves of trees, that it ravished their senses like the harmony of angels, and made them think they had entered the shades of gladsome Elysium. One while they wondered at the beauty of the woods, which nature adorned with a summer's livery, another while at the green and fragant grass, drawn out in round circles by fairies' dances, and were so bewildered that they lost themselves amongst the unknown passages, not knowing how, nor by what means to recover the perfect path of their journey, but were constrained to wander in the wilderness, like solitary pilgrims, spending their days with weary steps, and their nights with vain imaginations, even as the child, when he hath lost himself in a populous city, runneth up and down, not knowing how to return to his native dwelling ; even so it happened to these two lost, disconsolate travellers, for when they had wandered many days one way, and finding no end of their toils, they retired backward to the place of their first setting forth, where they were wont to hear the noise of people resounding in country villages, and to meet travellers passing from place to place ; but now they heard nothing but the blustering wind, rattling in the wood, making the brambles to whistle, and the trees to groan, and now and then to meet a speckled beast, like to the rainbow, stealing from his den to seek his natural sustenance ; in their travel by night they were wont to hear the crowing of the cock, recording glad tidings of the cheerful day's approach, the neighing of horses in pasture fields, and the barking of dogs in farmers' houses: but now they were affrighted with the roaring of lions, yelling of wolves, the croaking of toads in roots of rotten trees, and the rueful sound of Progne's defilement, recorded by the nightingale.

In this solitary manner wiled they the rolling time away, till thrice three times the silver moon had returned her borrowed light, by which time Sabra was reminded by premonitory symptoms that the hour of her delivery drew on, wherein she required Lucina's help, to make St. George the father of a princely son. Time called for midwives, to aid and bring her babe into the world, and to make her a happy mother ; but before the painful hour of her delivery approached, St. George had provided her a bower of vine-branches, which he erected between two pleasant hills, where, instead of a princely cabinet hung with arras, and rich tapestry, she was constrained to suffice herself with a simple lodging, covered with roses, and other fragrant flowers ; her bed he made of green moss and thistledown, beset curiously round about with olive-branches, and the sprigs of an orange-tree, which made it seem more beautiful than Flora's pavilion, or Diana's mansion. But at last, Sabra felt her pains grow intolerable, and her speedy delivery was at hand, and how she was in a wilderness void of women's company, that should be ready to assist her in so secret a matter, she cast herself down upon her mossy bed, and with a blushing countenance she discovered her mind in this manner to St. George.

"My most dear and loving lord," quoth she, "my true and

only champion at all times and seasons, except at this hour, for it is the painful hour of my delivery, therefore depart from out of the hearing of my cries, and commit my fortune to the pleasures of the heavens; for it is not convenient for any man's eye to behold the secrets of a woman in such a case: stay not, I say, dear lord, to see the infant, now moving in my womb, to be delivered from the bed of his creation; forsake my presence for a time, and let me, like the noble queen of France, obtain the favour of some fairy to be my midwife, that my babe may be as happily born iu this wilderness, as was her valiant sons, Valentine and Orson, the one of them was cherished by a king, and the other by a bear, yet both of them grew famous in their deeds."

At which words St. George sealed the agreement with a kiss, and departed silently without any reply, but with a thousand sighs, bade her adieu, and took his way to the top of a mountain, being in distance a quarter of a mile: there during the time of her travail, with his bare knees, upon the bosom of the earth, never ceasing prayers, but continually soliciting the assistance of God, to grant his lady a speedy and easy delivery. After whose departure the fury of her heart was constrained to heave so many scorching sighs, that they seemed to blast the leaves of the trees, and to wither the flowers which beautified her cabinet, her burthened torments caused her star-bright eyes, like fountains to distil down silver drops, and all the rest of her body, to tremble like a castle in a terrible earthquake

At last, her pitiful cries pierced down to the lowest vaults of direful Dis, where Proserpine, sits crowned amongst her fairies, and so prevailed, that in all haste she ascended to work this lady's safe delivery, and to make her mother of three goodly boys; who no sooner arrived in Sabra's lodging, but she practised the duty of a midwife, eased the burden of her womb, and safely brought her babes into the world.

This courteous deed of Proserpine was no sooner performed, but she laid the three boys in three sumptuous cradles, which she caused the fairies to fetch invisibly; and therewithal mantles of silk, with other things thereunto belonging; likewise she caused a winged satyr to fetch from the farthest borders of India, a covering of damask taffety embroidered with gold, the richest ornament that ever mortal eye beheld. With this rich and sumptuous ornament she covered the lady's child-bed, whereby it seemed to surpass in bravery the gorgeous bed of Juno the brave queen, when first she entertained imperious Jove. After this, Proserpine laid under every child's pillow a silver tablet, whereon were written, in letters of gold, their good and happy fortunes.

Under the first, who at that time lay frowning in his cradle like the god of war, were these lines:

> A soldier bold, a man of wonderous might
> A king likewise this royal babe shall die;
> Three golden diadems in bloody fight,
> By this brave prince shall also conquered be:
> The towers of old Jerusalem and Rome,
> Shall yield to him in happy time to come.

Under the pillow of the second babe, who lay in his cradle smiling like Cupid upon the lap of Dido, whom Venus transformed to the likeness of Ascanius, were these lines written:

> This child shall likewise live to be a king
> Time's wonder for device and courtly sport:
> His tilts and tournaments abroad shall ring,
> To every coast where noble knights resort:
> Queens shall attend, and humble at his feet,
> Thus love and beauty shall together meet.

Lastly, under the pillow of the third who blushed in his cradle, like Pallas when he strove for the golden apple with Venus, and the queen of heaven, were these lines:

> The muses' darling for true sapience,
> In princes' courts this babe shall spend his days;
> Kings shall admire his learned eloquence,
> And write in brazen books his endless praise:
> By Pallas' gifts he shall achieve a crown,
> Advance his fame, and lift him to renown.

Thus when the fairy queen had ended her prophecy upon the children, and had left them golden fortunes lying in their cradles, she vanished away, leaving the lady rejoicing at her safe delivery, and wondering at the gifts of Proserpine, which she conjectured to be but shadows to dazzle her eyes, and things of fading substance: but when she had laid her hands upon the rich covering of damask taffety, which covered her mossy bed, and felt that it was the self-same form that it seemed, she cast her eyes, with a cheerful look, up to the majesty of heaven, and not only gave thanks for received benefits, but for his merciful kindness in making her the happy mother of three such goodly children. But we will now return again to the noble champion St. George, who, after waiting some time, returned back to her sylvan cabin, which he found strangely decked with sumptuous habiliments, his lady lying in her childbed, as glorious as if she had been the greatest empress in the world, and three princely boys sweetly sleeping in their several cradles; at whose first sight his heart was so ravished with joy, that for a time it withheld the passage of his tongue: but at last, when he found the silver tablets lying under the pillows, and read the happy fortunes of his children, he ran unto his lady, embracing her lovingly, and kindly demanded the true disclosure of this accident, and by whose means' the bower was beautified so gorgeously, and the propounder of his childrens' prophesy; who, with a countenance blushing like the purple morning, replied in this manner:

"My most dear and well-beloved lord, the pains that I have endured to make you the happy father of three lovely boys, hath not been less painful, than the stroke of death, but yet my delivery more joyful than the pleasures of this world: the winds carried my groans to every corner of this wilderness, whereby both trees and herbs assisted my complaints, beasts, birds, and feathered fowls, with every senseless thing that nature framed on this earth, seemed to pity my moans; but in the midst of my torments, when my soul was ready to forsake this worldly habitation, there appeared to me a queen crowned with a golden diadem, in state and gesture like imperious Juno, and in beauty to divine Diana; her wisdom might compare with Apollo's, her judgment with Pallas' and her skill with Lucina's; for no sooner entered she my presence, but my travail ceased, my babes being brought to light by the virtue of her skill; she prepared these rich and sumptuous cradles, which were brought invisibly to my cabin; likewise these mantles, and this embroidered coverlet she frankly bestowed upon me, and so immediately vanished away."

At which words St. George gave her many kind embraces: at last, her hunger increased, and her desire thirsted so much after food, that, except she received some comfortable sustenance, her life would be in danger. This extreme desire of Sabra, caused St. George to buckle on his armour, and to unsheath his trusty sword, ready to gore the entrails of some deer; who swore, by the honour of true knighthood, never to rest in peace, till he had purchased her heart's content.

And thereupon, with his falchion ready charged, he traversed the woods, leaving no thorny brake nor mossy cave unsearched, till he had found a herd of fallow deer; from which number he singled out the fattest, to make his lady a bountiful banquet; but in the time of his absence there happened to Sabra a wonderful accident; for there came stealing into the cabin three most wild and monstrous beasts, a lioness, a tigress, and a she-wolf, which took the babes out of their cradles, and bore them to their secret dens.

At which sight, Sabra, like one bereft of sense, started from her bed, and as much as in her power offered to follow the beasts, but all in vain; for before she could get without her cabin, they were past sight, and the children's cry without her hearing; then, like a discontented woman, she turned back, beating her breast, rending her hair, and raging up and down her cabin, using all the fury at this time she could devise against herself; and had not St. George returned, she had most violently committed her own slaughter; but at his return, when he beheld her face stained with tears, her head disrobed of ornaments, and her ivory breast all rent, he cast down his venison in all haste, and asked the cause of her sorrow.

"Oh!" said she, "this is the most woful day that ever happened to me; for in the time of your unhappy hunting, a lioness, a tigress, and a wolf, came into the cabin, and took my children from their cradles: what is become of them I know not; but greatly fear I by this time they are entombed within their hungry bowels."

"Oh! simple monuments," quoth he, "for such sweet babes. Well, Sabra, if the monsters have bereaved me of my children this bloody sword, that dived into the entrails of the fallow deer, shall rive my woful heart in twain. Accursed be this fatal day, the planets that predominate, and sun that shines thereon; heaven blot it from the year, and let it never more be numbered, but accounted for a dismal day throughout the world; let all the trees be blasted in those accursed woods; let herbs and grass consume away and die, and all things perish in this wilderness. But why breathe I out these curses in vain, when methinks I hear my children in untamed lions' dens, crying for help and succour? I come, sweet babes! I come, either to redeem you from tiger's wrathful jaws, or make my grave within their hungry bowels!"

Then took he up his sword besmeared in blood, and like a man bereaved of wit and sense, ranged up and down the wilderness, searching every corner for his children; but his lady remained still in her cabin, lamenting for their loss, washing their cradles with her pearly tears.

In many paths wandered St. George, sometimes in valleys, where wolves and tigers lurk; sometimes on mountain tops, where lion's whelps do sport and play; and many times in dismal thickets, where snakes and serpents live.

Thus wandered St. George up and down the wilderness for the space of two days, hearing no news of his children. At last he approached the sight of a pleasant river, which smoothly glided down between two mountains, into whose streams he purposed to cast himself; and so by a desperate death put an end to his sorrows; but as he was committing his body to the mercy of the waters, and his soul to the pleasure of the heavens, he heard afar off the rueful shriek, as he thought, of a comfortless babe: which sudden noise caused him to refrain from his desperate purpose, and with more discretion to tender his own safety. Then casting his eyes aside, it was his happy destiny to spy three inhuman beasts lying at the foot of a hill, tumbling themselves against the warm sun, and his three pretty babes sucking from their dugs their most unnatural milk: which spectacle so encouraged the champion, that without farther advisement, with his single sword, he assailed at one time the three monsters, but so furiously they pursued him, that his success was trifling; and being almost breathless, was forced to get into an orange-tree, else he had been buried in their merciless bowels. But when the three wild beasts perceived him above their reach, and that by no means they could come near him with their wrathful jaws, they so rent and tore the root of the tree, that if by policy he had not prevented them, the tree had been pulled in pieces: for at that time it was so full of ripe oranges, and so overladen, that the branches seemed to bend, and the boughs to break; of which fruit he cast such abundance down to the beasts, whereby they restrained their furies, and fed so fast thereon that in a short time they grew tipsy, and quite overcome with a heavy sleep: this happy fortune caused St. George nimbly to leap off the tree, and with his keen-edged sword cut off their heads from their bodies; which being done, he went to his children, lying upon a mossy bank, who so pleasantly smiled in his face, that they made him greatly to rejoice: therefore taking them up in his arms, he spake the following words:

"Come, come, my pretty babes, your safe deliverance from these inhuman monsters will add long life unto your mother, and hath preserved your father from a desperate death; from henceforth let heaven be your guide, and send you as happy fortunes as Remus and Romulus, the first founders of imperious Rome, which in their infancies were nursed with the milk of a ravenous wolf."

And approaching the cabin, where he left his lady mourning for the loss of her children, he found her without sense or moving, being not able to give him a joyful welcome, whereat he fell into this extreme passion of sorrow.

"Oh Fortune! Fortune!" quoth he, "how many griefs heapest thou upon my head? Wilt thou needs enjoin me to an endless sorrow? See, Sabra, see, I have redeemed our sons, and freed them from the tigers' bloody jaws, whose wrathful countenance did threaten their death."

Which comfortable speech caused her presently to revive, and to take the infants in her arms, laying them sweetly upon her breasts. The kind embraces, loving speeches, and joyful conference that passed between the champion and his lady, were now too long to be discoursed; but to be short, they remained in the wilderness without farther disturbance, either of wild beasts, or other accident, till Sabra had recovered her child-bed sickness: and then, being conducted by happy stars, they returned back the ready way to Christendom, where, after some few days travel, they arrived in the Bohemian court, where the king of that country, with two other bordering princes, most royally christened the children, the eldest they named Guy, the second Alexander, and the third David; which being performed, and the triumphs ended, which in a most sumptuous manner continued for the space of one month, then the Bohemian king, for the great love he bore to St. George, provided most honourably for his sons' bringing up.

First, he appointed three several tutors who gave them all things necessary for so princely a charge, to conduct the three infants to three several countries. The first, and eldest, whose fortune was to be a soldier, he sent to the imperial city of of Rome (being then the wonder of the world for martial discipline), there by the emperor to be trained up. The second, whose fortune was to be a courtly prince, he sent to the rich and plentiful country of England, being the pride of Christendom for all delightful pleasures: the third and last, whose fortune was to be a scholar, he sent into Germany, unto the university of Wittenburg, being thought at that time to be the most appropriate place for learning that remained throughout the whole world.

Thus were St. George's children provided for by the Bohemian king; for when the ambassadors were in readiness, the ships for their passage furnished, and attendants appointed, St. George, in company with his lady, the king of Bohemia with his queen, and a train of lords, and gentlemen, and ladies, conducted them on ship-board, where the wind served them so prosperously, that in a short time they had bade adieu to the shore, and sailed cheerfully away. But as St. George returned back to the Bohemian court, it was his chance to come by an old ruined monastery, under whose walls in former time his father was buried, the which he knew by certain verses carved in stone over his grave, by the commons of the country, (as you may read before in the beginning of this history). Over the same he requested of the king that he might erect a stately monument, that the remembrance of his name might live for ever, and not be buried in the grave of obscurity. To which reasonable demand the king most willingly consented, and presently gave special command that the most cunning architects that remained within his dominion should forthwith be sent for, and withal gave a ton of gold out of his own treasury, towards the performance thereof. The sudden report of this memorable deed being noised abroad, caused workmen to come from every place of their own accord, with such willingness, that they in a short time finished it. The foundation of the tomb was of the purest marble, whereon was engraven the frame of the earth, and how the watery ocean was divided, with woods, groves, hills and dales; so lively pourtrayed, that it was a wonder to behold: the props and pinnacles of alabaster, beset with knobs of jasper-stone; the sides and pillars of the clearest jet; upon the top stood four golden lions, holding up as it were an element, wherein was curiously contrived the golden sun and moon, and how the heavens have their usual courses, with many other things wrought both in gold and silver, which for this time I omit, because I am forced at large to discourse of the princely proceedings of St. George, who, after the monument was finished, with his lady, most humbly took their leave of the king, thanked him for his love, kindness, and courtesy, and so departed towards Egypt and Persia, of whose adventures you shall hear more in the chapter following.

CHAPTER XVIII.

How St. George with his Lady arrived in Egypt; of their royal Entertainment in the City of Grand Cairo; and also how Sabra was crowned Queen of Egypt.

MANY strange accidents and dangerous adventures St. George with his lady passed through, before they arrived within the territories of Egypt, which I want memory to repeat, and art to describe. But at last when Fortune smiled, which before had long time crossed their intents with her constant changes, and had cast them happily upon the Egyptian shore, being the nurse and mother of Sabra's first creation; the twelve peers, unto whom St. George before-time committed the guarding of the land, and keeping of his crown, as you read before, now met him and his lady at the sea side, most richly mounted upon her costly trapped steeds, and willingly surrendered up his sceptre, crown, and regiment; and in company of many princely estates, both of dukes, earls, lords, knights, and royal gentlemen, attended them to the city of Grand Cairo, being then under the dominion of Egypt, and the greatest city in the world, for it was in breadth full three score miles, and had by just account, within the walls, twelve thousand churches, besides abbeys, priories, and houses of religion; but when St. George, with his stately attendants entered the gates, they were presently entertained with such joyful sounds of bells, trumpets, and drums, that it seemed like the inspiring music of heavenly angels, and to exceed the royalty of Cæsar in Rome, when he returned from the world's conquest: the streets were beautified with stately pageants, contrived by scholars of ingenious capacity, the pavement strewed with all manner of odoriferous flowers, and the walls hung with Indian coverlets, and curious tapestry.

Thus passed they the streets in great solemnity, wondering at the curiosity of the pageants, and listening to their learned orations, till they entered the gates of the palace, where, in the first entry of the court, was contrived overhead a golden pendant firmament, as it were supported by an hundred angels: from thence it seemed to rain nectar and ambrosia; likewise there descended, as it were from the clouds, Ceres, the goddess of plenty, sitting upon a throne of gold, beautified with all manner of springing things, as of corn, olives, herbs, flowers, grapes, and trees; who at the coming by of St. George and his lady, presented them with two garlands of wheat, bound up most curiously in bands of silver, to signify that they were happily returned to a plentiful country, both of wealth and of treasure. But at Ceres ascension up into the firmament, was seen most strange and pleasant fireworks shooting from place to place, as though the fiery planets had descended from heaven, and had generally consented to make them delightful pastimes: but as St. George with his lady, crowned with garlands of wheat, passed through the second court, they beheld a pageant most strangely contrived, wherein stood Mars, the angry god of war, environed with a camp of armed soldiers, as if they with their weapons were ready charged to assault some stronghold, or invincible city; their silver trumpets seemed to sound cheerfully, their thundering drums courageously, their silken streamer to flourish valiantly, and themselves to march triumphantly. All which seemed to give more content to St. George, than all the delightful pleasures before rehearsed; for there was nothing in all the world that more rejoiced his heart, than to hear the pleasant sounds of war, and to see the soldiers brandish forth their steeled weapons. After he had sufficiently delighted himself in these martial sports, and was ready to depart, the god of war descended his throne, and presented him with the richest armour that ever eye beheld, and the bravest sword that ever knight handled; for they have been kept within the city of Grand Cairo for the space of five hundred years, and held for the richest monuments in the country. Also he presented Sabra with a mirror of such an inestimable price, that it was valued at a king's ransom; for it was made by magic art: the virtues and qualities thereof were so precious, that it is almost incredible to report; for therein one might behold the secret mysteries of all the liberal sciences, and by art discourse what was practised in other princes' courts; if any hill or mountain within a thousand miles of the place where he remained, were enriched with a mine of gold, it would describe the place and country, and how deep it lay closed in the earth; by it one might truly calculate upon the birth of children, succession of princes, and continuance of commonwealths, with many other excellent gifts and virtues, which for this time I omit. Then in great state passed St. George to the third court, which was richly beautified with all gallant sights as the others were; for there was most lively pourtrayed the manner of Elysium, how Love and Juno sat invested in their royal thrones, and likewise how all the gods and goddesses took their places by degrees in parliament; pleasant was the sight and the device most excellent, their music admired, and their songs heavenly.

Thus passed St. George, with his lady through three courts, till they came to the palace; wherein was provided against their coming a more stately banquet than had the Macedonian monarch at his return into Babylon, when he had conquered the middle-earth; the curious cates, and well-replenished dishes, were so many that I want art and eloquence to describe them; but to be short, it was the most sumptuous banquet that ever they beheld since their departure from the English court, and so artificially served, as though all the world had been present. Many days continued this sumptuous cheer, and accompanied with such princely triumphs, as art herself wants memory to describe.

The coronation of Sabra, which was royally performed within three months following, requires a golden pen to write it, and a tongue washed in the conservatives of the Muses' honey to declare it: Egypt was honoured with triumphs, and Grand Cairo with tilts and tournaments. Through every town was proclaimed a solemn and festival day in the remembrance of their newly crowned queen; no tradesman nor artificer was suffered to work that day, but was charged, upon pain of death to hold it for a day of triumph, a day of joy, and a day of pleasure. In which royalties St. George was a principal performer, till the thirst of honour summoned him to arms; the remembrance of the Christian champions in Persia caused him to breviate the pastimes, and to buckle on his steel corslet, which had not glittered in the fields of Mars for four-and-twenty days; of which noble deeds, and adventurous proceedings, I will at large discourse, and leave all other pastimes to the new-invested queen and her ladies.

CHAPTER XIX.

The bloody battle between the Christians and Persians; and how the Necromancer, Osmand, raised up, by his magic art, an army of spirits to fight against the Christians; how the six Champions were enchanted, and recovered by St. George; the misery and death of the Conjurer, and how the Soldan brained himself against a marble pillar.

Now must we return to the Christian champions, and speak of their battles in Persia, and what happened to them in St. George's absence: for if you remember before, being in Egypt, when he had news, of his lady's condemnation in England, for the murder of the earl of Coventry, he caused them to march into Persia, and encouraged them to revenge his wrongful imprisonment upon the soldan's provinces; in which country, after they had marched about fifty miles, burning and spoiling his territories, they intercepted the soldan's power, which was about the number of three hundred thousand fighting men. But the muster-rolls of the Christians were likewise numbered, and they amounted not to above one hundred thousand able men: at which time between the Christians and Pagans a long and dangerous battle took place, the like in any age was seldom fought; for it continued for the space of five days, to the great loss of blood by both parties; but at last the Pagans had the worst; for when they beheld their fields covered with mangled bodies, and that the rivers for twenty miles flowed with blood, their courage began to fail, and they fled like sheep before the wolf. Then the valiant Christians, thirsting after revenge, speedily pursued them, sparing neither young nor old, till the ways were strewed with bodies, like heaps of scattered sand; in which pursuit and honourable conquest they burned two hundred forts and towns, battering their towers of stone as level with the ground as harvest-reapers do fields of ripe corn. But the soldan himself, with many of his approved soldiers, escaped alive, and fortified the city of Grand Belgor, being the strongest town in all the kingdom of Persia, before whose walls we leave the Christian champions planting their puissant forces, and speak of the abominable practices of Osmand within the town, where he accomplished many admirable acts by magic art: for when the Christians' army had long time assaulted the walls, sending their fiery bullets to the lofty battlements, like storms of winter's hail, whereby the Persian soldiers were not able any longer to resist, they began to yield, and commit their lives to the mercy of the Christian champions. But when the soldan perceived his soldiers' cowardice, and how they would willingly resign his happy government to foreign rule, he encouraged them still to resist the Christians' desperate encounters, and within thirty days, if they had not the honour of the war, then willingly to condescend to their country's conquest; which princely resolution encouraged the soldiers to resist, intending not to yield up the city till death had made triumph on their bodies. Then departed he unto a sacred tower, where he found Osmand sitting in a chair, studying by magic, how long Persia should remain unconquered, who at his entrance drove him from his charms with these speeches:

"Thou wondrous man of art," said the soldan, "whom for necromancy the world hath made famous! now is the time to express the love and loyalty thou bearest thy sovereign; now is the time thy charming spells must work for Persia's good; thou seest my fortunes are deprest, my soldiers dead, my captains slaughtered, my cities burned, my fields of corn consumed, and my country almost conquered. I that was wont to cover the seas with fleets of ships, now stand amazed to hear the Christians' drums, that sound forth doleful funerals for my soldiers. I that was wont with armed legions to drink up rivers as we marched, and made the earth to groan with bearing of our multitudes; I that was wont to make the whole kingdoms tremble at my frowns, and force imperious potentates to humble at my feet; I that have made the steets of many a city run with blood, and stood rejoicing when I saw their buildings burnt; I that have made the mothers' wombs the infants' tombs, and caused cradles to swim in streams of blood; may now behold my country's ruin, my kingdom's fall, and mine own fatal overthrow. Awake, great Osmand, from thy dreamy trance, awake, I say, and raise a troop of black infernal fiends, to fight against the cursed Christians, that like swarms of bees do flock about our walls; prevent, I say, my land's invasion, and, as I am great monarch of Asia, I'll make thee king of twenty provinces, and sole commander of the ocean: raise up, I say, thy charmed spirits, leaving burning Acheron empty for a time, to aid us in this bloody battle."

These words were no sooner ended, but there rattled such a peal of cannons against the city walls, that they made the very earth shake; whereat the necromancer started from his chair, and in this manner encouraged the soldan.

"It is not Europe, nor all the petty bands of armed knights, nor all the princes in the world, that shall abate your princely dignity: am not I the great magician of this age, that can both loose and bind the fiends, and call the black faced furies from low Cocytus? Am not I that skilful artist, which framed the charmed tower amongst the Amazonian dames, which all the witches in the world could never spoil? Therefore let learning, art, and all the secrets of the deep assist me in this enterprise, and then let frowning Europe do her worst; my charms shall cause the heavens to rain such rattling showers of stones upon their heads, whereby the earth shall be laden with their dead bodies, and hell filled with their hateful souls; senseless trees shall rise in human shapes, and fight for Persia. If wise Medea was ever famous for arts, that did the like for the safeguard of her father's state, then why should not Osmand practise wonders for his sovereign's happiness, I'll raise a troop of spirits from the lowest earth more black than dismal night, who in ugly shapes shall haunt them up and down, and when they sleep within their rich pavilions; legions of fiery spirits will I raise up from hell, that like to dragons spitting flames of fire, shall blast and burn the cursed Christians in their tents of war: down from the crystal firmaments I will conjure troops of airy spirits to descend, that like to virgins clad in princely ornaments shall link those Christian champions in the charms of love; their eyes shall be like the twinkling lamps of heaven, and so dazzle their warlike thoughts, and their lively countenances more bright than fairies, shall lead them captives to a tent of love, which shall be artificially erected by magic spells; their warlike weapons, that were wont to smoke in Pagans' blood, shall, in my charmed tent, be hung upon the bowers of Peace; their glittering armours, that were wont to shine within the fields of Africa, shall henceforth for evermore be stained with rust; and themselves, surnamed for martial discipline the wondrous champions of the world, shall surfeit with delightful loves, and sleep upon the laps of the airy spirits, that descend the elements in virgins' shapes; terror and despair shall so mightily oppress their merciless soldiers, that they shall yield the honourable conquest to your excellency: such strange and wonderful acts by art shall be accomplished that heaven shall frown at mine enchantments, and the earth tremble to hear my conjurations; therefore, most mighty Persian, number up thy scattered bands, and to-morrow in the morning set open thy gates, and march thitherwards, with thy armed soldiers; leave not a man within the city, but let every one that is able to bear arms, fight in the honour of Persia, and before the closing of the night I'll make thee conqueror, and yield up the bragging Christians as prisoners to thy mightiness."

"If this prove true, renowned Osmand, as thou hast promised," said the soldan, "earth shall not harbour that too dear for thee; for thou shalt have myself, my kingdoms, crowns, and sceptres, at command. The wealthy river Ganges shall pay thee yearly tribute with her treasure, the place where Midas washed her golden wish away. All things that nature framed precious, shalt thou be lord and sole commander of, if thou prevent the invasion of my country."

And thereupon he departed from the chamber, leaving the necromancer in his study; and as he gave commandment, his captains made ready their soldiers, and furnished their warlike horses, and by the sun's rise marched into the fields of Belgor, where, upon the north side of the enemy, they pitched their camp. On the other side, when the valiant Christians had intelligence, by their courts of guard, how the Persians had entered the fields ready to give them battle, sudden alarums sounded in their ears, rumours of conquest so encouraged the soldiers, that presently they were in readiness to entertain the Persians in a valorous contest. Both armies were in sight, with blood-red colours wavering in the air; the Christian champions, richly mounted on their warlike coursers, placed themselves in the fore-front of the battle, like courageous captains, fearing neither death nor inconstant change of fortune. But the soldan, with his petty princes, like cowards, were environed and compassed with a ring of armed knights, where, instead of nimble steeds, they sat in iron chariots. Divers heroical and many princely encouragements past between the two armies before they entered battle: but when the drums began to sound alarm, and the silver trumpets gave dreadful echoes of death; when the cross of Christendom began to flourish, and the arms of Mahomet began to be advanced; even then began so terrible and bloody a battle, that the like was never found in any age; for before the sun had mounted to the top of heaven, the Pagans received so great a massacre, that they were forced to wade up to the knees in blood, and their soldiers to fight upon heaps of slaughtered men: the fields were changed from a green colour to a purple hue, the dales were steeped in a crimson gore, and the hills and mountains covered with dead men's rattling bones. And let us not forget the necromancer Osmand, that during the time of that dangerous encounter kneeled in a low valley, near unto the camps, with his black hair hanging down unto his shoulders, like a wreath of snakes, and with his sliver wand circling the earth, where, when he heard the sounds of drums in the air, and the brazen trumpets giving dreadful sounds of war, he entered into these fatal speeches:

"Now is the battle furiously begun, for methinks I hear the soldan cry for help: now is the time my charming spells must work for Persia's victory, and Europe's fatal overthrow!" which being said, thrice did he kiss the earth, thrice beheld the elements, and thrice besprinkled the circle with his own blood, which with a silver razor he let from his left arm; and afterwards began again to speak in this manner:

"Stand still, you wandering lamps of heaven, move not, sweet stars, but linger on, till Osmand's charms be brought to full effect. O thou great Dæmon, prince of cursed ghosts; thou chief commander of those fearful shapes that nightly glide by misbelieving travellers; even thou that holdest the snaky sceptre in thy hand, sitting upon a throne of burning steel, even thou that tossest burning fire-brands abroad, even thou whose eyes are like to unlucky comets; even thee I charge to let my furies loose: open thy brazen gates, and leave thy boiling cauldron empty; send up such legions of infernal fiends that may in number countervail the blades of grass that beautify those blood-stained fields of Belgor."

These fatal speeches were no sooner finished, but there appeared such a multitude of spirits, both from the earth, water, air, and fire, that is almost incredible to report; which he caused to run into the Christian army; whose burning falchions not only annoyed the soldiers with fear and terror, but also fired the horses' manes, burned the trappings, consumed their banners, scorched trees and herbs, and dimmed the elements with such an extreme darkness, as though the earth had been covered with eternal night. He caused the spirits likewise to raise up such a tempest, that it tore up mighty oaks by the roots, removed hills and mountains, and blew up men into the air, horses and all; yet neither his magic arts, nor all the furies and wicked spirits, could one whit daunt the most noble and magnanimous minds of the six champions of Christendom; but, like unconquered lions, they purchased honour wherever they went, colouring their swords in Pagans' blood, making them the true witnesses of their victories and heroical proceedings, whom they had attired in a blood-red livery. And though St. George was absent in that terrible battle, yet merited they as much honour and renown, as though he had been there present; for the accursed Pagans fell before their warlike weapons, as leaves do from the trees, when the blustering storms of winter enter on the earth. But when the wicked necromancer, Osmand, perceived that his magic spells took no effect, and how, in despite of his enchantment, the Christians got the better of the day, he cursed his art, and banned the hour and time wherein he attempted so wicked an enterprise, thinking them to be preserved by angels, or else by some celestial means; but yet not purposing to leave off at the first repulse, he attempted another way, by necromancy, to overthrow the Christians.

First, he erected, by magic art, a stately tent, outwardly in show like to the compass of earth; but furnished inwardly with all the delightsome pleasures, that either art or reason could invent; only framed to enchant the Christian champions with enticing delight, whom he purposed to keep as prisoners therein. Then fell he again to his conjuration, and bound a hundred spirits by due obedience to transform themselves into the likeness of beautiful virgins; which in a moment they accomplished; and they were framed in form and beauty like to the darlings of Venus; in comeliness comparable with Thetis, dancing on the silver sands; and in all proportion like Daphne, whose beauty caused Apollo to descend the heavens; their limbs were like the lofty cedars, their cheeks to roses dipped in milk, and their eyes more bright than the stars of heaven; also they seemed to carry in their hands silver bows, and on their backs hung quivers of golden arrows; likewise upon their breasts they had pictured the god of love, dancing upon Mars' knees.

Thus, in the shape of beauteous damsels, caused he these spirits to enter the Christians' army, and, with the golden bait of their enticing smiles, to tangle the champions in the snares of love, and with their strong beauties lead them from their soldiers, and to bring them prisoners into this enchanted tent. Which commandment being no sooner given, but these virgins, more swift than the winds, glided into the Christians' army, where their glittering beauties so dazzled the eyes of the six champions, and their sober countenances so entrapped their hearts with desire, that their princely valours were abated, and they stood gazing at their excellent proportions, as though Medusa's shadow had been pictured upon their faces: to whom the enticing ladies spake in this manner:

"Come, princely gallants, come, away with your arms, forget the sounds of bloody war, and hang your angry weapons in the bower of Peace: Venus, you see, hath sent her messengers from Paphos, to lead you to the paradise of love; there heaven will rain down nectar and ambrosia sweet, for you to feed upon, and and there the melody of angels will make you music; there shall you fight upon beds of silk, and encounter with enticing kisses."

These golden promises so bewildered the champions, that they were enchanted with their loves, and vowed to take their last farewell of knighthood and magnanimous chivalry. Thus were they led from their warlike companies, to the necromancer's enchanted tent, leaving their soldiers without leaders, in danger of confusion. But the queen of chance so smiled upon the Christians, that at the same time St. George arrived in Persia, with a fresh supply of knights, of whose noble achievments I intend now to speak: for no sooner had he entered the battle, and placed his squadrons, but he had intelligence of the champions' misfortunes, and how they lay enchanted in the magic tent, sleeping in pleasure upon the laps of infernal furies, which Osmand had transformed, by his charms, into the likeness of beautiful damsels; which unexpected news constrained St. George to breathe from his sorrowful heart this woful lamentation:

"Unconstant Fortune, why dost thou entertain me with such bitter news? Are my fellow-champions come from Christendom to win immortal honour with their swords, and lie they now bewitched with beauty? O shame and great dishonour to Christendom! O stain to knighthood and true chivalry! This news is far more bitter to my soul, than were the poisoned dregs that Antipater gave to Alexander in his drunkenness, and a deadlier pain unto my heart, than was that juice that Hannibal sucked from his fatal ring. Come, soldiers, come, followers of those cowardly champions, unsheath your warlike weapons, and follow him whose soul hath vowed either to redeem them from the necromancer's charms, or die with honour in that enterprise. If ever mortal creatures warred with cursed furies, and made a passage to enchanted dales, where devils dance, and warlike shadows in the night, then, soldiers, let us march unto that pavilion, and chain the accursed charmer to some blasted oak, that hath so highly dishonoured Christendom."

These resolute speeches were no sooner finished, but the whole army, before daunted with fear, grew so courageous, that they protested to follow him through more dangers than did the Grecian knights with noble Jason in the isle of Colchos. Now began the battle again to renew, and the drums to sound fatal knells for the Pagan soldiers, whose souls the Christians' swords by numbers sent to burning Acheron. But St. George with his sword made lanes of slaughtered men, and with his strong arm made passage through the thickest of their troops, as though Death had been commander of the battle; he caused crowns and sceptres to swim in blood, and headless steeds with jointless men to fall as fast before his sword, as drops of rain before thunder; and ever in great danger he encouraged his soldiers in this manner: "Now, for the fame of Christendom, fight; captains, be now triumphant conquerors, or Christian martyrs."

These words so encouraged the soldiers' hearts, that they neither feared the necromancer's charms, nor all the flaming dragons, that filled the air with burning lights, nor daunted at the strange encounters of infernal legions, that like armed men, with burning falchions haunted them. So fortunate were their proceedings, that they followed the invincible champion to the enchanted tent; where the other champions lay surfeited in love, whilst thousands of their friends fought in coats of steel, and merited renown by their noble achievments; for no sooner arrived St. George, with his warlike followers, before the pavilion, but he heard, as it were, the melody of the Muses; likewise his ears almost betrayed his resolution because of the sweet songs of the enchanted virgins: so pleasant and delightful were the sights in the tent, and so charming in his eyes, that he had been enchanted with their beauty, if he had not continually borne the honour of knighthood in his thoughts, and that dishonour would redound to Christendom's reproach; therefore with his sword he cut the tent in a thousand pieces; which being done, he apparently beheld where the necromancer sat upon a block of steel, feeding his spirits with drops of blood; whom, when the champion beheld, he caused his soldiers to lay hold upon him, and after chaining him fast to the root of an old blasted oak, from whence neither art, nor the help of all his charms, nor all the legions of his devils, could ever after loose him, where we leave him to his lamentations, filling the air with echoes of cries, and speak how St. George delivered the champions from their enchantments.

First, when he beheld them disrobed of their warlike attire, their furniture hung up, and themselves secretly sleeping upon the laps of ladies, he fell into these discontented speeches:

"O heaven, how my soul abhors this spectacle! Champions of Christendom, arise, brave knights, stand up, I say, and look about like men. Are you the chosen captains of your countries, and will you bury all your honours upon ladies' laps? For shame, arise, I say; they have the tears of crocodiles, the songs of syrens to enchant. To arms, brave knights: let honour be your loves; blush to behold your friends in arms, and to see your native countrymen steeping the fields of Mavors with their blood. Champions, arise, St. George calls, the victory will tarry till you come! arise, and tear the womanish attire; surfeit not in silken robes; put on your steel corslets, your glittering burgonets, and unsheath your conquering weapons, that Mavors' field may be converted into a purple ocean."

These heroical speeches were no sooner finished, but the champions, like men amazed, arose, and being ashamed of their follies, they submissively craved pardon, and vowed by protestations never to sleep in beds of down, nor ever unbuckle their shields from their weary arms, till they had won credit in the field again, nor ever would be counted his deserved followers, till their triumphs were enrolled amongst the deeds of martial knights. So, arming themselves with approved corslets, and taking their trusty swords, they accompanied St. George to the thickest of their enemies, and left the necromancer chained to the tree, who at their departure, breathed forth these bitter curses:

"Let hell's horror, and tormenting pains, be their eternal punishment; let flaming fire descend with the elements, and consume them in their warlike triumphs, and let their ways be strewed with venomous thorns, that all their legs may rankle to the knees, before they march to their native country. But why exclaim I thus in vain, when heaven itself preserves their happiness? Now all my magic charms are ended, and all my spirits forsaken me in my need, and here I am fast chained to starve and die. Have I had power to rend the vale of earth, and shake the mighty mountains with my charms? Have I had power to raise up dead men's shapes from kingly tombs, and can I not unchain myself from this accursed tree? O no, for I am fettered up by the immortal power of the Christian's God; against whom I dared to rebel. I am now condemned to everlasting fire. Come, all ye necromancers in the world, come, all you sorcerers and charmers, come, all you scholars from the learned universities, come, all you witches, beldames, and fortune-tellers, and all that practise fiendish arts, come, take example by the story of my fate."

Having said this, he violently, with his own hands, tore his hair from off his head, as a sufficient revenge, because, by the direction of their wills, he was first trained in that cursed art. Then between his teeth he bit in two his loathsome tongue, because it muttered forth so many charms: then into his thirsty bowels he thrust his hands, because they had so often held the silver wand, wherewith he had made his charmed circles; and for every letter, mark, and character that belonged to his conjuration, he inflicted a severe torment upon himself: and at last, with sightless eyes, speechless tongue, handless arms, and dismembered body he was forced to give up the ghost; where after the breath of life was vanished from his body, the heavens seemed to smile at his sudden fall, and hell began to roar at his death; the ground whereon he died was ever after that time unfortunate, and to the present time it is called, in that country, "a vale of walking spirits."

Thus have you heard the cursed life and miserable death of this wicked necromancer Osmand, whom we will now leave to the punishment due to his offences, and speak of the seven noble and magnanimous Christian champions.

After St. George had ended these enchantments, they never sheathed up their swords, nor unlocked their armour, till the subversion of Persia was accomplished, and the soldan, with his petty kings, were taken prisoners. Seven days the battle continued without ceasing; they slew two hundred thousand soldiers, besides a number who fled away and were drowned; some cast themselves headlong down from the tops of high trees; some slew themselves, but the soldan, with his princes, riding in their iron chariots, endured the Christians' encounters, till the whole army was discomfited, and then by force and violence they were compelled to yield. The soldan happened to fall into the hands of St. George and six viceroys to the other six champions: where, after they had sworn allegiance to the Christian knights, and had promised to forsake their Mahomet, they were not only set at liberty, but used most honourably; but the soldan himself, having a heart fraught with despite and tyranny, contemned the champions' courtesies, and utterly disdained their Christian governments, protesting that the heavens should first lose their wonted brightness, and the seas forsake the false swelling tides, before his heart should yield to their intended desires; whereupon St. George, being resolved to revenge his injuries, commanded that the soldan should be disrobed from all his princely attire, and in base apparel sent to prison even to the dungeon where he himself had endured so long an imprisonment, as you read in the beginning of this history, which strict commandment was presently performed: in which dungeon the soldan had not long continued, sufficing his hungry stomach with the bread of musty bran, and stanching his thirst with channel water; but he began to grow desperate and weary of his life and at length ran his head against a marble pillar standing in the middle of the dungeon, and dashed out his brains; the news of whose death, when it came to the champions' ears, they offered no violence to his lifeless body, but entombed him in a sumptuous sepulchre; after that, St. George took upon him the government of Persia, and there established good and Christian laws; also he gave to the other six champions six several kingdoms belonging to the crown of Persia, and surnamed them six viceroys, or petty kings. This being done, he took truce with the world, and triumphantly marched towards Christendom with the conquest of three imperial diadems, that is to say, of Egypt, Persia, and Morocco; in which journey he erected many stately monuments, in remembrance of his victories and heroical achievements; and through every country that they marched, there flocked to them an innumerable company of Pagans, that desired to follow him into Christendom, and to be christened in their faith, protesting to forsake their gods, whose worshippers were none but tyrants, and such as delighted in nothing but shedding of blood: to whose requests St. George presently condescended, not only in granting them their desires, but also in honouring them with the favour of his princely countenance.

In this princely manner marched St. George with his warlike troops through the territories of Africa and Asia. But when the Christian champions approached the watery world, and began to go on board their ships, the earth seemed to mourn at their farewell, and the seas to rejoice at their presence; the waves couched as smooth as crystal ice, and the winds blew such gentle gales, as though the sea-gods had been the directors of their fleet.

Thus in great pleasure they passed the time away, committing their fortunes to the mercy of the winds and the waters, who did so favourably serve them, that in a short time they arrived upon the banks of Christendom; where, being no sooner come on shore, and past the dangers of the seas, but St. George, in presence of thousands, of his followers, kneeled down on the ground, and gave God praise for his happy arrival. After which he gave command that the army should be discharged, and every one rewarded according to his desert; which within seven weeks were performed, to the honour of Christendom.

After this, St. George earnestly requested the other six champions, that they would honour him with their company home to his country England, and there receive the comfort of joyful ease, after the bloody encounters of so many dangerous battles. This motion of St. George not only obtained their consents, but added a forwardness to their willing minds; so incontinently they set forward towards England, upon whose chalky cliffs they in a short time arrived; and their reception, and entertainments, were so honourably performed, that I want the eloquence of Cicero, and the rhetoric of Caliope, to describe it.

Thus, gentle reader, hast thou heard the first of the princely achievements, noble adventures, and honourable lives of these renowned and worthy champions. The second part relates the noble achievements and strange fortunes of St. George's three sons; the loves of many gallant ladies; the combats and tournaments of many valiant knights, and tragedies of mighty potentates. Likewise the rest of the noble adventures of the renowned champions; also the manner and place of the birth of the Seven Champions, their deaths, and how they came to be called the Seven Saints of Christendom.

PART II.

CHAPTER I.

How St. George's three sons were entertained in the famous city of London; and after how their mother was slain in a wood with the brambles of a thorny brake. The blessings she gave her sons. St. George's lamentation over her bleeding body. And likewise of the journey the seven Champions intended to Jerusalem, to visit the Sepulchre of Christ.

AFTER St. George, with the other six champions of Christendom, had brought into subjection all the eastern parts, as you heard in the former part of the history, they returned to England, where in the famous city of London they sojourned, a place not only beautified with sumptuous buildings, but graced with a number of valiant knights, and gallant gentlemen.

Here the Christian champions laid their arms aside, here hung they up their weapons in the bower of peace, here their glittering corslets rusted in their armouries, here was not heard the warlike sound of drums nor silver trumpets, here stood no sentinels nor courts of guard, nor barbed steeds prepared to do battle, but all things tended to a lasting peace.

But at last St. George's three sons, Guy, Alexander, and David, being all three born at one birth, in the wilderness, and sent into three several kingdoms by their careful father, to be trained up; being grown to some ripeness of age, they desired much to visit their parents whom they had not seen from their infancy.

This request so pleased their tutors, that they furnished

them with a stately train of knights, and sent them honourably into England, where they arrived all three at one time in the famous city of London, where their entertainments were most princely, and their welcome most honourable.

I omit what sumptuous pageants and delightful shows the citizens provided, and how the streets of London were beautified with tapestry, the bells that rung them joyful welcome, and the silver instruments that gave them pleasant entertainment. Also I pass over the father's joy, who prized their sights more precious in his eyes, than if he had been made sole monarch of the golden mines of rich America. Also their mother's welcome to her sons, who gave them many affectionate kisses.

The other champions' courtesies were not the least, nor the smallest in account, to these three young gentlemen: but to be short, St. George in his own person conducted them unto their lodgings, where they spent that day and the night following in royal banqueting amongst their princely friends.

But no sooner appeared the morning sun upon the mountain-tops, and the clear countenance of the elements made mention of some ensuing pastime, but St. George commanded a solemn hunting for the welcome of his sons.

Then began his knights to arm themselves in troops, and to mount upon their jennets, and some, with well-armed boar spears in their hands, prepared for game on foot; but St. George with his sons clad in green vestments, like Adonis, with silver horns hanging at their backs, in scarfs of coloured silk, were still the foremost in this exercise. Likewise Sabra (intending to see her sons valour displayed in the field, whether they were in courage like their father or no) caused a gentle palfry to be provided, whereon she mounted, to be witness of these Sylvan sports; she was armed with a curious breast-plate, wrought like to the scales of a dolphin, and in her hand she bore a silver bow of the Turkish fashion, like an Amazonian queen, or Diana hunting in the groves of Arcadia.

Thus, in this gay manner, rode forth these hunters to their princely pastimes, where, after they had ridden about six miles from the city of London, there fell from St. George's nose three drops of blood; whereat he suddenly started, and therewithal he heard the croaking of a flight of night ravens, that hovered by the forest side, all which he judged to be dismal signs of some ensuing tragedy; but having a princely mind, he was nothing discouraged thereat, nor little mistrusted the woful accident that afterwards happened, but with a noble resolution entered the forest, accounting such foretelling tokens for old wives' ceremonies, they had not passed the compass of half mile before they started a swift stag, at which they uncoupled their hounds, and gave bridle to their horses: but now behold how frowning fortune changed their pleasant pastime to a sad and bloody tragedy; for Sabra, proffering to keep pace with them, delighting to behold the valiant encounters of her young sons, and being careless of herself, through the overswiftness of her steed, she slipped beside her saddle, and fell directly upon a thorny brake of brambles, the pricks whereof (more sharp than spikes of iron) entered every part of her delicate body; some pierced the lovely closets of her starbright eyes, whereby there issued drops of purest blood; her face, before that blushed like the morning's radiant countenance, was now changed into a crimson red; her milk-white hands, that lately strained the ivory lute, did seem to wear a bloody scarlet glove; and her tender breast, that had often fed her sons with the milk of nature, were all rent and torn with those accursed brambles, from whose deep wounds there issued such a stream of purple gore, that it turned the grass from a lively green to a crimson hue, and the abundance of blood that fell from her breast began to enforce her soul to give the world a woful farewell. And when she perceived that she must of force commit herself to the fury of imperious death, she breathed forth this dying exhortation:

"Dear lord, in this unhappy hunting must you lose the truest wife that ever lay by any prince's side; yet mourn not, nor grieve you, my sons, nor you brave Christian knights; but let your warlike drums convey me royally to my tomb, that all the world may write in brazen books, how I have followed my lord, through many a bloody field, and for his sake have left my parents, friends, and country; but now the cruel Fates have wrought their last spite, and finished my life, because I am not able to perform what love he hath deserved of me. And now to you my sons this blessing do I leave behind; even by the pains that forty weeks I endured for your sakes, when you lay enclosed in my womb, and by a mother's love that ever since I have borne to you, imitate and follow your father in all his honourable attempts; harm not the infant, nor the helpless widow; defend the honour of distressed ladies, and give freely unto wounded soldiers; seek not to stain the unspotted virgins with your unholy desires, and adventure evermore to redeem true knights from captivity; live evermore professed enemies to Paganism, and spend your lives in the quarrel and defence of Christ, that babes, yet unborn, may speak of you, and record you in the books of Fame to be true Christian champions. This is my blessing, and this is the testament I leave behind; for now I feel the chillness of pale death closing the closets of mine eyes. Farewell, vain world; dear lord, farewell; sweet sons, you famous followers of my George and all true Christian knights, adieu."

These words were no sooner ended, but with a heavy sigh, she yielded up the ghost; whereat St. George fell upon her lifeless body, tearing his hair, and rending his hunter's attire from his back into many pieces.

His sons likewise whose sorrows were as great as his, protested never to neglect one day, but daily to weep some tears upon their mother's grave, till from the earth did spring some mournful flower, to bear remembrance of her death, as did the violet that sprung from Adonis' blood, where Venus wept to see him slain. Likewise the other six champions began now a little to recover themselves, and after protesting by the honour of true knighthood, to accompany St. George unto the Holy Land bare-footed, only clad in russet garberdines, like the usual pilgrims of the world, and not to return till they had paid their vows at that blessed sepulchre.

Thus in this sorrowful manner whiled they the time away, filling the wood with echoes of their lamentations, but at last, when black Night began to approach, and with her sable mantle to overspread the firmament, they retired with her dead body back to London, where the report of this tragical accident overwhelmed their friends in sorrow; for the news of her untimely death was no sooner noised abroad, but the same caused both old and young to lament the loss of so dear a lady.

This general grief of the citizens continued for the space of thirty days; at the end whereof, St. George with his sons and the other champions interred her body very honourably, and erected over the same a rich and costly monument (in sumptuous state, like the tomb of Mausolus, which was called one of the wonders of the world); for thereon was pourtrayed the queen of chastity with her maidens, bathing themselves in a crystal fountain, as a witness of her wondrous purity.

There was also lively pictured a turtle-dove sitting upon a tree of gold, in sign of the true love that she bore to her betrothed husband.

I will not speak of the curious workmanship of the pinnacles, that were framed all of the purest jet, enamelled with silver and jasper stones: and I omit the pendants of gold, the escutcheons of princes, and the arms of countries, that beautified her tomb. Her statue or picture was carved cunningly in alabaster, and laid as it were upon a pillow of green silk, like to Pygmalion's ivory image, and directly over the same hung a silver tablet, whereon, in letters of gold, was this epitaph written:

> Here lies the wonder of this worldly age,
> For beauty, wit, and princely majesty,
> Whom spiteful Death, in his imperious rage,
> Procur'd to fall through cursed cruelty:
> For as she sported in a fragrant wood,
> Upon a thorny brake she spilt her blood.

Let ladies fair, and princes of great might,
  With silver pearled tears bedew this tomb;
Accuse the fatal sisters of despite,
  For blasting thus the pride of nature's bloom:
For here she sleeps within the earthly grave,
Whose worth deserves a golden tomb to have.

Seven years she kept her pure virginity,
  In absence of her true betrothed knight,
When many did pursue her purity,
  Whilst he remained in prison day and night;
But yet we see that things of purest prize.
Forsake the earth and dwell above the skies.

Ladies, come mourn with doleful melody,
  And make this monument your settled bow'r;
Here shed your brackish tears eternally,
  Lament both year, month, week, day, hour:
For here she rests whose like can ne'er be found,
Here Beauty's pride lies buried in the ground.

Her wounded heart, that yet doth freshly bleed,
  Hath caus'd seven knights a journey for to take
To fair Jerusalem, in pilgrims' weeds,
  The fury of her angry ghost to slake;
Because their Sylvan sport was chiefest guilt,
And only 'cause her blood was timeless spilt.

Thus, after the tomb was erected, and all things performed according to St. George's direction, he left his sons in the city of London, under the government of the English king; and, in company of the other six champions, he took his journey towards Jerusalem.

They were attired after the manner of pilgrims, in russet gaberdines down to their feet; in their hands they bore staves of ebony wood, tipped at the ends with silver, the pikes whereof were of the strongest Lydian steel, of such a sharpness, that they were able to pierce a target of tortoise-shell; upon their breasts hung crosses of crimson silk, to signify that they were Christian pilgrims travelling to the sepulchre of Christ.

In this manner set they forward from England in the spring time of the year, when Flora had beautified the earth with nature's tapestry, and made their passage as pleasant as the gardens of Hesperides, adorned with all kinds of odoriferous flowers. When they crossed the seas, the silver waves seemed to lie as smooth as crystal ice, and the dolphins to dance above the waters as a sign of a prosperous journey. In travelling by land, their ways seemed so short and easy, and the chirping melody of birds made such music as they passed, that in a short season they arrived beyond the borders of Christendom, and had entered the confines of Africa.

There were they forced, instead of downy beds, nightly to rest their weary limbs upon heaps of sun-burnt moss; and instead of silken curtains and curious canopies, they had the clouds of heaven to cover them. Now their naked legs and bare feet, that had wont to stride the stately steeds, and to trample in fields of Pagan's blood, were forced to climb the craggy mountains, and to endure the torments of pricking briars, as they travelled through the desert places and comfortless solitary wildernesses.

Many were the dangers that happened to them in their journey before they arrived in Judea, princely their achievements, and most honourable their adventures which for this time I pass over, leaving the champions for a time in their travels towards the sepulchre of Christ, and speak of what happened to St. George's three sons in visiting their mother's tomb in the city of London.

CHAPTER II.

Of the strange gifts that St. George's sons offered at their mother's tomb, and what happened thereupon. How her ghost appeared to them, and counselled them to the pursuit of their father. Also how the king of England installed them with the honour of knighthood, and furnished them with habiliments of war.

THE swift-footed steeds of Titan's fiery car had almost finished a year since Sabra's funeral was solemnised; in which time St. George's three sons had visited their mother's tomb oftener than there were days in the year, and had shed more sorrowful tears thereon than are stars in the glittering horizon; but at last these three young princes fell into civil discord and mortal strife, which of them should bear the truest love to their mother's dead body, and which of them should be held in greatest esteem: for before many days were expired, they concluded to offer up their several devotions at her tomb; and he that devised a gift of the rarest price, and of the strangest quality, should be held worthy of the greatest honour, and accounted the noblest of them all.

The first, thinking to exceed his brothers in the strangeness of his gift, repaired unto a cunning enchantress, who abode in a secret cave adjoining to the city, whom he procured (through many rich gifts and large promises) by art to devise a means to get the honour from his brethren, and to give a gift of that strange nature, that all the world might wonder at the report thereof.

The enchantress (being won with his promises) by art and magic spells devised a garland containing all the diversity of flowers that ever grew in earthly gardens; and though it were then in the dead time of the winter, when the silver icicles had disrobed both herbs and flowers of their beauties, and the snow lay freezing on the mountain tops, yet was this garland contrived after the fashion of a rich imperial crown, with as many flowers as ever Flora placed upon the downs of rich Arcadia; in diversity of colours like the glittering rainbow, when shining in its greatest pride, and casting such an odoriferous scent and savour, as though the heavens had rained down showers of camphire, bis, or sweet-smelling ambergris.

This rare and exceeding garland was no sooner framed by enchantment, and delivered into his hands, but he left the enchantress sitting in her ebony chair, and upon a block of steel, practising her fatal arts, with her hair hanging about her shoulders like wreaths of snakes, or envenomed serpents; and so returned to his mother's tomb, where he hung it upon a pillar of silver that was placed in the middle of the monument.

The second brother also repaired to his mother's tomb, and brought in his hand an ivory lute, whereon he played such inspiring melody, that it seemed like the harmony of angels, or the celestial music of Apollo, when he descended from heaven for the love of Daphne, whom he turned into a bay-tree; the music being finished, he tied his lute in a damask scarf, and with great humility he hung it at the west end of the tomb, upon a knob of a jasper-stone.

Lastly, the third brother likewise repaired with no outward devotion, or worldly gift; but clad in a vesture of white silk, bearing in his hand an instrument of death, like an innocent lamb going to sacrifice, or one ready to be offered up for the love of his mother's soul.

This strange manner of repair caused his other brothers to stand and listen attentively, and with diligent eyes to behold his purpose.

First, after he had let fall a shower of tears from the cisterns of his eyes, in remembrance of his mother's timeless death; he pricked his naked breast with a silver bodkin, which he brought in his hand, from whence there trickled down about thirty drops of blood, which he after offered to his mother's tomb in a silver basin, as an evident sign that there could be nothing more dear, nor of more precious price, than to offer up his own blood for her love. This ceremonious gift caused his two other brothers to swell in hatred like to chafed lions, and run with fury upon him, intending to catch him by the hair of his head, and drag him round their mother's tomb, till his brains were dashed against a marble pavement, and his blood sprinkled upon her grave; but this wicked enterprise moved the majesty of heaven, and ere they could accomplish their intents, or stain their hands with his blood, they heard (as it were) the noise of dead men's bones rattling in the ground, whereupon looking fearfully about them, the tomb seemed of itself to open, and thereupon to appear a countenance resembling their mother, with her breast besmeared in blood, and her body wounded with a number of scars; and so with a dismal and rueful look, she spake unto her desperate sons in this manner:

"Oh you degenerate from nature's kind! Why do you seek to make a murder of yourselves? Can you endure to see my body rent in twain, my heart split asunder, and my womb dismembered? Abate this fury; stain not your hands with your own blood, nor make my tomb a spectacle of more death. Unite yourselves in concord, that my discontented soul may sleep in peace, and never more be troubled with your unbridled humours. Make haste, I say, arm yourselves in steel corslets, and follow your valiant father to Jerusalem, he is there in danger and distress of life; away, I say, or else my angry ghost shall never leave this world, but hunt you up and down with ghastly visions."

This being said, she vanished from their sight, into the brittle air; whereat for a time they stood amazed, and almost bereft of wit, through the terrors of her words; but at last recovering their former senses, they all vowed a continual unity, and never to proffer the like injury again, but to live in brotherly concord till the dissolution of their earthly bodies.

So in haste they went unto the king, and acquainted him with all things that had happened; and falling upon their knees before his majesty, requested at his hands the honour of knighthood, with leave to depart in pursuit of their father and the other champions, that were fallen into great distress.

The king, purposing to accomplish their desires, and to fulfil their requests, presently condescended, and not only gave them the honour of knighthood, but furnished them with rich habiliments of war, answerable to their magnanimous minds: first, he frankly bestowed upon them three stately palfreys, bred upon the bright mountains of Sardinia, in colour of an iron-grey, beautified with glossy hair, and in pace swifter than Spanish jennets; for boldness and courage like to Bucephalus, the horse of Alexander the Macedonian, or Cæsar's steed, that never daunted in the field; and they were trapped with rich trappings of gold, after the Morocco fashion, with saddles framed like unto iron chairs, with backs of steel, and their foreheads were beautified with spangled plumes of purple feathers, whereon hung many golden pendants. The king likewise bestowed upon them three costly swords, wrought of purest Lybian steel, with lances bound about with plates of brass; at the tops whereof hung silken streamers, beautified with the English cross, being the crimson badge of knighthood and honour of adventurous champions. Thus, in this royal manner, rode these three young knights from the city of London, in company of the king, with a train of knights and gallant gentlemen, who conducted them to the sea-side, where they left the young knights to their future fortunes, and returned back to the English court.

Now are St. George's sons floating upon the seas, making their first adventure in the world, that after ages might applaud their achievements, and enrol their fames in the records of honour. Fate, prosper them successfully; and, gentle fortune, smile upon their travels: for three braver knights did never cross the seas, nor make their adventures into strange countries.

CHAPTER III.

How St. George's sons, after they were knighted by the English king, travelled towards Barbary; and how they redeemed the Duke's daughter of Normandy from defilement, that was assailed in a wood by three tawny Moors.

NOT many days had these three magnanimous knights endured the danger of the swelling waves, but with a prosperous and successful wind they arrived upon the territories of France; where, being no sooner safely set on shore, but they bountifully rewarded their mariners, and betook themselves fully to their intended travels.

Now began their costly trapped steeds to pace it like the scudding winds, and with their warlike hoofs to thunder on the beaten passages; now began true honour to flourish in their royal breasts, and the renown of their father's achievements to encourage their desires. Although tender youth sat but budding on their cheeks, yet portly manhood triumphed in their hearts; and although their childish arms as yet never tried the painful adventure of knighthood, yet bore they high and princely cogitations in as great esteem, as when their father slew the burning dragon in Egypt for the preservation of their mother's life.

Thus travelled they to the farther part of the kingdom of France, guided only by the direction of fortune, without any adventure worth the noting, all at last, riding through a mighty forest standing on the borders of Lusitania, they heard (afar off as it were) the rueful cries of a distressed woman; which in this manner filled the air with echoes of her moans:

"O heavens!" said she, "be kind and pitiful unto a maiden in distress, and send some happy passenger that may deliver me from these inhuman monsters."

This woful and unexpected noise had caused the knights to alight from their horses, and to see the event of this accident: so after they had tied their steeds to the body of a pine-tree, by the reins of their bridles, they walked on foot into the thickest of the forest, with their weapons drawn, ready to withstand any assailment whatsoever; and, as they drew near to the distressed virgin, they heard her breathe forth this pitiful, moving lamentation, a second time:

"Come, come, some courteous knight! or else I must forego that precious jewel which all the world can never again recover."

These words caused them to make the more speed, and to run the nearest way for the maiden's succour. Where, approaching her presence, they found her tied by the locks of her own hair to the trunk of an orange tree, and three cruel and inhuman Negroes standing ready to despoil her of her purity and accomplish her ruin.

But when St. George's sons beheld her lovely countenance besmeared in dust, that before seemed to be as beautiful as roses in milk, and her crystal eyes filled with floods of tears, at one instant they ran upon the negroes, and sheathed their angry weapons in their loathsome bowels; the villains being slain, their blood sprinkled about the forest, and their bodies cast out as a prey for ravenous beasts to feed on, they unbound the maiden, and, like courteous knights, demanded the cause of her captivity, and by what means she came into that solitary forest.

"Most noble knights," quoth she, "and true renowned men at arms, to tell the cause of my former misery were a trouble unto my soul, for the discourse thereof would burst my heart with grief; but considering your nobility, which I do perceive by your princely behaviour, and kind courtesies extended towards me, being a virgin in distress, under the hands of these negroes, whom you have justly murdered, shall so much embolden me, though unto my heart's great grief, to discourse the first cause of my miserable fortune.

"My father," said she, "whilst gentle fortune smiled upon him, was duke and sole commander of the state of Normandy, a country now situated in the kingdom of France, whose lands and revenues in his prosperity were so great, that he continually kept as stately a train, both of knights and gentlemen, as any prince in Europe; wherefore the king of France greatly envied, and by bloody wars deposed my father from his princely dignity, who, for sake of his life in company of me his only heir and daughter, betook us to these solitary woods, where ever since we have secretly remained in a poor cell or hermitage, which by our industrious pains, hath been built with plants of vines and open boughs, and covered it over with clods of earth, and tufts of grass. Seven years have we continued in great extremities, sustaining our hunger with the fruits of trees and quenching our thirst with the dew of heaven, falling nightly upon fragrant flowers; and here, instead of princely attire, embroidered garments, and damask vestures, we have been constrained to clothe ourselves with flowers, which we have painfully woven up together: thus in this manner, continued we in that solitary wilderness, making both birds and beasts our chief companions; these merciless, tawny coloured Moors, who as you see, came into our cell, thinking to have found some store of treasure; but casting their gazing eyes upon my beauty, they were presently moved with wicked desires; then with furious and dismal countenances, and with hearts more cruel than was Nero's, the tyrannous Roman emperor, when he beheld the entrails of his natural mother laid open by his inhuman and merciless commandment, or when he stood upon the highest top of a mighty mountain, to see that famous and imperial city set on fire, by the remorseless hands of his unrelenting ministers, that added unhallowed flames to his unholy furies. In this kind, I say, these merciless and wicked-minded negroes with violent hands took my aged father, and most cruelly bound him to the blasted body of a withered oak, standing before the entry of his cell; where neither the reverend honour of his silver hairs, glittering like the frozen icicles upon the northern mountains, nor the strained sighs of his breast, wherein the pledge of wisdom was ever throned, nor all my tears or exclamations could any abate their cruelties; but (grim dogs of Barbary) they left my father fast bound unto the tree, and like egregious vipers took me by my golden hair, dragging me like a silly lamb unto the slaughtering place, intending to satisfy their lust at the expense of my defilement. Being used thus, I made my humble supplication to the Almighty, to be revenged upon their cruelties: I spoke to them of the rewards of base defilements; yet neither the fears of heaven, nor the terrible threats of hell, could mollify their bloody minds; but they proceeded to persevere in that wickedness, and vowed, that if all the leaves of the trees, that grew within the wood, were turned into Indian pearls, yet should they not redeem my chastity from the stain of their insatiable and base desires. This being said, they bound me with the trammels of my hair to this orange-tree, and at the very instant they proffered to defile my unspotted body, you happily approached, and not only redeemed me from their tyrannous desires, but quit the world of three of the wickedest creatures that ever nature framed; for which, most noble and invincible knights, if ever virgin's prayers may prevail, humbly will I make my supplications to the deities, that you may prove as valiant champions as ever put on helmet, and that your fames may ring to every prince's ear, as far as bright Hyperion doth show his golden face."

This tragical tale was no sooner ended, but the three knights embraced the sorrowful maiden between their arms, and requested her to conduct them unto the place where she left her father bound unto the withered oak; to which she willingly consented, and thanked them highly for their kindness; but before they approached the old man's presence, what for the grief of his banishment, and violent usage of his daughter, he was forced to yield up his miserable life to the mercy of unavoidable death.

When St. George's valiant sons, in company of this sorrowful maiden, came to the tree, and contrary to their expectations, found her father cold and stiff, void of sense and feeling, also his hands and face covered with green moss, which they supposed to be done by the robin-redbreast, and some other little birds, who do use naturally to cover the bare parts of any body that they find dead in the field, they all fell into a new confused extremity of grief; but especially his daughter, having lost all joy and comfort in this world, made both heaven and earth resound with her exceeding lamentations. Thus when the three young knights perceived the comfortless sorrow of the virgin, and how she had vowed never to depart from those solitary groves, but to spend the remnant of her days in company of her father's dead body, they courteously assisted her to bury him under a chestnut tree, where they left her behind them bathing his grave with her tears, and returned back to their horses, where they left them at the entry of the forest tied to a lofty pine, and so departed on their journey; where we will leave them for a time, and speak of the Seven Champions of Christendom, that were gone on pilgrimage to the city of Jerusalem, and what strange adventures happened to them in their travels.

CHAPTER IV.

Of the adventures at the golden fountain in Damasco. How six of the Christian champions were taken prisoners by a mighty Giant; and how, after, they were delivered by St. George. And also how he redeemed fourteen Jews out of Prison. With divers other strange incidents that happened.

LET us now speak of the favourable clemency that smiling Fortune showed to the Christian champions in their travels to Jerusalem; for after they had departed from England, and had journied in their pilgrim's attire through many strange countries, at last they arrived upon the confines of Damasco, which is a country not only beautified with sumptuous, costly buildings, framed by the curious architecture of man's device, but also furnished with all precious gifts that nature in her greatest liberality could bestow.

In this fruitful dominion long time the Christian champions rested their weary steps, and made their abode in the house

of a rich Jew, a man that spent his wealth chiefly for the
succour and comfort of travellers and wandering pilgrims;
his house was not curiously erected of carved timber-work,
but framed with quarries of blue stones, and supported with
many stately pillars of the purest marble. The gates and
entry of his house were continually kept open, in sign of his
bountiful mind; over the portal thereof did hang a brazen
tablet, whereon was most curiously engraven the picture of
Ceres, the goddess of plenty, decked with garlands of wheat,
wreaths of olives, bunches of vines, and with all manner of
fruitful things; the chamber wherein they slept, was garnished with as many windows of crystal glass as there are days in
the year, and the walls painted with as many stories as were
years since the world's creation. It was likewise built four-
square, after the form of the pyramids in Greece; on the
north side were painted high mountains of snow, whose tops
seemed to reach the clouds, and mighty woods overhung with
silver icicles, which is the nature of the northern climate.
Lastly, upon the west side of the chamber sat the god of the
seas, riding upon a dolphin's back, a troop of mermaids following him with their golden trammels floating upon the silver
waves. Thus in this chamber rested these weary champions
a long season, where their food was not delicious, but wholesome, and their services not curious, but comely. The courteous Jew, their friendly host, whom nature had honoured
with seven comely sons, not only kept them company, and
showed them the curiosities of his habitation, but also described the pleasant situation of his country.

Some days were spent in this manner, to the exceeding
great pleasure of the Christian knights; and when the dark
night approached, and the wonted time of sleep summoned
them to their silent and quiet rest, the Jew's children, being
seven as brave and comely boys as ever Dame Nature framed,
filled the seven champions ears with such sweet and delicate
melodies, gently strained from their ivory lutes, that not
Arion, when all the art of sweet music consented with his
tune, voice and hand, when he won favour of the dolphin,
being forsaken of men, was comparable thereto; whereby the
Christians were enchanted with such delights, that their sleep
seemed to be as pleasant as were the sweet joys of Elysium.
But upon a time, after the courteous Jew had intelligence
that they were Christian knights, and such admirable martial
champions, whom Fame had canonized to be the wonders of
the world for martial discipline and knightly adventures; and
finding a fit opportunity, as he walked in their companies,
upon an evening, under an harbour of vine-branches, he
revealed to them the secrets of his soul, and the cause of his so
sad and solitary dwelling. So standing bare-headed in the

middle of the champions, with his white hair hanging down to his shoulders, in colour like the silver swan, and softer than the down of thistles, or Median silk untwisted, he began, with a sober countenance and gallant demeanour, to speak as follows:

"I am sure," quoth he, "you invincible knights, that you marvel at my solitary course of living, and that you greatly muse wherefore I exempt myself from the company of worldlings, except my seven sons, whose sights are my chief comfort, and the only prolongers of my life; therefore prepare your ears to entertain the strangest discourse that ever tongue pronounced, or wearied old man in the height of his extremity delivered.—I was, in my former years, whilst fortune smiled upon my happiness, the principal commander and chief owner of a certain fountain, and of such wonderful and precious virtue, the water thereof was so strange in its operation, that in four-and-twenty hours it would convert any metal, as brass, copper, iron, lead, or tin, into rich refined gold; the stony flint into pure silver, and all kinds of earth into excellent metal. By the virtue thereof, I have made the leaves of trees a flourishing forest of riches, and the blades of grass valuable as the jewels that are found in the country of America. The virtue thereof was no sooner noised through the world, but it caused many foreign knights to try the adventure, and by force of arms to bereave me of the honour of this fountain. But at that time nature graced me with one-and-twenty sons, whereof seven are yet living, and the only comfort of my age: but the other fourteen, whom frowning fortune hath bereaved me of, by their valiant powers and matchless fortitude, defended the fountain from many great and furious assailers; for there was no knight in all the world that was found so hardy, or of such invincible courage, that if they but once attempted to encounter with any of my valiant sons, they were either taken prisoners, or slain in the combat. The fame of their valour, and the riches of the fountain, ran through many strange countries; and lastly, came to the ears of a furious giant, dwelling upon the borders of Arabia; who at the report thereof came, armed with his steel coat, with a mighty bar of iron on his neck, like to furious Hercules, that burst the brazen gates of Cerberus, and bore the mighty mountain Altas upon his shoulders; he was the conqueror of my sons, and the first cause of my sudden downfall. But when I thus had intelligence of the overthrow of fourteen of my sons, and that he had made conquest of my wealthy fountain, I, with my children, thinking all hope of recovery to be past, betook ourselves to this solitary course of life, where ever since, in this mansion or hermitage we have made our abode and residence, spending our wealth to the relief of travelling knights and wandering pilgrims, hoping once again that smiling fortune would advance us to some better hap; and, to be plain, right worthy champions, since then my hope was never at the height of full perfection till this present time, wherein your excellent presence almost assures me that the hideous monster shall be conquered, the fountain restored, and my sons' death revenged."

The champions with great admiration gave ear to the strange discourse of this reverend Jew, and proffered in requital of his extraordinary kindness, to undertake this adventure; and the more to encourage the other, St. George began in this manner to utter his mind, speaking both to the Jew and their host, and his valiant fellow-champions:

"I have not without great wonder, most reverend and courteous old man, heard the strange discourse of thy admirable fountain, and do not a little lament, that one of so kind and liberal a disposition should be dispossessed of such exceeding riches; neither am I less sorry that so inhuman a monster, and known enemy to all courtesy and kindness, should have the fruition of so exceeding great treasure; for to the wicked, wealth is the cause of their greater wickedness. But that which most grieveth us is that having had so many valiant knights to fight, they all so unfortunately fell into the hands of that relentless monster; but be comforted, kind old man, for I hope, by the power of my Maker, we were directed hither to punish that hateful giant; revenge the injuries offered to thine age; satisfy with his death the death of thy children, if they be dead; and restore to thy bounteous possession, that admirably rich fountain again.

"And now to you, my valiant champions, I speak, that with me through many dangers have adventured: let us courageously attempt this rare adventure, where such honours to our names, such happiness to our friends, such glory to God consists, in recovering right to the wronged, and punishing rightfully the wrongers of the oppressed; and that there be no contention among us, who shall begin this adventure, for I know all of you thirst after honour, therefore let lots be cast, on whomsoever the chief lot falleth, let him be foremost in assailing the giant, and so good Fortune be our guide."

The champions, without more words disrobed themselves from their pilgrim's attire, every one putting on other habiliments, then ready in the Jew's house; instead of their ebony staves tipped with silver, they wielded in their hands steel blades; and their feet, that had endured many painful pilgrimages upon the bare ground, were now ready to mount the lofty stirrup; but as I said, they purposed not all to assail the giant, but singly, every one to try his own fortune thereby to obtain great honour, and their deeds to merit higher fame: therefore lots being cast among themselves, which should begin the adventure, the lot fell first to St. Denis, the noble champion of France, who greatly rejoiced at his fortune, and so departed for that night, to get things in readiness; the next morning, no sooner had the golden sun displayed his beauty in the east, but St. Denis arose from his sluggish bed, and attired himself in costly armour, and mounted upon a steed of iron-grey, with a spangled plume of purple feathers on his burgonet, with a shining star of gold, resembling the azure firmament, beautified with glittering stars. Where after he had taken leave of the other champions, and had demanded of the Jew where the giant had his residence, he departed forward on his journey, and before the sun had mounted to the top of heaven, he approached the giant's presence, who then sat upon a block of steel, directly before the soldan's fountain, satisfying his hunger with raw flesh, and quenching his thirst with the juice of ripe grapes.

The first sight of his ugly and deformed proportion, almost daunted the valour of the French champion, that he stood in amaze, doubting to try the adventure, or return with dishonour back to his other fellow-knights; but having a heart filled with true magnanimity, he chose rather to die in the encounter, than to return with infamy; so committing his trust to the inconstant queen of chance, he spurred his horse, and assailed the giant so furiously that the strokes of his sword sounded like weighty blows hammered upon an anvil: but so disregarded the giant the puissant force of this single knight, that he would scarce rise from the place where he sat; but yet remembering a strange dream, that a little before he had in his sleep, which revealed unto him how that a knight would come from the northern climates of the earth, which should alone end the adventure of the fountain, and vanquish him by fortitude; therefore, not minding to be taken at any advantage, he suddenly started up, and with a grim countenance he ran upon St. Denis, and took him, horse, armour, furniture and all, under his arm, as lightly as a strong man would take a sucking infant from his cradle, and bore him to a hollow rock bound about with bars of iron, standing near unto the fountain, in a valley betwixt two mighty mountains: in which prison he enclosed the French champion, amongst fourteen other knights, that were sons to the courteous Jew, as you heard before discoursed; and being proud of that attempt, he returned to the block of steel; where we will leave him sitting, glorying in his own conceit, and speak of the other champions remaining in the Jew's house, expecting the French knight's fortunate return; but when night had taken possession of the elements, and no news was heard of the champion's success, they judged presently that either he was slain in the adventure, or else discomfited and taken prisoner; and therefore they cast lots again, which of them the next morning should try his fortune, and revenge the French knight's quarrel; so the lot fell to St. James, the noble champion of Spain, whereat his heart rejoiced more than if he had been made king of the western world. So, in like manner, on the next morning by break of day, he attired himself in rich and costly armour like the other champion, and mounted upon a Spanish jennet, in pace most swift and speedy, and in portly state like to Bucephalus, the proud steed of Macedonian Alexander; his caparison was in colour like to the waves of the sea; his burgonet was beautified with a spangled plume of feathers, and upon his breast he bore the arms of Spain. Thus in this gallant manner departed he from the Jew's habitation, leaving the other champions at their divine contemplations for his happy success; but his fortune chanced contrary to his wishes, for at the giant's first encounter he was likewise borne to the rock to join St. Denis.

This giant was the strongest and hardiest knight at arms that ever set foot upon the confines of Damasco; his strength was so invincible, that at one time he durst encounter with a hundred knights. But we return again to the other champions, whom, when night approached, and likewise missing St. James, they cast lots the third time, and it fell to the noble champion of Italy, St. Anthony, who on the next morning attired himself in the costly habiliments of war, and mounted upon a Barbarian palfrey, as richly as did the valiant Jason, when he adventured into the isle of Colchos for the golden fleece and for Medea's love; his helmet glittered like an icy mountain, decked with a plume of ginger-coloured feathers and beautified with many silver pendants. But his shining glory was soon blemished with a cloud of mischance, for although he was as valiant a knight as ever brandished weapon in the field of Mars, yet he found a disability in his fortitude to withstand the furious blows of the giant, that he was forced to yield himself prisoner like the former champions.

The next lot there was cast fell to St. Andrew of Scotland, a knight as highly honoured for martial discipline as any of the rest; his steed was clad with a caparison after the manner of the Grecians; his armour varnished with green oils, like the colour of the summer fields; upon his breast he bore a cross of purple silk, and on his burgonet a goodly plume of feathers; but yet Fortune so frowned upon his enterprise, that he did not prevail, but committed his life to the mercy of the giant, who likewise imprisoned him with the other knights. The fifth lot fell unto St.

Patrick of Ireland, as brave a knight as ever nature created, and as adventurous in his achievements. If ever Hector upon his Phrygian steed pranced up and down the streets of Troy, and made that age admire his fortitude, this Irish knight might countervail his valor: for no sooner had the moon forsook the azure firmament, and had committed her charge to the golden burnished sun, but St. Patrick approached the sight of the giant, mounted upon his Irish hobby, clad in a corslet proof, beautified with silver nails; his plume of feathers of the colour of virgin's hair; his horse covered with an orange-tawny silk, and his saddle bound about with steel, like an iron chair. The sight of this valiant champion so daunted the courage of the giant, that he thought him to be the knight that the vision had revealed, and by whom the adventure should be accomplished; therefore with no cowardly fortitude he assailed the Irish knight, who with as princely valour endured the encounter; but the unkind destinies not intending to give him the honour of the victory, compelled his strength to submit to the giant's force, and likewise to join the other imprisoned champions. The next lot fell to St. David of Wales, who nothing discouraged at the other Christian knights, but at the morning sun's uprise into the azure firmament glittered in his silver armour before the fountain with a golden griffin shining on his breast, where he endured a long and dangerous combat with the giant, making the skies resound with echoes of their strokes; but at last, again the giant perceived that St. David was constrained, like to the other Christian champions to yield to the giant's mercy.

But now the heroical champion of England, St. George, he that was Fame's true knight, and the world's wonder, remaining in the Jew's pavilion, and pondering in his mind the bad success of the other six champions and that it was his turn to try his fortune the next morning in the adventure, he fell into great contemplation: "I that have fought for Christendom in fields of blood, and made my enemies to swim in streams of crimson gore, shall I not now confound this inhuman monster, that hath discomfited six of the bravest knights that ever nature framed? I slew the burning dragon in Egypt; I conquered the terrible giant that kept the enchanted castle amongst the Amazonians: then Fortune, let me accomplish this dangerous adventure, that all Christians and Christian knights may applaud my name."

In this manner spent he the night, hoping for the happy success of the next day's enterprise, whereon he vowed by the honour of his golden garter, either to return a worthy conqueror, or to die with honour valiantly. And when the sun began to beautify the eastern elements with a fair purple colour, he repaired to the Jew's armoury, and clad himself in a black corslet, mounting himself upon a pitchy-coloured steed, adorned with a blood-red caparison, in sign of a bloody and tragical adventure; his plume of feathers was like a flame of fire quenched in blood, as a token of speedy revenge; he armed himself, not with a sturdy lance, bound about with plates of brass, but took a javelin made of steel, the one end sharpened like the point of a needle, at the other end a ball of iron, in fashion like a mace or club. Being thus armed, according to his desires, he took leave of the Jew and his seven sons, all attired in black and mournful ornaments, praying for his happy and fortunate success, and so departed speedily to the golden fountain, where he found the giant sleeping carelessly upon his block of steel, dreading no ensuing danger. But when the valiant champion St. George was alighted from his horse, and sufficiently beheld the deformed proportion of the giant, how the hair of his head stood upright, like the bristles of a wild boar, his eyes gazing open like two blazing comets, and teeth long and sharp, like to spikes of steel, the nails of his hands like the talons of an eagle, over which were drawn a pair of iron gloves; and every other limb huge and strongly proportioned, like to the body of some mighty oak; the worthy champion awakened him in this order: "Arise, unreasonable, deformed monster, and either deliver the captive knights, whom thou hast wrongfully detained, or prepare thy ugly self to abide the strongest force of my warlike arm and death-prepared weapon."

At which words the furious giant started up, as one suddenly amazed or affrighted from his sleep, and without making any reply took his iron mace fast in both hands, and with great strength struck at the most worthy English champion, who with exceeding cunning and nimbleness defended himself from the danger, by speedily avoiding the violent blow; and withal returned on his adversary a mighty thrust, with the sharp end of his javelin, which rebounded from the giant's body, as if it had been run against an adamantine pillar. Which St. George perceiving, turned the heavy round ball end of his massy javelin, and so mightly assailed the giant, redoubling his heavy blows with such courageous fortitude, that at last he beat the brains out of his deformed head, whereby the giant was constrained to yield up the ghost, and give such a hideous roar, as though the whole frame of the earth had been shaken with the violence of some clap of thunder. This being done, St. George cast his loathsome carcase as a prey to the fowls and ravenous beasts to seize upon; and after diligently searching up and down, till he found the rock where all the knights and champions were imprisoned; which with his steel javelin he burst asunder, and delivered them presently from their servitude, and after-

"And as might be expected this small disadvantage was met with such courageous fortitude that at last he laid his claims full at his deformed feet."

CHAP II PART 2

wards returning most triumphantly to the Jew's pavilion, in as great majesty and royalty as Vespasian with his Roman nobles and peers returned into the confines of flourishing Italy, from the admired and glorious conquest of Jerusalem and Judea.

But when the reverend Jew saw the English champion return with victory, together with the other six fellow-champions, and likewise, beheld his fourteen sons safely delivered, his joy so mightily exceeded the bounds of reason, that he suddenly swooned, and lay for a time in a trance, with the exceeding great pleasure he received. But having a little recovered his decayed senses, he gladly conducted them into their several lodgings, and there they were presently unarmed, and their wounds washed in white wine and new milk, and afterwards banqueted them in the best manner he could devise; at which banquet there wanted not all the excellency of music that the Jew's seven younger sons could devise; extolling in their sweet sonnets the excellent fortitude of the English champion, that had not only delivered their captured brethren, but restored, by that ugly giant's deserved death, their aged father to the re-possession of his golden fountain. Thus after St. George, with the other six champions, had sojourned there for the space of thirty days, having placed the Jew with his sons in their former desired dignities—that is, in the government of the fountain—they clothed themselves again in their pilgrim's attire, and so departed forward on their intended journey to visit the holy sepulchre at Jerusalem.

CHAPTER V.

Of the Champions, return to Jerusalem. and after how they were almost famished in a wood; and how St. George obtained them food by his valour in a giant's house.

THE champions after this battle of the golden fountain, never rested travelling till they arrived at the holy hill of Sion, and had visited the sepulchre, which they found most richly built of the purest marble, garnished curiously by cunning architecture, with many carbuncles of jasper, and pillars of jet. The temple gates were of burnished gold, and the portals refined silver: and in it commonly burned a sweet smelling taper, always maintained by twelve of the noblest virgins dwelling in Judea, clad in silken ornaments. Many days these worthy champions offered up their ceremonious devotions to that sacred tomb, washing the marble pavements with their true and unfeigned tears, and witnessing their true and hearty zeal, with their continual volleys of discharged sighs. But at last, upon an evening, when Titan's golden beams began to descend the western element, as those princely-minded champions, in company of these twelve admired maidens, kneeled before the sepulchre, offering up their evening orisons, an unseen voice from a hollow vault in the temple uttered these words:

"You magnanimous knights of Christendom whose true nobilities hath circled the earth with reports of fame, whose bare feet for the love of our sweet Saviour have set more weary steps upon the parched earth, than there are stars within the canopy of heaven, return, return into the bloody fields of war, and spend not the honours of your time in this ceremonious manner, for great things by you must be accomplished, such as in time to come shall fill large chronicles, and cause babes as yet unborn. to speak of your achievements. And you chaste maidens, that spend your time in the service of God, even by the plighted promise you have made to true virginity, I charge you to furnish these warlike champions with such approved furniture as hath been afforded to this royal sepulchre by these travelling knights, which have fought under the banner of Christendom. This is the pleasure of high Fates, and this, for the redress of all wronged innocents in earth, must be with all immediate dispatch forthwith accomplished."

This unexpected voice was no sooner ended, but the temple seemed strangely to resound, like the melody of celestial angels, or the holy harmony of cherubims; whereupon the twelve arose from their contemplations, and conducted the seven champions to the further side of Mount Sion, and there bestowed upon them seven of the bravest steeds that ever they beheld, with martial furniture answerable thereunto, befitting knights of such esteem. Thus the Christian champions, being proud of their good fortunes, attired themselves in rich and sumptuous corslets, kindly bidding the ladies adieu, betook themselves to the world's wide journey. Their travels began at that time of the year when the summer's queen began to spread her beauteous mantle amongst the green and fresh boughs of the high and mighty cedars, when all kinds of small birds flew round about, recreating themselves in the beauty of the day, and with their well-tuned notes making a sweet and heavenly melody. At which time, I say, these mighty and well-esteemed knights, the Seven Champions of Christendom, betook the way from Jerusalem, which they thought to be most used ; in which they had not many days travelled through the deserts, and over many a mountain top, but they grew feeble for lack of their accustomed victuals, and could not hide nor dissemble their great hunger. But one evening, when they had spent the day in great extremity, and night drew on, they happened to be in a thicket of tall trees, when the silver moon with her bright beams glittered most clearly; yet to them it seemed as dark as pitch, for they were sorely troubled for the lack of that which should sustain them, and their faces did show their hungry state. So they sat down upon the green herbs, and studied their extreme necessity, providing to take rest for the night; but all was in vain, for their corporal necessities would not consent thereunto; but without sleeping for that night, till the next day in the morning they turned to their accustomed travel and journey, thinking to find some food for the cherishing of their stomachs, and had their eyes always gazing about to spy some village or house where they might satisfy their hunger and take rest. In this helpless manner spent they the next day, till the close of the evening light, by which time they grew so faint that they fell on the ground with feebleness.

The next morning, by that time the golden sun had almost mounted to the top of heaven, and the glorious prime of the day began to approach, they travelled on till they came to a field, out of which there appeared a great smoke, which gave them to understand that there should be some habitation near that place. Then the princely-minded St. George said to the other champions: "Take comfort with yourselves, and by little and little come forward with an easy pace, for I will ride before to see who shall be our host this night; and of this, brave knights and champions, be assured, whether he be pleased or no, he shall give us lodgings and entertainment like travelling knights;" and therewithal he set spurs to his horse, and swiftly scoured away; his beast was so speedy, that in a short time he approached the mountain, where, at the noise of his horse in running, there arose from the ground a terrible giant, of such great height, that he seemed to be a grown tree, and for hugeness like to a rock; but when he cast his eyes upon the English knight, who seemed to him like two brazen plates, or two torches ever flaming, he laid his hand upon a mighty club of iron which lay by him, and came with great lightness to meet St. George; but when he approached his presence, thinking him to be a knight of but small valour and fortitude, he threw away his iron bat, and came towards the champion, intending with his fists to buffet out his brains; but the courage of the English champion so exceeded, that he forgot the extremity of hunger, and like a courageous knight raised himself in his stirrups, otherwise he could not reach his head, and gave him such a blow upon the forehead, with his falchion, that he cut his head half asunder, and his brains in great abundance ran down his deformed body, so that he fell to the ground, and presently died: his fall seemed to make the ground shake, as though a stone tower had been overturned;

for as he lay upon the earth he seemed to be a great oak blown up by the roots with a tempestuous whirlwind.

At that instant the rest of the champions came to that place, with as much joy, as before they were sad and sorrowful.

When St. Denis, with the other knights, saw the size of the giant, and the deformity of his body, they thought his valour beyond imagination; but afterwards St. George desired the rest of the champions to go and see what store of victuals the giant had prepared for him.

Whereupon they entered the giant's house, which was cut out of hard stone, and wrought out of a rock: therein they found a very large copper cauldron standing upon a trevet of steel, the feet and supporters thereof were as big as great iron pillars, under the same burned a huge flaming fire, which sparkled like a fiery furnace in burning Acheron.

Within the cauldron were boiling the flesh of two fat bullocks, prepared only for the giant's dinner.

The sight of this ensuing banquet gave them great comfort, all fell to work, hoping for their trouble to eat part of the meat; one turned the beef in the cauldron, another increased the fire, and others pulled out the coals, so that none were idle, in hopes of the benefit to come.

The hunger they had, and their desire to eat, caused them to fall to the meat before it was half ready, though it had been over-sodden; the two knights of Wales and Ireland, not intending to dine without bread and drink, searched in a secret hollow cave, where they found two great loaves of bread, as big in compass as the circle of a well, and two great flaggons full of as good wine as ever they tasted, which with great joy and pleasure they brought from the cave, to the exceeding contentment of the other champions. And after they had thus satisfied their hunger, St. George requested the champions to take horse, and mounted himself upon his palfrey; they travelled from thence through a narrow path, which seemed to be used by the giant, and so with great delight they travelled all the rest of that day, till night closed in the beauty of the heavens; at which time they had got to the top of a high mountain, from whence, a little before night, they discovered marvellous great plains, which were inhabited with fair cities and towns, at which sight these Christian champions received great contentment and joy: and so without staying they hastened onward on their journey, till such time as they came to a low valley lying between two running rivers, where, in the midst of the way, they found an image of fine crystal, the picture and lively form of a beautiful virgin, which seemed to be wrought by the hands of some most excellent workman, all bespotted with blood.

And it appeared by the wounds that were cunningly formed

in the same picture, that it was the image of some lady that had suffered torments, as well with terrible cuttings of irons, as cruel whippings; the lady's legs and arms seemed as though they had been wrung with cords, and about the neck, as though she had been forcibly strangled with a napkin. The crystal picture lay upon a richly adorned bed of black cloths, under an arbour of purple roses; by the curious fair-formed image sat a goodly aged man, in a chair of cypress wood; his attire was after the manner of the Arcadian shepherds, not curious but comely, yet of a black and sable colour, a sure sign of some deadly discontentment: his hair hung down below his shoulders, like untwisted silk, in white-ness like down of thistles; his beard over-grown, dangling down as it were frozen icicles upon a hawthorn tree; his face wrinkled and over-worn with age, and his eyes almost blind, bewailing the griefs and sorrows of his heart.

Which strange and woful spectacle, when the Christian champions earnestly beheld, they could not by any means, refrain from the shedding of tears, in seeing before them the picture of a woman of such excellent beauty, which had been oppressed with cruelty; but the pitiful English knight had the greatest compassion when he beheld the counterfeit of this sorrowful heart, he courteously desired the old father, sitting by this woful spectacle, to tell the cause of his sorrow, and discourse of that lady's past fortune, for whose sake he seemed to spend his days in that solitary manner; to whom the old man, with sighs, thus kindly replied:

"Brave knights, to tell you the story of my bitter woes, and the causes of my endless sorrows, will constrain a spring of tears to trickle from the conduits of my aged eyes, and make the mansion of my heart rive in twain, in remembrance of my undeserved miseries; but now Fortune, I see, hath smiled upon me, sending you hither to work just revenge for the inhuman murder of my daughter, whose perfect image lieth here carved in fine crystal, as the continual object of my grief; and that you should understand the true discourse of her timeless tragedy, I have written it down in a paper book, that which my tongue is not able to reveal."

And thereupon he pulled from his bosom a gold-covered book, with silver clasps, and requested St. George to read it to the rest of the knights, to which he willingly condescended; so sitting down amongst the other champions upon the grass, he opened the book, and read over the contents, which contained the sorrowful words following.

CHAPTER VI.

What happened to the Champions after they had found an Image of fine crystal in the form of a murdered maiden; where St. George had a gold book given him, wherein was written the true tragedies of two Sisters. Likewise how the Champions intended a speedy revenge upon the Knight of the Black Castle for the deaths of the two ladies.

"In former time, whilst fortune smiled upon me, I was a wealthy shepherd, dwelling in this unhappy country, not only held in great estimation for my wealth, but also for two fair daughters, whom nature had made most excellent in beauty, in whom I took such exceeding joy and delight, that I accounted them my chief happiness; but yet in the end, that which I thought should most content me, was the occasion of these my endless sorrows.

"My two daughters were endowed with wonderful beauty, accompanied with no less modesty; the fame of whose virtues was much blazed in many parts of the world; by reason of which there came to my cottage divers strange and worthy knights, with wishes to marry with my daughters; but above all, there was one named Leoger, knight of the Black Castle, in distance from this place two hundred leagues, in an island encompassed by the sea.

"This Leoger, I say, was so entangled with the beauty of my daughters, that he desired me to give him one of them in marriage; when I, little mistrusting the treason and cruelty that afterwards followed, but rather considering the great honour that might redound therefrom, for he was a worthy knight as I thought, and of much fortitude, I quickly fulfilled his desire, and granted to him my eldest daughter in marriage; where after Hymen's holy rites were solemnized in great pomp and state, she was conducted, in the company of her newly-wedded lord, to the Black Castle, more like a princess in state, than a shepherd's daughter of such low degree.

"But still I retained in my company the youngest who was more beautiful than her eldest sister; of which this traitorous and unnatural knight was informed, and her surpassing beauty so excelled, that in a short time he forgot his newly-married wife and sweet companion, and wholly gave himself over to my other daughter's love, without considering that he had married her sister. So this inordinate and lustful love kindled and increased in him every day; and he was so troubled with his new desire, that he daily planned with himself by what means he might obtain her, and keep her in despite of all the world. In the end he used this policy and deceit to get her home into his castle: when the time drew on, that my eldest daughter, his wife, should be delivered, he came in great pomp, with a stately train of followers, to my cottage, and certified me that his wife was delivered of a goodly boy, and thereupon requested me, with very fair and loving words, that I would let my daughter go unto her sister, to give her that contentment which she desired, for that she did love her more dearly than her own soul. Thus his crafty and subtle persuasions so much prevailed, that I could not frame an excuse to the contrary, but must needs consent to his demands; so straightway when he had in his power that which his soul so much desired, he presently departed, giving me to understand that he would carry her to his wife, for whose sight she had so much desired, and at whose coming she would receive so much joy and contentment: her sudden departure caused such sorrow in my heart (being the only stay and comfort of my declining age) that the fountains of my eyes rained down a shower of salt tears upon my aged breast, so dear is the love of a father unto his child; but to be short, when this lustful-minded caitiff, with his pompous train, came in sight of the castle, he commanded his followers to ride forwards, that with my daughter he might have private conference. And entering with her into the most private part of a thick wood, he there began to open his evil thoughts to her, persuading her to submit to his wicked desires; but when his fair words and enticing speeches could not prevail, he whipped her tender body, after stripping her to the waist, with the reins of his bridle, in such a cruel manner, that she fainted away. After she had a little recovered herself, he thus expostulated with her:

"'Hadst not thou better consent to my pleasure, than suffer thyself to be tormented? Dost thou think it better to endure this torment, than to live a most loving, sweet, and contented life?'

"And therewith his anger so increased, that he stared in her face with his accursed eyes, so fixed that he could not draw them back. Which being perceived by this distressed virgin, as one far more desirous of death than of life, with a furious voice she said, 'Oh traitor, thou wicked monster, thou utter enemy to all humanity, thou shameless creature, more cruel than the lion-deserts of Hyrcania; thou stain of knighthood, and the bloodiest wretch that ever nature framed in this world! wherein dost thou contemplate thyself? Thou fleshly butcher, thou unmerciful tiger, thou lecherous hog, and dishonour of thy progeny! make an end, I say, of these my torments, for now it is too late to repent thee; gore my unspotted breast with thy bloody weapon, and send my soul into the bosom of Diana, whom I behold sitting in her celestial palace, accompanied with numberless troops of vestal virgins, ready to entertain my bleeding ghost in her pleasant mansion.'

"This merciless knight seeing the stedfastness that she had in the defence of her honour, with a cruel and infernal heart took a silken scarf which the damsel had girded at her waist, and with a brutal anger doubled it about her neck, and pinched it so strait that her soul departed from her body. O you valiant knights, that by your prowess come to the reading of this dismal tragedy, and come to the hearing the lines contained in this gold book, consider the great constancy and purity of this unfortunate maiden, and let the grief thereof move you to take vengeance of this cruelty shown without any desert.

"So when this infernal knight saw that she was dead, he took his horse and rode after his fellows, and in a short time overtook them, and looked so furious and ireful, that none durst be so hard as to ask him where my daughter was; only one of his squires, that bore me great affection for the kindness and courtesy I offered to him at his lady's and my daughter's nuptials, who having suspicion, by the great alteration that appeared in his master, and being very desirous to know what was become of the damsel, because he came without bringing the damsel with him, he then presently drew himself back, and followed the foot-falls of the horse, and ceased not until he came to the place where this cruelty was wrought; whereat he found the maiden dead; at the sight of which he remained almost beside himself, so that he had nearly fallen to the ground. The sorrowful squire remained thus a good while before he could speak; but at last, when he came to himself again he began with a dolorous complaint to cry out against Fortune, because she had suffered such cruelty to this damsel. And making his sorrowful lamentation, he unloosed her from the tree, and laid her upon part of her apparel which he found lying by, all besmeared in blood. He afterwards cut down branches from trees, and gathered grass from the ground to cover her body, left it laying so, that it seemed to be a mountain of green grass, or a thicket of springing trees, and then determined, in the best manner that he could, to let me know of the cruel act. So he took horse and rode the nearest way towards the castle, in which he rode so fast, that he overtook the knight and his company entering the gates, where the wicked tyrant alighted, and without speaking to any person entered into his closet; by reason whereof this kind and courteous squire had time to declare all the things he had seen to the new married lady, and the dolorous end of her sister.

"This sudden and unlooked-for sorrow, mixed with anger and wrath, was such to the lady, that she would not allow the squire to depart from the castle, as occasion served, and to keep all things in secret that he had seen: she remained very sorrowful, making great lamentation to herself in secret, as if she would not be perceived, yet with a soft voice she said:

"'Oh unfortunate lady, born in a sorrowful hour, when some blazing and unlucky comet reigned! O unhappy destinies, that made me wife unto so cruel a knight, whose foul misdeeds have made the very elements blush! but yet I know that Fortune will not be so unkind, but that she will procure strange revenge upon his stained soul. Oh you immortal powers! revenge me on this wicked homicide; if not, I swear that I will with mine own hands perform such an enterprise, and so stain my unspotted heart with wilful murder, that all the Fates above, and all the bright celestial planets, shall sit, and look from their immortal palaces, and tremble at the strength of my hate.'

"This being said, she took in her hand a dagger of the knight's, and in her arms her young son, being of the age of forty days, saying, 'Now do I wish so much evil unto the world, that I will not leave a son of so wicked a father alive; for I will wash my hands in their accursed blood, were they in number as many as king Priam's children.'

"And entering the chamber where the knight her husband was, and finding him tumbling on his bed from one side to the other, without taking any rest, but in his fury rending and tearing the silken ornaments; where, with a sorrowful, weeping, and terrible voice, she called him traitor, and, like a fierce tigress, with the dagger that she brought in her hand before his face she cut the throat of the innocent babe, and threw it to him on the bed, and then said, 'Take, thou traitor, the fruit that thy wicked seed created in my body,' and then she threw the dagger at him also, in hopes of killing him; but fortune would not that it should take effect, for it struck against the tester of the bed and rebounded back unto her hand, which when the lady saw, she turned upon herself with outrageous fury: taking the bloody dagger, she thrust it into her heart so it parted in two, and she fell dead into his arms who was the occasion of all this bloody cruelty. The great sorrow that this false and unhappy king received, was so strong that he knew not what course to take; but thinking upon a severe vengeance that might succeed his cruel acts, he straightway devised that the body of the lady should be secretly buried; which being done by himself, in the darkest time of night, in a solitary garden under the castle wall, he heard a hollow voice, breathe from the deep vaults of the earth this speech:

"'For the bloody act which thou so lately hast committed, thy life draws near to a shameful end; and thy castle, with all thy treasure therein, shall be destroyed, or fall into the hands of him whose daughter thou hast so cruelly murdered.'

"Upon this, he determined to use a secret policy, which was, to set a watch, and guard every passage near to his castle, and to arrest all such travellers as by adventure landed upon that island, not suffering them to pass until such time has they had promised by oath to aid and assist him, even unto death, against all his enemies. In the mean time the aforenamed squire, which had seen and heard all the tragical dealings that have been here declared, in the best way he could, returned again unto my cottage, and told me all that you have heard, which was unto me very sorrowful and heavy news. Judge then, gentle knights, and ye beholders of this woful tragedy, what sorrow I, an unfortunate wretch, sustained, and what anguish I received; for at the hearing thereof I fell into a swoon, and being come again to myself I besmeared my white hairs in dust, that before were as clean as tried silver; and with my tears, the true signs of sorrow, I bathed the bosom of my mother earth, and my sighs passed in such abundance from my tormented heart, that they stayed the passage of my speech, and my tongue could not reveal the grief that my woful thoughts conceived. In silence and sorrow of mind I remained three days and three nights, numbering my silent passions with the minutes of the day, and my nightly griefs with the stars when frost-bearded Winter has clad the elements with sparkling diamonds; but at last, when my griefs were somewhat abated, my eyes requiring some sleep, to mitigate the sorrows of my heart I repaired to a certain meadow near to my cottage, where in the green springing downs I purposed taking some rest, and to lock up the closets of my eyes with slumber, thinking it to be the greatest content my sobbing heart required; but before I could settle my senses to a quiet sleep, I was constrained to breathe this woful lamentation from my oppressed soul:

"'Oh unhappy chance! Oh cruel, and most spiteful Fortune! why didst thou not make me lose this bitter and sorrowful life in my childhood? Or why didst thou not permit and suffer me to be strangled in my mother's womb, or to have perished in my cradle or on my nurse's knee? Then had my heart never felt this sorrow, my ears heard of the murder of my children, nor mine eyes had ever wept so many helpless tears.'

"At the end of this sorrowful lamentation, for want of natural rest, my eyes closed together, and my senses fell into a heavy sleep.

"But as I lay slumbering in the green meadows, I dreamed that there was a great and fierce and wild man, stood before me, with a sharp falchion in his hand, as though he would kill me; whereat I was so frightened, that I gave many shrieks, calling for succour to the empty air. Then methought there appeared before my face a company of courteous knights, who said unto me—Fear not, old man, for we are come from thy daughter to aid and succour thee: but yet for all this the wild man vanished not, but struck with his falchion upon my breast, whereat it seemed to open, and then the wild Centaur put his hand into the wound, and pulled out my bleeding heart; at the same instant, methought that one of the knights likewise laid hold upon my heart, and they strove together with much contention, who should pull it from the other's hands; but in the end each of them remained with a piece in his hand, and my heart parted in two.

"Then the piece which remained in the wild man's keeping turned into a stone, and the piece which remained in the power of the knight was changed into red blood, and so they vanished away. Then after this, there appeared before mine eyes the image of my murdered daughter, in the same form as you behold her pourtrayed; who, with a naked body besmeared in blood, reported unto me the true discourse of her unhappy fortunes, and told me what place and where her body lay in the woods, dishonoured for want of burial: also desiring me not of myself to attempt revenge, for it was impossible, but to entomb her corpse by her mother, and cause the picture of her body to be most lively pourtrayed and wrought in fine crystal, in the same manner that you found it in the woods, and afterwards erected it near unto a common passage, where adventurous knights do usually travel; and assuring me that thither would come some certain Christian champions that should revenge this injury and inhuman murder. Which words being finished, methought she vanished with a grievous and heavy groan, leaving behind her certain drops of blood sprinkled upon the grass: whereat, with great perplexity and sorrow, I awaked out of my dream, bearing it in my grieved mind, not telling it to any one, but with all expedition performed her bleeding soul's request. Where ever since, most courteous and noble knights, I have here lamented her untimely death and my unhappy fortune, spending the time in writing this doleful tragedy in blood-red lines, which I see with great grief you have read in this book of gold. Therefore, most curious knights, if ever honour encouraged you to fight in noble adventures, I now most earnestly entreat you, with your magnanimous fortitude, to assist me to take revenge for the great cruelty that hath been used against my unfortunate daughter."

At the reading of this sorrowful history, St. George with the other champions shed many tears, increasing in them a further desire of revenge; and, being moved with great compassion, they protested by their promises made to the honour of knighthood, to persevere speedily on their vowed revenge and determined purpose: so sealing up a promise to their plighted oaths, protesting that sooner should the lives of all the famous Romans be raised from the dead, from the time of Romulus to Cæsar, and all the rest unto this time, than they be persuaded to return from their promises, and never to travel back into Christendom till they had performed their vows; and thus burning with desire to see the end of this sorrowful adventure, St. George clasped up the blood-written book, and gave it again to the shepherd; and so they proceeded forward towards the island where the knight of the Black Castle had his residence, guided only by the direction of the old man, whose aged limbs seemed so lusty in travelling, that it prognosticated a lucky event: in which journey we will leave the champions for a time, with the wonderful provision that the knight of the Black Castle made in his defence, the success whereof will be the strangest that ever was reported.

CHAPTER VII.

A wonderful and strange adventure that happened to St. George's sons, in the pursuit of their father, by finding certain drops of blood, with virgin's hair scattered in the field; and how they were informed of the injurious dealings of the Knight of the Black Castle against the Queen of Armenia.

MANY and dangerous were the adventures of the three young princes in the pursuit of their father, St. George, and many were the countries, islands, and princes' courts they had searched to obtain a sight of his martial countenance, but all to no purpose, for fortune neither cast them happily upon that coast where he and the famous champions had their residence, nor sounded in their ears the place of his arrival. In which pursuit I pass over many noble adventures these three princes achieved, as well upon the raging ocean as upon the land, and only tell of an accident that happened to them in an island bordered upon the confines of Armenia, near unto the island where the knight of the Black Castle remained, as you heard in the last chapter; upon which coast after they arrived, they travelled in a broad and straight path, until such time as they came to a very large forest, where sundry creeping birds had gathered themselves together, to refresh and shroud themselves from the parching heat of the golden sun, filling the air with the pleasures of their shrill-tuned notes. In this forest they travelled almost two hours: they went up to the top of a small mountain which was near, from which they discovered very fair and well-towered towns, princely palaces, very sumptuous to behold; likewise they discovered from the hill a fair fountain all of marble, like unto a pillar, out of which proceeded four spouts running with water, which fell into a great cistern, and coming to it, they washed their hands, refreshed their faces, and departed.

After they had looked round on every side, towards their right hand, they espied, amongst a number of green trees, a small tent of black cloth, towards which these young princes directed their course with an easy pace; but when they had entered the tent, and saw nobody therein, they remained silent for a while listening if they could hear anything stirring, but they could neither see nor hear any thing, only they found the print of little feet upon the sand, which caused them more earnestly to desire to know whose footsteps these were, for they seemed to be some lady's or damsels's: so finding the track, they followed them, and the more the knights followed, the more the ladies seemed to haste; so long they pursued the track, that at the end they approached a little mountain, where they found scattered about locks of yellow hair, which seemed like threads of gold, and, stooping to gather them up, they saw that some of them were wet with drops of blood, by which they well understood that in great anger they had been pulled from some lady's head: likewise they saw how the earth was spotted with crimson blood. They went up to the top of that little mountain, and having lost the footprints, they recovered them again by gathering up the hair; where they had not travelled far upon the mountain, but towards the water's-side they heard a grievous complaint, which seemed to be the voice of a woman in great distress, and the words which the knights did understand were these:

"O Love! now shalt thou no more rejoice, nor have any longer dominion over me, for Death, I see, is ready to cut my thread of life, and finish these my sorrowful lamentations. How often have I asked vengeance at the hands of Fortune against that wicked wretch who hath caused my banishment, but yet she will not hear my request: how often have I made my sad complaints to Hell, yet have the fatal Furies stopped their ears against my mournful cries." And then she held her peace, giving a sorrowful sigh; which being done, the three Christian knights turned their eyes to the place from whence they heard this complaint, and discovered among certain green trees a lady who was endued with singular beauty, being so excellent that it almost deprived them of their hearts, and captivated their senses in the snares of love, which liberty as yet they had not lost. She had her hair about her ears, which hung down her comely shoulders through the violence she used against herself, and leaning her cheek upon her delicate white hand, that was bespotted with blood, which was occasioned by the scratching of her nails upon her rose-coloured face; by her stood another damsel, which they conjectured to be her daughter, for she was clad in virgin-coloured silk, as white as the lilies of the fields, and as pleasant to see as the glittering moon in a clear winter's night: notwithstanding all this delectable sight, the three princely knights would not discover themselves, but stood closely behind three pine trees which grew near to the mountain, to hear the event of this sad accident; where, as they stood cloaked in silence, they heard her thus confer with her beautiful daughter:

"Oh my Rosana! the unhappy figure of him that without pity hath wounded my heart, and left me comfortless with the greatest cruelty that ever knight or gentleman left lady! how hath it been possible that I have had the power to bring up thee, the child of such a father who hath bereaved me of my liberty! O you sovereign powers, grant that I may establish in my mind the remembrance of the love of thy adulterous father! O girl! born to further grief, here do I desire the guiders of thy fortunes, that thy glittering beauty may have such force and power, whereby the shining beams may take vengeance of the dishonour of thy mother. Give ear, dear child, I say, unto thy dying mother, thou that art born in the dishonour of thy generation, by the loss of my virginity, here do I charge thee, even at the hour of my death, and swear by the band of nature, never to suffer thy beauty to be enjoyed by any one, until thy disloyal father's head be offered up in sacrifice to my grave, thereby somewhat to appease the fury of my discontented soul, and recover part of my former honour.

These and such like words spake the afflicted queen, to the great amazement of the three young knights, who as yet intended not to discover themselves, but still to mark the event, for they conjectured that her woful complaints were the induction of some strange accident. Thus, as they stood obscurely behind the trees, they saw the young and beautiful damsel give unto her dying mother, paper, pen, and ink, which she pulled from her fair bosom, with which the grieved queen subscribed certain sorrowful lines unto him that was the cause of her banishment, and making an end of her writing, they heard her, with a dying breath, speak unto her daughter these sorrowful words:

"Come, daughter, behold thy mother at her last gasp, and imprint my dying request on thy heart, as on a table of brass, that it never may be forgotten; time will not give longer respite, that with words I may show to thee my deep affection, for I feel my death approaching, insomuch that I, a most miserable creature, do feel my soul trembling in my flesh, and my heart quivering at this my last and fatal hour: but one thing, my sweet and tender child, I do desire of thee before I die, which is, that thou wouldest see this letter given to that cruel knight, thy disloyal father, giving him to understand this my troublesome death, the occasion whereof was his unreasonable cruelty."

And making an end of saying this, the miserable queen fell down, not having strength to sit up, and the letter fell out of her hand; which her sorrowful daughter took up, and falling upon her mother's breast, she replied in this sorrowful manner:

"O, my sweet mother, tell me not that you will die, for it adds a torment more grievous unto my soul than the punishment which Danaus's daughters felt in hell; I had rather be torn in pieces by the fury of some merciless monster, or have my heart parted in twain by the hands of him that is my greatest enemy, than remain without your company. Sweet mother, let these my youthful years and this green budding beauty encourage you that you may revive, and not leave me comfortless, like an exile in the world; but if the gloomy Fates do triumph in your death, and abridge your breath of life, and your soul must needs go wander in the Elysian shades, with Trusa's shadow, and with Dido's ghost; here I protest, by the great and tender love I bear you, and by the due obedience that I owe unto your age, either to deliver this your letter into the hand of my unkind father, or with these my rueful fingers to rend my heart asunder; and before I will break my vow, the silver-streamed Tygris shall forsake her course, the sea her tides, and the glittering queen of night her usual changes, neither shall any forgetfulness be an occasion to withdraw my mind from performing your dying requests."

Then this weak queen, whose power and strength were wholly decayed, and her hour of death drew near, with a feeble voice, she said, "O you sacred and immortal gods! and all you bright celestial powers of happiness, into your divine bosoms now do I commend my soul, asking no other vengeance against the cause of my death, but that he may die like me for want of love."

After this, the dying queen never spoke a word more, for at that instant the cruel Destinies gave an end unto her life; but when Rosana perceived her to be dead, and she left in the world devoid of comfort, she began to tear the golden tresses from her head, and furiously to beat her white ivory breast, filling the empty air with clamours of her moans, making the skies echo to her lamentations, and at last taking her mother's letter in her hands, washing it with floods of tears and putting it next to her naked breast, she said "Here lie thou, adjoining my bleeding heart, never be removed until I have

performed my dying mother's testament. Oh works, and the
last work of those her dying hands, here do I swear by the
honour of true a virgin, not to part it from my bosom, until
such time as love has rent the disloyal heart of my unkind
father;" and speaking this, she kissed it a thousand times,
breathing forth sighs, and so with a blushing countenance, as
red as Aurora's glittering beams, she rose, and said to herself,
"What is this, Rosana? Dost thou think to recal thy
mother's life with ceremonious complaints, and not perform that which by her was commanded thee? Arise, I say,
gather unto thyself strength and courage, and wander up and
down the world, till thou hast found thy disloyal father,
as thy true heart hath promised to do."

These words were no sooner finished, but St. George's sons,
like men whose hearts were almost overcome with grief, came
from the pine trees, and discovered themselves to the damsel,
and courteously requested her to discourse of the story of all her
past miseries, and as they were true Christian knights they
promised her, if it lay in their power, to lessen her sorrows,
and give end unto her miseries. Rosana, when she beheld
these courteous and well-demeanoured knights, which in her
conceit carried relenting minds, and considering how kindly
they desired to be partners in her griefs, she stood not upon
curious terms, nor upon excellencies, but most willingly condescended to their requests; so when they had prepared
their ears to entertain her sad and sorrowful discourse, with
a sober countenance, she began in this manner:

"Lately I was, whilst Fortune smiled on me, the only child
and daughter of this lifeless queen, whom you behold lying
dead; and she, before my birth, whilst fortune granted her
prosperity, was the maiden queen of the country called
Armenia, adjoining this unhappy island; who in her young
years, when her beauty began to flourish, and her high renown
to mount upon the wings of Fame, she was so entrapped with
the golden bait of blind Cupid, and so entangled with the
love of a disloyal knight, called the knight of the Black
Castle; who, after he had become her husband, and had
proved his affection by the fruit of lawful wedlock becoming
apparent, he grew weary of her love, and most discourteously
left her as a shame unto her country, and a stain to her
kindred, and afterwards gave himself to a lustful and lascivi-
ous manner of life, he unlawfully married a shepherd's
daughter in a foreign land, and likewise violated her own
sister, and afterwards committed her to a most inhuman
slaughter in a desert wood. This being done, he fortified
himself in his Black Castle, and has consorted with a cunning
necromancer, whose skill in magic has grown so excellent,
that all the knights in the world can never conquer the castle,

where ever since he hath remained, in spite of the whole earth.

"But now I speak of the tragical story of my unhappy mother. When I, her unfortunate babe, began first to struggle in her womb, wherein I wish I had been strangled, she heard news of her knight's bad conduct, who had for ever left her love, never intending to return; the grief whereof so troubled her mind, that she could not in any wise dissemble it; and so being amongst her ladies, calling to remembrance her shame, and the seed of dishonour placed in her womb, she fell into a wonderful trance, as though she had been oppressed with sudden death; which when her ladies and damsels beheld, they presently determined to love her more, and stripping her of her rich ornaments, carried her to her bed, but she made signs with her hands that they should depart and leave her alone, whose commandment was straightway obeyed, not without their great sorrow, for they were dear unto her. This afflicted queen, when she saw that she was alone, began to exclaim against her fortune, and the Fates, with bitter exclamation.

"'O unconstant queen of chance, thou that hast warped such strange webs in my kingdom; thou who gave my honour to that tyrant's pleasure, which without all remorse hath left me comfortless, it is thou that didst constrain me to set my life to sale, and to sell my honour as it were with the cryer, and to do that which hath spotted my princely estate, and stained my bright honour with infamy. Woe is me for purity! that which my parents gave me charge to have respect unto—but I have carelessly kept it, and had small regard to it: I will therefore chastise my body, for thus forgetting myself, and be so revenged for the little regard that I have made of my honour, that it shall be an example to all noble ladies and princes of high estate in the whole world. Oh miserable queen! oh fond and unhappy lady! thy speeches are too foolish; for although thy desperate hand should pull out thy despised heart from thy bleeding breast, yet can it not make satisfaction for thy dishonour. O you clouds, why do you not cast some fiery thunder-bolt down upon my head! Or why doth not the earth gape and swallow my infamous body! Oh false and deceitful lord, I would thy loving and amorous words had never being spoken, nor thy quick sighted-eyes ever gazed upon my beauty! then had I flourished still with glory and renown, and lived a happy virgin.'

"With these and other like lamentations this grieved queen passed away the time from day to day, till pregnancy appeared. At which she received double pain, for that it was impossible to cover or hide it: and seeing herself thus like a woman hated and abhorred, she determined to discover herself publicly unto her subjects, and deliver her body unto them to be sacrificed unto the gods; with this determination one day she caused certain of her nobles to be sent for, who straightway came, according to her commandment; but when she perceived her lords, knights, and gentlemen of honour were come thither before her, she covered herself with a rich robe, and sat up in bed in her private chamber, being so pale and lean, that all they that saw her had great compassion upon her sorrow. Being all sat round about her bed, and keeping silence, she revealed to them the cause of her grief in this manner:

"'My lords, I shame to entitle myself your queen and sovereign, in that I have defamed the honour of my country, and disregarded the welfare of my commonwealth: my glittering crown methinks is shaded with a cloud of dire disgrace, and my princely attire converted into unsound habiliments, in which I have both lost the liberty of my heart, and my wonted joy, and now am I constrained to endure perpetual pain, and an ever-pining death; for I have lost my honour, and reaped nothing but shame and infamy. To conclude, I have foregone the liberty of a queen, and sold myself to a slavish sin. Only mine own is the fault, and mine own shall be the punishment. Therefore, without making any excuse, I surrender up my body into your power, that you may, as an evil queen, sacrifice me unto your gods, for now, my lords, you shall understand, that I am dishonoured by the Knight of the Black Castle; he it is that hath taken away my purity, but with my consent I must confess, and left me, for a testimony of this my evil deed, my pregnancy is plainly apparent. And with this she made an end of her lamentable speech.

"But when those earls, lords, and honourable personages that were present, had understood all the queen had said unto them, like men greatly amazed, they changed their colours, in sign of anger, looking one upon another, without speaking any word, but impressed in their hearts of the fault done by the queen, to the great disgrace of the country; without any further consideration, deprived her of all princely royalty, both of crown and dignity, and pronounced her perpetual banishment from Armenia, like subjects not to be governed by such a defamed princess.

"So when the time arrived, like a woman forlorn and hated of every one, she prepared herself for her appointed banishment. After her departure, the Armenians proceeded to elect another prince, and left their deposed queen wandering in unknown islands, void of succour and relief, where, instead of her princely bed, covered with canopies of silk, she took her nightly repose upon the green grass, shadowed with the sable curtains of the skies; and the nurses that were provided against her delivery were nymphs and fairies dancing in the night by Proserpine's commandment. Though in great grief continued she many days, contenting herself with her appointed banishment, making her lamentations to the whispering winds, which seemed to re-answer her complaints; at length the glittering moon had ten times borrowed light of golden Phœbus, and the night's clear candle was now almost extinguished, by which time approached the hour of her travail; where, without help of a woman, she was delivered of me her unhappy daughter, where ever since I have been nourished in these unfrequented woods, and many times, when I came to years of discretion, my woful mother would discourse unto me this lamentable story of both our miseries, which I have most truly declared unto you.

"Likewise she told me, that many times in my infancy, when she wanted milk in her breasts to nourish me, there would come a lioness, and sometimes a she-bear, and gently give me such, and, contrary to the nature of wild beasts, they would many times sport with me; whereby she conjectured that the immortal powers had preserved me for strange fortune: likewise at my birth nature had pictured upon my breast, the lively form of a purple rose, which as yet doth beautify my bosom with a vermilion colour; and this was the cause that my mother named me Rosana, answerable to my nature's mark. After this, we lived many years in great distress, penury, and want, entreating time to redress our woes more often than we had lived hours; the abundance of our tears might suffice to make watery seas, and our sighs countervail the stars. But at last, the fatal sisters, listening to my mother's moans, and to my great sorrow, deprived her of life; where now I am left a comfortless orphan to the world, until I find some courteous knight that may conduct me to the Black Castle, where my disloyal father hath his residence, that I may there perform my mother's dying will."

These words being finished, Rosana stood silent, for her extreme grief hindered the passage of her tongue, and her eyes rained such a shower of pearled tears upon the lifeless body of her mother, that it constrained St. George's sons to express the like sorrow; where, after they had let fall a few tears from their eyes, and had taken truce for a time with grief, they took Rosana by the hand, and protested never to depart from her company till they had safely conducted her to the Black Castle. Thus after this, when the Christian knights had pitifully bewailed the misery and untimely death of her mother, they took their daggers and digged a grave under a bay-tree, and buried her body therein, that hungry ravens might not seize upon it, nor furious bears tear it in pieces, nor ravenous harpies devour; and after, with the point of their daggers, they engraved this epitaph in the bark of the bay-tree:

> Here lies the body of a hapless queen,
> Whose great good will to her small joy did bring;
> Her willing mind requited was with teen,
> Though she deserve'd, for love, a regal king:
> And, as her corpse enclosed here doth lie,
> Her luckless fate and fame shall never die.

So when they had made this epitaph, and covered her grave with green turf, they departed towards the Black Castle, where we leave them in their travels, and return to the disloyal Leoger, and how he fortified his castle by magic art, according to the learned skill of a cunning necromancer.

CHAPTER VIII.

Of the preparations that the Knight of the Black Castle made by Magic Art to withdraw his enemies; and how the seven Champions entered the castle, where they were enchanted into a deep sleep so long as seven lamps burned; which could be not quenched but by the water of an enchanted Fountain.

THE wicked Leoger, when he grew detested and abhorred in every company, as well by noble as gallant ladies, for the spoil and murder of those three virgins, whose pitiful stories you heard in the two former chapters, and fearing sudden vengeance would fall upon his head, he fortified himself strongly in his castle, and with his treasure hired many furious giants to defend it; wherein if they failed, and should be overcome, he consorted with a wicked necromancer, that he with charms and spells should work wonders in his castle: which magical accomplishments we will pass over till a more convenient time, because I purpose to explain the history in good order to the reader.

First, we will speak of St. George, with the other Christian knights, that came to revenge the shepherd and his unfortunate daughter, who arrived upon the shore of the island where this wicked Leoger and the magician had fortified the Black Castle, in which country the champions, like the invincible followers of Mars, fearing no danger, nor the frowns of inconstant Fortune, betook themselves to the readiest way towards the castle; in which journey they entered into a narrow and straight lane, garnished on both sides with trees of divers sorts, they heard the summer birds recording their pleasant melodies, and making their sweet and accustomed songs without fear of man to molest them. In which row of pleasant trees, there wanted not the green laurel, so much esteemed among learned scholars; nor the sweet myrtle beloved by ladies; nor the high cypress, so much regarded by lovers; nor the stately pine, which for his flourishing height is called the prince of trees: by which they judged it to be an habitation for gods and goddesses rather than a terrestial country, for the golden sun with his glittering beams past through those green and pleasant trees without any hindrance of clouds, for the skies were as clear as tried silver: likewise the western wind did softly shake the shivering leaves, which made a sweet harmony as if they had been celestial cherubims: a thousand little streamed brooks ran upon the enamelled ground, making sundry works by their crooked turnings; and joining one water with another, with a very gentle meeting, made sweet music, that the champions with the pleasure thereof were highly pleased and disregarded whether their horses went right or no; and travelling in this sort, they rode forward till they came to a wide meadow, being of such exceeding fairness, that I am not able with a pen to tell the excellency thereof; where were feeding both wild and tame harts, adorned with great horns: likewise the furious wild boar, the fierce lion, and the simple lamb, were altogether feeding with such great friendship, as by nature they were not enemies.

The noble champions were almost overcome in their own conceits, and amazed in their imaginations, to see such strange love, quite contrary to nature, and that there was no difference between wild beasts and tame. In this manner they travelled along, till they arrived before the buildings of the Black Castle. Below, under the castle, there was an arch with a gate which seemed to be of diamonds, and was encompassed about with a moat or ditch, and almost two hundred paces broad, and every gate had its draw-bridge, all made of red boards, which seemed as though they had been all bathed in blood. After this, the champions rode to the other side of this goodly castle, wondering at the curious workmanship, when they espied a pillar of beautiful jasper-stone, all wrought full of precious stones of strange works, which pillar was of great value, and was garnished with chains of gold, that were made fast unto it by magic art; at which pillar likewise hung a very costly silver trumpet, with certain letters carved about, which contained the words following:

> If any dare attempt this place to see,
> By sounding this, the gate shall open'd be;
> A trumpet here enchain'd by magic art,
> To daunt with fear the proudest champion's heart:
> Look thou for blows that enterest in this gate,
> Return in time, repentance comes too late.

Which when St. George beheld, and had understood the meaning of those mystical letters, without any more tarrying, he set the silver trumpet to his lips, and sounded such a vehement blast, that it seemed to echo in the foundation of the castle; when the principal gate presently opened, and the draw-bridge was let down, without the help of any visible hand, which made the champions wonder, and stand amazed at the strange incident; but yet, intending not to return like cowards daunted with a puff of wind, they alighted from their warlike steeds, and delivered them into the old shepherd's hands, to be fed upon the fragrant and green grass, till they had performed the adventure of the castle, which they vowed either to accomplish or never to return : so locking down their beavers, and drawing their falchions, they entered the gates, and being safe, the champions looked about them to see if they could espy any body, but they saw nothing but a pair of winding stairs, which they descended. They had not gone far before they were enveloped in a thick darkness, that seemed darker than any other worldly place; yet, groping by the walls, they kept going down those narrow and turning stairs, which were very dark, and of such length, that they thought they descended into the middle of the earth.

They spent a long time in descending those stairs, but in the end they came into a very fair and large court, compassed with iron gates like unto a prison, or a place provided to keep untamed lions, when, casting their eyes up to the top of the castle, they beheld the wicked knight walking with the necromancer upon a large gallery, supported with great pillars of brass; likewise they were attended by seven giants, clothed in iron coats, holding in their hands bats of steel: to whom the bold and venturous champion of England spake with an undaunted courage and loud voice in this manner, "Come down, thou wicked knight, thou spoiler of virginity, thou that art environed with monstrous giants, these wonderful works of nature. Come down, I say, from thy brazen gallery, and take to thee thy armour. Thou that hast a heart to commit a virgin's rape, for whose revenge we come; now likewise have courage in thy defence, for we vow never to depart out of thy castle till we have confounded thee, or been by thy force discomfited."

At these words he held his peace, expecting an answer; but the wicked knight, when he heard St. George, began to fret and fume like a starved lion, famished with hunger, even Leoger knight of the Black Castle, raging and threatening fury from his sparkling eyes, and in this manner reanswered the noble champion of England:

"Proud knight, or peasant, whatsoever thou art, I pass not the smallest hair of my head, for thy upbraiding me with thy unruly tongue. I will return thy unruly speeches on thyself, for he pavements of my castle shall be sprinkled with thy cursed blood, and the bones of those thy unhappy followers shall be buried in the sinks of my channels. If thou hadst brought the army of Cæsar, that made all lands to tremble where he came, yet were they but as a blast of wind unto my force. Seest thou not my giants, who stand like oaks upon our brazen gallery? they at my command shall take you from the places where you stand, and throw you over the walls of my castle, so that they shall make you flee into the air more than ten falchions high. And for what thou hast upbraided me with, the disgrace done unto a virgin, I tell thee, if I had thy mother here, of whom thou took first the air of life, my hand should rend her womb, as Nero did in Rome: or if thy wife and children were present before thy face, I would abridge their lives, that thy accursed eyes might be witnesses of their murders: so much wrath and hate rageth in my heart that all the blood in thy body cannot wash it thence."

At these words the giants, whom he hired to defend him from his foes, came unto him very strongly armed, with weapons in their hands, and requested him to be quiet, and to abate his incensed anger, and they would fetch unto his presence all those brave knights that were the occasion of his disquietude and anger; and without tarrying for an answer, they departed down to the court, and left the knight of the castle with the magician standing still upon the gallery to behold the following encounters. But when the giants approached the champions' presence, and saw them so well proportioned and furnished, of such statures, they flourished about their knotty clubs, and purposed not to spend the time in words but in blows.

Then one of the fiercest and cruelest giants of them all (which was called Brandamond) seeing St. George to be most forward in the enterprise, and judging him to be the knight that had so braved his lord, he began with a stern countenance to speak unto him in this manner:

"Art thou that bold knight, that with thy witless words hath so angered the mighty Leoger, the lord of this castle? If thou be, I advise thee by submission to seek to appease his furious wrath before revenge be taken upon thy person, also I charge thee (if thou wilt remain with thy life) that thou dost leave thy armour, and yield thyself, with all thy followers, with their hands bound behind them, and go and ask forgiveness at his feet."

To which St. George, with a smiling countenance, answered: "Giant, thy counsel I do not like, nor thy advice will I receive; but rather do we hope to send thee and all thy followers without tongues to the infernal king of Phlegethon; and for that you shall not have any more time to speak such folly and foolishness, either return your ways from whence you came, and repent of this you have said, or else prepare yourselves to a mortal battle."

The giants, when they heard the champions' resolutions, and how slightly they regarded their proffers, without any longer tarrying they straightway fell upon St. George and his company, intending with their bats of steel to beat them as small as flesh unto the pot: but the queen of chance so smiled upon the Christian champions, that the giants did not prevail, for between them was fought a long and terrible battle, in such danger, that the victory hung waving on both sides, not knowing to whom it would fall; the bats and falchions made such a noise upon each other's armour, that they sounded like to the blows of Cyclops working upon their anvils; and at every blow they gave, fire flew from their steel corslets like sparks from their flaming furnaces in hell; the skies resounded back the echoes of their strokes; the ground shook as though it had been oppressed with an earthquake; the pavement of the court was overspread with an intermixture of blood and sweat, and the walls of the castle were mightily battered with the giants' clubs. By the time that glittering Sol began to decline from the top of heaven, the giants began to faint; whereupon the Christian knights with more courage began to increase in strength, and with such vigour assailed the giants, that before the golden sun had dived to the western world, the giants were quite discomfited and slain: some lay with their hands dismembered from their bodies, weltering in purple gore; some had their brains sprinkled against the walls; some lay with their entrails trailing down in streams of blood; and some jointless, with bodies cut in pieces, so that there was not one left alive to withstand the Christian champions.

Whereupon St. George with the other six knights fell upon their knees, and thanked the Immortal Rector of all good chance for their victory. But when the knight of the Black Castle, who stood upon the gallery during all the time of the encounter, saw how all the giants were slain by the prowess of those strange knights, he raged in great wrath, wishing that the ground might gape and swallow him, before he should be delivered into the hands of his enemies, and presently would have cast himself headlong from the top of the gallery, and dashed out his brains against the pavement, had not the necromancer, who likewise beheld the eventual encounter, intercepted him in his intended drift, promising to perform by art what the giants could not do by force. So the necromancer fell to his magic charms, by which the Christian champions were much troubled and molested, and brought in danger of their lives in a fearful and strange manner, as shall be hereafter shown : for as they stood after their long encounter unbuckling their armour to take the fresh air and dress the bloody wounds received in their last conflict, the magician caused by his art a spirit, in the likeness of a lady of a marvellous and fair beauty, to look through an iron grate, who seemed to lean her face upon her hand very pensively, and shed from her crystal eyes abundance of tears. When the champions saw this beautiful creature, they remained in great admiration, thinking within themselves that by some hard misfortune she was imprisoned. At which this lady seemed to open her fair and crystalline eyes, looking earnestly at St. George; and giving a grievous sigh, she withdrew herself from the grate; whose sudden departure caused the Christian knights to have a great desire to know who it should be, suspecting that by the force of some enchantment they should be overthrown. But casting up their eyes again to see if they could see her, they could not, but they saw, in the very same place, a woman of great and princely stature, who was armed all in silver plates, with a sword girded at her waist, sheathed in a golden scabbard, she had hanging at her neck an ivory bow and a gilt quiver : this lady was of such great beauty, that she seemed almost to exceed the other ; but, in the same sort as the other did, upon a sudden vanished away, leaving the champions no less troubled in their thoughts than they were before. The Christian knights had not long time bewailed the absence of the two ladies, but without seeing any body, they were struck with such furious blows upon their backs, that they were constrained to stoop with one knee upon the ground ; yet in a trice they rose again, and looking then to see who they were that struck them, they perceived them to be the likeness of certain knights, who in great haste seemed to run in at the door that was at one of the corners of the court : and with such great anger that the champions were deceived, seeing themselves so hardly entreated, they followed with their accustomed lightness after the knights, in at the same door ; wherein they had not entered three steps, but that they fell down into a deep cave, which was covered over in such a subtle manner, that whoever trod in it, straightway fell into the cave, except he was advertised thereof before. Within the cave it was as dark as the silent night, and no light at all appeared : but when the champions saw themselves treacherously betrayed, they greatly feared some further mischief would follow, to their overthrow ; so with their swords drawn, they stood ready charged to make their defence against whatever should afterwards happen : but by reason of the great darkness they could not see any thing, neither discover wherein they were fallen, they determined to settle themselves against something, either post, pillar, or wall, and groping about the cave, they searched in every place for some other door, that might bring them from out of the darksome den.

As they went groping and feeling up and down, they found that they stood upon no other things but dead men's bones, which caused them to stand still; and not long after they espied a secret window, at which entered a little light into the den where they were, by which they espied a bed most richly furnished with curtains of silk, and golden pendants, which stood in a secret room of the cave, hung with rich tapestry of a sable colour; which bed when the champions beheld, and being weary of the long fight which they had with the giants in the court of the castle, they required some rest, and desired to sleep upon the bed, but not all at one instant, for they feared some danger to be at hand; and therefore St. George, as one most willing to be their watchman, and keep sentinel in so dangerous a place, to give the other champions their repose upon the bed, he would be as wakeful as the cock against all dangerous accidents; so the six Christian knights repaired to the bed, whereon they were no sooner laid, but presently they fell into a heavy sleep, so that they could not be awaked by any manner of violence. The bed was enchanted by the necromancer's charms in such a manner, that whoever but sat upon the sides, or but touched the furniture of the bed, were presently cast into as heavy a sleep as if they had drunk the juice of owaile or the seed of the poppy. Where we leave them for a time, like men cast into a trance, and speak of the terrible adventure that happened to St. George in the cave, who, little mistrusting their enchantments, stood like a careful guard, keeping the furious wolf from the spoil of the sleeping sheep : but suddenly his heart began to throb, and his hair to stand upright on his head, but having a heart fraught with invincible courage, he purposed not to wake the other knights, but himself to withstand whatever happened; being in these princely cogitations, there appeared to him, as he thought, a magician, with a visage lean, pale, and full of wrinkles, with locks of black hair hanging down to his shoulders, like wreaths of envenomed snakes, his body seemed to have nothing upon it but skin and bones, who spake unto St. George in this spiteful manner:

"In an evil hour, camest thou hither, and so shall thy lodgings be, and thy entertainment worse; for now thou art in a place where thou shalt look for no other thing but to be meat to some furious beast, and thy overcoming strength shall not be able to make any defence."

The English champion, whose heart was oppressed with great wrath, answered: "O false and accursed charmer, may ill chance confound thy condemned arts, and for whom the fiends have prepared a place in hell, what fury hath incensed thee, that with thy false charms thou dost practise so much evil against travelling and adventurous knights? I hope to obtain my liberty in spite of all thy mischief, and with the strength of this arm to break all thy bones asunder."

"All that thou dost or can do, I will suffer at thy hand," replied the necromancer, "only for the revenge that I will take of thee for the slaughter of my master's giants, which yet lie murdered in the court, and that very quickly;" and with that he went out of the cave: so not long after he heard a sudden noise, and beheld as it were a window opening by little and little, whereat there appeared a clear light, by which St. George plainly perceived that the walls were dashed with blood, and likewise that the bones whereon they trod at their first entry into the den were human bodies, which appeared not to be very long since their flesh was torn off; but this consideration could not long affright him, then he heard a great rushing, and looking what it could be, he saw coming from another den a mighty serpent with wings, as large in body as an elephant; she had only two feet, which appeared out of her monstrous body a span in length, and each foot had three claws three spans long; she came with open mouth, of such size and so deformed, that an armed knight, horse and all, might enter in; she had upon her jaws two tusks, which seemed to be as sharp as needles, and all her body was covered with sharp scales of divers colours, with great fury she came with her wings spread. St. George, although he had a valiant and undaunted mind, yet he could not help but be troubled at the sight of such a monstrous beast. But considering with himself, that it was then time to have courage, and to be expert and valiant to make his defence, he took his good sword in his hand, and shielded himself under his hard and strong shield, and waited the coming of the ugly monster. When the furious beast saw that there was a prey whereon she might employ her sharp teeth, she struck with her venomous wings, and with her piercing claw she griped, and laid fast hold upon St. George's hard shield, intending to have swallowed this courageous warrior whole; and fastening her sharp tusks upon his helmet, which she found so hard that she let go her hold, and furiously pulling at his target with great strength she drew it from his arm: with that the English knight struck at her head a strong blow with his sword, but in no wise hurt her by reason of the hard scales wherewith it was covered, and though he gave her no wound, yet for all that she felt the blow and fell to the ground: then this valiant knight made great haste to redouble his force to strike another blow, but all was vain, for upon a sudden she stretched herself so high, that he could not reach her head. But yet kind Fortune so favoured his hand, that he struck her upon the belly, where she had no defence with scales, nor any other thing but feathers, thence issued such abundance of black blood, that it sprinkled all about the den.

This terrible and furious serpent, when she felt herself sorely wounded, struck at St. George such a terrible blow with her tail, that if he had not seen it coming, it had been sufficient to have cut his body in pieces; the knight, to clear himself from the blow, fell flat upon the ground ; for he had no time to make any other defence. Thus, that most terrible blow had no sooner passed over him, but straightway he recovered his feet, in time to see the furious serpent come towards him. Here St. George, having great confidence in his strength, performed such a valiant exploit, that all former adventures that have ever been done by any knight may be put in oblivion, and this kept in perpetual memory. He threw his sword out of his hand, and ran upon the serpent, and caught her between his arms, and so squeezed her, that the furious beast could not help herself with her sharp claws, but only with her wings she beat him on every side. This valiant champion and noble warrior would not let her lose, but still remained holding her between his arms, continuing the perilous and dangerous fight, till all his bright armour was imbrued with her bestial blood, by which occasion she lost a great part of her strength, and was not able long to continue.

Long endured this great and dangerous encounter, and the infernal serpent remained fast unto the noble and valiant breast of the English knight, till such time as he plainly perceived that the monster began to grow faint, and to lose strength. Likewise it could not be otherwise, but St. George waxed somewhat weary, considering the fight he had so lately with the giants. Notwithstanding, when he felt the great weakness of the serpent, he animated himself with courage, and having opportunity, by reason of the quantity of blood that issued from her wounds, he took his trusty sword and thrust it into her heart with such violence, that he clove it in two. So this infernal monster fell dead to the ground, and carried the Christian champion with her, for they were fast together; but by reason of the serpent lacking strength, he quickly cleared himself of her claws, and recovered his sword. When he saw he was clear from the monster, and that she had yielded up her breath into the air, he kneeled down, and gave thanks to the happy queen of chance for his delivery.

After the victory was obtained, and the monster dead, he

grew very weary and faint, and was constrained to sit and cool himself by a well of water, standing in a corner of the cave, from which the monstrous serpent came forth. And when he found himself refreshed, he repaired to the enchanted bed, whereon the six champions lay sleeping, and dreamed of no such strange incident as had happened to him, to whom he purposed to reveal the truth, of all the dangers that had befallen him in that incident.

But no sooner had he approached the enchanted bed, and setting himself down upon one end of it, thinking to discourse, but he fell into a heavy and dead slumber.

There will we leave them sleeping and dreaming upon the enchanted bed, not to be wakened by any means, and return to the necromancer, who was busied all the time of the serpent's encounter, with Leoger, in burying of the dead giants; but he knew by his art that the serpent was slain, and likewise St. George oppressed with a charmed sleep in company of the other champions upon the enchanted bed, from whence he purposed that they never more should awake, but spend the rest of their fortunes in eternal sleep.

Whereupon by his fiendish arts he caused lamps to burn continually before the entry of the cave, the properties of which were so strange, that as long as the lamps continued burning, the champions could never be waked; and the fires never quenched but by the water of an enchanted fountain, which he by magic art had erected in the middle of the court, guarded most strongly with sprites; and the water should never be obtained but by a virgin which at her birth should have the form of a rose lively pictured upon her breast.

These things being performed by the secrets of the magician's skill, added such a pleasure to Leoger's heart, that he thought himself elevated higher than the towers of his dwelling; for he accounted no joy so pleasing unto his soul, as to see his mortal enemies captured into his power, and that the magician had done by his art, more than all the knights in Asia could perform by prowess.

We will now not only leave the champions in their sleep, dreaming of no mishap, but also the magician with Leoger in the Black Castle, spending their time securely, careless of all ensuing danger, and speak now of the old shepherd, whom the champions, at first entering in at the gates of the castle, left to look unto their warlike palfreys, as they fed upon the green grass; which old man, when he could hear no news of the champions' return, he greatly mistrusted their confusion, and that by some treachery they were intercepted in their vowed revenge; therefore he concluded, if that for his sake so many brave champions had lost their lives, never to depart out of those fields, but to spend his days in sorrow. In this deep distress we will likewise leave this old shepherd mourning for the long absence of the English champion, and the other Christian knights.

CHAPTER IX.

How St. George's three sons, after their departure from the Queen of Armenia's sepulchre, in company of her daughter Rosana, met with a wild man, with whom there happened a strange adventure.

THE valiant sons of St. George, to perform their knightly promises, and accomplish what they had protested to Rosana, at her mother's grave, which was, to bring her safely unto the Black Castle, where her unkind father had his residence; first, they provided her a palfrey, which was furnished with black caparisons, in sign of her heavy and discontented mind, and his forehead beautified with a spangled plume of feathers.

Where in her company they travelled day and night from the confines of Armenia, with successful fortune, till they happily arrived upon the island of the Black Castle, where they were constrained to rest themselves many nights under the shadows of green-leaved trees, and instead of delicate fare, they were forced to satisfy their hunger with sweet oranges and ripe pomegranates, that grew very plentifully in that island.

But at last, upon a morning, when the skies appeared in their sight very clear and pleasant, and at such time as the sun began to spread his glittering beams upon the lofty mountains and stately cedars, they set forward on their journey, hoping before the close of day to arrive at the Black Castle, being their long-wished-for haven and desired port. But entering into an unknown way and narrow path, not much used, they were intercepted by a strange and wonderful adventure.

For as they travelled in those untrodden passages, spending the time in pleasant conference, without mistrusting any thing that should happen to them in that pleasant island, upon a sudden not knowing the occasion, their horses started, and rose up with their fore-feet, and turned backward into the air in such a manner, that they had almost unsaddled their masters: whereat the valiant knights suddenly looked round to see who or what it was that caused so much fear; but they perceived nothing, nor could conjecture what was the occasion of such terror, they grew wonderfully troubled in mind. Then one began to encourage the rest, saying, "Believe me, brethren, I much wonder what should be the cause of this alteration in our horses: hath some spirit glided by us? or remaineth some fiend among these bushes? Whatever it be, let us, by the power and favour of all good luck, attempt to know, and with our warlike weapons revenge the fright of our horses, for our minds are not daunted by the prowess of men, nor are we afraid of the fury of demons."

These words being spoken with great courage and majesty, caused Rosana to smile, and to embolden her heart against all ensuing accidents. And now they came up to a river which was both clear and deep, which they judged ran quite through the middle of the island: and so travelling along by the river side, where in a little while their horses began again to start, and to be afraid. Whereupon the knights, casting about their eyes to see if they could perceive what it was that made their horses so timorous, they espied a terrible monster in the shape of a satyr, or wild man, who crossed over the island, of a wonderful great and strange make, who was as big and broad as any giant; for he was almost four-square. His face was three feet in length, he had but one eye, and that was in his forehead, which glittered like a blazing comet or fiery planet; his body was covered all over with long and shaggy hair, and in his breast there was as though it had been glass, out of which there seemed to proceed a great and shining light.

This monster directed his way towards certain rocks which stood in the island, and by reason of the struggling and great noise that the horses made, he cast his head aside, and espied the three knights travelling in company of the lady. Upon whom he had no sooner cast his blazing eye, but with a fiendish fury he ran towards them, and instead of a club, he bore in his hand a great and knotty maple tree.

These valiant knights were not dismayed at the sight of this deformed creature, but against his coming they cheered up their horses, and pricked their sides with their spurs, giving a great shout, as in sign of encouragement; and withal drawing forth their sharp swords, they stood attending the fury of the monster, who came roaring like a bull, and discharging his knotty tree amongst the magnanimous knights, who with light leaps cleared themselves from his violent blows, so that his club fell down to the ground with a terrible fall, as though with the violence it would have overthrown a castle.

With that, the knights alighted from their horses, thinking thereby more nimbly to defend themselves, and more courageously to assail the satyr. Many were the blows on both sides, and dangerous the encounter, without sign of victory to either party.

But St. George's sons so manfully behaved themselves in this encounter, bearing the prowess of their father in mind, that they made very deep wounds in the monster's flesh, and such terrible gashes in his body, the green grass was covered with his black blood, and the ground besmeared and strewed with his mangled flesh.

When the monster felt himself wounded, and saw his blood upon the earth like congealed gore, he fled from them more swift than a whirlwind, or like an arrow forced from a bow, and ran in great haste to the rocks that stood near, where, presently he threw himself into a cave, pulling down after him a rock, which closed up the entry, which was done in such haste, that the knights had not time to strike; but after a while, wondering within themselves to see such a strange and sudden thing, they essayed by strength to remove the stone, and clear the mouth of the cave, which they did not without great difficulty.

Yet for all that, they could not find which way they might enter, but like unto angry lions, fretting and chafing, they went searching around the rock, to see if they could espy any entry, and at last they found a great cleft on the one side of the rock, and looking in, espied the monster lying upon the floor, licking of his wounds with his tongue.

And seeing him, one of the knights said: "O thou traitor and destroyer by the high-ways! O thou infernal fiend and enemy to the world! thou that art the devourer of human flesh, and drinker of man's blood, think not that the strong and fast closing up of thyself in this rock shall avail thee, or that thy devilish body shall escape unslaughtered. No, no, our bloody weapons shall be sheathed in thy bowels, and tear thy heart asunder;" and therewithal they thrust their weapons through the cleft of the rock, and pierced his throat so, that the monster died: which being done, they returned in triumph to Rosana, who they found half dead lying upon her palfrey.

The next morning, by the break of day, they approached the sight of the Black Castle, before whose walls they found seven steeds, feeding in a green pasture, and by them an old man, bearing in his face the true picture of sorrow, and carving in the barks of trees the true subject of all his past grief. This man was the old shepherd whom the Seven Champions of Christendom, before their enchanted sleep in the castle, left without the gates to look after their horses, as you heard before in the last chapter.

But St. George's sons, after they had beheld the manner of the shepherd's silent lamentations, demanded the cause of his grief, and why he remained so near the danger of the castle. To whose demands the courteous old man answered in this manner:

"Brave knights, for you seem to be no less by your princely demeanours, within this castle remaineth a bloody tyrant, and a wicked homicide, called Leoger, whose tyranny and lust hath not only ravished, but murdered, two of my daughters, with whom I was honoured in my younger years; in whose revenge there came with me seven Christian knights, of seven several countries, that entered his accursed castle about seven days since, appointing me to stay without the gates, and to have a vigilant care of their horses, till I heard either news of the tyrant's confusion, or their overthrows. But never since by any means could I learn whether good or bad were befallen them."

These words struck such a terror to their hearts, that for a time they stood speechless, imagining that those seven knights were the Seven Champions of Christendom, in whose pursuit they had travelled so many countries. But at last, when St. George's sons had recovered their speech, one of them (though not intending to reveal what they imagined) said to the old shepherd:

"That likewise they came to be revenged upon that accursed knight, for the spoil of a beauteous and worthy virgin queen, done by the same lust-inflamed tyrant."

Then the lady and the three knights alighted from their horses, and likewise committed them to the keeping of the old shepherd; who courteously received them, and earnestly prayed for their prosperous proceedings.

CHAPTER X.

How St. George's three sons and Rosana entered the Black Castle; where they quenched the lamps, and awakened the Seven Champions of Christendom after they had slept seven days upon an enchanted bed.

THE three knights buckled close their armour, laced on their helmets, and put their shields upon their arms, and in company of Rosana they went to the castle-gate, which glittered against the sun like burnished gold; where hung a mighty copper ring, with which they beat so vehemently against the gate, that it seemed to rattle like a violent storm of thunder.

Then there appeared, looking out of a marble-pillared window, the magician, newly risen from his bed, in a wrought shirt with black silk, and covered with a night-gown of damask velvet; and seeing the knights with the lady standing before the gate, he thus discourteously greeted them.

"You knights of strange countries, for so doth it appear by your strange demeanours, if you desire to have the gates opened, and your bones buried in the vaults of our castle, turn back unto the jasper pillar behind you, and sound the silver trumpet that hangs upon it, so shall your entry be easy, but your coming forth miraculous." And thereupon the magican left the window.

Whereupon one of the knights went unto the jasper pillar, and with a vehement breath sounded the enchanted trumpet, as St. George did before, when the gates flew open in like

manner; without disturbance they entered; and coming to
the same court where the champions had fought with the
giants, they spied the enchanted lamps, which burned before
the entry of the cave where the champions lay upon the
enchanted bed. Under the lamps hung a silver tablet in an
iron chain: on it was written these words:

> The fatal lamps, with their enchanted lights,
> In death's sad sleep have cast seven Christian knights:
> Within this cave they lie with sloth confounded,
> Whose fame but late in every place resounded:
> Except the flaming lamps extinguish'd be,
> Their golden thoughts shall sleep eternally.
>
> A fountain fram'd by Furies rais'd from hell,
> About whose spring doth Fear and Terror dwell.
>
> No earthly water may suffice but this,
> To quench the lamps, where Art commander is;
> No wight alive this water may procure,
> But she that is a virgin chaste and pure,
> And Nature at her birth did so dispose,
> Upon her breast to print a purple rose.

These verses being perused by the three knights, and finding them, as it were, contrived in the manner of a mystical oracle, they could not imagine what they should signify. But Rosana, being of a quick understanding, presently knew that by her the adventures should be finished; and therefore she encouraged them to seek out the enchanted fountain, that by the water thereof the lamps might be quenched, and the seven champions delivered out of captivity.

This importunate desire of Rosana caused the three young knights not to lose any time, but to search in every corner of the castle, till they had found the place where the fountain was. For as they went towards the north side of the court, they espied another little door standing in the wall, and when they came to it they saw that it was all made of very strong iron, with a portal of steel, and in the key-hole thereof was a brazen key, with which they opened it, when they heard a very sad and sorrowful voice breathe forth these words.

"Let no man be so foolhardy, as to enter here; for it is a place of terror and confusion."

In spite of all this they entered, and would not be daunted with any fear, but, like knights of heroical estimation, they went forward: and had no sooner entered, but they saw that it was very dark, and seemed unto them that it was a very large hall, and they heard very fearful howlings, as though there had been a legion of hounds, or that Pluto's dog had been vicegerent of that place. Yet these valiant knights did not lose any of their accustomed courage, nor would the lady leave their company for any danger at all; but they advanced and took off the gauntlets from their left hands, whereon they wore marvellous great and fine diamonds set in rings, that gave so much light that they might plainly see all things that were in the hall, which was very great and wide, and upon the walls were painted the figures of many furious fiends, with other strange visions, framed by magic art, only to terrify the beholders. But looking very circumspectly about them on every side, they espied the enchanted fountain standing directly in the middle of the hall, to which they went with their shields braced on their left arms, and their good swords charged in their right hands, ready to withstand any dangerous incident that might happen.

But coming to the fountain, and offering to fill their helmets with water, there appeared before them a strange and terrible griffin, which seemed to be all of fire, who struck all the three knights, one after another, so that they were forced to recoil. Yet notwithstanding, with discretion they kept themselves upright, and with a wonderful lightness, accompanied with no less anger, they threw their shields at their backs, and taking their swords in both hands, they began most fiercely to assail the griffin with strong blows. Then there appeared before them a whole legion of devils with flesh-hooks in their hands, spitting forth flames of fire, and breathing from their nostrils smoking sulphur and brimstone. In this way tormented they these three valiant knights, whose years although they were but few, yet with great wrath and redoubled force adventured they themselves against this fiendish crew, striking such terrible blows that in spite of them they came to the fountain, and proffered to take off the water; but all in vain, for they were not only put from it by this devilish company, but the water itself glided from their hands.

But during the time of these dangerous encounters, Rosana stood like one bereft of sense, through the terror of the same; but at last, remembering the superscription written in the silver tablet, which the knight perused by the enchanted lamps; the signification of which was, "That the quenching of the lights should be accomplished by a pure virgin that had the lively form of a rose naturally pictured upon her breast;" all which Rosana knew most certainly to be comprehended in herself: therefore, whilst they continued in their dangerous fight, she took up a helmet that was pulled from one of the knight's heads by the furious force of the griffin, and ran unto the fountain, and filled it with water, wherewith she quenched the enchanted lamps, with as much ease as though one had dipped a waxen torch in a mighty river of water.

This was no sooner done and finished, to Rosana's satisfaction, but the skies grew dark, and overspread with a black and thick cloud, and thunderings and lightnings, and such terrible noises, as though the earth would have sunk ; and the longer it endured, the more was the fury thereof : so that the griffin, with all that deluded generation of spirits vanished away, and the knights forsook their encounters, and fell upon their knees, and with great humility they desired in their hearts to be delivered from the fury of that exceeding terrible tempest.

By the sudden alteration of the heavens, the Knight of the Castle knew that the lamps were extinguished, the champions redeemed from their enchanted sleep, the castle yielded to the pleasure of the three knights, and his own life to the fury of their swords, except he preserved it by sudden flight; so he departed from the castle, and secretly fled out of the island unexpected by any one : of whose after fortunes, miseries, and death, you shall hear more.

The necromancer by his art likewise knew that the castle was yielded into his enemies' power, and his charms and magic spells nothing prevailed, therefore he caused two airy spirits, in the likeness of two dragons, to carry him swiftly through the air in an ebony chariot.

Here we likewise will leave him, in his wicked and fiendish attempts and enterprises, because it belongeth to our history now to speak of the seven renowned Champions of Christendom, who by the quenching of the lamps were awaked from their enchantments, wherein they had lain in obscurity for the space of seven days. For when they were risen from their sleep, and had roused up their drowsy spirits, like men newly recovered from a trance, being ashamed of that dishonourable enterprise, they long time gazed on each other's faces, not being able to express their minds, but by blushing looks, being the silent speakers of their extreme sorrows ; at last St. George began to express the extremity of his grief in this manner :

"What is become of you, brave European champions ? where is now your wonted valour, of late so much renowned throughout the world ? what is become of your great strength, which hath bruised enchanted helmets, and quelled the power of mighty multitudes ? what is become of your terrible blows, that have subdued mountains, hewed asunder diamond armours, and brought whole kingdoms under your subjection ? Now I see that all is forgotten, and nothing worth, for that we have buried all our honours, dignities, and fame, in slothful slumbers upon a silken bed."

And with this he fell upon his knees, and said, "Thou art the Guider of all our fortunes, unto thee I invocate and call, and desire thee to help us, and do not permit us to have our fame taken away for this dishonour; and let us merit dignity by our victories, and that our bright renown may ride upon the glorious wings of Fame; whereby babes yet unborn may speak of us, and in time to come fill whole volumes with our princely achievements."

These and such-like speeches pronounced this discontented champion, till such time as the element cleared, and that golden-faced Phœbus glittering with resplendent brightness into the cave through a secret hole, which seemed to dance about the veil of heaven, and to rejoice at their happy delivery.

In this joyful manner returned they up to the court of the castle, with their armours buckled fast unto their bodies, which had not been loosed for seven days before; where they met with the three knights coming to salute them and to give them the courtesies of knighthood.

But when St. George saw his sons, whom he had not seen for two years before, he was so delighted with joy, that he swooned in their bosoms, being not able, to give them his blessing; so great was the pleasure he took at the sight.

Here I leave the joyful greeting between the father and his sons, to those that know the secret love of parents to their children, and what dear affection long absence breedeth. For when they had sufficiently opened the integrity of their souls to each other, and had explained how many dangers every knight and champion had passed since their departure from England, when they began their first intended pilgrimage to Jerusalem, as you heard in the begining of this book, they determined to search the castle, and to find out Leoger, with his associate, the wicked enchanter, that they might receive due punishments for their offences; but they, like wily foxes, were fled from the hunter's traps, and left the empty castle to the spoil of the Christian champions. But when Rosana saw she was frustrated in her purpose, and that she could not perform her mother's will against her disloyal father, she protested by a mother's name, "never to close her cheerful eyes with quiet slumbers, nor even rest her weary limbs on bed of down, but travel up and down the circled earth, till she enjoyed a sight of her disloyal father, whom as yet her eyes had never seen."

Therefore she conjured the champions, by the love and honour that knights bear unto poor distressed ladies, to grant her liberty to depart, and not to hinder her intended travel.

The knights considered with themselves that she was a lady, born under some strange fortune, and one by heaven appointed, who had redeemed them from a wonderful misery: therefore they condescended to her desires; and not only gave her leave to depart, but furnished her with all things belonging to a lady of so brave a mind.

First, they found within the castle an armour fit for a woman, which the enchanter had caused to be made by magic art, of such a singular nature that no weapon could pierce it, and so light in wearing that it weighed no heavier than a tiger's skin. It was contrived after the Amazonian fashion; plated before with silver plates, like the scales of a dolphin, and riveted together with gold nails. So that when she had it upon her back, she seemed like Diana hunting in the forest of transformed Acteon.

Likewise they found standing in the stable, at the east end of the castle, a lusty-limbed steed, big of stature, and a very good air; for the half part forwards was of the colour of a wolf, and the other half all black, saving that here and there it was spotted with little white spots. His feet was cloven, so that he needed not at any time to be shod: his neck was somewhat long, having a little head, with great ears hanging down, like a hound. His pace was with great majesty; and he so doubled his neck, that his mouth touched his breast: there came out of his mouth two great tusks, like unto an elephant. This likewise they gave the lady, which she received with great pleasure. Also the ten Christian knights gave her, at her departure, ten diamond rings, continually to wear upon her fingers, in the remembrance of her courtesy.

This done, without any longer stay, but only to thank them for the great kindness shown unto her in her distress, she leaped into the saddle without the help of stirrup, and rode speedily away from their sight.

After her departure the champions remembered the old shepherd, whom they had almost forgotten through the joy that they had in their happy meetings: he as yet remained without the castle gates, carefully keeping their horses; whom now they caused to come in, and not only gave him the honour due unto his age, but bestowed frankly upon him the state and government of the castle, with stores of jewels, pearls, and treasures, only to be maintained and kept for the relief of poor travellers.

This being performed with their general consents, they spent the rest of the day in banquetting and other pleasant conference of their past adventures: and when the night with her sable clouds had overspread the day's delightful countenance, they betook them to their rest.

CHAPTER XL

How, after the Christian knights were gone to bed in the Black Castle, St. George was awakened from his sleep in the dead time of the night, in a most fearful manner; and likewise how he found a knight lying upon a tomb that stood over a flaming fire.

LONG was the sleep that these princely-minded champions took in the castle, the first part of the night; but between twelve and one, such a strange alteration worked in St. George's thoughts, that he could no longer enjoy the benefit of sweet sleep, but was forced to lie awake, like one disquieted by sudden fear: but as he lay with wakeful eyes, thinking upon his past fortunes, he heard as it were a cry of ravens, beating their fatal wings against the windows of his lodging, by which he imagined some direful accident was near at hand: yet not being frightened with this fearful noise, nor daunted with the croaking of the ravens, he lay still silent, not revealing it to any of the other champions, that lay in the six several beds in the same chamber; but at last, being between sleeping and waking, he heard, as it were, the voice of a sorrowful knight, that constrained these bitter passions from his soul, contained in these words:

"O thou invincible knight of England, thou that art not frightened with this sorrowful dwelling, wherein thou canst see nothing but torments, rise up, I say, from thy sluggish bed, and with thy undaunted courage and strong arm, break the charms of my enchantment."

And therewithal he seemed to give a most terrible groan, and then ceased. This unexpected noise caused St. George to arise from bed, and buckle on his armour, search about the castle to see if he might find the place that harboured the knight that made such sorrowful lamentations.

So going up and down in the castle all the latter part of the night, without finding the adventure of this strange voice, or disturbance by any other means, but that he was hindered from his natural and quiet sleep; by the break of day, when the dark Night began to withdraw her sable curtains, and to give Aurora liberty to display her purple brightness, he entered a four-square parlour, hung round with black cloth, and other mournful habiliments; where on the one side of the same he saw a tomb, covered with black, and upon it lay a man with a pale colour, who at certain times gave most grievous sighs, caused by burning flames that proceeded from under the tomb, being such that it seemed that his body therewith should be converted into coals: the flame thereof was so nauseous that it made St. George retire from the place where he saw that most fearful spectacle.

He lay upon the tomb, casting his eyes aside, espied St.

George, and knowing him to be a human creature, with an afflicted voice he said, "Who art thou, sir knight, that art come into this place of sorrow, where nothing is heard but clamours of fear and terror?"

"Nay, tell me," said St. George, "who thou art, that with so much grief dost demand of me that which I stand in doubt to reveal to thee."

"I am the king of Babylon," answered he, "which, without all consideration, with my cruel hand did pierce through the white and delicate breast of my beloved daughter. Woe be to me, and woe unto my soul therefore: for at once she did pay her offence by death, but I, a most miserable wretch, with many torments do die living."

When this worthy champion, St. George was about to answer him, he saw come forth from the tomb a damsel, who had her hair of a yellow colour, hanging down about her shoulders; and by her face she seemed very strangely afflicted with torments; and in a sorrowful voice she said:

"O unfortunate knight, what dost thou seek in this infernal lodging, where cannot be given thee any other pleasure but mortal torment! and there is but one thing that can clear thee from it, and this cannot be told thee by any but by me; yet I will not express it, except thou wilt grant me one thing, which I will ask of thee."

The English champion, with a sad countenance, stood beholding the sorrowful damsel, and being greatly amazed at the sight which he had seen, answered and said:

"The powers which govern my liberty will do their pleasures; but touching the grant of thy request, I never denied any lawful thing to either lady or gentlewoman, but with all my power and strength I was made to fulfil the same: therefore say what thy pleasure is?" and with that the damsel threw herself into the sepulchre, and with a grievous voice she said: "Now, most courteous knight, perform thy promise; strike but three strokes upon this fatal tomb, and thou shalt deliver us from a world of misery, and make an end of our continual torments."

Then the invincible knight replied: "Whether you be human creatures placed in this sepulchre by enchantment, or furies raised from fiery Acheron to work my confusion, I know not; and there is so little truth of all your past fortunes, that by what means you were brought into this place, and as I am a true knight, and one that fights in the quarrel of Christendom, I vow to accomplish whatever lieth in my power."

Then the damsel began with a sorrowful lamentation to declare as strange a tragedy as ever was told; and lying in the fatal sepulchre, unseen of St. George, with a hollow voice, like a murdered lady whose soul as yet felt the terrible stroke of her death, she repeated the following pitiful tale.

CHAPTER XII.

Of a tragical discourse pronounced by a lady in a tomb, and how her enchantment was finished by St. George.

In famous Babylon reigned a king, who had only one daughter, who was very fair, whose name was Angelica, humble, wise, and chaste; the beloved of a duke, a man cunning in the Black Art. This magician better deserved the government than any other in the kingdom, and was very well esteemed throughout all Babylon, almost equally with the king: for which there engendered in the king's heart, a secret rancour and hatred towards him. The magician cast his love upon the young princess Angelica, which she repaid with the same affection; so that both their hearts being wounded with love, the one to the other, they endured sundry great passions.

"Then Love, which continually seeks occasions, set before this magician a waiting-maid of Angelica's, named Fidelia, which seemed to be wrought by the immortal power of the goddess Venus. Oh in what fear the magician was to discover all his heart, and to bewray the secrets of his love-sick soul! But in the end, by great industry and diligence of the waiting-maid (whose name was answerable unto her mind), there was orders given that these two lovers should meet together.

"This fair Angelica, because she could not at her ease enjoy her true lover, determined to leave her own country and father; and with this intention, being one night with her lover, she cast her arms about his neck, and said:

"'O my sweet and well-beloved friend, seeing my destinies have been so kind to me as to link my heart into thy breast, let no man find in thee ingratitude, for I cannot live except continually I see thee; and do not muse, my lord, at these words, for the entire love that I bear to you constraineth me to make it manifest: and this believe of a certainty that if thy sight be absent from me, it will be an occasion that my heart will lack its vital recreation, and my soul forsake its earthly habitation. You know, my lord, how that the king my father doth bear you no good will, but hates you from his soul; which will occasion our separation: for the which I have determined (if you think well thereof) to leave both my father and native country, and go live with you in a strange land. If you deny me this, you shall very quickly see your loving lady without life. But I know you will not deny me, for in it consists my welfare, and my chief prosperity.' And shedding a few tears, she held her peace.

"The magician, answered and said: My love and sweet mistress, wherefore have you any doubt that I will not fulfil and accomplish your desire in all things? Therefore put out of hand all things in readiness that is your pleasure to have done; for what more benefit or content can I receive, than to enjoy your sight continually, that neither of us may depart from the other's company, till the fatal Destinies give an end to our lives?

"After this, within a few days, the magician by enchantment caused a chariot to be made, that was drawn by flying dragons; into which, without being seen by any one, they put themselves, together with their trusty waiting-maid, and in great secrecy departed out of the king's palace, and took their journey towards the country of Armenia; into which country in a short time they arrived, and came without any misfortune unto a place where deep rivers continually strike upon a rock, upon which stood an old building, which they intended to inhabit, as a most convenient place for their dwelling, that they might, without fear of being found, live peaceably, enjoying each other's love.

"Not far from that place there was a small village, from whence they might have necessary provision for the maintainance of their bodies.

"Great joy and pleasure these two lovers received, when they found themselves in such a place where they might satisfy each other's loves. The magician delighted in nothing but hunting with certain country dwellers that inhabited the village, leaving his sweet Angelica, accompanied with her trusty Fidelia, in the house.

"So they lived together four years, spending their days in great pleasure; but in the end, time (who never rested in one degree) took from them their rest, and repaid them with sorrow and extreme misery. For when the king her father knew she was missing, his sorrow and grief was so much, that he kept his chamber a long time, and would not be comforted by any body.

"Four years passed away in great heaviness, filling the court with echoes of his beloved daughter, and making the skies resound his lamentations. But at last, as he sat in his chair, lamenting her absence with great distress, and being overcharged with grief, he chanced to fall into a troublesome dream; for after quiet sleep had closed up his eyes, he dreamed that he saw his daughter standing upon a rock by the sea-side, offering to cast her body into the waves before she would return to Babylon, and that he beheld her lover, with an army of satyrs and wild men, ready furnished with habiliments of war to pull him from his throne, and deprive him of his kingdom.

"Out of this vision he presently started from his chair, as though he had been frightened with a legion of spirits, and caused four of the chief peers of his land to be sent for, to whom he committed the government of his country, certifying them that he intended taking a voyage to the sepulchre at Memphis, thereby to pacify the fury of his daughter's ghost, whom he dreamed was drowned in the seas, and except he sought by true submission to appease the angry Fates, whom he had offended, he should be deposed from his kingdom.

"None could withdraw him from his determination, though it was to the prejudice of the whole land: therefore within twenty days he furnished himself with all necessaries, as well of armour and martial furniture as of gold and treasure, and so departed from Babylon privately and alone, not suffering any one to bear him company.

"But he travelled not as he told his lords, after any ceremonious order, but like a blood-hound, searching country after country, nation by nation, and kingdom by kingdom, that he might be revenged upon his daughter for her disobedience; and as he travelled, there was no cave, den, wood, or wilderness, which he did not furiously enter, and diligently search for his Angelica.

"At last, by chance he happened to be in Armenia, near unto the place where his daughter had her residence: where, after he had intelligence, by the commons of the country, that she remained in an old ruined building on the top of a rock, without more delay he travelled to the place, at such a time as the magician her husband was gone about his accustomed hunting; coming to the gate, and finding it locked, he knocked so furiously, that he made the noise resound all over the house.

"When Angelica heard the knock, she came to the gate, and with all speed opened it; where she thought to embrace him (thinking it to be her lover), she saw that it was her father, and with a sudden alteration she gave a shriek, and ran with all speed she could back into the house.

"Her father being angry, like a furious lion followed her, saying, 'It doth little avail thee, Angelica, to run away, for that thou shalt die by this revengeful hand, paying me with thy dishonour what my crown hath received by thy flight.'

"So he followed till he came to the chamber where her waiting-maid Fidelia was, who likewise knew the king; upon whose wrathful countenance appeared the image of pale death; and fearing the harm that might happen to her lady, she put herself over the lady's body, and gave several loud shrieks.

"The king, then forgetting the natural love of a father

towards his child, laid hands upon his sword, and said: 'It doth not profit thee, Angelica, to fly from death, for thy desert is such that thou canst not escape it; for mine own arm shall be the killer of my own flesh, and I unnaturally hate that which nature itself commandeth me especially to love.'

"Then Angelica, with a countenance more red than scarlet, answered and said: 'Ah my lord and father! will you be now as cruel unto me, as you had wont to be kind? Appease your wrath, and withdraw your unmerciful sword, hearken unto this which I say, in discharging myself of that you charge me withal. You shall understand, my lord and father, that I was overcome and constrained by love for to love, forgetting all fatherly love and duty towards your majesty: yet for all that, having power to accomplish the same, it was not to your dishonour, in that I live honourably with my husband.' Then the king (with a visage fraught with terrible anger, more like a dragon in the woods of Hyrcania than a man by nature) answered:

"'Thou viperous brat, degenerate from nature's kind! thou wicked traitor to thy generation! what reason hast thou to make this excuse, when thou hast committed a crime that deserves more punishment than human nature can inflict?'

"And saying these words, he lifted up his sword, intending to strike her in the heart, and to bathe his weapon in his own daughter's blood; when Fidelia, being present, gave a terrible shriek, and threw herself upon the body of unhappy Angelica, offering her tender breast to the fury of his sharp sword, only to set at liberty her dear lady and mistress.

"But when the furious king saw her make this defence, he pulled her off by the hair of her head, offering to trample her delicate body under his feet, thereby to make a way, that he might execute his determined purpose without resistance.

"Fidelia, when she saw the king determined to kill his daughter, like a lioness, she hung about his neck, and said: 'Thou monstrous murderer, more cruel than the mad dogs in Egypt, dost thou determine to slaughter the most chaste lady in the world, even she within whose lap untamed lions will come and sleep. Thou art thyself, the occasion of all this evil, and thine only is the fault; for thou thyself art so malicious, and so full of mischief, that she durst not let thee understand her love.'

"These words and tears of Fidelia did little profit to mollify the king's heart, who, rather like a wild boar in the wilderness being surrounded with a company of dogs, most irefully trembled, and threw Fidelia from him, so that he had almost dashed her brains against the chamber walls; and with double wrath he proceeded to execute his fury. Fidelia with terrible shrieks sought to hinder him, till such time as with his cruel hand he thrust his sword into her lady's breast, so that it came out at her back, whereby her soul was forced to leave her body.

"The wrathful king, when he beheld his daughter's blood sprinkled about the chamber, and that by his own hands it was committed, he repented himself of the deed, and cursed the hour wherein the first motive of such a crime entered his mind, wishing the hand that did it ever after might be lame, and the heart that contrived it to be plagued with more extremities than was miserable Œdipus.

"In this manner the unfortunate king repented of his daughter's bloody tragedy, with this determination, not to stay till the magician returned from his hunting exercise, but to exclude himself from the company of men, and to spend the remnant of his life among untamed beasts in some wilderness. Upon this resolution he departed to his chamber, and said; 'Farewell thou lifeless body of my Angelica; and may thy blood, which I may have spilt, crave vengeance of the Fates against my guilty soul; for my earthly body shall endure a miserable punishment.'

"Fidelia, after the departure of the king, used such fury against herself, both by rending her hair, and tearing her face with her nails, that she seemed rather an infernal fury, subject to wrath, than an earthly creature furnished with clemency. She sat over Angelica's body, wiping her bleeding breast with a damask scarf, which she had pulled from her waist, and bathing her dead body in tears, which forcibly ran down from her eyes like an overflowing fountain.

"In this woful manner spent the sorrowful Fidelia that unhappy day, till bright Phœbus went into the eastern part of the horizon. At which time the magician returned from his accustomed hunting, and finding the door open, he entered into Angelica's chamber, where, when he found her body weltering in congealed blood, and beheld how Fidelia sat weeping over her bleeding wounds, he cursed himself, for he accounted his negligence the occasion of her death, in that he had not left her in more safety. But when Fidelia had certified him, how that by the hands of her own father she was slaughtered, he began like a frantic tyrant to rage against Destiny, and to fill the air with terrible exclamations.

"'Oh cruel murderer!' said he, 'crept from the bowels of some untamed tiger; I will be so revenged upon thee, O unnatural king, that all ages shall wonder at thy misery. And likewise thou unhappy virgin, shalt endure like punishment, in that thy accursed tongue hath noised this fatal deed in my ears; the one for committing the crime, and the other for reporting it. For I will cast such deserved vengeance upon your heads, and place your bodies in such continual torments, that you shall lament my lady's death, leaving alive the fame of her with your lamentations.'

"And saying these words, he drew a book out of his breast, and reading certain charms and enchantments, that were therein contained, he made a great and very black cloud appear in the skies, which was brought by terrible high winds, in which he took them up both, and brought them into the enchanted castle, where ever since they have remained in this tomb cruelly tormented with unquenchable fire, and must for ever continue in the same extremity, except some courteous knight will vouchsafe to give but three blows upon the tomb, and break the enchantment.

"Thus have you heard, magnanimous knight, the true discourse of my unhappy fortune. And the virgin which for the true love she bore unto her lady was committed to this torment is myself, and this pale body lying upon the tomb is the unhappy Babylonian king, who unnaturally murdered his own daughter; and the magician who committed all these villanies is that accursed wretch, which by his charms and fiendish enchantments hath so strongly withstood your encounters."

These words were no sooner finished, but St. George drew out his sharp sword, and gave three blows upon the enchanted tomb; when presently appeared the Babylonian king standing before him, attired in rich robes, with an imperial diadem upon his head, and that lady standing by him, with a countenance more beautiful than damask rose.

When St. George beheld them, he was not able to speak for joy, nor to utter his mind, so great was the pleasure that he took in the sights; without any longer ceremony, he led them into the chamber, where he found the other knights newly risen from their beds; to whom he revealed the true nature of the adventure, and by what means he had redeemed the king and lady from their enchantments; which was as great joy as before it was to St. George.

So, after they had for six days refreshed themselves in the castle, they all intended to accompany the Babylonian king to his country, and to place him again in his kingdom.

CHAPTER XIII.

How the Knight of the Black Castle, after conquest of the same by the Christian Champions, wandered up and down the world in great terror of conscience; and after how he was found in a wood by his own daughter, in whose presence he desperately slew himself.

THE Christian champions had slain the seven giants in the enchanted castle, and had made conquest thereof. Disloyal Leoger, being the lord of the same, secretly fled, not for anger at the loss, but for the preservation of his life. In grief and terror of conscience he wandered, like a fugitive, up and down the world; sometimes remembering his past prosperity, at other times thinking upon the rapes he had committed, how disloyally in former times he had left the queen of Armenia, with the stain of dishonour and the curse of her lost reputation. Sometimes his guilty mind imagined that the bleeding ghosts of the two sisters, whom he both defiled and murdered, followed him up and down, haunting him with fearful exclamations, and filling each corner of the earth with clamours of revenge. Such fear and terror raged in his soul, that he thought all places where he travelled were filled with multitudes of knights, and that the strength of countries pursued him to heap vengeance upon his guilty head for those wronged ladies; whereby he cursed the hour of his birth, and blamed the cause of his creation, wishing the Fates to consume his body with a fire, or that the earth would gape and swallow him.

In this manner he travelled up and down, filling all places with echoes of his sorrow and grief; which brought him to such a perplexity, that many times he would have slain himself, and have rid himself from a world of miseries.

But it happened that one morning very early, by the first light of Titan's golden torch, he entered a narrow and straight path, which conducted him into a very thick and solitary forest; where with much sorrow he travelled till such time as glittering Phœbus had passed the half way of his journey: and being weary with the long road, and the great weight of his armour, he was forced to take rest and ease under some green myrtle trees; whose leaves shadowed a very fair and clear fountain, the stream of which made a bubbling murmur on the pebbles: and down upon the green grass, he closed his eyes, in hopes to repose himself in a quiet sleep, and to abandon his discontented thoughts: in which silent contemplations we will leave him for a while, and return to Rosana, the queen's daughter of Armenia, whom you remember likewise departed from the Black Castle in the pursuit of her disloyal father, whom she never in her life beheld.

This courteous lady travelled in many strange countries with weary steps, yet never could she meet with her unkind father, unto whom she was commanded to give her mother's letter; neither could she hear, in any place where she came where she might find him. In her travels she met with strange adventures, which ended to her great honour: still she wandered over hills and dales, mountains and valleys, through many solitary woods, till at last she came to the wilderness where this discontented king lay sleeping upon the grass; near to which place she likewise reposed herself under the branches of a chesnut tree, wishing to take rest after a long travel.

But suddenly being awaked, she heard a very dolorous groan, as it were of some sorrowful knight, which was so terrible, heavy, and bitter, that it made her give an attentive ear to the sound, and see if she could hear and understand what it could be; without making the least noise, she arose, and went towards the place, where she might see who it was; and there she beheld a knight, well armed, lying upon the grass, under a green myrtle tree. His armour was all russet, and full of bars of black steel, which showed a very sad, sorrowful, and heavy enamelling, agreeable to the sadness of the heart. He was of big stature in body, and well proportioned, and seemed by his disposition to be in great grief. Where, after she had awhile stood in secret, beholding his sorrowful countenance, in a woful manner he tumbled his restless body upon the grass, and with a sad and heavy look he breathed forth his lamentation:

"Oh heavy and perverse Fortune, why dost thou cause me, so vile and cruel a wretch, to breathe so long upon the earth; upon whose wicked head the sun disdains to shine, and the glittering elements deny their cheerful light! O that some ravenous harpy would come from his den, and make his loathsome bowels my fatal tomb; or that my eyes were sightless, like the miserable king of Thebes', that I never might again behold this earth, whereon I have long lived and committed so many cruelties. I am confounded with the curse of sad mischance, for wronging that maiden queen of Armenia, in the spoil of whose purity I made a triumphant conquest. Where was thine understanding, when thou forsook that gracious princess, who not only yielded to thee her liberty, love, and honour, but therewith a kingdom and a golden diadem? And therefore woe unto me, traitor! may more woes fall upon my soul than there are hairs upon my head! and may the sorrows of old Priam be my last punishment! What doth it profit me to fill the air with lamentations, when that the crime is already past, without all remedy or hope of comfort?" This being said, he gave a terrible sigh, and so held his peace.

Rosana, by sorrowful lamentations, knew him to be her disloyal father, whom she had so long travelled to find out: but when she remembered how his unfaithfulness and unkindness were the death of her mother, she felt such extreme pain and sorrow, that she was constrained to fall to the ground.

But yet her courageous heart could not let her remain long in that position, but straightway she rose again upon her feet, with a desire to perform her mother's will, yet not intending to discover her name, nor to reveal to him that she was his daughter. So with this thought and determination she went to the place where Leoger was; who when he heard the noise of her coming, straightway started upon his feet.

Then Rosana saluted him with a voice somewhat heavy, and Leoger returned the salutation with no less show of grace.

Then the Amazonian lady took the letter from her breast, where she had kept it, and delivered it into his hands, and said:

"Art thou that forgetful and disloyal knight, who left the unfortunate queen of Armenia, in such great pain and sorrow, among those unmerciful tyrants her countrymen, who banished her from her country, in revenge of thy crime where ever since she had been companion with wild beasts, that their natures have lamented her banishment?"

Leoger, when he heard these words, began to look at her; and though his eyes were blubbered with weeping, yet he earnestly gazed in her face, and answered her in this manner:

"I will not deny thee, gentle Amazonian, that which the very clouds do blush at, and the earth mourns for. Thou shalt understand that I am the same knight whom thou hast demanded: tell me what is thy will."

"My will is, thou most ungrateful knight, that thou read here this letter, the last work of the white hand of the unhappy Armenian queen."

At which words the knight was so troubled in thought, and grieved in mind, that it almost occasioned his death; and putting forth his hand, somewhat tremblingly, he took the letter, and sat down very sorrowful upon the green grass, without any power to the contrary, his grief so exceeded the bounds of reason

No sooner had he opened the letter but he knew it to be written by the wronged lady, the Armenian queen; and with great alteration both of heart and mind he read the same. But when he had read it, he could not refrain from tears, so great was the grief that his heart sustained. Rosana did likewise bear him company, to solemnize his heaviness, with as many tears trickling from the conduits of her eyes.

Their great sorrow and lamentation were such, that for a long time, the one could not speak unto the other; but afterwards, their griefs being somewhat extenuated, Leoger began to say:

"O messenger from her, with the remembrance of whose wrong my heart is wounded, being undeservedly of me evil rewarded, tell me (even by the nature of true love) if thou dost know where she is: show to me her abiding place, that I may go, and give a discharge of this my great fault by yielding unto death."

"O cruel and without love," answered Rosana, "what

discharge canst thou give unto her that already, through thy cruelty, is dead and buried, only by the occasion of such a forsworn knight?"

This penitent and grieved knight, when he understood the certainty of her death, with a sudden and hasty fury struck himself on the breast with his fist; and lifting his eyes unto the clouds, in manner of exclamation against the Fates, giving sorrowful sighs, he threw himself to the ground; tumbling and wallowing from one side to the other, without taking any ease, or having any power or strength to declare the inward grief which at that time he felt; but with lamentation, which did torment his heart, he called continually on the Armenian queen; and in the fury wherein he was, drew out his dagger, and lifting up the skirt of his coat of mail, he thrust it into his body, and calling upon his wronged lady he finished his life, and fell to the ground.

This sad and heavy lady, when she beheld him so desperately pierce his martial breast, and fall lifeless to the earth, she repented herself that she had not discovered her name, and revealed to him how that she was his unfortunate daughter, whose face before that time he had never beheld; and as a lion who seeing before her a young lioness hard pressed by the hunter, she ran to her murdered father, and with great speed pulled off his helmet, and unbraced his armour, which was in colour to his passion, but as strong as any diamond, made by magic art. She took away his shield, which had on it a russet flag, and in the midst thereof was pourtrayed the god of love with two faces; the one was very fair and bound with a cloth about his eyes, and the other was made fierce and furious. This being done, with a fair linen cloth she wiped off the blood from his wounded body. And when she was certain that it was he for whom she had travelled so far, and that he was dead, with a furious madness she tore her hair, and then returned again and wiped his bleeding body; making such sorrowful lamentation, that whoever had seen her would have been moved with compassion.

Then she took his head between her hands, striving to lift it up, and lay it upon her lap; but seeing, for all, that there was no moving him, she joined her face to his pale cheeks, and with sorrowful words she said:

"Dear father, open thine eyes and behold me; open them, sweet father, and look upon me, thy sorrowful daughter. If Fortune be so favourable, let me receive some contentment whilst life remaineth. O strengthen thyself to look upon me, that such delight may come to me that we may one accompany the other. Oh my lord and only father, seeing that in former times my unfortunate mother's tears were not sufficient to reclaim thee, give satisfaction for the great travail which I have taken in seeking thee out. Come now in death, and rejoice in the sight of thy unhappy daughter, and die not without seeing her: open thine eyes, that she may gratify thee in dying with thee."

This being said, Rosana began to wipe his body, for it was all bathed in blood, and felt his eyes and mouth, and his face and head, till such time as she touched his breast, and put her hand on the mortal wound, where she held it still, and looked upon him whether he moved or no.

At length she perceived his dim eyes open; and his senses now a little gathered; and when he saw himself in her arms, and understood by her words that she was his daughter, whom he had by the unfortunate queen of Armenia, he suddenly strove against weakness: he cast his arms about the neck of the fair Rosana; and then, with a feeble and weak voice, the wounded knight said:

"O my daughter, unfortunate by my disloyalty! I do confess that I have been pitiless unto thy mother, and unkind to thee; thou hast travelled with great sorrow in search of me; and now thou hast found me, I must leave thee alone in this sorrowful place. Yet before my death, sweet girl, give me a few gentle kisses. This only delight I crave for the little time I have to tarry; and afterwards I desire thee to entomb my body in thy mother's grave, though it be far in distance from this unlucky country."

"O my dear lord," answered she, "do you request me to give your body a sepulchre? I think it more requisite to seek some one to give it unto us both: for I know my life cannot continue long, if the angry Fates deprive me of your company." And without strength to proceed anything further, she kissed his face with many sighs; and having a terrible conflict within she tarried for the answer of her dying father, who, with pain and great anguish of death, said:

"Oh my child, how happy should I be, that thus embracing one in the other's arms we might depart together. Then should I be joyful in thy company, and account myself happy in my death. But, alas! I must leave thee to the world! Daughter, farewell! Good Fortune preserve thee; and for ever may she take thee to her favour." And when he had said this, inclining his neck upon the face of Rosana, he died. Which when this sorrowful lady saw, she kissed his pale lips; and giving sorrowful sighs, she began a most heavy lamentation, calling herself unhappy and unfortunate, and laid herself upon the dead body, cursing her destinies, so that it was lamentable to hear her.

At length, remembering the promise that she made him, which was to bury him in her mother's tomb; on which occasion she did somewhat cease her lamentation; and taking to herself more courage than her sorrowful grief would consent to, she put the body under a broad pine-apple tree, and covered it with leaves and green grass, and hung his armour upon the boughs, in hope that the sight thereof would cause some adventurous knight to approach her presence, that in kindness would assist her to entomb him. This done, here we will leave Rosana weeping over her father's body, and speak of the necromancer after his flight from the Black Castle.

CHAPTER XIV.

How the magician found Leoger's armour hanging upon a pine-tree, kept by Rosana the queen's daughter of Armenia, between whom happened a terrible battle; also of the desperate death of the lady.

I AM sure you well remember, when the Christian knights conquered the Black Castle, which was kept by enchantment, how the furious necromancer, to preserve his life, fled from the same, carried by his art through the air in an iron chariot drawn by two flying dragons; in which he crossed over many parts of the eastern countries.

At last, being weary of his journey, he put himself into the thickest part of a forest, wherein he never rested till he came to a broad river. There he alighted from his chariot to refresh himself. And as he found himself alone, there came into his mind many thoughts of his past life, and how he was vanquished by the Christian knights; for which with great anger he gave terrible sighs, and began to curse, not only the hour of his birth, but the whole world, and all the generations of mankind.

Likewise he remembered the sorrow and travail that he had ever since endured, and what toil travelling knights do endure. In these variable cogitations spent he the time away, till night came on. All that night passed away with such sorrowful lamentations for his late disgrace, that the woods and mountains resounded his woful exclamations, till Sol, with his glittering beams began again to cover the earth. Which being seen by the magician, he arose up, intending to prosecute his journey; but lifting up his eyes towards the elements, he discovered hanging upon a high pine-apple tree the armour of Leoger.

This armour was hung there by Rosana, in the remembrance of his death, as you heard in the last chapter. And though it had almost lost its wonted colour, and begun to rust, through the abundance of rain that had fallen thereon, yet for all that it seemed of a great value and of a wonderful richness. So without further circumspection or regard, he took down the knight's armour, and armed himself therewith;

and when he had lacked no more to put on but the helmet, he heard a voice that said:

"Be not so hardy, thou knight, as to undo this trophy, except thou prepare thyself to win it by the sword."

The magician at this unexpected noise cast his head on one side, and espied Rosana newly awaked from a heavy sleep, most richly armed with a strong enchanted armour, after the manner of the Amazonians; but for all that, he made an end of arming himself; and having laced on his burgonet, he went towards the demander, with his sword ready drawn in his hand, inviting her to a mortal battle.

Rosana, who saw his determination, prepared to defend herself and offend her enemy.

The valiant Amazonian, when her enemy came unto her, struck him so terrible a blow upon the visor of his helmet, that the fury thereof made sparkles of fire to fly out in great abundance, and forced him to bow his head unto his breast. The magician returned her his salutation, and struck her such a blow upon her helmet, that with the great noise thereof it made a sound in all the mountains; and so began between them a fearful battle. Fortune, not willing to use her utmost extremity, inclined the foil to neither party, nor yet gave the conquest to any. All the time of the conflict, the furious magician and the valiant Amazonian thought on no other thing, but either of them endeavoured to bring the other to an overthrow, striking such terrible blows, and with such fury, that it made either of them senseless: and both seeing the great force one of the other, were greatly incensed with anger.

Then the valiant lady threw her shield at her back, that with more force she might strike and hurt her enemy; and then she gave him so strong a blow upon the helmet, that he fell to the earth quite stunned.

But when the magician came again to himself, he returned Rosana such a terrible blow, that if it had chanced to hit right upon her, it would have cloven her head in pieces; but with great discretion she cleared her head, so that it was struck in vain; and with great lightness she retired, and struck the magician so furiously, that she made him once again fall senseless, and there appeared at the visor of his helmet abundance of blood, that issued from his mouth; but presently he revived and got up with great anger.

Then the furious necromancer, blaspheming against his mishap, having his sharp sword very fast in his hand, ran towards his enemy, who, without any fear of his fury, advanced to receive him; and when they met together, they discharged their blows at once: but it happened that the Amazonian's blow did first fasten, with such great strength,

P

that for all the helmet of the magician, which was wrought of the strongest steel, it was not sufficient to make defence, but the force wherewith it was charged, bent it in, so that it brake in pieces; and the magician's head was so sorely wounded, that streams of blood ran down his armour, and he was forced to yield to the mercy of the valiant lady; who quickly condescended to his request, upon this condition, that he would be a means to convey her father's dead body to an island near adjoining the borders of Armenia, and there entomb it in her mother's grave, as she promised when that his air of life fleeted from his body.

The magician, for safety of his life, presently agreed to perform her desires, and accomplish whatever she demanded.

Then by his art he prepared his iron chariot, with his flying dragons in readiness; wherein he laid the murdered body of Leoger, and placing themselves in; they were no sooner entered, with necessaries belonging to their travels, but they fled through the air more swift than a whirlwind, or a ship sailing on the seas in a tempest.

Thus was Rosana, with her father's dead body, carried through the air by magic art, over hills and dales, mountains and valleys, woods and forests, towns and cities, and through many wonderful and strange places and countries.

At last they arrived near unto the confines of Armenia, being the place of their long desired rest. But when they approached unto the queen of Armenia's grave, they descended from the enchanted chariot, and bore Leoger's body to his burying-place, which they found overgrown with moss and withered brambles: for all that, they opened the sepulchre, and laid his body near the lady, the magician covered the grave again with earth, and laid thereon green turfs, which made it as though it had never been opened.

All the time the magician was performing the ceremonious funeral, Rosana watered the earth with her tears, never withdrawing her eyes from the grave; and when it was finished, she took a naked sword, which she had ready for the purpose, and putting the pummel to the ground, cast her breast upon the point; which she did with such furious violence, that the magician could not prevent her committing so bloody an act.

This sudden suicide so amazed him, that for a time, he could not speak one word to express his passion. But he took up the dead body of Rosana, bathed all in blood, and likewise buried her in her parent's grave; and over the same hung an epitaph, that declared the occasion of their deaths.

This being done, to express the sorrows of his heart for the desperate death of such a magnanimous lady, and to exempt himself from the company of all human creatures, he erected over the grave, by magic art, a stately tomb, which was in this order framed:—First, there were fixed four pillars, every one of a very fine ruby; upon which was placed a sepulchre of crystal. Within the sepulchre there seemed to be two fair ladies; the one having her breast pierced through with a sword; and the other with a crown of gold upon her head, and so lean of body that she seemed to pine away. And upon the sepulchre there lay a knight with his face looking up to the heavens, and armed in a corslet of fine steel, of a russet enamelling. Under the sepulchre there was spread a great carpet of gold, and upon it two pillars of the same; and between them lay an old shepherd, and his sheep-hook lying at his feet: his eyes were shut, and out of them were distilled many pearly tears. At either pillar there was a gentlewoman of a comely feature; one of them seemed to be murdered, and the other defiled. And near unto the sepulchre, there lay a great beast, like a lion, his breast and body like a wolf, and his tail like a scorpion; which seemed to spit continually flames of fire. The sepulchre was compassed about with a wall of iron, with four gates for to enter in thereat: the gates were after the manner and colour of fine diamonds; and directly over the top of the chief gate stood a marble pillar, whereon hung a table written with red letters, the contents whereof were as follow:

> So long shall breathe upon this brutal earth,
> The framer of this stately monument,
> Till that three children of a wond'rous birth,
> Out of a northern climate shall be sent:
> They shall obscure his name, as Fates agree,
> And by his fall the fiends shall tamed be.

This monument was no sooner framed, but the necromancer enclosed himself within the walls; where he consorted chiefly with furious evil spirits, that continually fed upon his blood, and their execrable seals sticking upon his left side, as a sure token and witness that he had given both his soul and body to their governments after the date of his mortal life was finished.

In which enchanted sepulchre we will leave him for a time, conferring with his infamous mates, and return to the Christian knights, where we left them travelling towards Babylon, to place the king again in his kingdom.

CHAPTER XV.

How the Seven Champions of Christendom restored the Babylonian king unto his kingdom; and after how honourably they were received at Rome, where St. George fell in love with the Emperor's daughter.

THE valiant Christian champions having, as you heard before, performed the adventure of the enchanted monument, accompanied the Babylonian king to his kingdom of Assyria, as they had solemnly promised him.

But when they approached the confines of Babylon, and made no question of princely entertainment, there was neither sign of peace nor likelihood of joyful and friendly welcome, for all the country raged with intestine war, four several competitors unjustly striking for what unto the king properly and rightfully belonged.

The unnatural causers and stirrers-up to this blood-devouring controversy were four noblemen, unto whom the king unadvisedly committed the government of his realm, when he went in the tragical pursuit of his fair daughter, after his dreamy illusion, that caused him so cruelly to seek her death.

Two years after the king's departure these deputies governed the public state in great peace, and with prudent policy, till no tidings of the king could be heard, notwithstanding so many messengers as were in every quarter of the world sent to inquire after him : then did ambition kindle in all their hearts, each striving to take into his hand the sole possession of the Babylonian kingdom. To this end they all made several friends; for this had they contended in many fights; and now, they intended to set all their hopes upon this main chance of war, intending to fight till three fell, and one remained victor over the rest; whose head should be beautified with a crown.

But to traitors and treason the end is sudden and shameful; for no sooner had St. George (placing himself between the battles) in a brief oration showed the adventures of the king, and he himself to the people discovered his reverend face, but they all shouted for joy; and hailing the usurpers presently to death, they reinstalled him in the ancient dignity, their true, lawful, and long-looked-for king.

The king being thus restored, married Fidelia for her faithfulness; and after the nuptial feasts, the champions (at the earnest request of St. Anthony) departed towards Italy; where, in Rome, the emperor spared no cost, honourably and most sumptuously to entertain those never-daunted knights, the famous wonders of Christendom.

At that time of the year when the summer's queen had beautified the earth with interchangeable ornaments, St. George (in company of the emperor, with the rest of the champions) chanced to walk along by the side of the river Tiber, to delight themselves with the pleasant meads and beautiful prospect of the country. Before they had walked half a mile from the city, they approached an ancient nunnery, which was a stately building, and likewise encompassed about with crystal streams and many green meadows, furnished with all manner of beautiful trees and fragrant flowers.

This nunnery was consecrated to Diana, the queen of chastity, and none were suffered to live therein but such chaste ladies and virgins as had vowed themselves to a single life. In this place the emperor's only daughter lived as a professed nun, and exempted herself from all company, except it were the fellowship of chaste and religious virgins.

This virtuous Lucina (for so was she called) having intelligence before, by the overseers of the nunnery, that the emperor her father, with many other knights, were coming to visit her religious habitation, against their approach she attired herself in a gown of white satin, all laid over with gold lace, having also her golden locks of hair somewhat laid forth: and upon her head was knit a garland of sweet-smelling flowers. Her beauty was so excellent, that it might have quailed the heart of Cupid, and her bravery exceeded the Paphian queen's. Never could Nature, with all her cunning, bestow more beauty on any one creature, than was in her face; nor ever could the flattering Sirens more beguile the travellers, than did her bright countenance enchant the English champion; for in entering the nunnery, he was so delighted with her beauty, that he was unable to withdraw his eyes from her, but stood gazing at her, like one bewitched with Medusa's shadows, and her beauty so filled his heart, that he must either enjoy her company, or end his life by some untimely means.

St. George, thus being wounded with the dart of love, dissembled his grief, and revealed it not to any one, but departed with the emperor back to the city, leaving his heart behind him, closed in the stone monastery with his lovely Lucina.

All that night he could not enjoy the benefit of sleep, but contemplated upon the great beauty of the lady, fraught was his mind with a thousand cogitations how he might attain to his love, being a chaste virgin and a professed nun.

In this way he spent the night, and no sooner appeared the morning's brightness, but he arose, and attired himself in velvet, and wandered alone to the monastery; where he revealed his deep affection unto the lady, who was as far from granting his request as the skies from the earth; for she protested, while life remained within her body, never to yield her love to any one, but to remain a pure virgin, of Diana's train.

No other resolution could St. George get of the chaste nun, which caused him to leave in great discontent, intending to seek by other means to obtain her love. So coming to the rest of the Christian champions, he revealed to them the truth of all things that had happened; who in this manner counselled him: that he should provide a multitude of armed knights, every one bearing in his hand a sword ready drawn; and to enter the monastery at such time as she little mistrusted; and first with promises, and fair and kind speeches to seek her love, but if she would not yield, to fill her ears with threatenings, protesting, that if she refused to requite his love with like affections, he would not leave one stone of that monastery standing upon another, and likewise make her a bloody offering to Diana.

This policy well pleased St. George, though he intended not to prosecute such cruelty: so the next morning by break of day he went to the nunnery, in company of no other but the Christian champions, armed in bright armour, with their glittering swords ready drawn, which they carried under their cloaks, to prevent suspicion.

But when they came to the monastery, and had entered into the chamber of Lucina, St. George first proffered her kindness by fair promises; but finding that nothing prevailed, he then made known his pretended unmerciful purpose; and thereupon all of them shaking their bright swords against her breast, they protested (though contrary to their intents) that except she would yield to St. George her unconquered love, they would bathe their weapons in her dearest blood.

At which words the distressed virgin, being overcharged with fear, sunk down to the ground, and lay for a time in agony; but in the end recovering herself, she lifted up herself, and in this manner declared her mind:

"Most renowned knight," said she, "it is as difficult for me to climb up to the highest top of heaven, as to persuade my mind to yield to the fulfilling of your requests. The pure and chaste goddess Diana, that sits now crowned amongst the golden stars, will revenge my perjured promise, if I yield to your desires; for I have since deeply vowed to spend my days in this religious house, in honour of her deity, and not to yield the flower of my virginity to any one; which vow I will not infringe for all the wealth of Rome. You know, brave champions, that in time the water drops will mollify the hardest diamond; and time may root this resolution out of my heart. Therefore I request you, by honour of true knighthood, and by the love you bear to your native country, to grant me the liberty of seven days, that I may fully consider before I give an answer to your demands, and that I may make some sacrifices, as well to appease the wrath which the goddess Diana may conceive against me, as to satisfy my own soul for not fulfilling my vow."

These words were no sooner ended, but the champions, without any more delay, joyfully consented, and moreover proffered themselves to be all present at the sacrifice; and so they departed from the monastery with great comfort.

The champions being gone, Lucina called together all the rest of the nuns, and declared to them the whole discourse; after which, amongst this religious company, with the advice of some other of their approved friends, they devised a most strange sacrifice, which hath since been the occasion of many inhuman and bloody sacrifices being committed.

The next morning, after six days were finished, no sooner did bright Phœbus show his golden beams abroad, but the nuns began to prepare all things in readiness for the sacrifice: for directly before the door of the monastery they hired cunning workmen to erect a scaffold, all very richly covered with a cloth of gold; and upon the scaffold, about the middle thereof, was placed a fair table, covered also with a carpet of gold, and upon it a chafing-dish of coals burning. All this being set in good order, the emperor, with the Christian champions, and many other Roman knights, being present to behold the ceremonious sacrifice, little thought of the doleful tragedy that afterwards happened.

The assembly being silent, there was immediately heard a sweet and harmonious sound of clarions and trumpets, and sundry other kinds of instruments: these entered first upon the scaffold; and next to them were brought seven rams, all adorned with fine white wool, more soft than Arabian silk, with huge horns, bound about with garlands of flowers; them followed a number of nuns attired in black vestures singing their accustomed songs in honour of Diana, after them followed an ancient matron, drawn in a chariot by four comely virgins, bringing in her hands the image of Diana; and on either side of her, two ancient nuns of great esteem, each of them bearing in their hands rich vessels of gold, full of precious and sweet wines; then, came the beautiful Lucina, apparelled with a rich robe of state, being of great and inestimable value.

Thus ceremoniously she ascended the scaffold, where the matron placed the image of Diana behind the chafing-dish of coals that was there burning; and the rest of the nuns continued still singing their songs, and drinking of the precious wines that were brought in the golden vessels. This being done, they all at once brought low the necks of the rams, by cutting their throats; the blood they sprinkled round the scaffold, and opened their bowels, and burned the inward parts in the chafing-dish of coals.

Thus they made sacrifice to the queen of chastity; at the sight whereof was present the surfeiting lover St. George, with the other six Christian knights, armed all in bright armour, and all very attentive.

This sacrifice ended, Lucina commanded silence to be made; and when all the company were still, she raised herself upon her feet, and with a heavy voice, shedding many tears, she said:

"O most excellent and chaste Diana, in whose blessed bosom we undefiled virgins do recreate ourselves, unto thy most divine excellency do I now commend this my last sacrifice, calling to record all the gods, that I have done my best to continue a spotless maiden of thy most beautiful train. O heavens! shall I consent to deliver my purity to him whose soul desires to have the use of it? Or shall I myself consent to my utter ruin and sorrowful destruction, which proceedeth only by the means of flourishing beauty? I would it had been as the night ravens, or like to the tawny tanned Moors in the farthest mountain of India.

"O sacred Diana! thou blessed queen of chastity, is it possible that thou dost consent that a virgin, descended from so royal a race as I am, should suffer the worthiness of her predecessors to be spotted by yielding her virgin honour to the conquest of love, without respecting the chaste vow I made unto thy deity? And to thee I speak, thou valiant knight of England: behold here I yield unto thy hands my lifeless body, to use according to thy will and pleasure; requesting only this thing at thy hand, that as thou lovest me living, thou wilt love me dead, and, like a merciful champion, suffer me to receive a princely burial.

"And last of all, to thee, divine Diana, do I speak; accept of this my bleeding soul, that with so much blood is offered to thee."

So finishing this sorrowful speech, she drew out a shining sword, which she had hidden secretly under her gown; and, setting the hilt against the scaffold, she suddenly threw herself upon the point of the sword, in such a furious manner, that it parted her heart asunder, and so rent her soul to the tuition of her unto whom she offered her most bloody sacrifice.

What, shall I here declare the lamentable sorows and pitiful lamentations that were made by her father and other Roman knights that were present at this unhappy mischance? So great it was, that the wall of the monastery echoed, and their pitiful shrieks ascended to the clouds.

But none was more grieved in mind than the afflicted English champion, who with great fury rushed amongst the people, throwing them down on every side, till he ascended upon the scaffold; and approaching the dead body of Lucina, he took her up in his arms, and with a sorrowful and passionate voice he said:

"O my beloved joy, and late my own heart's delight! is this the sacrifice wherein thou hast deceived me, who loved thee more than my life! Is this the respite that thou requiredst for seven days, wherein thou hast concluded thy own death, and my utter confusion!

"O Diana, accursed be this mischance! because thou hast caused so bloody a tragedy: for I do here protest, that never more shalt thou be worshipped; but in thy stead, in every land and country where the English champion cometh, shall Lucina be adored. From henceforth will I seek to diminish thy name, and blot it from the firmament; yea, and utterly extinguish it for ever, so that there shall never more memory remain of thee, for this bloody tyranny, in suffering so lamentable a sacrifice."

No sooner had he delivered these speeches, but, incensed with fury, he drew his sword, and parted the image of Diana into two pieces; protesting to ruinate the monastery within whose walls the device of this bloody sacrifice was concluded.

The sorrow and extreme grief of the Roman emperor was so great for the murder of his daughter, that he fell to the earth in a swoon, and was carried by certain of his knights half-dead with grief, home to his palace, where he remained speechless for the space of thirty days.

The emperor had a son, as valiant in arms as any born Italian, except St. Anthony. This young prince, whose name was Lucius, seeing his sister's death, and by what means it was occasioned, he presently intended, with a train of one hundred armed knights, which continually attended upon his person, to assail the discontented champions, and by force of arms to revenge his sister's death.

This resolution so encouraged the Roman knights, that between these two companies began as terrible a battle as ever was fought by any knights; the fierceness of their blows so exceeded the one side against the other, that the resounding echoes yielded a terrible noise in the neighbouring woods.

This battle continued between them both sharp and fierce for two hours, by which time the valour of the incensed champions so prevailed, that most of the Roman knights were discomfited and slain: some had their heads severed from their shoulders, some had their arms and legs lopped off, and some lay weltering in their own blood; in which encounter many a Roman lady lost her husband, many a widow was bereaved of her son, and many a child left fatherless, to the great sorrow of the whole country.

But when the valiant young prince of Rome saw his knights discomfited, and he left alone to withstand so many noble champions, he set spurs to his horse, and fled.

After whom the champions would not pursue, accounting it no glory to their names to triumph in the overthrow of a single knight, but remained by the scaffold, where they buried the sacrificed virgin, under a marble stone close by the monastery wall; which being done to their satisfaction, St.

George engraved this epitaph upon the same stone with the point of his dagger, which was in the following manner:

> Under this marble stone interr'd doth lie,
>   Luckless Lucina, yet of beauty bright;
> Who, to maintain her spotless purity
>   Against th' assailment of an English knight,
> Upon a blade her tender breast she cast;
> A bloody offering to Diana chaste.

So when he had written this epitaph, the Christian champions mounted upon their swift-footed steeds, bade adieu to unhappy Italy, hoping to find better fortunes in other countries. In which travel we will leave them for a time, and speak of the prince of Rome, who after the discomfiture of the Roman knights fled from the warlike champions; after which, he traversed along by the river Tybris, filling all places with his melancholy passions, until such time as he entered a thick grove; where he purposed to rest his weary limbs, and lament his misfortunes. After he had unlaced his helmet, he cast up his wretched eyes unto the skies, and said:

"O you fatal torches of the elements, why are you not clad in mournful habiliments, to cloak my wandering steps in eternal darkness? Or shall I be made a scorn in Rome for my cowardice? Or shall I return and accompany my Roman friends in death, whose blood methinks I see sprinkled about the fields of Italy? Methinks I hear their blows fill every corner of the earth with my base flight: therefore will I not live to be termed a fearful coward but die by my own hands; whereby those accursed champions shall not obtain the conquest of my death, nor triumph in my fall."

This being said, he drew out his dagger, and clave his heart asunder. The news of whose death being soon brought to his father's ears, he interred his body with his sister Lucina's, and erected over them a stately chapel, wherein the nuns and ceremonious monks, during their lives, sung dirges for his children's souls.

After this, the emperor made a proclamation through all his dominions, that if any knight was so hardy as to travel in pursuit after the English champion, and by force of arms to bring him back, or deliver his head to the emperor, he should not only be held in great estimation through the land, but receive the government of the empire after his decease: which rich proffer so encouraged the minds of many adventurous knights, that they went from sundry provinces in the pursuit of St. George; but their attempts were all in vain.

CHAPTER XVI

Of the triumphs, tilts, and tournaments, that were solemnly held in Constantinople by the Grecian Emperor; and of the honourable adventures that were there achieved by the Christian Champions.

In the eastern parts of the world the fame and valiant deeds of the champions of Christendom were noised, with their heroical acts and feats of arms, naming them as the mirror of nobility, and the types of bright honour. All kings and princes, to whose ears the report of their valour was known, desired much to behold them. And when the emperor of Greece, keeping his court in the city of Constantinople, heard of their mighty and valiant deeds, he wished to see them, and his mind could never be satisfied until he had devised a means to bring them to his court, not only that he might enjoy their company, but that he might have his court honoured with the presence of such renowned knights; and in this manner it was accomplished:

The emperor despatched messengers to diverse parts of the world, and charged them to publish, throughout every country and province as they went, an honourable tournament, that should be held in the city of Constantinople, within six months; thereby to accomplish his intent, and to bring the Christian champions, whose company he so much desired, to his court.

This charge of the Grecian emperor, as he commanded, was performed with such diligence, that in a short time it came to the ears of the Christian knights, as they travelled between the provinces of Asia and Africa, who, at the time appointed, came in great pomp to Constantinople, to furnish the honourable triumphs.

At the fame whereof likewise resorted thither a great number of knights of great valour and strength; among whom were the prince of Argier, with a goodly company of noble persons, and the prince of Fez, with many well proportioned knights: likewise came thither the king of Arabia in great state; and with no less majesty came the king of Sicily, and a brother of his, both giants. Many other brave and valiant knights came to honour the Grecian emperor. They came also to prove their fortitude, and to get fame and a name, and the praise that belongeth to adventurous knights. It was supposed of all the company, that the king of Sicily would gain by his prowess the dignity from the rest, for that he was a giant of very big limb; although his brother was taken to be the most furious knight, who determined it not to be just that his brother should get the honour and praise from all the knights that came;—but it fell out otherwise, as hereafter you shall hear.

For when the day of tournament was come, all the ladies and damsels put themselves in places to behold the jousting, and attired themselves in the greatest bravery, that they could devise, and the great court swarmed with people that came thither to behold the triumphant tournament.

What shall I say here of the emperor's daughter, the fair Alcida, who sat glittering in rich ornaments amongst the other ladies, like unto Phœbus in the crystal firmament? When the emperor was seated upon the imperial throne, under a tent of green velvet, the knights began to enter into the lists, and he that first entered was the king of Arabia, mounted upon a very fair and well-adorned courser. He was armed with black armour all bespotted with silver knobs, and he brought with him fifty knights, apparelled with the same livery: and thus with great majesty he rode around about the palace, making great obeisance unto all the honourable ladies and damsels.

After him entered the Pagan knight who was lord of Syria, armed with armour of lion's colour, who passed round about the palace, showing unto the ladies great friendship and courtesy, as the other did.

Which being done, he beheld the king of Arabia tarrying to receive him at the joust; the trumpets began to sound, giving them to understand that they must prepare themselves to the encounter; whereto these two knights were not unwilling, but spurred on their coursers with great fury, and closed together with courageous valour. The king of Arabia most strongly made his encounter, and struck the Pagan upon his breast; but the Pagan at the next race struck him so surely with his lance, that he heaved him out of his saddle, and he fell to the ground: after which the Pagan knight rode up and down with great pride and gladness.

The Arabian king being thus overthrown, there entered into the lists the king of Argier, armed with no other furniture but a silver mail, and a breast-plate of bright steel before his breast: his pomp and pride exceeded all the knights that were then present: but yet to small purpose his pride and arrogancy served; for at the first encounter he was overthrown to the ground. In like sort did that Pagan use fifteen other knights of fifteen provinces, to the great amazement of the emperor and all the assembly.

During all these valiant encounters, St. George, with the other Christian champions, stood afar off upon a high gallery beholding them, intending not as yet to be seen in the tilt.

But now this valiant Pagan, after he had rode about six courses up and down the place, and seeing none entered the tilt-yard, he thought to bear all the fame and honour away for that day. But at the same instant there entered the noble-minded prince of Fez, being for courage the only pride of his country. He was a very well-proportioned knight, and was armed all in white armour, wrought with excellent knots of gold; and he brought in his company a hundred knights, all attired in white satin; and riding about the place, he showed his obeisance unto the emperor, and to all the ladies, and thereupon the trumpets began to sound. At the noise whereof the two knights spurred their coursers, and made their encounters so strong, and with such great fury, that the proud Pagan was cast to the ground, and so departed the lists with great dishonour.

Straightway entered the brave king of Sicily, who was armed in a glittering corslet of very fine steel, and mounted upon a mighty and strong courser; and brought in his company two hundred knights, all apparelled with cloths of gold, having every one an instrument of music in his hand, sounding thereon a most delightsome melody.

And after the Sicilian king had made his accustomed compass and courtesy in the place, he locked down his beaver, and put himself in readiness to fight. When the sign was given by the chief herald at arms, they spurred their horses, and made their encounters so valiantly, that at the first race, their lances shivered in the air, and the pieces thereof scattered abroad like aspen leaves in a whirlwind. At the second course, the young prince of Fez was carried over his horse's buttocks, and the saddle with him between his legs; which was a great grief unto the emperor and all the company, for he was well-beloved of them all, and held for a knight of great estimation.

The Sicilian king grew proud at the prince of Fez's overthrow, and he was so enraged and furious, that in a short time he left not a knight remaining on horseback in the saddle, that durst attempt to fight with him; but everyone, of what country or nation soever, he unhorsed in the attempt: so that there was no question, among either nobles or the multitude, but that unto him the undoubted honour of the victory in triumph would be attributed.

But being in this arrogant pride, he heard a great noise, in the manner of a tumult, drawing near, which was the occasion that he stood still; and expecting some strange accident, and looking about what it could be, he beheld St. George entering the lists, as he came from the gallery; who was armed with strong armour all of purple, full of gold stars; and before him rode the champions of France, Italy, Spain, and Scotland, all on stately coursers, bearing in their hands four silken streamers of four different colours, and there followed him the champion of Wales, carrying his shield, whereon was pourtrayed a golden lion in a sable field; and the champion of Ireland likewise carried his spear, being of knotty ash, strongly bound about with plates of steel.

When St. George had passed by the royal seat where the emperor sat, in company of many princes, he rode along by the other side, where Alcida the emperor's fair daughter sat, amongst many ladies and fair damsels, richly apparelled in vestures of gold; to whom he veiled his bonnet, showing them the courtesy of a knight; and so passed by Alcida, who at the sight of this noble champion could not refrain herself, but with an high and bold voice, said unto the emperor:

"Most mighty emperor, and royal father, this is the knight in whose power and strength all Christendom put their fortunes, and this is he whom the whole world admires for chivalry."

Which words of the lovely princess although St. George heard them very well, yet passed he on as though he had heard nothing. Now when he came before the face of his adversary, he took his shield and spear, and prepared himself in readiness to joust; and so provided, the trumpets began to sound; whereat with great fury these two warlike knights met together, and neither of them missed their blows at their encounter; but yet, by reason that St. George had a desire to extol his fame, and to make his name resound through the world, he struck the giant such a mighty blow upon his breast, that he presently overthrew him; and so with great state and majesty he passed along, without any show of disdain; whereat the people gave so great a shout, that it resounded like an echo in the air, and in this manner he said: "The great and furious boaster is overthrown, and his mighty strength hath little availed him."

After this, many princes proved their adventures against the English champion, and every knight that was of any estimation fought with him, but with ease he overcame them all, in less than two hours, time. But when the day drew to an end, there entered the lists the brave and mighty giant, brother to the Sicilian king, with a great spear in his hand, whose glimmering point of steel glittered through all the court. He brought with him but one squire, attired in silver mail, bringing in his hand another lance.

So this furious giant, without any care or courtesy due unto the emperor, or any of his knights there present, entered the place; which being done, the squire that brought the other spear went to the English champion, and said:

"Sir knight, yonder brave and valiant giant, my lord and master, doth send unto thee this warlike spear, and therewith he willeth thee to defend thyself to the utmost of thy power and strength, for he hath vowed before the sun set be either lord of thy fortunes, or a vassal to thy prowess;

"He struck the giant such a mighty blow upon his helmet that he nearly overthrew him to the ground, and so with great state and majesty he passed on."

CHAPTER PART I

and likewise saith, that he doth not only defy thee in the tournament, but also challenge thee to a mortal battle."

This braving message caused St. George to smile, and bred in his breast a new desire for honour, and so returned he him this answer: "Friend, go thy ways, and tell the giant that sent thee that I accept his demand, although it doth grieve my very soul to hear this arrogant defiance, to the great disturbance of this royal company, in the presence of so mighty an emperor. But seeing he is gorged with so much pride, tell him, that St. George of England is ready to make his defence, and also that shortly he shall repent him, by the pledge of my knighthood.

In saying these words he took the spear from the squire, and delivered him his gauntlet from his hand, to carry to his master, and then put himself to the standing for the encounter. At that time he was very nigh the place where the emperor sat, who heard the answer which the English knight made to the squire, and was much displeased that the giant would so defy St. George, without any occasion. But it was no time then to speak, but to keep silence, and to mark what became of his great pride and arrogance.

At this time the two warriors, mounted upon their steeds, tarried for the sign to be made by the trumpets; which being given, they set forward their coursers, with their spears in their rests, with so great fury and desire, the one to unhorse the other, that they both failed. The giant, who was very strong and proud, when he saw that he had missed his intent, returned against St. George, carrying his spear upon his shoulder; and coming nigh unto him, upon a sudden, before he could clear himself, he struck him such a mighty blow upon the corslet, that his staff broke in pieces, by reason of the fineness of his armour, and made the English knight to double his body backwards upon his horse's crupper. But when he saw the great villainy that the giant had used against him, his anger increased very much; and so, taking his spear in the same sort, he went towards the giant and said:

"Thou furious and proud beast, thou scorn of nature and enemy to true knighthood, thinkest thou for to entrap me treacherously, and to gore me at unawares like a savage boar? Know, as I am a Christian knight, if my knotty spear have good success, I will revenge me on thy incivility."

And saying this, he struck him so furiously on the breast, that the spear passed through his body, and appeared forth at his back, whereby he fell down dead to the ground. All that were present were very much amazed thereat, and wondered greatly at the strength and force of St. George, accounting him the most fortunate knight that ever wielded lance, and the very pattern of true nobility.

At this time the golden sun had finished his course, having nothing above the horizon but his glittering beams; whereby the judge of the tournament commanded, with sound of trumpets, that the jousts should cease, and make an end for that day.

So the emperor descended from the imperial throne into the tilting place, where all the knights and gentlemen were, to receive the noble champion of England, and desired him that he would go with them into his palace, there to receive all honours due unto a knight of such desert. To which he could not make any denial, but most willingly consented. After this, the emperor's daughter, in company of many courtly virgins, likewise descended from her place; where Alcida bestowed upon St. George her glove, which he wore for her favour many days after in his burgonet.

The other six Christian champions, although they merited no honour by this tournament, because they did not try their adventures therein, yet obtained they such good liking among the Grecian ladies, that every one had his mistress; and in their presence they long time fixed their chief delights: where we must leave the champions in the emperor's court for a time, and return to St. George's sons travelling in the world to seek out adventures.

CHAPTER XVII.

How a Knight with two Heads tormented a beautiful Maiden, that had betrothed herself to the Emperor's son of Constantinople; and how she was rescued by St. George's Sons; and how they were brought by a strange adventure into the company of the Christian Champions.

THIS renowned emperor, within whose court the Christian champions made their abode, had a son named Pollemus, in all virtues and knightly demeanours equal with any man living. This prince in his youth fell in love with a maiden of mean parentage, but in beauty and other precious gifts of nature most excellent.

This Dulcippa (for so she was called), being but daughter to a country gentleman, was restrained from the emperor's court, and denied the sight of her beloved Pollemus; and he forbidden to set his affection so low, upon the displeasure of the emperor his father; for he being the son of so mighty a potentate, and she the daughter of so mean a gentleman, it was thought to be an unfit match, and contrary to the laws of the country; and therefore they were not suffered to manifest their loves as they would, but were constrained by stealth to enjoy each other's company.

At this time these two lovers concluded to meet together in valley between two hills, in distance from the emperor's t about three miles, where they might in secret unite and fix both their hearts in one knot of true love, and so to prevent the determination of their parents, who so unkindly thought to cross them. And when the appointed day drew near, Dulcippa attired herself in costly apparel, as though she was going to perform her nuptial ceremonies; and in this manner she entered the valley, when the sun began to appear out of the golden horizon; likewise the calm western winds did very sweetly blow upon the green leaves, and made a delicate harmony, at such time the fairest Dulcippa approached the place of their appointed meeting.

But when she found not prince Pollemus present, she determined to spend the time till he came, in trimming her golden hair, and decking her delicate body. So sitting down upon a green bank, under the shadow of a myrtle tree, she pulled a golden caul from her head, wherein her hair was wrapped, and taking out an ivory comb she began to comb her hair.

But mark, gentle reader, how frowning Fortune crossed her desires, and changed her wished-for joys into unexpected sorrows; for as she sat, there came wandering by, an inhuman tyrant surnamed the knight with two heads, who was a defiler of virgins, an oppressor of infants, and an enemy to virtuous ladies and strange travelling knights. This tyrant was bodied like a man, but covered all over with locks of hair: he had two heads, two mouths, and four eyes, all red as blood. This deformed creature presently ran to the virgin, and caught her under his arms, and carried her over the mountain into another country, where he intended to torment her, as you shall hear more at large hereafter.

But to return to prince Pollemus, who at the time appointed likewise prepared to meet his betrothed; but going to the place, he found nothing but a silver scarf, which Dulcippa had let fall in her fearful fright at the sight of the two-headed knight.

No sooner had he found her scarf but he was oppressed with extreme sorrow, fearing Dulcippa was murdered by some inhuman means, had left her scarf as a token that she infringed not her promise, but performed it to the loss of her own life. Therefore taking it up, and putting it next his heart, he breathed forth this lamentation:

"Here rest thou near to my true loving heart, thou precious token and remembrance of my dearest lady, never to be hence removed till such time as my eyes may either behold her, or my ears hear certain news of her untimely death, that I may in death consort with her. And for her sake I vow to travel through the world, as far as ever golden Phœbus lends his light, filling each corner of the earth with her name, and make the elements resound with my lamentation."

Q

In which resolution he returned home to his father's palace, dissembling his grief in such a manner, that none could suspect his sorrows, nor the strange accident that had happened to the beauteous Dulcippa.

One day, as he was meditating with himself, seeing the small comfort that he took in the court, considering the want of her presence whom he so much desired, he determined, in great secrecy, as soon as it was possible, to depart from the court. Which determination he straightway put in practice, and took out of the emperor's armoury, very secretly, an exceeding good corslet, which was all russet enamelled with black, and embroidered round about with a gilded edge, very curiously and artificially graven and carved. Also he took a shield of the same make, except that it was not graven as the armour was; and commanded a young gentleman, who was son to an ancient knight of Constantinople, of a good disposition and hardy, that he should keep them safely, and gave him to understand of his determination.

Although it grieved the young man very much, for all that, seeing the great friendship that he used towards him, in telling his secrets to him before any other, without replying to the contrary he took the armour, and hid it, till he found a convenient time to put it into a ship very secretly. Likewise he put into the same ship two of the best horses which the emperor had; and forthwith he gave the prince to understand, that all things were then in readiness, and in good order. Pollemus, dissembling with the accustomed sorrow that he used, withdrew himself into his chamber, till such time as dark night came. When it was come, he made himself ready with his apparel; and when all the people of the court were at their rest, he alone, with his page, who was named Mercutio, departed from the palace, and went to the sea-side. His page called the mariners of the ship, who straightway brought unto them their boat, into which they entered, and went straight aboard. And being therein, he commanded them to weigh anchor, hoist up their sails, and commit themselves to the mercy of the waters. As he commanded, all was done; and in a short time they found themselves far from the sight of land.

But when the emperor his father knew his secret departure his lamentation was very great; and he commanded his knights to go to the sea-side, to ask if any ship had departed that night; and when it was told them that there was a bark that heaved anchor, and hoisted sail, they supposed straightway that the prince was gone away.

I cannot here declare the grief and sorrow which the emperor felt for the absence of his son. But when the departure of Pollemus was noised through all Constantinople, all sports and feasts ceased, and all the people of the country were overcome with sorrow.

So Pollemus sailed through the seas three days, and three nights, with a fair and prosperous wind. The fourth day, in the evening, being calm, and no wind at all, the mariners went to take their rest, some on the poop, and some on the fore-ship, to ease their wearied bodies. The prince, who sat upon the poop of the ship, asked his page for his lute, which was straightway given him, and sung so sweetly, that it seemed to be a most heavenly melody; and being in this sweet music, he heard a very lamentable cry, as it were of a woman; and leaving his delicate music, he gave a listening ear to what this sorrowful creature said; and by reason of the stillness of the night, he might easily hear as it were a woman uttering these words: "It will little profit thee, thou cruel tyrant, this, thy bold hardiness, for I am beloved of so worthy a knight as will undoubtedly revenge this tyrannous cruelty proffered me."

Then he heard another voice, which seemed to answer:

"Now I have thee in my power there is no human creature of strength able enough to deliver or redeem thee from the torments that, in my determination, I have purposed thou shalt endure."

Pollemus could hear no more, by reason of their passing by so swiftly; but he supposed it was his lady's voice which he heard, and that she was carried away by force. So laying down his lute, he began to fall into great thought, and was very heavy and sorrowful, so that he knew not how to adventure for her recovery.

Being in this cogitation, he returned to his page, who was asleep, and struck him with his foot, and awaked him, saying:

"What, didst thou not hear the great lamentation that my lady Dulcippa made, being in a small bark that has passed by, and gone forwards to the seas?" To which the page Mercutio answered nothing, for he was still in a sound sleep. To whom the prince called again, saying: "Arise, I say; bring forth my armour; call upon the mariners, that they may launch their boat into the sea; for by Jupiter I swear, that I will not be called the son of my father if I suffer such violence to be done against my love, and not proceed with all my strength to revenge the same."

Mercutio would have replied, but the furious countenance of the prince would not give him leave, no, not once to look upon his face: so he brought forth his armour and buckled it on.

In the mean time the mariners had launched their boat into the sea; into it he leaped in hasty fury, and carried with him his page, and four of the mariners to row the bark, and he commanded them to make their way towards the other company that had passed by them.

So they laboured all night, till such time as bright Phœbus with his glittering beams gave them such light that they might discover the other bark, although afar off.

So they laboured with great courage till the day was far spent; at which time they saw coming after them a galley, which was rowed with eight oars upon a side; and of such great speed, that in a trice they were with them, and he saw that there were in her three knights, in bright armour; to whom Pollemus called with a loud voice, saying: "Most courteous knights, I request you to take me into your galley, that I may the better accomplish my desire."

The knights who were in the galley passed by the prince without making any answer. These three knights were the sons of the English champion, who left their father in his journey towards Babylon to set the king again in his kingdom.

But now to follow our history: The prince of Constantinople, seeing the little account they made of him, with great anger and fury he took an oar in one hand, and with such strength he struck the water, that he made the bark almost fly and laboured so much at the oars, that they were soon equal with the galley.

So leaving the oars, with a light leap he put himself into the galley, with his helmet on and his shield at his shoulder; he said, "Now shall you do that by force, which before you would not yield to."

This being said, one of St. George's sons encountered him, thinking it a blemish to the honour of knighthood by multitudes to assail him. So the two knights, without any advantage of one another, fought so valiantly, that it was a wonder to the beholders. The prince of Constantinople struck the English knight such a furious blow, that he recoiled backwards two or three steps; but he came quickly again to himself, and returned him so strong a blow upon his helmet, that he made his teeth chatter in his head.

With great policy and strength they endured the bickering all day, and when they saw the dark night come upon them they strove with more courage and strength to finish the battle.

The prince of Constantinople, puffing and blowing like an enraged bull, lifted up his sword with both hands, and discharged it so strongly upon his enemy, that he made him fall to the ground, and therewith offered to pull his helmet from his head. But when the English knight saw himself in that sort, he threw his shield from him, and very strongly caught the other about the neck, and held him fast; so that between them began a terrible wrestling, tumbling, and wallowing up and down the galley.

At this time the night began to grow very dark, wherefore they called for lights, which were brought them by the mariners: In the mean time the knights rested themselves, although it was not much. So when the lights were brought, they returned to their old combat with new force and strength.

"O heavens," said Pollemus, "I cannot believe the contrary that this is Mars the god of war, that doth contend in battle with me; and for the envy he bears against me, he goeth about to dishonour me." And with these words they thickened their blows with great desperation. And though this last assault continued more than two hours, neither of them did faint; but at last, they both together lifted up their swords, and charged them together, the one upon the other's helmet, with such great strength, that both of them fell down upon the hatches senseless.

The rest looking upon them, believed they were both dead, by reason of the abundance of blood that came from their visors; but it was quickly perceived that there was some hope of life in them. Then there was an agreement made between the knights of the galley and mariners of the bark, that they should join together and travel whither Fortune would conduct them. In this order carried they these two knights without any remembrance.

But when the prince of Constantinople came to himself, with a loud voice he said: "O Love, is it true that I am overthrown in this first encounter and assault of my knighthood? Here I curse the day of my creation, and the hour when first I merited the name of knight: henceforth I'll bury all my honours in disgrace, and spend the remnant of my life in base cowardice." And in speaking these words, he cast his eye aside, and beheld the English knight as one newly risen from a trance, who likewise breathed forth these discontented speeches: "O unhappy son of St. George! now a coward and of little valour, I know not how thou canst name thyself to be the son of any knight in the world, for that thou hast lost thy honour in the last assault."

Then the two weary knights concluded a peace between them, and revealed to each other their names, and wherefore they adventured to travel; which when it was known, they sailed forward that way the sorrowful woman went. So they travelled all the rest of the night that remained, till such time as the day began to break, and they descried land; to which place they speedily rowed.

And coming to land, they found no beaten way; but one narrow path: wherein they had not travelled far when they met with a poor countryman, with a new-ground hatchet, in his hand, and he was going to cut some fire-wood off the high and broad spreading trees; and of whom they demanded what country and land it was. "This country," said he, "is called Armenia; but yet, most courteous knights, you must pardon me, for that I do request you to return again, and proceed no further, if you do esteem your lives; for in going this way there is nothing to be had but death: for the king of this country is a furious monster, called the two-headed Knight, he is so furious in his tyranny, that never any stranger could as yet escape out of his hands alive; and for proof of his cruelty, no longer than yesterday he brought a lady prisoner, who, at her first coming on shore, he whipped and beat so much, that it would make a tyrant relent and pity her distress, swearing that every day he would torment her, till her life and body made their separation."

Pollemus, the prince of Constantinople, was very attentive to the old man's words, thinking the lady to be his Dulcippa, after whom he travelled. The grief he received at this report struck such a terror to his heart, that he fell into a swoon, and was not able to go any further: but St. George's sons encouraged him, and swore, by the honour of knighthood, never to forsake his company till they saw his lady delivered from her torments, and safely conducted home into his own country.

So travelling with this resolution, the night came on, and it was so dark, that they were constrained to seek some convenient place to take rest; and laying themselves down under a broad-branched oak tree, they passed the night, pondering in their minds a thousand imaginations.

When the morning came, and the diamond of heaven began to shine upon the mountain tops, these martial knights were not slothful, but rose up and followed their journey.

After this, they had travelled scarce half a mile, when they heard the pitiful lamentation of a woman: so they staid to hear from whence that lamentable noise came. And afar off, they beheld a high pillar of stone, out of which there came forth a spout of clear water; and thereat was bound a woman, naked; her back fastened to the pillar, her arms backwards embracing it, with her hands fast bound behind her.

These warlike knights laced on their helmets, and came unto the place where she was; but when the prince of Constantinople saw her, he knew her to be his lady and lovely mistress: for by reason of the coldness of the night, and with her great lamentation and weeping, she was so full of sorrows and affliction, that she could scarce speak. Likewise the prince's heart so yearned at the sight of his unhappy lady, that he could not look upon her for weeping.

At last, with a sorrowful sigh he said: "O cruel hands, is it possible that there should remain in you so much mischief, that where there is such great beauty and fairness you should use such baseness and villany! She doth more deserve to be loved and served, than to be thus badly treated."

This woful prince with much sorrow beheld her white skin and back spotted with blood; and taking a cloak from one of the mariners, he threw it upon her, and covering her body, he took her in his arms, whilst the other knights loosed her.

This unhappy lady never felt nor knew what was done unto her, till such time as she was loosed from her bands, and in the arms of her lover; but she thought she had been in the arms of the two-headed knight, and therefore she gave a terrible sigh, saying: "O Pollemus, my true betrothed husband, where art thou now, that thou comest not to succour me!" and therewith ceased her speeches.

The prince, hearing these words, would have answered her, but he was disturbed by hearing a great noise of a horse, which seemed to be in the woods amongst the trees. The rest of the knights, intending to see what it was, left the lady lying upon the green grass in keeping of prince Pollemus and the mariners, and St. George's sons went towards the place where they heard the rushing noise; and as they looked about them, they beheld the two-headed monster, mounted upon a furious palfrey, who was returning to see if the lady was alive, to torment her anew.

When he came to the pillar, and saw not the lady, with an ireful look he cast his eyes, round about him on every side; and at last he saw the three knights coming towards him with a slow pace, and the lady untied from the pillar where he left her, and in the arms of another knight, making her sorrowful complaint.

The two-headed knight, seeing them, with great wrath came riding towards them; and when he was near them, he said: "Fond knights, what wretched folly and madness hath bewitched you, that without any leave you have untied the lady from the pillar where I left her? Or come you to offer up your blood in sacrifice upon my falchion?" To whom one of the three valiant brothers answered: "We be knights of a strange country, that at the sorrowful complaint of this lady arrived at this place; and seeing her to be a beautiful woman, and without any desert to be thus badly treated, it moved us to put our persons in adventure against them that may further ill use her."

While the knight was speaking these words, the ugly monster beheld him, and knitting his brows with the anger he received in hearing his speeches; and with great fury he spurring his monstrous beast, so that he made him give a mighty leap, had almost fallen on the English knight, who with great lightness delivered himself: and, drawing out his sword, he would have struck him, had not the beast passed by with such great swiftness that he could not reach them.

Here began as terrible a battle, between the two-headed knight and St. George's sons, as ever was fought by any knights: their mighty blows seemed to rattle in the elements like terrible thunder, and their swords to strike sparkling fire in such abundance, as though from a smith's anvil.

During this conflict, the English knights were so grievously wounded, that their bright armour was stained with blood, and their helmets bruised with the terrible strokes of the monster's falchion; whereat they grew so enraged, that one of them struck a blow with his trusty sword upon his knee; and his armour being not very good, he cut it clean asunder, so that leg and all fell to the ground, and the two-headed knight fell on the other side to the earth, and with great roaring began to rage and stare like a beast, and to blaspheme the Fates for this his sudden mishap.

The other two brethren, seeing this, presently cut off his two heads.

There was another knight that came with this monster, who, when he saw all that had passed, with great fear returned the way from whence he came.

These victorious conquerors, when they saw that they were delivered from the tyrant's cruelty, with joyful hearts departed with conquest to the prince of Constantinople, where they left him comforting his distressed mistress.

So when they were all together, they commanded the mariners to provide them something to eat, for they had great need thereof; who presently prepared it, for continually they bore their provision about them. Of this banquet the knights were very glad, and rejoiced much at that which they had achieved, and commanded that the lady should be very well looked to, and healed of her harm received.

At the end of three days, when the princely lady had recovered her health, they left the country of Armenia, and departed back to the seas, where they had left their ships, and tarried there until their coming. They had no sooner entered the vessels, but the mariners hoisted sail, and took their way towards Constantinople, as the knights commanded. The wind served them so prosperously, that within a short time they arrived in Greece, and landed within two days' journey of the court, which lay then about a mile from Constantinople.

Being on land, the prince Pollemus consulted with St. George's three sons what course was best to be taken for their proceeding in the court: "For," saith he "unless I may with the emperor my father's consent enjoy my dearest Dulcippa,

I will live unknown in her company, rather than delight in the heritage of ten such empires."

At last they concluded that the lady should be covered with a black veil, that Pollemus should appear in black arms, and the other knights be attired suitably, and that all should ride together; which accordingly they did, and about ten in the morning entered the palace; where they found the emperor, and the seven champions, with many other princes, in the great hall; to whom one of St. George's sons thus spake:

"Great emperor, and noble knights, this knight, that leadeth the lady, hath long loved her; in their births there is great difference, so that their parents crossed their affections; for him she hath endured much sorrow, and for her he will and hath suffered many hazards. His coming thus to your court is to this end, to approve her the only deserving lady in the world, himself the most faithful knight, against all knights whatsoever; which, with your imperial leave, he, myself, and these two my associates, will maintain; desiring your majesty to give judgment as we deserve."

The emperor condescended; and on the green before the palace, those four overthrew more than four hundred knights: so that St. George and three other of the champions entered the list, and ran three violent courses against the black knights, without moving them; who never suffered the points of their spears to touch the armour of the champions; which the emperor perceiving, guessed them to be of acquaintance: wherefore, giving judgment that the knight should possess his lady, at his request they discovered themselves.

To describe the delightful comfort that the English champion felt in the presence of his children, and the joy that the emperor received at the return of his lost son, requires more art and eloquence than my tired senses can afford: I am therefore here forced to leave the flower of chivalry in the city of Constantinople.

Of whose following adventures I will at large discourse hereafter; and how all these famous champions came to their deaths, and for what cause they were called the Seven Saints of Christendom.

CHAPTER XVIII.

Of the praiseworthy death of St. Patrick; how he buried himself; and for what cause the Irishmen to this day, wear their red cross upon St. Patrick's day.

HERE must you suppose, gentle readers, that time had run a long race before these aforesaid thrice-honoured champions had purchased so many victories: and being now wearied with age, death with his gloomy countenance, began to challenge an end of all their worldly achievements, and to draw their noble names to a full perfection : therefore preparing a black stage to act his last scene out, thus it followed:

The valiant champion St. Patrick, feeling himself weakened with time and age, not able any longer to endure the bruises of princely achievements, became an hermit; and wandering up and down the world in poor habiliments, he came at last to the country of his birth, which is now called Ireland, but in former times Hibernia; where, instead of martial achievements, he offered up, in the name of his Redeemer, devout orisons, daily making petitions to the Deity of Glory, in behalf of his desired peace: a life more delightful to his aged heart, than all his former accomplishments. And now, willing to bid farewell to the world, he desired an enclosure to be made, and to be pent up in a stony wall from the sight of all earthly objects. To which request of this holy father (now no soldier, but a man of peace) the inhabitants condescended, and built him a foursquare house of stone, without either window or door, only a little hole to receive his food in; wherein they closed him up, never to be seen any more alive by the eyes of mortal man. Also appointing several persons to bring him, at convenient times, food to maintain nature, they delivered it in at the aforesaid hole, which they thought to be a deed of more than common charity, and he, the receiver, to be an honour to the country, by the severe and strict course of life he put himself to. Thus lived he, the servant of his God; day and night kneeling on the bare ground, till thrice the winter's cold had taken departure, and as oft the summer's warmth had cheered up the cold earth, making his knees hard with kneeling, and his eyes dim with lamentations for his former offences. In which time the hairs of his head were all overgrown, and the nails of his fingers seemed like the talons and claws of an old raven; with which, by little and little, he dug his own grave, preparing it against the hour of his death to be buried in: which in process of time came to effect as follows:

When he had wasted, as I have said before, thrice twelve months in divine contemplations, by inspiration (as it seemed) he laid him down in the grave that his own nails had dug, and gave up the ghost.

Thus being changed from a lively substance to a dead body, his attenders, as their usual custom was, came with food to relieve him, and calling at the hole where he was wont to receive it, they heard nothing but empty air blowing in and out, which made them conjecture presently that death had prevailed, and the fatal sisters had finished their labours. So calling together more company, they made an entrance therein; and finding what had happened, by a common consent of the whole kingdom they pulled down the house or tower, and in the same place built a most sumptuous chapel, calling it St. Patrick's Chapel; and in the place where this holy father had buried himself, they likewise erected a costly monument framed upon pillars of pure gold, beautified with many artificial ornaments, most pleasant to behold; where for many years after resorted distressed people, such as were commonly molested with loathsome diseases; where making their orisons at St. Patrick's tomb, they found help, and were restored to their former healths.

By which means the name of St. Patrick is grown so famous through the world, that to this day he is entitled one of our Christian champions, and the saint for Ireland; where, in remembrance of him, and of his honourable achievements done in his lifetime, the Irishmen, as well in England as in that country, do as yet, in honour of his name, keep one day in the year a festival, wearing upon their hats each of them a cross of red silk, in token of his many adventures under the Christian cross, as you have read in the former history at large discoursed: whose noble deeds, both in life and death, we will leave sleeping with him in the grave, and speak of our next renowned tragedy, which Heaven and Fate had allotted St. David, the champion of Wales, at that time entitled Cambro-Britanus.

CHAPTER XIX.

Of the honourable victory won by St. David in Wales; of his death, and the cause why leeks are by custom, worn on St. David's day, by Welshmen.

SOME months after the departure of St. Patrick from the city of Constantinople, St. David, having a heart still fired with fame, thirsted even to his dying day for honourable achievements; and although age and time had almost wearied him away, yet would he once more make his adventure in the field of Mars, and seal up his honours in the records of fame with a noble farewell.

One morning, framing himself for a knightly enterprise, he took his leave of the other champions, all alone, well mounted upon a lusty courser, furnished with sufficient habiliments, and began a journey towards his own country, accounting that his best joy, and the soil for most comfort.

But he had not travelled long, ere he heard of the distresses of his native land; how Wales was beset with a people of savage nature, thirsting for blood, and the ruin of that brave kingdom; and how many battles had been fought to the disparagement of Christian knighthood. Whereupon, arming himself with true resolution, he went forward with a courageous mind, either to redeem the fame, or to lose his best blood in the honour of the country.

Upon which, all the way as he travelled, he drew to his aid and assistance all the best knights he could find, of any nation whatever, giving them promises of noble rewards, and entertainment as befitted so worthy a fellowship. By this means, before he came upon the borders of Wales he had gathered together the number of five hundred knights, of such noble resolution, that all Christendom could not afford better, the Seven Champions excepted. And these, all furnished for battle, entered the country ; where they found many towns unpeopled, houses subverted, monasteries defaced, cities ruined, fields of corn consumed with fire—yea, every thing so out of order, as if the country had never been inhabited. Whereupon, with a grieved mind, seeing the region of his birth-place so confounded, that nothing but uproars of murder and death sounded in his ears, he summoned his knights together, placing them in battle array to travel high up into the country, for the performance of his desired hopes. But as they marched along with an easy pace, to prevent dangers, there resorted to them people of all ages, both young and old, bitterly complaining of the wrongs thus done to their country. Where, when they knew him to be the champion of Wales, whom so long they had desired to see, their joy so abounded that all former woes were abolished, and they emboldened to nothing but revenge.

The rest of the knights that came with St. David, perceiving their forces and numbers increase, purposed an onset and to show themselves before their enemies; who lay encamped among the mountains, with such strength and policy that it was hard to make an assailment.

Whereupon the noble champion, being then their general and leader, called his captains together, and with bold courage said as follows:

"Now is the time, brave knights, to be canonized the sons of Fame ; this is the day of dignity or dishonour; an enterprise to make us ever live, or to end our names for ever. Let not fear pull us back from the golden throne, where the adventurous soldier sits in glory deservedly. We are to trample in the field of death and dead men's bones, and to battle with an enemy of great strength, a Pagan's power, that seeks to overrun all Christian kingdoms, and to wash our Cambrian fields with innocent blood. To arms ! I say, brave followers ; I will be the first to give death the onset; and for my colours or ensign do I wear upon my burgonet, you see, a green leek beset with gold, which shall, if we win the victory, hereafter be an honour to Wales ; and on this day, being the first of March, be it for ever worn by the Welshmen in remembrance hereof."

Which words were no sooner spoken by the champion, but all the royal army, of every degree and calling got themselves the like recognizance—having each of them a green leek upon their hats or beavers, which they wore all the time of the battle; and by that means the champion's followers were known from the others. It was not long before St. David and his company beheld, descending from the mountains, an army of Pagans, as it seemed numberless; people of such mighty stature, whose appearance might have daunted their noble resolutions, had not the brave champion still animated them with princely encouragements. The battle soon commenced; and the Pagans, with their iron clubs and bats of steel, so laid about them, that had not our Christian army been preserved by miracle, such a slaughter had been made of the champion and the knights that well might have caused the whole world to wonder.

But chance so favoured St. David and his followers, that, what with their lances, keen darts and arrows, shot from their bows, and Welsh hooks in great abundance, (the sun also lying in the pagans' faces, to their great disadvantage), in a short time the noble champion won a worthy victory. The ground lay all covered with mangled carcasses; the grassy fields changed from green into red colour, with the streams of blood that ran from horse and man. It was a noble policy for the Christians in that battle to wear green leeks in their burgonets for their colours; by which they were all known and preserved from the slaughter of each other's swords; only St. David himself excepted, who, being victor, in the highest pride of his glory, was at last vanquished. O unhappy fate, to cut off his honour, that was the only darling of Honour! Help me, Melpomene, to bewail his loss, that, having won all, lost his dear life. Oh fatal chance! For, coming from the battle, over-heated in blood, so sudden a cold congealed in all his life's members, that he was forced to yield unto Death, to the great grief of all his knights and followers, who for the space of forty days mourned for him in great heaviness, and afterwards attended him to his grave with much sorrow.

CHAPTER XX.

How St. Denis was beheaded in his own country, and by a miracle shewn at his Death, the whole Kingdom of France received the Christian Faith.

ST. DENIS, being the third in this our pilgrimage of death, was likewise desirous of the sight of his own country, which he had not seen for many years; and purposing a toilsome travel to the same, took leave of the other champions, who were not altogether willing to leave so noble a brother knight; yet considering the desire of his mind they quickly agreed, wishing him the best welfare of knighthood : and so parting, they to their princely pavilions, and he to his restless journey, as well mounted, and as richly furnished with habiliments of knighthood, as any martialist in all Arabia, in which country he then was. But leaving that place, to satisfy his desires, he travelled day by day towards the kingdom of France, without any adventure worth reporting, till he arrived upon the borders of that fair country that he had so long wished to behold. But now see how Fate frowned! for there was remaining in the French king's favour a knight of St. Michael's order, who in former times hearing of the honourable adventures of this noble champion St. Denis, and thinking him to be a disparagement to his knighthood and the rest of the order, conspired to betray him, and to bring all his former honours with his life to an end.

Whereupon this envious knight of St. Michael went unto the king (being as then a Pagan prince, one that had no true knowledge of the Deity), and said : " There has come into this kingdom a strange knight, a false believer, one that in time would draw the love of his subjects from him to the worship of a strange god ; and that, in despite of him and his country, he would establish false opinions ; and that he wore upon his breast the Christian cross; with many other things, contrary to the laws of his kingdom.

Upon these false informations the king grew so enraged, that, without any more consideration, he caused the good knight St. Denis to be attacked in his bed chamber—otherwise a score of the best knights of France had not been sufficient to bring him prisoner to the king's presence: before whom being no sooner come, but with more than human fury, without cause, he sentenced him to a speedy death, and by martial law, without any further trial, to receive the same.

The good champion St. Denis, even in death having a most noble resolution, nothing at all dismayed, and knowing his cause to be good, and that he should suffer for the name of his sweet Redeemer, most willingly accepted the judgment, saying : " Most mighty, but yet cruel king, think not but that this exceeding tyranny will be requited in a strange manner. Thy censure I take with much joy, in that I die for Him, whose colours I have worn from my infancy ; and this my death seals up the obligation of all my comforts. And thou, sweet country, where I first took life, receive it again, a legacy due unto thee; for this my blood, which here I offer up into thy bosom, as the best gift I can bestow upon thee. Farewell, knighthood; farewell, honourable adventures and princely achievements: never may this dauntless arm brandish weapon more in honour of the Christian cross; for death awaiteth me to cut off all such noble hopes, and I by tyranny am betrayed thereunto."

These speeches being uttered, he was forced to stand silent; and in the presence of the king, with many hundreds more, was constrained to yield his body to the fatal stroke; where his head being laid upon the block, was by a base executioner, quickly severed from the rest of his manly members. Which being no sooner done, and the champion lifeless, but the elements, beset with cloudy exhalations, sent down such a thunder clap, that struck dead the knight of St. Michael who accused him, and the executioner, with others who had assisted at the death of the brave knight. At which fearful spectacle the king grew so amazed, that he deemed him to be a blessed creature; that he had suffered wrongfully; and that his cause, for which he so willingly rendered up his life, was the true cause, which all must have a desire to die in: wherefore instantly, from a Pagan, the king turned Christian, and caused it to be proclaimed through all his provinces, ordaining churches to be built in remembrance of this great man.

CHAPTER XXI.
Of the infamous Death that the Spanish Champion was put to.

HERE, gentle reader, prepare to give entertainment to the sorrowful manner of the Spanish champion's death, who by tyranny and cruel dealing of the infidels was likewise made away: for age and time, as upon the former knights, grew upon him, and so enfeebled his strength, that he was no longer able to sustain the adventures of chivalry, nor fight the battles of his Saviour. Wherefore, resolving to spend the remnant of his days in peace, he desired leave to commit his fortunes to the queen of chance, which, he quickly obtained: and so, leaving Constantinople, he travelled towards the country of his first being, not decked in his shining armour, nor mounted on his Spanish jennet, but poor and in outward bare habit, though inwardly furnished with gold and jewels of an inestimable value, which he had sewed up in the patches of a russet gabardine, the better to travel with. Where, instead of a bright shining battle-axe, his pilgrim's staff served him to walk with; and for his burgonet of glittering steel, he covered his head (now as white as thistle down, with age) with a hat of grey colour, broached with a broad scallop-shell. His princely lodgings were changed to green pastures, and his canopies to the skies' azured covering, where the nightingale and lark told the time's passage.

In which manner travelling many days, giving as he went to the poor and needy such small pieces of silver as he could well spare, he arrived at last upon the confines of Spain: where, in honour of that God for whom he had fought so many battles, he built up, at his own charge, a sumptuous chapel, to this day bearing the name of St. Jaque's chapel; (which is the same as our James); and, for the maintenance of the said chapel, he purchased divers lands adjoining; and placed choristers to sing day and night therein, Allelujah to his Redeemer.

This gift begot such love of the meaner sort of people, that they esteemed him more than a man; with such reverence and regard that his very name won greater admiration than the high tilts of their country's king; who being then cruel and proud, maintaining atheism in his government, grew so envious thereat, that he caused good St. Jaques, with the whole choir of celestial singers, to be closed up together in the chapel which the champion had erected, and so starved them to death. Oh bloody butchery, and inhuman cruelty! But, to be brief, hunger prevailed, and they died, their bodies putrified, and in time consumed away to dust and mould; whereupon the Lord, to show how they died in his favour and the love of Heaven, caused a light to shine in the chapel, day and night with such an ardent brightness, as if it had been the glorious palace of the sun: and likewise was heard therein continually (though no creature remained) such a choir of melodious harmony, as if it had been the sound of celestial music. Which strange pleasures, both to the eyes and ears, bred so great an amazement in the whole country, that all with common consent blamed their king for tyrannically putting to death these good men, but especially the noble St. Jaques, whom they purposed to hold for their country's saint and champion till the world's dissolution. The proud king, perceiving now his own rashness, and the common hate against him for his misdeed, took such an inward conceit of grief, that, without taking any food ever after, he languished away and died.

CHAPTER XXII.

The honourable and worthy death of the Italian Champion.

AFTER all these proceedings, Nature, the common nurse of us all, so wrought in the heart of St. Anthony, the champion for Italy, that he undertook the next tragical enterprise; and leaving St. George, with St. Andrew, in the emperor's court of Constantinople, he took his journey towards Italy; and knowing, by the course of nature, that his days were not many, he purposed there to finish all his earthly troubles. So coming, after a long journey, to the city of Rome, where the emperor Domitian kept his court; and the city being then in her chief pomp and glory, won great desire in the champion's mind to see the monuments of the same.

So in the morning, going from his lodgings, he walked up and down the streets with admiration, and fed his eyes with many delightful objects. First, with great wonder he stood gazing upon the monuments that were erected in honour of all their famous emperors, consuls, orators, and conquerors, things which yielded him great pleasnre. The next thing that his eyes delighted in, was the temple of the twelve Sibyls, a most miraculous building; in which temple were all their prophecies enrolled; as also the beginning and ending of the whole catalogue of the heathen gods, as Mars, Jupiter, Saturn, Apollo, and such like; with their manner of worship. The next that he saw was the house of Remus and Romulus, who built Rome; a building of much grandeur. Next unto it stood an ancient prison (an old rotten thing) where the man lay that was condemned to death, and could have no one come to him to succour him but was searched, yet he was kept alive a long space by sucking his daughter's breasts. After this, he saw Pompey's theatre, reputed one of the nine wonders of the world: the emperor Nero's tomb, maintained with disgrace, for the offence he did in setting Rome on fire. To conclude, he spent many days in viewing the martyrs' tombs, and other reliques brought from Jerusalem. Amongst many other delightful sights, he came into a chapel dedicated unto himself, called, "The Honour of St. Anthony;" wherein were pourtrayed, in alabaster pictures, the true forms of all the champions of Christendom, with the stories of all their adventures, combats, tournaments, and battles; their imprisonments, dangers, and enchantments; all pictured up by enchantments and witchcraft; whereupon ran a prophecy, that the patron of this chapel should ever live unconquered, and never embrace death, till his eyes were witness of the same portraitures; which in golden letters were inscribed over the chapel door or entrance. Which when St. Anthony beheld, and knowing himself to be the man, with a meek mind he embraced his own end, and never after departed the chapel, but remained kneeling in the same, upon the bare marble, making his orisons of repentance to the Eternal Deity, till pale Destiny had cut off the threads of his old days. And thus being converted to mouldy earth the emperor caused him to be entombed in the same chapel; and over his grave to be set a magnificent chair, in which chair, for many years after, the Roman conquerors received their laurel rewards of martial victory.

CHAPTER XXIII.

Of the Martyrdom of St. Andrew the Scottish Champion.

ST. GEORGE and St. Andrew were the two last champions that staid together, and, as it seemed, the dearest love remained between these two ; but yet rusty Time with his swift course would needs part them, and break their united fellowship. The summons of honour so animated the bold heart of the Scottish champion, that he burned with desire to see his native country, and to behold the place of his first being. Leaving Constantinople, only honoured with the presence of St. George and his three sons, he travelled day by day, till Time and Fate set him happily in the kingdom of Scotland; where not having been for many years before, he received such entertainment as if he had been the greatest emperor in the world : for all the streets and passages where he went were crowded with people of the best estate, to give him a gracious' welcome to his native home ; the king especially, who for the love and honour he bore unto his name and knighthood, lodged him in his own palace, and proclaimed for his noble welcome a princely tournament to be holden for the space of fifteen days ; in which time all the nobility and martial knights of Scotland performed such well-approved achievements, that neither Greece, Constantinople, Rome, nor Jerusalem, could equal them in the least. St. Andrew being now aged, and unfit for such princely encounters, sat as a beholder, censuring the deserver, and giving such commendations as befitted so gallant a company: and for a farewell of such time-honoured pastimes, he desired leave of the king to depart, and to spend the remnant of his life in private contemplations, for the good of his soul, and to wash away, with the water of true penitence, all the blood he had spilt in his travels about the world in the maintenance of knighthood : a request so reasonable, that the king could not but give his consent to. So taking leave of his majesty, and the rest of the nobility and knights present, he departed up to a mountain, far from the king's court, under which by nature was erected a cave or hollow vault ; wherein he remained for the space of a year, studying divinity and the commands of his Redeemer. Scotland being then a rude and heathenish country, where the common sort of people dwelt, he was supposed to be sent from some place unknown, as a messenger to bring them evil tidings: whereupon those misbelieving people, by a common consent (taking him for some subtle conspirer against their Pagan gods, which they worshipped) put him secretly to death ; and after cutting off his head, in hope of reward bore it to the king, deeming they had done a deed which deserved commendation. When the king saw their inhuman cruelty he deeply lamented the loss of this good man, and with all speed, in revenge of his death, raised a power of his best resolved knights of war, putting every one to the sword, both man, woman, and child, that in any manner consented to the champion's death; and after, in process of time, appointed a monastery to be built in the same place where he died.

CHAPTER XXIV.

Of the Adventure performed by St. George: how he received his Death by the Sting of a venomous Dragon.

Now droops my weary muse, for she has come unto her latest tragedy. St. George is summoned to the bar of Death, where Honour stands ready to give his name a noble renown to all future ages.

This illustrious champion, when he was left by the other six, in the company of his three sons, Guy, Alexander, and David, strange imaginations day by day possessed his mind, so that he could not rest nor sleep: sometimes supposing his companions were in great distress; at other times that they had won the chiefest goal of honour, little needing his knightly service and assistance: sometimes one thing, sometimes another, so molested him, that he must needs follow them.

Whereupon, calling his three sons together, he went to the Grecian emperor, and requested that they might all four depart, for knightly adventures had challenged them all to appear in some foreign region, where noble achievements were to be performed; but where and in what country his destiny had not yet revealed to him.

So dressing themselves in habiliments of shining steel, they left Constantinople, as it were, guided by Fate, until they came into England, then called Britain, whose chalky cliffs St. George had not seen for twice twelve years: and now coming to his native country, he gave his three sons a most joyful welcome, showing them, to their great comfort, the situation of the towns and cities, and the pleasant prospects of the fields as they passed, until they came within sight of the city of Coventry, where he was born; upon whose glittering pinnacles he no sooner cast his eyes, but the inhabitants interrupted his delights with a doleful report, how upon Dunsmore-Heath was an infectious dragon, that so annoyed the country that the inhabitants thereabout could not pass the heath without great danger; and how that fifteen knights of the kingdom had lost their lives in adventuring to destroy the same. Also giving him to understand a prophecy, "That a Christian knight never born of a woman should be the destroyer thereof, and his name in after ages, for accomplishing the adventure, should be held for an eternal honour to the kingdom. St. George no sooner heard this, and what wrongs his native country received by this infectious dragon, than, knowing himself to be the knight, he felt so encouraged, that he purposed presently to put the adventure in trial, and either to free his country from such great danger, or to finish his days in the attempt; so taking leave of his sons, and the rest there present, he rode forward with as noble a spirit as he did in Egypt, when he there combatted with the burning dragon.

So coming to the middle of the plain, where his infectious enemy lay couching on the ground in a deep cave, who by a strange instinct of nature knowing his death to draw near, made such a yelling noise, as if the element had burst with thunder, or the earth had shook with a terrible explosion; and coming from his den, and espying the champion, ran with such fury against him, as if he would have devoured both man and horse in a moment; but the champion being quick and nimble, gave the dragon such way that he missed him, and with his sting ran full two feet into the earth: but recovering, he returned again with such rage upon St. George, that he had almost turned his horse over: but the dragon, having no stay of his strength, fell with his back downward to the ground, and his feet upward: whereat the champion taking advantage, kept him still down, with his horse standing upon him, fighting as you see in the plate of St. George, with his lance goring him through in divers parts of the body: and the dragon's sting annoyed the good knight so much, that the dragon being no sooner slain, but St. George likewise took his death wound by the deep strokes of the dragon's sting which he received in various parts of the body, and bled in such abundance, that his strength began to fail: yet, retaining the true nobleness of mind, valiantly returned victor to the city of Coventry; where his three sons, with the whole inhabitants, stood without the gates in great royalty, to receive him, and to give him the honour that belonged to so worthy a conqueror; who no sooner arrived before the city, and presented them with the dragon's head which so long had annoyed the country, but, from the loss of blood from his wounds, he was forced to yield up his breath. His three princely sons long lamented his death, and the whole country, from the king to the shepherd, mourned for him for the space of a month: which heavy time being ended, the king of this country, being a virtuous and noble prince, advanced St. George's three sons to noble offices: first, the eldest of them, named

Guy, to be earl of Warwick, and high chamberlain of his household: the next, named Alexander, according to his name, to be captain-general of his knight of chivalry: and the youngest, named David, to be his cup-bearer, and comptroller of all his revels and delights. And likewise, in remembrance of their noble father, the Christian champion, he ordained for ever after to be kept a solemn procession about the king's court, by all the princes and chief nobility of the country, upon the twenty-third day of April, naming it St. George's Day, upon which day he was most solemnly interred in the city where he was born: and caused a stately monument to be erected in honour of him, though now by time defaced and abolished. He likewise decreed, by the consent of the whole kingdom, that the patron of the land should be named St. George, our Christian champion, in that he fought so many battles in the honour of Christendom.

Leaving thus the Christian champions in their graves, we proceed now to relate the surprising adventures that befel St. George's three sons; as also the martial exploits of the sons of the other champions, in defence of the Christian religion, and relief of distressed knights and ladies.

PART III.

CHAPTER I.

The great joy of the Infidels at the death of the seven champions. The Soldan of Persia's letter for the mustering up of an Army; with the effects thereupon.

SOON had wide-mouthed Fame dispersed the news of the death of the Seven Champions into all the countries and kingdoms of the earth; which caused a universal joy and rejoicing among those miscreants, and infidels, who had felt the weight of their victorious arms, insomuch that they published a day of thanksgiving, to praise their gods, Mahomet, Termagant, and Apollo, for the deliverance of their countries out of the hands of such mortal enemies. Next they provided for the invasion of Christendom, and by a mutual consent to muster up such an army as should extirpate Christianity, and root out those seven nations from off the earth, whereof those worthies were the heroic champions; and to this end the soldan of Persia wrote the following letter to those kingdoms and nations which were therein concerned:

To all those Potentates and Followers of the sect of Mahomet, the high and mighty emperor the Soldan of Persia sendeth greeting:

" KNOW ye, that our gods have now at last sent the messenger of death, which hath arrested those terrors of our people, the Seven Champions of Christendom, by whom we have sustained so many harms and damages ; by which means opportunity is left, whereby we may revenge our wrongs and injuries. To this purpose, we therefore desire you to meet us, with what power of men ye can raise, on the plains of Babylon ; there to join with the forces of other kings and princes, to be revenged on the Christians, by slaying their people, burning their towns and cities, and utterly destroying them from off the face of the earth."

The copy of this letter being sent into several nations and kingdoms, the kings of those countries assembled together all the forces they could, and with the greatest expedition they could use marched to the plains of Babylon. The first that came thither was the king of Arabia, attended with an army of twenty thousand men, whereof eight thousand were mounted on Arabian coursers, being armed with spears and targets, so swift and dexterous in their undertakings, that they seldom missed of achieving any business they were about. His pavilion was of a violet colour, fringed with yellow, to distinguish what country he was of.

The next was the soldan of Persia himself, with an army of ten thousand horsemen and thirty thousand foot, of which nine thousand were pioneers, to level the way for the armies marching, and to dig trenches for the assaulting of any castle or city. His pavilion was red, fringed with orange-tawny; being mounted on a hill, to be the more conspicuous to the beholders.

Next was the king of Egypt, with twenty-five thousand men, of which three hundred were magicians or soothsayers, to charm and bewitch the Christian army, that they might not fight. His pavilion was blue, fringed with black, and was placed on the right hand of the king of Arabia.

Soon came the great cham of Tartary, with an army of thirty thousand men, all in quilted jackets, so thick wrought that no arrow could pierce them. They were all armed with steel gauntlets, and had swords of a hand's breadth, and withal so sharp, that they would cut off a man at the middle with a blow. His pavilion was of a primrose colour, with a white fringe, which was placed on the left hand of the soldan of Persia.

Next came the king of Morocco, with two thousand horsemen, mounted all on Barbary steeds, armed with the skins of stags, so thick and tough that no sword could cut through them : he had also ten thousand footmen, with iron maces having round balls at the end of them of four or five pounds weight, therewith to dash out the Christians' brains. His pavilion and the fringe thereof were all black, to signify black and dismal days to ensue. He was placed next to the king of Egypt.

The next that arrived in the fruitful fields of Babylon, was the king of Parthia, with an army consisting of fifteen thousand men; he had also an hundred elephants, carrying towers on their backs, in each of which ten men might stand and fight. This king was in stature four feet higher than most men, having each limb answerable thereto; so that he wore a sword two yards in length, the pummel whereof weighed twenty pounds. His pavilion was sky-colour, fringed with sea-green, and was placed next to the king of Morocco.

Next was the emperor or grand signior of the Turks, accompanied with ten thousand janisaries, armed with sharp scimitars, so keen that they could cut a bolt of iron asunder. He was armed in a coat of mail of burnished silver, having on his head a white turban, and a pendant on it, whereon was pictured a half-moon, with this motto, "Still increasing." His pavilion was green, with silver and gold fringe, and was placed on the right hand of the soldan of Persia.

After him came the prince of Tripoli, accompanied with four giants of a marvellous size, whose names were, Garian, Caras, Phidon, and Raphsarus. These bore on their necks great knotty oaks, with which they could strike two yards deep into the ground, and were most dreadful to behold. He had also with him a deformed creature called a Sagittary, being half a man and half a horse, who could run as swift as a ship can sail having wind and weather: his offensive weapon was a bow, with which he shot poisoned arrows; and was so expert therein, that he could shoot to a hair's-breadth. This prince of Tripoli was encamped next to the king of Parthia, and had a pavilion of a pea-blossom colour, fringed with murrey.

After him came the Count Palatine of Trebizon, with fifteen hundred cross-bowmen, all armed in steel corslets. He had also three thousand men that used slings, with which they could exactly hit whatever they aimed at, and that at a great distance from them. On his shield was painted a griffin grasping a Christian, with this motto, "Seized of his prey." His pavilion was of an azure colour, fringed with red, and was placed next to the emperor or grand signior of the Turks.

The next that appeared on the Babylonian plains, for the destruction of the Christians, was the bassa of Aleppo, who brought with him an hundred waggons laden with balls of wild-fire, sulphur, and certain engines called caltrops, being little things made with four iron points of such a fashion, that which way soever they were thrown one point would always stick up like a nail; and these were to be thrown into the Christians' army, to spoil the feet of their horses. His pavilion was of an iron-grey colour, and was placed next to the Count Palatine of Trebizond.

Next was the mameluke of Damascus, attended with six thousand horse and six thousand footmen. He had also in his army a deformed monster, from the shoulders downwards shaped like a man, but his head and face like that of a horse, being a present sent him from the cham of Tartary, and from whom descended the horse-faced Tartar killed by count Sereni. This mameluke's pavilion was of yellow intermixed with black, and fringed with red, being placed next to the bassa of Aleppo.

Many other kings, princes, and emperors were engaged in this enterprise, whose names would be too tedious here to recite; insomuch that there was assembled such an army as made the earth to shake under the weight thereof; being more in number than that of Xerxes, which drank up all rivers dry as they went; or than that of the Macedonian Alexander, with which he conquered the greatest part of the world.

Being in this manner assembled together, the soldan of Persia, as one of the chief of the association, gathered the greatest princes and captains to his pavilion, where he entertained them with a costly banquet, and then he made this following oration:

"Most mighty kings, princes, and captains of this invincible army, it is not unknown to you what injuries and mischiefs we have received from the Christian armies, under the conduct of those persons whom they called the Seven Champions of Christendom : to enumerate them all in particular, would make my oration too tedious unto you ; I shall therefore only give some few instances. What injury did St. George, the champion of England, unto Ptolemy king of Egypt, by stealing away his daughter ; as also from Almidor, king of Morocco, his dearest lady and mistress! Did not the king's daughter of Thessaly run away from her country by the sly insinuations of St. Denis of France ; as also the king of Jerusalem's daughter by the like persuasions of St. James of Spain? What intolerable injury was it to the king of Thrace, to have his fair daughter Rosaline tempted away from her country by the brave Italian champion, to be deprived of his other six daughters. Did not the Welsh champion slay the Count Palatine of Tartary in his father's court? Besides infinite other mischiefs, losses, and disgraces we have received from them ; all which, whilst they lived, we were not able to revenge ; but now, since Death hath being so kind to take them out of the world, let us pluck up our courage, and manfully fight in revenge of our injuries. Let pity be exiled from our thoughts, neither sparing old age for their hoary heads, nor the tender infant for its pitiful cry : let not the tears of matrons find regard, nor the wailings of widows any respect; but let all be destined to the sword, that we may have a general triumph in their utter confusion."

This oration was received with general applause, each one protesting his utmost endeavours for the extirpation of Christianity, and never to sheath his sword till they had laid the European cities equal with the dust, and their stately monuments in ruin, like to the lofty pyramids of Troy. And now, considering, by experience, the fatal effects of their former discord in electing a general, and how necessary it was to have a commander-in-chief; to avoid all controversy, it was decreed amongst them, that six of the most renowned should be picked out, and from them one to be chosen by lot to be commander-in-chief; the king of Arabia, the king of Persia, the soldan of Babylon, the king of Egypt, the emperor of the Turks, and the king of Morocco. The lots being cast, it fell to the share of the soldan of Babylon to be their general, the king of Persia major-general, and the king of Arabia, by reason of the swiftness of his coursers, scout-master-general.

Other kings and princes had appointed unto them several other offices, according to the quality and capacity they had in the feats of war. So that, all things considered, they seemed to be an army invincible, being for number like the army of Xerxes, which drank all rivers dry; and for warlike provisions, so much and plentiful, as far exceeded all number of arithmetic.

Here will we leave this mighty army in the plains of Babylon, and come to tell you of the great preparations the Christians made to resist them. But first we shall describe the valiant acts of St. George's three sons, and how they, hearing of this great army intended for the ruin of Christendom, returned home to fight in defence of their country

CHAPTER II.

How St. George's three sons left England to seek adventures in Foreign Countries; how they arrived in Sicily, and killed a terrible monster, named Pongo; how Urania, the king of Sicily's daughter, fell in love with Sir Guy; with the other things which happened.

You may remember, in the second part of this famous history, we left St. George's three sons in the English court; where they had not long continued after their father's death, but growing weary of idleness, and being more desirous to follow the camp of Mars than to dally with ladies in the court of Venus, they resolved to betake themselves to travel, and to seek out adventures in foreign countries; and having imparted their minds to the king, they furnished themselves with all things necessary for such a journey, and bidding the fruitful soil of England adieu, they in a few weeks' sailing, arrived on the coasts of Sicily; where marching up higher into the country, they saw many houses, but no inhabitants—yea, whole towns of empty houses, but neither man, woman, nor child within them: which made them jealous that some grievous pestilence had overspread that country, and made it desolate of inhabitants; wherefore, to avoid any infection which might happen unto them, they took up their lodging in the open fields, having only the starry firmament for their canopy. Thus sweetly reposing on their mother earth, they slept as soundly as if they had laid on beds of down, and been surrounded with curtains of the purest Arabian silk. Thus did they sleep securely, until such time as Aurora began to gild the firmament with her bright rays, and to usher in Phœbus's golden light; when suddenly they were awaked with a most horrible noise, which seemed to be sent from the deep abyss, and to be able to rend the rocks asunder: whereupon they suddenly buckled on their armour, and stood upon their guard; and indeed it was high time, for at that instant they saw coming towards them a most deformed monster, of an excessive size and terrible shape, having eyes like burning saucers, and claws sharper than eagles' talons. He seemed to move like a high tower or pyramid, and with his weight to make the earth tremble. The sight of this ugly monster so startled their horses, that they would hardly endure the bit; but, snorting and stamping the earth with their feet, showed the dread they had of such a sight. But these three valiant knights, in whom were sown the seeds of true magnanimity, stood fearless to abide what danger soever might happen.

The first whom this fierce monster made unto, was the valiant knight Sir Guy, who, nothing daunted at his hideous shape, having put his spear in his rest, ran furiously against him; but the monster being armed with scales far harder than brass, his spear shivered in a thousand pieces. Then drawing out his trusty falchion, he assailed the monster with manly strokes; who on his part, not backward in defence, but bolting upright with his tail, stretched forth one of his paws, and with the same grasped so hard on the arm of Sir Guy, that he had well near siezed him, had not Sir David at that instant come in and with his sword cut the monster's paw quite off, leaving the claws so firmly fixed on Sir Guy's arm, that, notwithstanding the goodness of his armour, it was very hard to get off. In the mean time the valiant and renowned knight Sir Alexander, with great force set upon the monster, giving him such blows upon the head as made him reel; who with his tail striking at Sir Alexander, so wrapped the same about his horse's legs, that, not able to stand, he came over and over with the knight. The monster seeing him on the ground, was making towards him; when Sir David met him with such a lusty thrust on the breast, though it pierced not the same, it laid the monster flat on his back; which was no sooner done, but Sir Guy, nimbly leaping from off his horse, thrust his sword down the monster's throat, who lay gasping for breath, when he tore his heart asunder: yet notwithstanding the same, the monster's teeth were so keen, that he bit the knight's sword in two, leaving the one half in his throat; and withal sent forth such a hideous yell, as surpassed the roaring of the cataracts of the Nile, or the greatest crack of the loudest thunder: but having received his death wound, with some little struggling he yielded his life up to the victors; who surveying his body, found it to be, from the head to the tail full ten yards in length: his bulk at least a ton weight; having paws and claws answerable to it; and each part so armed with scales, as scarcely was penetrable with any sword.

The knights having obtained this victory, returned thanks to the immortal powers, and leaving the carcass of the hideous monster, travelled up higher into the country, hoping to meet with some of the inhabitants thereof, who, now they saw, had left their houses for dread of this monster. Having travelled some few miles, and desirous of refreshment after this encounter, they saw some smoke ascending out of the tunnel of a little cell near unto them; whither bending their course, they saw standing at the door an aged hermit, in a gown of frieze reaching to the ground; his hair as white as the down of swans, or driven snow, which in a careless manner hung down his shoulders: in his face you might read the map of sorrow, charactered out in deep-furrowed wrinkles: whom the knights courteously saluted, desiring to know the reason why so fruitful a country as they had passed was left destitute of inhabitants. The aged hermit, having viewed them well, and perceived by their habit that they were outlandish knights bent upon martial adventures, and seemed to be persons who dreaded no danger, he desired them to alight from their warlike steeds, and for a while to repose themselves in his lowly cell, and he would endeavour to satisfy their desires: "In the mean time," said he, "I would desire you to take such homely refreshment as my cell affords;" and thereupon he brought them forth such country viands as that place afforded; which they courteously accepted; and having satisfied their hunger, the hermit began to speak to them in this manner:

"Sir knights," said he, "for so you seem by your outward habiliments, if we may judge of the goodness of the apple by the fairness of the rind; know that this country wherein you now are, is the land of Sicily; once so fruitful and abounding in all things, that it well might be called the granary of the world, and now still retaining its virtue, did the inhabitants manure the same. But now our plenty is turned into misery, our mirth into mourning; our streets, which were wont to be replenished with throngs of people, now destitute and empty of inhabitants; and all by reason of a most ghastly dreadful monster, sent, I think, from the infernal regions for the punishment of mankind, whom the country people term by the name of Pongo. This direful monster or rather fiend incarnate, begotten, as it is thought, between a land tiger and a sea-shark, so that it participates of both elements, swimming in the sea near our Sicilian coasts, espied some herdsmen near on the shore, who with great wonder beheld this monster as he sported himself on the waves of the sea: but when they saw that he made towards them, and beheld the monstrousness of his proportion, fear, standing at the gates of their eyes, put back all further persuasions of beholding him, and, adding wings to their fear, they flew away in the greatest haste they possibly could make. But in vain was all their speed, for he, soon recovering the shore, seized upon some of the hindmost of them, whom he made a prey to his devouring paunch; and having tasted the sweetness of human blood, he ever since hath haunted our coasts, raging up higher into the country, devouring all wheresoever he came: and herein is his cruelty most exemplary, that he delights more in the slaughter of men than of beasts; so that it is judged he hath devoured no less than five hundred persons; and for twenty miles' space left all desolate and uninhabited; the dread of him being so very great, that the women, to terrify their children from crying, used to say, 'the Pongo cometh.'

"Thus, renowned knights, have you heard the cause of our country's misery; not one of our stoutest champions having the heart to encounter with him; so that with freedom he wastes and destroys all before him, until such time as it shall please Providence to send us some more redoubted knights than ours, to free us of him: for which our king hath promised great rewards, the spur to honourable achievements; besides the great good (a reward in itself) which it will do to mankind, in freeing us from so terrible an enemy."

The hermit concluding his speeches with a deep sigh for a period, the valiant knight Sir Guy, with a smiling countenance, thus answered him: "Now then," said he, "are the stars so benign unto Sicily, that your country is freed from this direful misery; for, the cause being taken away, the effect must needs cease. Know then, that by the victorious arms of me, and my two brothers, the monster is dead; and there is no more dread of your being affrighted by a dead Pongo, than is to be feared from a living grasshopper, or butterfly."

Scarcely had Sir Guy ended his speech, when the hermit, transported with an excessive joy, fell down at his feet, being almost in as great an ecstasy for joy as was that father, who, having three sons returned victors from the Olympic games, his overjoyed spirit could not contain itself in the bounds of reason, but by the excessiveness thereof yielded up the ghost. "And is our land," said he, "capable of so great a benefit! Does so good fortune attend our country! Then thanks to the immortal Powers above, who hath sent you hither to be the means of our future happiness! How is our nation bound to your manhood, and what victims shall we offer for your fortunate success!"

As the hermit was thus discoursing, there was passing by his cell an herald at arms, well accoutred, and attended by four knights clad all in mourning armour, who were sent by the king into foreign countries, to proclaim in every place where they came, that if any knight would be so hardy as to encounter with the Pongo, and overcome him, he should be made a peer of the realm, and have a golden hermit for his reward. This their errand being made known to the three knights, they declared unto them how the Pongo was already killed; which put a stop to their further journey: and sending back one of the knights to the king, to inform him thereof, the rest went to view the dead carcase of the Pongo; which having surveyed with great admiration, the three Sicilian knights invited Sir Guy, Sir Alexander, and Sir David to the city of Syracuse, where the king then kept his court; who courteously accepting of their proffer, taking leave of the aged hermit, who returned to his cell, mounting their warlike steeds, with an easy pace they marched on. But when the king heard the news of the monster's death, he caused the bells to be rung, and bonfires to be made, for joy thereof; and hearing how the three knights were coming towards him, he went forth to meet them, attended in this manner:—First, went two trumpeters clad in the arms of Sicily, being two plaunches argent, charged with as many eagles' sable. Then followed a band of pensioners with golden streamers, which they displayed as they marched along. After them went four score knights, mounted on their barbed steeds, and armed with bright glistering falchions. Next went the king's life-guard, in buff coats edged with silver fringe, and wearing on their shoulders coronation scarfs, inlaid with gold. After them the king himself, in a costly chariot studded with pillars of silver, and lined with carnation velvet; being followed by an innumerable train of lords and gentlemen, and their attendants.

With this stately train did the king go to meet these three victorious knights; who, at his coming, alighted from their steeds, whom the king courteously embraced; and after some short discourse, had them into his chariot, and so triumphantly returned back to Syracuse; all the way the bells ringing, the bonfires blazing, and the people making such loud acclamations of joy, that the earth rang with the noise thereof.

Being come to the king's palace, they were met by the queen Berenice, and her beautiful daughter Urania, the flower of courtesy, and paragon of rare perfection; who, as she excelled the other Sicilian virgins in dignity and honour, so did she surpass them all in beauty, and other ornaments of nature; to which were joined such rare endowments of the mind, as completed her a princess of admirable parts. After they were alighted from the chariot, they were conducted to a stately room, where was provided for them a costly banquet; which being ended, their ears were saluted with most sweet music; after which the ladies presented them with a stately mask. All this while the princess Urania fed her eyes with beholding Sir Guy, whose perfections she so contemplated, that love, entering in at her eyes so wounded her heart, that she became wholly captured in the bonds of Cupid. Sir Guy, on the other side, was so pierced with her transcendant beauty, and her other rare accomplishments, that he wholly resigned up himself to her devotion, she being the loadstone of his affections, attracting all the faculties of his soul in obedience to her commands.

Thus did these two princely persons reciprocally bear true love to each other, though neither of them knew each other's mind. But as fire will not be long hid under combustible matter, so love, where it is ardent, will show itself through all the disguises they can put upon it. These heroic knights had not been many weeks in the Sicilian court, feasting and revelling in all the delights and pleasures which that fruitful country afforded, but such pleasures grew too tedious unto them, especially to Sir Guy, whose love to the princess Urania made sports and company distasteful unto him: so one evening, at such time as the golden charioteer of heaven had finished his diurnal course, and driven his panting steeds down the western hill, he intended to take a solitary walk in the garden, when, coming under the princess Urania's chamber window, he heard the music of a lute, which with harmonious airs saluted his ears; and, listening awhile, a voice delivered itself in these words:

> Now woe is me, poor hapless virgin, I
> Am forc'd to yield to Cupid's deity;
> All striving is in vain;
> Love the conquest he will gain,
> And I a vassal must to him remain.

> Yet, gentle Cupid, let me thee desire
> To wound his breast, like mine, with equal fire,
>   That so our loves, together join'd,
>   May settle in a quiet mind,
> And we in them may true contentment find.

As Sir Guy was listening to this harmonious voice, there passed by him one of the princess Urania's ladies, which put a stop unto her singing: but pondering well in his mind the substance of her sonnet, it gave him great hopes of her affections to him; and as every lover flatters himself in his own imagination, so did he imagine himself sole monarch of the princess's heart. That night the ladies had provided a stately mask, which at the end of every scene was attended with most rare music and excellent dancing; to which mask the three brothers were invited. The time being come for the mask to begin, it was performed in this manner:

First began a most excellent concert of music. Then entered four maskers in cloth of gold, most richly embroidered; three of them personating the goddesses, Juno, Pallas, and Venus, when they strove for the golden apple on the mount of Ida; the fourth represented the shepherd Paris, who having heard their several pleas, which they made for the obtaining of the apple, he adjudged it to Venus. Having danced a carouse about the room they withdrew.

After a little space, the music playing again, according as it was appointed, the three knights took each of them a lady by the hand to lead them in a dance: and now had Sir Guy the happiness to converse with his dear lady and mistress: for, taking the princess Urania by the hand, he with great courtesy and humility kissed it; and she kindly accepting his proffer, he led her a course about the room in as great majesty and state as did Æneas, when he revelled it in the court of queen Dido; and she following him with as much grace, as might become the queen of love to have acted: and so having showed the spectators that he could as well tread a measure in a dance, as handle the warlike lance, he with the princess Urania withdrew into a corner of that spacious room; whilst Sir Alexander, having associated himself with a gallant lady named Alsatia, the daughter to the viceroy of Naples, began a second course to the music; which whilst they were performing, Sir Guy courted the princess Urania in these words:

"Most peerless princess," said Sir Guy, "if the bleeding wounds of my heart could speak, which you have pierced by the beams of your matchless beauty, then would it save my tongue the labour to declare the affection which I bear to your noble person. If I have aimed too high, blame your matchless beauty and virtues, that have caused it. Let me therefore conjure you, by all the rights and charms of love, and by those fair eyes that have enthralled mine, not to prove obdurate in thy love, though I must confess myself unworthy of so high a bliss: yet shall the sun sooner cease to run his course, the stars to give light, and every thing alter from its wonted course, ere Guy will prove false, or cease to honour the perfections of the princess Urania."

Although this speech was very welcome to the love-sick princess, yet, that she might not seem too forward, with a maidenly modesty she thus replied:

"Sir, you must pardon me, if I look before I leap. That myself, together with our whole country, is indebted to your prowess, we shall for ever acknowledge. But to love, and so to love as to make you a promise of being my husband (for I hope you mean no other thing but what tends to my honour.) you must excuse me, having no other assurance of your quality and truth, but only your own verbal expressions: besides, you being a stranger, and I an heir to a crown, were your estate answerable to your (I must confess) excellent qualification, yet could I not be so at my own disposal to conclude of what you desire, seeing not only my parents, but my country, have so great a share in me."

She would have proceeded further, but Sir Alexander and the lady Alsatia having finished their dance, the cornets and other wind music sounding aloud, they were called away to behold another scene of fresh maskers, who in this way entertained the beholders. First entered the likeness of a stately fabric, made of a pasteboard, and adorned with many golden streamers, which represented the temple of Honour. This being drawn to the further side of that spacious room, soon after entered another fabric, but lower and not so richly adorned, which represented the temple of Virtue, and was so placed that none could enter the temple of Honour but must first pass through the temple of Virtue. Afterwards entered several persons, who attempted to get into the temple of Honour, but were loth to go through the temple of Virtue, therefore they missed of their aim. Those who went through the temple of Virtue, were richly adorned and rewarded, and and greatly honoured of the people; but those who would climb up to the temple of Honour, and not enter it by the temple of Virtue, it was made so slippery on the top, that with the least treading away they fell down and broke their necks.

This show being ended, and the cornets and other loud music ceasing, the valiant and renowned knight Sir David, taking a most beautiful damsel by the hand, named Artesia, and niece to the king of Sicily, by his sister Rodelentia, whose husband was a renowned knight at arms, and master of the strong castle of Angelo: this noble lady, who had not her superior for beauty on the face of the earth, most willingly gave her hand to Sir David; and so, with as much portly majesty as the god of war led the stately Venus, they danced a galliard: which whilst they were doing, Sir Guy having a further opportunity to speak to the goddess of his affections, accosted her in this manner:

"Most excellent lady, do not entertain a heart more hard than flint, which the tears of my true love cannot mollify; nor think my affections to you to be like breath on steel, soon on and soon off: no, I protest by all the sacred oaths of religion, and by yourself—that is, by all that is good—my love shall be as durable and firm as whatsoever is most permanent. Nor do not think, because some have proved treacherous and disloyal to their loves, that once so unworthy a thought should ever enter into my heart. No, although Æneas proved false to Dido, yet will Guy be as true to his Urania, as ever was Pyramus to his beloved Thisbe, or Leander to Hero. What though Jason basely forsook his Medea, by whose means he obtained the golden fleece, yet shall my faith always remain firm, and be as constant to thee as was Ulysses' to his Penelope."

The princess, hearing these asseverations, and being willing he should not be too much dejected, but that some beams of comfort should reflect on him, she told him, that time, the mother of truth, would prove the reality of his affections; in the mean time that he should not despair, since, being a soldier, he must needs know that the strongest castles by continual batteries are forced to yield.

By this time the night was so far spent as summoned them all to go to their beds; where no sooner were they laid, but Somnus, the god of sleep, closed up their eyes in golden slumbers. Next morning, no sooner did Aurora from the glowing east display her purple; and that Hyperion, with his ruddy rays began to gild the horizon with his radiant beams, than the shrill noise of a silver trumpet sounding at the court gates raised them from their beds, to know what was the meaning of it; when they were quickly informed, that it was a knight of Thessaly, attended by a squire and a trumpeter, who desired to speak with the king of Sicily; who being admitted into his presence delivered himself in these words:

"Most noble prince, my coming hither to you, is to desire of you assistance for our distressed country of Thessaly, oppressed, and made almost desolate, by the encroachments and tyranny of the king of Thrace: the cause of which quarrel he pretends to be, for that our king having but one daughter, named Mariana, the heiress to his crown and dominions: being a lady not only endued with the excellency of Nature's gifts, but withal so virtuous, affable, and every way complete in knowledge, that she may well be said to be the darling of her sex, and admiration of all that know her. This peerless princess, the king of Thrace, who is famed as a man given over to all licentiousness, and so far degenerate from royalty that he commits actions unbeseeming a peasant, desired of her father to have her in marriage; but she, loathing to link herself in such marriage bonds, where love and true honour did not mutually embrace each other, refused so loathsome a proffer, and that with such indignation, that, upon his ambassador's return, and acquainted with his slighting, he resolved to do that by force which he could not obtain by favour; and to that end mustered up a most puissant army; which was done in such an instant, that he has marched into the midst of our land before we were prepared to meet him on our borders: nay, his horse, consisting of ten thousand well-approved soldiers, excellently armed, both with offensive and defensive weapons, had by their incursion so affrighted our people, that our strongest citadels were not held sufficient to guard them from danger, and all left to the spoil of the enemy. At last this news was brought to our king, who held himself secure, by reason there was a mutual league of peace between them, which at that time was not half expired; so that he was altogether unprovided for the present (a great fault in princes, to think any estate so permanent that it may not be soon overturned): but upon the news thereof he bestirs himself; fortifies his chief city, Larissa, where he kept his court; and raises as puissant an army as he could, in so short a time, which he marched against his enemies. The king of Thrace had with him a mighty giant, named Predo, in whom he put great confidence. This giant had the strength of ten men, and was for stature and shape very terrible to behold. In the valley of Tempe they joined battle, where, notwithstanding our men did what in them lay, as fighting for the liberty of their country, yet, being overpowered and borne down by the strength and valour of the giant Predo, they received a dismal overthrow; the greatest part of the army were slain, and most of the rest taken prisoners; amongst whom our woful king was one; who encountering Predo, who had on him a coat of mail, and over that an armour of two hundred pounds weight, being on foot (for no horse was able to bear him), our king running against him with his lance, it shivered in a thousand pieces; nor could his sword aught avail against the giant's armour, although he laid on such strokes, that sparks flew from it as from a piece of hot iron when a smith is working it. But the giant valued his blows so little, finding him to be the Thessalian king, and now almost spent with long fighting, that he made no more ado, but, clasping his arms about him, he carried both horse and man together into his tent; which our men seeing, fled, and dispersed themselves as well as they could for their own safety. And now the Thracians being absolute victors, it was agreed amongst them, that the giant Predo should carry our king prisoner with him into his castle where he lives, being a place strongly situated in an island, having one associated with him, famous for his skill in the Black Art; so that what by the strength of the one, and devilish cunning of the other, we despair of ever having our king again. As for the king of Thrace, he, with the remains of his army, marched up to the city of Larissa, wherein our princess Mariana is enclosed, and so straitly besieged it, that without speedy help the city is in danger to be lost, and with it the liberty and welfare of our whole country, which now lies bleeding in a pitiful manner, unless (most noble prince) your goodness will be pleased to lend us any aid or assistance, which now both our nobles and commons do most humbly implore at your hands."

This woful tale being finished, moved great pity and compassion in all the hearers thereof, especially in the three English brothers, whose princely minds being endowed with the true seeds of magnanimity, they vowed, by the honour of true knighthood, and all that was most dear unto them, to use their utmost endeavours, were it to the spending of their most precious blood, for the relieving of the princess Mariana and her captive father. The Thessalian king promising his best assistance to join with them, they with all speed made what haste they could for the mustering up of an army; and notwithstanding the great strength and terribleness of the giant Predo, strike some dread and terror into the hearts of many, yet being accompanied with such invincible knights as were these three brothers, they dreaded no danger, but with a valiant courage resolved to venture their lives with them, whose valiant acts and noble achievements, deserving to be recorded in the books of Fame, Calliope assisting, shall be recorded in the next chapter.

CHAPTER III.

How Sir Guy took his leave of the Princess Urania; the battle between the Sicilians and Thracians; the Message of the Princess Mariana to the enchanted castle, and how Sir Alexander courted the Princess.

THE captains and other officers made such expedition in mustering up an army, that in a fortnight's time they had gotten together twenty thousand men: all which the king completely armed out of his royal armoury, being a magazine sufficiently stored with all necessary habiliments of war. To the three brothers he gave each a silver helmet studded with gold, and inlaid with precious stones, as a reward for their victory in conquering the monster Pongo, appointing to their valiant conduct the management of the whole army. Whilst thus this preparation was in hand, the courageous knight, Sir Guy, although his heart was full fraught with valour, and bent to the performance of noble achievements, yet had love taken such impression in his thoughts, that it was death unto him to part with his Urania. Whilst thus honour on the one hand invited him to buckle on his armour, and love on the other side pleaded for his stay, he resolved not to desist from the performance of honourable achievements, since the attainment of love was by hazardous attempts in actions which were truly honourable.

Accordingly he bestirred himself in mustering his men, showing them how to handle their weapons, and use them to the best advantage; also how to gain ground in fight, and when to retreat, with other things belonging to martial discipline. And now being ready for their march, he went to take his solemn leave of the princess Urania, who bestowed on him a very valuable diamond ring, to wear for her sake, as also a medal of herself very curiously wrought with great art, and exceeding costly, which he afterwards constantly wore in his bosom, next his heart. But now seeing he could not have the opportunity of expressing his mind unto her as he would have done, he wrote the following letter, which, by a waiting gentlewoman that attended on her, was delivered unto her about the time of his departure.

"Excellent Princess,

"Blame me not that for a while I am summoned by the highest tie of honour to depart from you; being in such a cause to help the injured, which all true knights are bound to perform: yet, madam, know that no distance of place can remove the affection I bear to your virtues; and this I swear by all that is sacred, and can make an oath. Let me desire you therefore to cherish a good opinion of me, until, crowned with victory, I return again to evidence myself to be,

"Your most loyal servant,
GUY."

This letter was very welcome to the princess Urania who now began to set such a high esteem on Sir Guy, that she judged him worthy of the empire of the world. And now, he being the sole monarch of her heart, she could not but breathe forth some sighs for his absence; but then, considering upon what an honourable account he was engaged, she could not but applaud his undertaking: yet, to give him some more clear demonstration of her affection to him, upon his marching away, she went in her chariot to speak to him, whom she found at the head of his troops, and kindly bade him farewell in these words:

"Most courteous knight, may Heaven prosper your undertaking, according to the justice of your cause, and that your return may be both speedy and honourable; and for your prosperous proceeding, assure yourself you shall have a virgin's prayers day and night. In the mean time, let me request you to wear this scarf for my sake, that by looking on the same, I may not be altogether, out of your remembrance."

In delivering of which the tears began to flow into her eyes for grief of his departure; which that they might not be seen by Sir Guy, she made the more haste back to her palace, where from one of the highest turrets she might behold in what goodly array the army passed along; the valiant Guy, like a second Hector, prince of Troy, conducting them in as much state as the Macedonian monarch, when he returned from the conquest of the Indian Empire.

The distressed state of the Thessalians was such as called aloud for help and succour, which made the Sicilians make such haste, that in four days' time they had got into the bounds of pleasant Thessaly; a country formerly enriched with all the delights that art and nature could afford, but now, by the miseries of war, so ruined and devastated, that it looked like to a barren wilderness. The first place they came to was the city of Larissa, wherein the princess Mariana was besieged; for the relief of which Sir Alexander was sent before, with a choice part of the army, to give them an assault in the night-season, the rest of the army marching at more leisure to second them, if they should be overpowered: and one of the Thessalians, who was well acquainted with the country, was sent into the city to give them notice of their coming, and that at such a time they should make what strength they could, and give a sally out upon the Thracians. This Thessalian, who was thus sent in, brought great comfort unto the besieged, who accordingly prepared against the time: and so about midnight, when Sir Alexander with his army was come within sight of the city, and held up a blazing torch to give them notice of their approach, they issued out of their gates and manfully set upon the Thracians. Sir Alexander, on the other side, coming upon their backs, fell on them with such fury as sent such numbers of the Thracian's souls to the lower regions, that Charon's boat was overburthened with their numbers. Sir Alexander laid about him with such incredible valour, that he made a lane of slaughtered carcasses, till he came to the Thracian king's pavilion, who, not dreaming of any enemy's approach, was at that time in his bed; but being alarmed by the dreadful cry of his soldiers, he suddenly started up: but before he could put on his clothers, Sir Alexander had entered his pavilion, and took him prisoner. Then fell the hearts of the Thracians, nothing being heard but cries and lamentations of wounded men. Here was one who would have run away, but had one leg cut off and the other deeply wounded; here another having both his arms cut off. Here lay the trunk of a body without a head; and there a head gasping, as if it would speak to what body it belonged. In some, death appeared in so many shapes, and all of them so horrid, that to any but a very unrelenting heart indeed the sight would appear very pitiful.

By this time was Sir Guy come up with the rest of the forces, where he found an absolute victory obtained to his hand; so that all which they had to do, was only to take prisoners, and divide the spoil among the soldiers. By this time Hyperion with his golden chariot had enlightened our lower hemisphere; wherefore the army marched into the city to refresh themselves; Sir Alexander, as he worthily deserved the honour of the victory, leading his royal prisoner, to present him to the princess Mariana, who was ready to receive him, with all due acknowledgments to the three brothers; but in an especial manner to Sir Alexander, for his magnanimity and martial conduct in the rescuing of her and the kingdom from so implacable an enemy.

"Most heroic knight," said the lovely princess, "although my tongue is not able to express how much I am indebted to your victorious arm, nor set forth your well deserved merits, whose worth transcends all encomium of praise; yet shall the remembrance of these so great kindnesses never be out of my heart, nor the thoughts of them out of my mind, without a grateful acknowledgment."

Then turning to the Thracian king, with as much of a wrathful countenance as such lovely beauty would admit, she thus spake:

"And as for you, Sir, the causer of all this mischief, what just reason of hatred I may have unto you, you can surely but imagine; for could you think this the way to come a wooing? I am sure if you did, you might well think it was not the way to come a speeding: and now, Sir, since we have you (and I must confess, rather as an enemy than a lover), you must not be angry if we safely secure you, until we hear how our royal father is used by those that belong unto you."

And so she committed him to the custody of the marshal of her household, to be kept prisoner in a strong tower near adjoining to her palace, but with the charge that he should be accommodated as a king. This being done, she invited the three brothers, with many of the other chief commanders, into her palace; where having disarmed themselves, and being refreshed with some bowls of Greek wine, there was provided for them a banquet of the choicest fare which they had about them at that time; the long and strait siege which they had endured having eaten up the most part of their provision. The banquet being ended, they were entertained with most excellent music, intermixed with songs in praise of the Sicilians' valour, for in the art of poetry Thessalians are very expert. The common soldiers were highly feasted by the citizens: and, in fine, such universal joy did so possess the hearts of the people, that had I the skill of Homer the Grecian poet, and as many hands to express that skill as Argus had eyes, and as many pens to write withal as Briarius had hands, yet were all insufficient to express the same.

Amidst this joy, the princess Mariana was not forgetful of her father's safety; and therefore she presently dispatched a messenger to the giant Predo, at his castle in the enchanted island, offering the Thracian king to be exchanged for him; which if it should be denied, the messenger was to learn in what state the king was in, and (if it were possible) to speak with him, and to acquaint him how matters stood, with resolutions of using their utmost power for his relief.

Whilst the messenger was gone on this message, the soldiers took their repose in safety—only each of the days they exercised, that if the giant Predo should be averse to any good conclusion, they might be the more expert at their arms: and indeed it was good policy so to do, for the messenger arriving at the enchanted island, could find no access into the castle, it being so formed by magic art, that whosoever approached within twelve yards of the gate was taken with such a deep sleep, as if he had drunk opium, or the juice of aconitum. Before the gate was a pillar of brass, supported by two lions, and curiously engraved; on which these verses were inscribed.

> "By magic spells this castle shall remain,
> Supported by infernal fiends below,
> Until three brothers shall the same attain,
> Whose power shall be this castle's overthrow.
> Whoe'er thou art, forbear to draw too near;
> Thy life's at stake, than which there's nought more dear."

Near attached to this brazen pillar stood a rock of alabaster, in which were enclosed three swords, richly enchased, and beset with precious stones in the pummels; on the handle of the first sword were these lines written:

> "Hard closed in this rock I firmly stand,
> Until drawn out by the First Brother's hand."

On the pummel of the second sword were these lines incribed:

> "The Second Brother shall, by Fate's decree,
> Draw from the rock this sword, and none but he."

On the pummel of the third sword, which was more artificially wrought than any of the other two, having a rich sapphire set therein, which cast forth a most radiant lustre, were these words engraved:

> "When the Third Brother he shall draw me forth,
> Then is our necromantic skill no worth;
> All magic charms and spells shall be in vain,
> And then shall be the end of giant Predo's reign."

The messenger, notwithstanding he had read the writing on the brazen pillar, yet ventured to go forwards; but coming into the enchanted ground, before he could come at the castle-gate he fell into such a sound sleep, that had twenty pieces of ordnance being shot off at his ears, they would not have wakened him. The necromancer, who by his skill in the Black Art knew what had happened, fetched his body into the castle, laying it by the Thessalian king, who also, as soon as he came into the enchanted ground, had fallen into a deep sleep. And now being there laid together, we will leave them taking their rest, and come to speak of the proceedings of the Sicilian army at the city of Larissa.

The princess Mariana, hearing no news of her messenger, and doubting the worst which might befal her father, consulting with the three brothers, it was agreed amongst them to march with their army into Thrace, although at that time love had taken so deep an impression in her heart that it was almost death unto her to part with Sir Alexander. On the other side, Sir Alexander, upon the first sight of the princess was so stricken with her admirable perfections, her beauty being such an attractive loadstone, as captured his heart in the allurements of love; so that now, as the poet hath it,

> ——"The treasure of his heart did lie
> In the fair casket of his mistress' eye."

Cupid having thus stricken him with his youthful dart, so that he became a stranger to rest, he resolved yet to declare his admiration before he betook himself to arms; and to that purpose, finding one day the princess all alone, he accosted her in this manner:

"Most gracious princess, I think the stars could have allotted me no greater good than to behold the surpassing work of nature in you; your excellencies having so captivated my heart, that to live without your good liking will be but a lingering death unto me. I must confess my presumption great, in aiming so high; but who can look on such perfections without liking, and who can like without loving? And though the small trial you have of the real affection wherewith I honour your virtues may discourage you to credit my words, yet, I hope, in the trying of me how willing I shall be to merit your favour, you will not find my deserts altogether unworthy of your regard, since the utmost of my abilities is, and shall be, devoted to your service."

To which the princess returned this answer:

"Most courteous knight, to whom I stand so much obliged for former courtesies, that all which I can do will not stand in competition of your deserts, yet the natural affection which I bear to my aged father compels me at this time humbly to implore your further assistance, which as I doubt not (the gods being just in rightful cases) you will perform: so assure yourself your extraordinary kindness, afforded to me in such a time of necessity, shall never be from my heart; and therefore of this you may be assured, that no one whatsoever hath so large a possession therein as yourself: so that should you (as the gods forbid!) miscarry therein, when I am dead (as death must assuredly ensue thereon) they will find the name of Alexander written on my heart."

Their minds being made known to each other, gave great contentment to them both, especially to Sir Alexander, who humbly kissing the hands of the princess, replied thus unto her:

"Madam, there is no danger in the world so great which I shall not adventure on for your sake; were it to perform the twelve labours of Hercules, or with Æneas to encounter with the giant Turnus. Be pleased therefore to accept me as your knight and servant; and I hope to behave myself so, that hereafter you shall have no cause to repent you thereof." To whom the princess, smiling, said, "Sir, I do accept you for my knight; and hope the gods will be so propitious to you for my sake, that you shall have no enemy to withstand you."

With which words, taking a rich diamond ring from off her finger and giving it him, she said, "Wear this for my sake, that whensoever hereafter you look on it, it may add fresh courage into your breast by the remembrance of me."

Much other discourse they had, but the army being now upon the march, they summoned Sir Alexander to march along with them. Wherefore, taking a gentle farewell of the princess, having vowed constancy on both sides, he joined himself to the army; whose knightly adventures, with those of his two brothers, we shall record in the next chapter.

CHAPTER IV.

The great Battle between the three English Knights and the Sicilians on the one side, and the three Giants and Count Brandamil on the other side; the finishing of an adventure of the enchanted Castle; with the story of the wicked Sir Vuylon.

THE necromancer Soto, who lived with the giant Predo in the enchanted castle, knowing by his magic spells that the Sicilian army had beaten the king's troops and taken him prisoner; as also how they were marching towards the country of Thrace; he acquainted the giant with his knowledge; who thereupon bestirred himself in all haste to their assistance; who no sooner had notice thereof, but with the forces belonging unto them they hastened away. In like manner he sent unto count Brandamil, whom the king of Thrace had left deputy at such a time as he made his expedition into Thessaly, to raise what power he could against the Sicilians. And now nothing was heard but the loud sound of the thundering drum, and the shrill noise of the sounding trumpet: horror and amazement seized on the stoutest hearts, and the foreboding ravens foretold the fall of slaughtered carcasses.

Whilst these things were acting in Thrace, the Sicilian army, being joined with the Thessalians, and making in all the number of forty thousand men, armed in a just cause, marched in great confidence of an assured victory. And now being entered into the territories of Thrace, the first that marched against them was count Brandamil, with an army of fifty thousand Thracians; where joining battle together, it was fought with much eager courage on both sides, each of them striving to outvie the other in valour; the one side to defend their native country, the other to revenge losses sustained by the enemy. Victory thus for a long while stood hovering over the heads of both armies, till in the end the valiant knight Sir David, who had the honour that day to lead the van-guard, encountering with Count Brandamil, by main strength overthrew him, bearing him with his lance quite over the crupper of his horse, whereby his fall was so great that the blood gushed forth out of his mouth: whereupon the Sicilians gave such a shout, that the earth rang at the sound thereof, and the Thracians' courage was quite cast down; for the loss of a general is a general loss. And now the Thracians began to turn their backs and flee; when in that instant came to their rescue the two giants Brandamore and Pandaphilo, with the forces they had; which though but few, yet gave such proof of their valour, that the almost routed Thracians, rallying again, set so fiercely upon the Sicilians, that in great disorder they began to give back. And now did Sir Guy bestir himself, encouraging those that were about to flee to stand to it manfully, himself doing such execution upon his enemies, that they flew from before his conquering sword as a flock of sheep from the devouring wolf.

Whilst thus he drove the Thracians before him, he at last met with the giant Brandamore, to whom he cried, "Defend thyself, thou misshapen fiend, whose bulk is a weight too heavy for the earth to bear; and therefore prepare thyself, for I intend thou shalt this night sup with thy master, grim Pluto."

The giant, making little account of his person, and less of his words, thought to snap him at one morsel; and coming up to Sir Guy, intended to take him up, horse and man, under his arm, and carry him away; but ere he could lay hold of him, Sir Guy gave him such a blow on his head, that had not his helmet been of approved metal, he had cleft him down unto the middle: however, it made him to stagger, and recoil two or three steps backwards. And finding by this he had a stronger foe to encounter than he thought of, he waxed more wary, not only to assail but defend himself. And now the giant began to use his club, which was of a wondrous length, and so weighty, that had it lighted on Sir Guy it would at one blow have crushed him to pieces. After long fighting, the giant being angry to be thus repulsed, which never before in his life he had been, he struck at Sir Guy with all the strength he had; but missing his blow, he struck his club so deep into the earth that he could not readily draw it out again; which advantage Sir Guy espying, spurred up his horse, and with his lance gave such a violent punch upon the giant's breast, that he tumbled backwards over the dead carcasses of two or three slaughtered soldiers. Then Sir Guy, nimbly alighting from his horse, intended with his sword to have smitten off his head; but at that instant Pandaphilo, the other giant, came running to his brother's rescue, and undoubtedly had done Sir Guy much injury, being then almost spent with fighting, had not Sir David timely succoured him; who, searching out for Pandaphilo, finding his brother so hard beset, he engaged with him in fight, which was performed with such manhood on both sides, that I can scarcely describe the same. Pandaphilo, trusting to his strength, laid on his strokes with great fury; which blows Sir David nimbly avoided, and withal gave his adversary ever and anon such lusty knocks, that he well perceived he had a valiant foe to encounter withal. In the mean time the giant Brandamore had scrambled up, and began a fresh encounter with Sir Guy. Whilst these four were busy in fighting, the valiant knight Sir Alexander had made such havock amongst the Thracians, that they began to turn their backs and flee. The two giants, seeing their army in this running posture, ran also, to bear them company; whom the brothers hotly pursued, dealing such blows with their trusty falchions, that they made arms and legs complain to the earth how ill their masters kept them. The giant Predo, who was at the time of the battle in the enchanted castle, hearing how hardly his brothers fared, hastened with all the speed he could to their relief; whose coming put a stop to the Sicilians, being almost weary with pursuing them; so that, a retreat being sounded, the giants had time with the remainder of their broken army to secure themselves in their castle, cursing their fortune, and invoking their false gods for their future success.

Sir Alexander presently dispatched a messenger to the princess Mariana, giving her an account of their success in this following letter.

Most gracious princess,

"Guarded by the almighty power, and influenced by your divine beauty, we have given the Thracians a great overthrow; which we do not impute so much to the strength of our arms, as to the justness of our cause, and fighting under the banner of such a perfection of excellencies. As for the king your father, of whom I know you are impatient to hear, all we can understand of him is by some prisoners we have taken, that he is confined in the enchanted castle, from which we hope ere long to free him. Till then, most dear princess, rest in hope, assuring yourself, for the effecting thereof there shall not be wanting the utmost endeavours of

"Your most true and loyal knight,
"ALEXANDER."

The army having refreshed themselves for the space of two days, they then marched against the enchanted castle; but before they had come within a quarter of a mile of it, they were encountered by the giant Predo and his two brothers, with what forces had escaped from the battle: and now began a most terrible fight, insomuch that the earth was changed from a verdant green to a crimson dye, and the heaps of slaughtered carcasses overspread the fields. In the heat of this fight it was Sir Alexander's fortune to meet with the giant Brandamore, between whom began a most fierce combat, in which art and valour strove who should have the mastery: for the giant being of an incredible strength, was therein an overmatch for Sir Alexander; and he, on the other side, so nimble and skilful, that he returned him blow for blow with advantage. Thus they continued fighting for some space, till in the end, Brandamore, what through the weight of his armour and the hotness of the weather, sweat so abundantly, that it ran into his eyes, and quite blinded him. Sir Alexander, taking the best of the opportunity, gave him such a blow on the head as made him to stagger, and redoubling his stroke, at the next blow fetched him down headlong; who in his fall gave such hideous yells, as made a noise like to the cataracts of the Nile. This overthrow of the giant, in whom they put so much confidence, so discouraged the soldiers, that, notwithstanding Predo and Pandaphilo did what they could to persuade them, they would no longer abide by it; so that they were forced to retreat unto their castle for shelter; whom the Sicilians, being over-wearied with fighting, did not instantly pursue, but contented themselves at present with what they had then gotten.

Sir Alexander, after the fight of the Thracians, cut off the giant Brandamore's head, and despoiling him of his armour, sent it as a trophy to the city of Larissa, to be presented to his lady, the princess Mariana, who received the same very joyfully, wondering at the large proportion thereof, and caused it to be hung up in one of the principal temples of their city, as a monument to posterity; and having richly rewarded the messenger, she returned Sir Alexander thanks by him in the following letter:

" Most dear knight,

" That good fortune is always attendant upon virtue, your actions demonstrate; and for your valour shown against my enemies, I shall for ever stand obliged to you. For the present you sent me, I could not but view it with admiration, as by the same having an idea of the vast bulk of that unwieldly monster, and therein your invincible courage to encounter with him, and happy success in his overthrow. May the Heavens prosper your future endeavours with good success, and that your actions may be crowned with victory; which to effect shall be the hearty prayers of,

" Your dearest lady and mistress,
" MARIANA."

But to return again to speak of the army,—After they had sufficiently refreshed themselves, and taken care of the wounded soldiers, they marched up to the enchanted castle, wherein now the defenders had strongly enclosed themselves, trusting more to the strength of the place than to their own supposed invincible valour, which now they saw was overmatched by the three victorious knights.

And now no opposition was made till they came to the castle-gate, on the top of which were two giants, with massive stones in their hands, to tumble on the heads of any who should offer to scale the walls. The three brothers, approaching near thereunto, espied the brazen pillar, as also the rock of alabaster; and having read the several writings inscribed on them, with a matchless resolution resolved to try the adventure: and first the undaunted venturous knight Sir Guy, putting his hand to the pummel of the first sword, he drew it out with much ease; notwithstanding, he had no sooner laid his hand thereon but he was encountered by a terrible griffin; but Sir Guy so nimbly bestirred himself, that having deeply wounded the griffin, he flew from him; and immediatley was heard a sound out of the enchanted castle, as if it had been the noise of thunder.

The three brothers were much amazed at this terrible noise, expecting some dreadful encounter to ensue presently thereupon; having waited some time, and seeing nothing follow, they proceeded on in the adventure. And next Sir Alexander attempted to draw out the second sword; but ere he could well fasten his hand on the pummel, there came flying against him a most dreadful fierce dragon, which smote him with such a force that he could hardly stand upright on his legs; but having once drawn the sword, the dragon immediately vanished away; and at that instant proceeded a more terrible noise from the castle, which made the very foundation thereof to shake, and the walls to stagger and totter about.

This terrible noise being ended, the valiant and undaunted knight Sir David going to pull out the third sword, was in his passage assailed by a most furious dreadful monster; between whom began a cruel combat, which lasted long; but in the end, Sir David cutting off one of the monster's legs, he nimbly drew it out; which was no sooner done, but presently the heavens seemed to be rent asunder with dreadful claps of thunder, intermixed with terrible flashes of lightning; the earth quaked, and terrible groans and yells were heard of damned spirits; then fell a horrible nauseous smoke, and all on a sudden the castle, together with the brazen pillar and alabaster rock, were vanished away. The two giants, which before appeared so terrible, now fell down on their knees to the three brothers, begging for mercy. The necromancer Soto, who knew by this that his charms were at an end, sought to fly from deserved vengeance, but all in vain, for his spells now would do him no good, but he was forced to yield up his loathed carcass to the mercy of the conquerors. The Thessalian king, who had slept for so long a space, now awaked, wondering at what had happened, not knowing whether he was in the hands of friends or foes. Also the messenger that came from the princess Mariana who (as related before) was sent on an embassage to the giant Predo. With them also awaked many others, who by the necromancer's charms, coming within the compass of the castle, were there cast into this lasting sleep.

The first thing the three princely brothers did, was, by the help of some of the Thessalians then in the camp, to find out their king; who being known, he was entertained with all respect due to his princely majesty. The two giants were committed unto safe custody, under a guard of valiant soldiers; but as for the necromancer Soto, notwithstanding he pleaded with much rhetoric to have his life saved, his practices were so notorious and diabolical as would admit of no pardon; whereupon, by the command of the three brothers, he had his head severed from his body. At which instant appeared a great number of fiends as if come from hell, some of which seized upon his body, and some upon his head, which they carried away with them; leaving behind them such an intolerable stench of sulphur and brimstone, enough to have suffocated all that were near them, had they not run from the place as fast as their legs would bear them.

All things being thus ordered for the present, and no enemy appearing against them, they left this accursed place, where the castle stood, which had for a long space been the habitation of fiends and wicked persons, and marched to the city of Galata, there to refresh their wearied army; from whence they sent letters both into Thessaly, and also to Sicily, to certify them of their good success, and intention to return as soon as opportunity would permit them.

Amongst others which by finishing this enchantment were awaked out of their long sleeping, there was only one gentlewoman, who, now though something overworn through grief and age, yet by the remains of her visage showed she had once a face which might have been accounted Nature's proud master-piece, and an attractive loadstone wherein the god of love sat enthroned. All the company, especially the king of Thessaly, were very inquisitive to know what she was, and by what accident she came to be enchanted in that castle; and therefore requested she would be so courteous with them, as to give them a relation thereof. To which, after a deep sigh, she said:

"Although, noble gentlemen, the rehearsal of my misfortunes cannot but breed sorrow in the hearers, much more in the relator: yet to satisfy your curiosity, and in part of recompense for the favours I have received from you, I shall the more willingly impart them to you. Know then, that I am a native of this country, and was, at the time when Fortune smiled on me, wife to a noble knight named Fonteious, a man renowned through all Thrace for his learning and liberality, two special ornaments of a noble mind. Rich he was both in wealth and virtue, which two, though they seldom go together, yet in him they had their residence. At the age of sixteen years I was married unto him. Now whether liking be the cause of love, or love the cause of liking, I know not; but so it was, that reciprocal love passed between us; I loving him because he was kind unto me, and he being kind to me because I loved him. Long time thus lovingly lived we together, until Atropos cutting off the thread of his life, gave an *ultimum vale* to my good fortune; for my husband leaving me very rich, and I being withal young and beautiful, you may be sure such a widow would not be long without suitors. And indeed it was not long before I had plenty of them; so that the famous Ulysses's house, during his ten years' absence at the siege of Troy, was not more thronged with them to court the chaste Penelope, than was my house to gain my favour. Amongst others of this gallant crew, was one Sir Vylon, a man who, had he been endued with internal virtues as he was adorned with a comely outside, he might have been a match fit for a princess. The multiplicity of his vows, the protestations of his love, his gifts upon gifts, were as so many snares to entrap me. To be short, with the catching oratory of his words, and language strewed with flowers, he won me, and matched me. But long had not we been married together, although no cause given on my part, but his smiles were turned into frowns. No just pretence could he make therefore, though many were pretended. At last he found means to accomplish his desire, which he brought to pass in this manner: he hearing of the fame of this enchanted castle, with the dire effects attending upon those who came near it, pretended a letter, as come from a brother of mine, who had been long absent, and was thought (as indeed he was) dead. The letter contained these words:

'Dear sister.

'After many dangers and troubles past in peregrination, it was my hap to come into this country, with great expectation of enjoying your happy society; but hearing how crossly you are matched, and how your husband undervalues your kindred; because I cannot appear so splendid before him as stands to your credit, I would desire you to come to me as privately as you can to the castle in the island, commanded by my special friend Brandamore, where we may confer together in safety. Thus desiring your presence as soon as possible you can, I remain,

'Your affectionate brother,
'BRUDO.

"This letter was conveyed privately to my hands; and to give me the better opportunity to go thither, my husband pretended a journey to Bœtia, where he said he should stay a fortnight. All things did, as I then thought, conspire to my happiness, whereas the Fates had decreed quite the contrary; for taking only one servant for my guide, in whom I could repose confidence; coming within sight of the castle, I sent him back again, with instructions how to excuse my absence from home, as being gone to see a near relation. Then boldly I approached the castle gate; but ere I could come at it, a deep sleep seized on me, which how long it hath lasted, I am ignorant of; but I never awaked until both sleep and castle were vanished away.

"And thus, gentlemen, have you heard the sad story of my misfortunes. What hath befallen at home since, I am fearful to think, having left behind me two young children, a son and a daughter, the dear pledges of my first husband, who I fear may speed the worse for my sake; for those who love not the stock of the tree, will never affect the branches thereof."

Whilst she was thus discoursing, there chanced to be a Thracian knight, whose dwelling was not far from Sir Vylon's, who hearing the relation of her misfortunes; "Madam," said he, "for what you are so doubtful of, I can in the greatest part resolve you. Know, then, that since the time you were missing, during which space I conceive you have slept, is now fully two years: but what will add most grief to your hearing is, that soon after your husband had thus subtilly disposed of you, which he thought to be for a longer space, he began to revel in all sensual delights, spending his time and coin in such riotous manner, as if he had had the riches of Crœsus, and were to have lived the years of Nestor. But had his wickedness terminated in himself, it had been the more tolerable, but it extended to others in a most barbarous cruelty; for he being conscious of his own guilt, thinking if your children lived he might be brought to an account for his riotousness and debauchery, he found a means to make them away, and that in this manner:

"He had in his house a servant named Barco, one as ripe for mischief as himself, and to whom he bare a special affection, as being a companion with him in lewdness; those two, complotting together, enticed the children to the sea-side, where they had provided an empty boat, into which putting the two innocent babes, they launched them into the sea, and so committed them to the mercy of the waves; which how they dealt with them is only known to the Almighty Powers. But it was not long ere the children's being missing caused a suspicion amongst the neighbours of hard usage towards them by some belonging to Sir Vylon; nay, there were those who stickled not openly to accuse Barco as one prompt for any villany, and would receive any impression his master put upon him. Now this was so openly buzzed about, that at last it came to Sir Vylon's ear, who, fearing to be detected, thought if Barco were put to the rack, he would discover all; wherefore he found means to have him poisoned: a just reward for such bloody villainies, had it been done by a juster hand than did it.

"But see how divine vengeance pursues wicked actions! Sir Vylon, now revelling in all excess without controul, was stricken with a sudden phrensy, the use of his limbs also being taken from him, so that he lay raving and cursing in a most fearful manner: in one of which fits he discovered all the circumstances I have related unto you, and soon after in a desperate horror of conscience yielded up the ghost."

This mournful story moved all the company to great compassion: whereupon it was determined that the knight who had related this story, and who had been taken prisoner by the Sicilians, should have his freedom, and accompany the lady to her habitation; who in a mournful manner took her leave of the Thracian king, and the three English knights, and returned homewards. In which journey we will leave her for the present, to relate the further achievements of those renowned sons of Mars, Sir Guy, Sir Alexander, and Sir David.

CHAPTER V.

How Sir Guy conducted the army of Sicilians into their own country, and Sir Alexander that of the Thessalians; how, hearing of the great preparation of the Infidels, they returned into Christendom, to raise Forces to withstand them.

SOON after the departure of Sir Vylon's widow, and that the army were sufficiently refreshed, being highly satisfied for all the pains they had taken with the rich booties they had gained; the Thessalian king, and the three English brothers, thinking themselves revenged with advantage on the Thracians, they determined to march home into their own countries; and having settled their affairs in Thrace, Sir Guy with his brother David, marched with the army of the Sicilians back into that fruitful country, to which Sir Guy longed to come to enjoy the company of his beloved Urania: in which journey we will leave them for a time, to accompany Sir Alexander home with the Thessalian army, who had a great desire to see his beloved Mariana; and therefore, having secured the chief forts of the kingdom, they took their march, carrying with them the two giants, Predo and Pandaphilo, prisoners, who for their huge stature and vast proportion were gazed on by the people with admiration wheresoever they came, multitudes from all places flocking to see them.

Before they came to the city of Larissa, where the princess Mariana resided, they were met by the chief magistrates of the city in their scarlet gowns, gold chains, and their horses caparisoned with foot cloths of black velvet; besides multitudes of common people, who all with one voice echoed forth "Long live the king of Thessaly, and the renowned knight, Sir Alexander of England." The bells rung, the bonfires blazed, the conduits ran with pure Greek wine, the streets were hung with rich suits of tapestry; and all the windows along as they passed were filled with abundance of spectators to behold the return of their king, and to have a sight of the noble champion Sir Alexander, whom they styled the deliverer of their country, the flower of chivalry, the darling of mankind, with all the epithets which might conduce to his praise and magnanimity.

At the palace gate they were met by the princess Mariana, who in dutiful manner welcomed home her royal father, and with many expressions of love and affection entertained her noble champion Sir Alexander. Here did they spend several days in feasting, banqueting, and all the delights that art and cost could invent : but in the midst of all this jollity, there came news to the court of the great preparations which were made by the infidels against the Christians, as you read in a former chapter of this most excellent history. This news struck a sudden damp upon their mirth ; for the love of his native country was so dear unto Sir Alexander, that, notwithstanding the entire affection he bare to the princess Mariana, he resolved to give what succour he could unto the place wherein his father received his first breath, and from whence his own honour was derived. So making his mind known to the Thessalian king, and taking his solemn leave of his beloved Mariana, with great asseverations of his fidelity to her, and promise of return when those wars were finished, he prepared for his journey to Sicily to acquaint his two brothers with his resolution ; being accompanied therein by divers of the prime Thessalian nobility, who resolved to spend their lives in the company and under the conduct of so noble a champion.

In which journey we will leave them for a time, and return to speak of Sir Guy and Sir David ; who having conducted their army back to Sicily, were entertained with all demonstrations of joy imaginable, especially by the peerless princess Urania, in whose heart the love of Sir Guy was so deeply engraven, that nothing but death was able to blot it out. But here likewise, as well as to Thessaly, soon came news of the infidels' great preparations for the invasion of Christendom ; which when Sir Guy heard, he resolved to send to his brother Alexander, to prepare to march homewards ; but ere the messenger was fully dispatched, Sir Alexander with the Thessalian lords were arrived at the Sicilian court, to the great joy of Sir Guy and Sir David, and other martial spirits ; only the princess Urania was deeply melancholy that now she should part with her dear knight, whose company she prized far above all the riches of the mines of America ; wherefore retiring to her chamber, and taking her lute in her hand, she warbled forth this mournful ditty :

> My mournful mind doth crave some sweet delight,
> And Fancy fain would lend me some, I see ;
> But Fortune frowns, and sends me foul despite,
> And Care doth keep all comfort quite from me :
> Such passions strange do still perplex my mind,
> As I despair of any ease to find.
>
> But let me see : I must not yet despair,
> Dame Fortune's wheel may hap to turn again ;
> When storms are past, the weather may be fair,
> And pleasure comes unlook'd for after pain.
> Things at the worst, the proverb saith, will mend ;
> Why should not, then, my sorrows have an end!

But old wives' tales are yet not Scripture all,
  For things at worst, are past all mending quite;
To pining hearts all pleasure seemeth small,
  What mirth can do the pining heart delight?
When Fates do frown, and Fortune is our foe,
Nought can be thought to rid the mind of woe.

Scarcely had she ended her song, when Sir Guy came to take his leave of her: finding her sitting in such a disconsolate manner, one would have thought silence, solitariness, and melancholy, were come under the ensign of mishap to conquer his delight, and drive him from his natural seat of beauty. But now to describe the grief of these two lovers at their parting, I must implore the help of Melpomene, the most mournful of the nine Muses, to guide my pen; the sorrow of Orpheus for his beloved Eurydice, Andromache for Hector, Ægeus for his supposed dead Theseus, Antigone leading her blind father Œdipus, or that of weeping Niobe for the loss of her children, compared to this, deserves not the name of grief. At last, having vented their sorrows through the conduits of their eyes, and that a lovely beauty began again a little to dress herself in her face, the peerless Urania brake silence, and said:

"My dearest Guy, I must confess the excess of my sorrow doth scarce give way to the relief of words, being forced down with cares in the seas of woe; so that I am in effect but a living corpse, for which I can only blame your unkindness. Hath my prayers prevailed so far with the Divine Powers, to bring me unto you again in safety, and now will you leave me to enter into fresh dangers? Did you not swear by all that is divine and human, sooner should Phœbus cease to shine by day, or Luna lend us her light by night, than your heart should be separated from mine, which then you pretended to be dearer unto you than victuals to the almost famished soul, or drink to those whose throats are parched with thirst? If my love was so dear to you then, what change have you found in me, that, after the accomplishment of your Thessalian journey, we should not then enjoy the fruition of our loves, but that you will adventure again on new engagements, preferring your honour and desire of fame before my unstained love, which hath been as ever was that of the chaste Penelope to her wandering Ulysses."

Sir Guy, after many protestations of his constant affection, and how nearly this imminent danger, wherein all Christendom was involved, concerned his honour, which would be for ever stained should he decline such an honourable action, at last drew her consent, although with much reluctancy; so giving her a sweet kiss for a farewell, leaving her in tears for his departure, he went to accompany his two brothers, and those other martial heroes who were now ready prepared to join with him against the enemies of Christendom; and having with great ceremony taken their leave of the Sicilian king, they took ship, and coasting along the fruitful banks of Italy, befriended both by Neptune and Æolus, they in a short time arrived in England, the happy port whereto their desires tended. At the time of their arrival the whole people were in mourning, hearing of those vast forces prepared against them, whom the three brothers comforted in the best manner they might; and with what expedition they could make, went to the court, where the noble king Edgar then resided: who entertained them in a most sumptuous manner, being overjoyed for their arrival at such an exigency. Then having consulted together, they sent messengers unto all the rest of the countries of Christendom, to raise what forces they could make, and to be ready to join together in the country of Naples against the common enemy, and this to be done within one month at the farthest: who accordingly raised great forces in each country, and with them marched into Naples at the time appointed. But now, Calliope, the sacred sister of the Muses, assist my pen in setting forth the valiant acts of these renowned knights, which they performed to their own eternal fame and honour, and the general good and benefit of all Christendom.

CHAPTER VI.

How the Christian Army assembled together in Naples: the Oration of Sir Guy unto the soldiers; and how they marched against the Pagan Army.

YOU read in the last chapter how messengers were sent into all countries of Christendom, for the raising of forces against the infidels; which severally arrived at the place of rendezvous in the fruitful country of Naples; and first (as being nearest) was an army of thirty thousand Italians, conducted by the valiant knight Sir Orlando, whom the renowned champion St. Anthony had begotten on the princess Rosalinde, daughter to the king of Thrace. This martial knight, marching before his companies in as much state as did Hector when he traced the fields of Ilium, pitched up his tent in a large plain near unto the city of Nicosia. His pavilion was of a silver colour, adorned with a silken streamer, waving in the air, wherein was pourtrayed a lion rampant, beating his back with his tail, and from his mouth proceeded these lines:

"Incensed with anger just,
For victory we hope and trust."

The very next day after these Italians had encamped themselves, came marching into the field twenty-five thousand

Spaniards, conducted by a valiant knight named Sir Predo, son unto St. James the champion of Spain, whom he begat on the princess Celestine, the beautiful daughter of the king of Jerusalem. After courteous embracements between him and Sir Orlando, he pitched his camp on the west side of the Italians. His pavilion was blue; and for his device he had a griffin seizing on his prey, with this motto:

> "Thus griffin-like I do oppose;
> Defend myself, offend my foes."

The third nation that appeared in these warlike preparations was twenty thousand gallant Frenchmen, on warlike horses, and most bravely accoutred with offensive and defensive weapons. They had for their commander a most heroic knight, named Sir Turpin, begotten by St. Denis, the renowned champion of France, on Eglantine, the king's daughter of Thessaly, and who for her pride was transformed into a mulberry tree. He was with more than ordinary compliments entertained by Sir Orlando and Sir Predo, and pitched his camp on the east side of Sir Orlando. His pavilion was orange-tawny, embroidered with purple; and for his device he had lilies, the arms of France, with this motto:

> "The lily's glory of the field;
> Unto the lily all must yield."

The fourth nation that engaged in this quarrel for the honour of Christendom, was the hardy Scotchmen, who to the number of fifteen thousand arrived on the fruitful banks of Naples, conducted by that valiant and renowned knight Sir Ewin, son to St. Andrew, the famous champion of Scotland, and by him begotten on Artesia, one of the six daughters of the king of Thrace, who were transformed into the likeness of swans, as you may read in the first part of this honourable history. At his first arrival he was highly entertained and feasted by the other captains, and pitched his camp next to the Spaniards. His pavilion was of a red colour, fringed with blue, whereout hung a golden streamer in which was pourtrayed the effigies of Mars, looking with a stern countenance, and breathing forth these words:

> "Armed for victory."

The next that arrived on the fruitful banks of Naples, were a band of valiant Irishmen, to the number of ten thousand, attired in quilted jackets, and slops of blue cotton, being so swift of foot that few horses could out-run them. These were conducted by a valiant knight named Sir Phelim, whom the Irish champion, St. Patrick, begat on another of the six Thracian ladies, whom he had redeemed out of the hands of thirty bloody satyrs, as was related in the First Part. This courageous knight was of stature somewhat more than ordinary, and withal of such strength that he would seize on a wild bull, or any other beast, though never so fierce and strong. At his first approach unto the camp he was welcomed with a great shout of the soldiers, being a goodly person, and having his head adorned with a plume of ostrich feathers. He pitched his camp next to the Scottish army, having a tent of green, intermixed with scarlet, and richly adorned with gold fringe. In his streamer was pourtrayed a kite hovering, with a chicken in her claws, with these words:

> "'Tis common seen, the weakest they
> Unto the strong become a prey."

Scarce were the Irish well settled in their tents, when there arrived the like number of Welshmen, conducted by a valiant knight, named Sir Owen of the Mountains, the son of the renowned champion St. David of Wales, begotten on the beautiful Estrild, daughter of the king of Powisland; who had been bred up in all warlike affairs by the appointment of his grandfather, so that for martial prowess he was accounted as valiant a knight as most in Christendom. He was likewise received with the usual ceremonies by the other captains, and pitched his tent next to the Irish. His pavilion was of a blood-red colour, fringed with white, signifying peace to the yielding and blood and destruction to the obstinate; the words were these:

> "The doom of either life or death,
> Consisteth in the conqueror's breath."

Next came the English army, consisting of four score thousand experienced soldiers. They were divided into three battalions, whereof Sir Alexander led the van-guard, Sir Guy the main battle, and Sir David brought up the rear. Of these were twenty thousand horsemen, armed in rich corslets of steel, to defend themselves, and lances and darts to offend their enemies. There were of the foot thirty thousand stout archers, having bows of the strongest yew, and arrows of a full yard long, headed with steel, with which they would shoot a full half mile in length. Also twenty thousand pikemen, with pikes of the strongest ash, headed with steel, as sharp as Spanish needles, to defend the archers from the enemy's horse, and to oppose an army in a straight passage. The rest of the army were pioneers, waggoners, victuallers, and such others as are commonly attendant on an army. At their first landing they were entertained by the other commanders with such a shout of joy, that the earth rang with the sound thereof, and the hollow caverns of the hills reverberated with such an echo, as if Jupiter had sent his thundering artillery to welcome these English heroes. They pitched their camp near unto the army of the Italians; Sir Guy's pavilion being of watchet, embroidered with silver, and fringed with gold; and to distinguish it from others, it was adorned with the red cross, the ancient arms of England. His two brothers were not far different in their devices; and for the motto of them all, it was to this effect:

> "Arm'd with a righteous cause, we fear no foe,
> No foil, nor flight, much less an overthrow."

Divers captains of other nations came also in aid of the Christians' army; as, Sir Lando the Warlike, with five thousand stout Swedish soldiers; Sir Pandrasus the Dane, having in his company a giant named Wonder, for his matchless strength, which was such, that he would lift a weight that twelve ordinary men could hardly stir; besides many others, too many to enumerate; the whole sum amounting to three hundred thousand.

After they had consulted awhile together, it was concluded unanimously among them all, that every captain should have the command of those soldiers he brought out of his country; but that, in difficult matters, and wherein diversity of opinions might breed confusion, it should be referred to Sir Guy's ordering, who was generalissimo of the whole army. And now, having nothing else to do but to march against their enemies, Sir Guy, to encourage them the more, being all the chief of them assembled together, made unto them this following oration:

"Fellow-soldiers, and brethren in arms, I think I shall not need many words to stir you up to magnanimity; the justness of our cause being such as, rightly considered, is enough to make a coward valiant. I hope that you are not so forgetful, that you now go to fight for your parents, your wives, your children, your country, and, what should be most dear unto you, the Christian religion; against pagans, infidels, and miscreants, enemies to God and goodness; whose delight is only in blood and rapine, whose trade and practice are the burning and destroying of towns and villages, murdering of matrons, ravishing wives and virgins, tossing of sprawling infants on the tops of their merciless pikes: in short, such people as act all that barbarism and cruelty prompt them to. Therefore, if you are not willing to see these miseries fall upon you, be valiant and courageous; and so let us willingly go on, armed with a just cause, and doubt not in the least but the just God will give us victory."

No sooner had he ended this oration, but it was received with a general acclamation, each one vowed to live and die in such a cause, and under the conduct of such a general.

Being thus resolved, they prepared to dislodge the enemy; and having furnished themselves with a store of provision, which was freely given them by the Neapolitan king, besides to the number of five hundred waggons for carriage of their ammunition and other necessaries, they embarked in several galleys; and cutting the briny face of Neptune, after about a fortnight's prosperous sailing, they came upon the fruitful coasts of Asia; where soon they heard tidings of the Pagans' army, and how they were advanced as far as Galatia, within a hundred leagues of the place where the Christians were landed. And now having brought the armies thus near together, we will look back again into Europe, and show you by what a wonderful miracle the Christians' army were supplied with an unexpected assistance.

CHAPTER VII.

How the Seven Champions, being raised from their graves, resolved to follow the Christian Army; how by tempest they were cast upon the coast of Thessaly. The great battle fought between the Thessalians. How afterwards they went to the Christian Army, and of the great battle fought between the Christians and Pagans.

Now, notwithstanding this great preparation to withstand the Pagan army, a great fear and consternation still continued in the hearts of the people; for the report of the vastness of the Pagan's army was spread abroad in each place, so that it was deemed so numerous as not to be encountered withal: the best remedy therefore, as they thought, was by prayers to God, to crave his assistance against such potent enemies; so that in every place intercessions were sent up to heaven for succour in this exigency of time.

Now it so chanced, that at the same time there lived in the north country a certain holy hermit, named Sylvanus. To this man it was revealed in a dream, how that the Seven famous Champions were not wholly dead, but for the good of Christendom they should again wake, and help to overcome the Pagan army; and that by opening their tombs, and laying the herb bazil to the roots of their tongues, they should revive again in good strength and vigour. This dream he declared unto an abbot of an abbey near adjoining, and he to the governor of that province, who all together went to the English court, and declared the same unto the king; whereupon it was determined that the experiment should soon be tried; and accordingly messengers were dispatched to France, Spain, Italy, Scotland, Ireland, and Wales; which message was no sooner delivered in those several countries, but that they soon applied the same, and found the effect answerable to what the hermit had dreamed; for immediately thereupon the champions arose as out of a sweet sleep; and having awhile discoursed of those matters we have in the former chapters declared unto you, the messengers were returned back again with this agreement, that with all expedition they should meet together in the country of Naples aforesaid, that with the better celerity they might overtake and join themselves with the Christians' army. This determination being accordingly made known to each other, they with all speed provided themselves with armour and other necessaries for their journey; and taking the holy hermit Sylvanus along with them, they in a little space met together in the land of Naples. To recite the great joy at this their so unexpected meeting, is beyond the skill of my pen to express; but having congratulated one another, they agreed to hasten after the Christian army, with all the expedition they could make: so being furnished with a stately ship, they put forth to sea: but they had not sailed long, when a dreadful tempest overtook them, so that they expected every minute to be engulfed, and to make their graves in that merciless element. At last the weather clearing, they found themselves on the coast of fruitful Thessaly; where being landed, they gave thanks to the powers above, for their safe deliverance: next they provided for the refreshing of their bodies, having in two days before taken no sustenance, for so long had the tempest endured.

Now whilst they were at their collation, they thought they heard the rattling of armour, trampling of horses, shrieks of wounded soldiers, with divers other symptoms of an army fighting not far off; wherefore, to be resolved, they called to a Thessalian, who by his running posture seemed to fly from some danger near at hand; from whom they understood, that about some half a mile from that place the king of Thrace and the king of Thessaly were engaged in a bloody fight. For so it happened, that soon after the departure of St. George's three sons (either through a generous disposition in the king of Thessaly, not willing that kings should be too close confined, or through the negligence of them that should have looked after him) the king of Thrace made his escape out of prison: and having a band of his soldiers in readiness, they surprised the place wherein the two giants Predo and Pandaphilo were likewise kept in hold, and set them at liberty; and being thus set free, they went into Thrace, where they soon raised an army; and being accompanied with the two giants aforesaid, they entered Thessaly, harassing the same with fire and sword: to oppose whom the king of Thessaly had raised an army, and both parties were at that time engaged in a fierce and bloody battle.

The Christian champions having heard in what danger the

king of Thessaly stood, resolved to succour him: and so buckling on their armour, being guided by the Thessalian, who had fled from the fight, they came to the army just as they were in a running posture; but soon by their valour they made it known what difference there is between multitude and manhood; for laying about them with their keen-edged falchions, they soon made lanes of slaughtered carcasses, so that the Thracians fled from before their blows, as flocks of sheep from before the wolf, or chickens at the sight of the kite. The two giants, seeing the Thessalians thus make head again, whom just before they accounted vanquished, they made up to the head of their army; whom when the champions had beheld, St. George singled out the giant Predo, and St. Denis encountered with Pandaphilo: and now such blows were dealt amongst them, that Mars himself might have been a spectator of the fight: here Strength and Courage seemed to strive for superiority, Fury and Valour encountered each other, giving and receiving such mighty strokes as none but themselves were able to sustain. At length St. George with his battle-axe gave the giant Predo such a blow, as dashed out his brains, and made way for Death to take possession of his body. Pandaphilo, seeing his brother's fall, upon his knees desired mercy, which the noble champion St. Denis granted him. In the mean time the other champions had made such dreadful havock among the Thracians, that all the field lay strewed with their slaughtered carcasses; the king himself, being deadly wounded was taken prisoner.

The king of Thessaly, in the mean time, was in great admiration and wished to know who these strangers could be, who had brought Victory to his side, which was taking her wings to fly to his adversaries; and therefore, now the field being cleared of all enemies, he went unto them, desiring to know to whose valour he was so much indebted, as the rescue of his life and kingdom. But when he understood they were the renowned champions of Christendom, whose fame was spread all the world over, and who were supposed to be dead; and how that St. George was the father of those three princely brothers who had before so valiantly fought for him; he was transported with an ecstasy of joy, as was that father whose three sons returned home victors from the Olympic games. And having congratulated each other, they took order for their prisoners, which were in a manner the remainder of the whole army. Then marched they in good array to the city of Larissa, being met by the princess Mariana, attended with a train of five hundred virgins, attired all in suits of white sarsenet; who having done her obeisance to her father, she most courteously welcomed the

Christian champions, especially St. George, for the entire affection which she bore to Sir Alexander.

Here did they spend some few days in mirth and jollity; when one night, at such a time when the bright charioteer of heaven had set his fiery brass-hoofed coursers to their meat, and that the jetty sable Night had overspread his golden glistering locks; Morpheus the god of sleep, having locked up the eyes of mortals, and cast them into deep slumbers; as St. George lay sleeping on his bed, there appeared to him the likeness of a beautiful angel, which breathed forth these words:

> "Brave English champions, make you no delay,
> But to the Christians' army post away:
> Fame calls aloud, and Mars doth beat alarms:
> Then leave off court delights, and fall to arms."

Next morning, no sooner had Phœbus with his refulgent beams enlightened the hemisphere, but St. George arose from his drowsy bed, and relating his vision to the other champions, they agreed with all speed to hasten to the Christian army; and having acquainted the king of Thessaly with their determination, they prepared to be gone, being accompanied to the sea-side with the chief of the Thessalians. On their entering into the ship, the king presented each of the champions with rich diamond rings, and to St. George he gave, over and above, a rich collar of esses, having hanging thereon a medal of gold, beset with precious stones, and in it the picture of an elephant, for giant-like valour showed in his defence. The princess Mariana at the same time sent unto Sir Alexander a signet made of polished jasper, wherein was engraven a heart wounded with a sword, and crowned with a wreath, with this word, "Amarete."

So taking their solemn leaves of each other, the wind standing fair, they set sail: where we will leave them for a while, to speak of what befel the Christian army in the mean time, whom, you may remember, we left upon the coasts of Asia; who, hearing the Pagans' army was so near, provided themselves to assail and withstand their enemy; and so by slow marches drew near unto them. And now did Sir Guy send out twenty of his nimblest horsemen to discover what they could of the enemy; who returning back, brought with them six Persians, whom they had taken prisoners, by whom they understood that the whole army was encamped on a spacious plain not far off, unconcious of an approaching foe: whereupon it was determined, that the next morning before the break of day, they should fall upon them; which they did in this manner: First in the van was Sir Alexander, with the choicest of the English horsemen: on his right hand the famous French knight Sir Turpin, with the flower of the French cavalry; on the left hand Sir Predo commanded a gallant party of Spaniards, mounted on such speedy-paced jennets, for their swiftness were said to be equal with the wind. And that their army might spread the further, lest they should be surrounded by the numerous forces of their enemies, they had four outwings, on the one side five thousand Swedes, conducted by Sir Lando the Warlike, and six thousand Germans on the other side, led by a valiant knight named count Primaleon. The main battle was conducted by the matchless knight Sir Guy, with thirty thousand foot of bows and pikemen, whose warlike resolution carried victory in their very looks. On his right hand marched the warlike Danes, commanded by Sir Pandrasus, having in his company the giant Wonder. On his left hand was placed the valiant Scottish men, conducted by their valiant leader Sir Ewin. The rest was brought up by Sir David, with the rest of the English, having on his right hand the stout Sir Phelim, with his nimble Irishmen, and on his left Sir Owen, with the hardy Welsh. Being thus marshalled, they set forward; but ere they came to the camp, their enemies had notice of their approach, who thereupon instantly armed themselves, and put themselves in as good a posture as on the sudden, they could.

The first that encountered each other were the valiant knight Sir Predo, with his resolute Spaniards, against the bassa of Aleppo; by these was fought such a terrible battle, that the earth resounded with the noise of their blows. Next day the magnanimous knight Sir Alexander encountered with the soldan of Babylon, sending him such a flight of arrows as would have darkened the sky on a clear day. The Babylonians, on the other side, laid on with great courage, seeking with their horse to trample them under foot; but that the pikemen kept them off with such courage, as cast many riders to the ground, and put the troops in great disorder. On the other side Sir Turpin, with the French, gave a lusty charge on the king of Egypt, insomuch that he was in great danger of a total rout, had he not been timely succoured by the king of Morocco, who, stoutly interposed, and drove the French back in great confusion; whereupon Sir Lando the Warlike set upon them with undaunted courage, which gave a check to their proceedings; who with his warlike Swedes he so stoutly followed, that coming up to the king of Morocco, after a fierce encounter between these two, in which Mars himself might have been a looker-on, at length the king of Morocco, being deeply wounded, surrendered up his life and body to the victor's disposal.

And now the main battle came forward, by which time the sun with his beams had gilded the hemisphere, so that they could see to fight with more eagerness than they had done before. The valiant knight Sir Guy charged strongly upon the Persians, who with courage and skill defended themselves. Count Primaleon, with his Germans, encountered the Arabians. And now generally both armies were fully engaged ; so that death began to appear in its greatest horror: then was cutting, hacking, and slashing on every side; the renowned Christian champions dealing such blows with their swords, and giving to many Mahometans their deaths, as if they intended to overcharge Charon's boat in ferrying them over the Stygian river. The infidels, on the other side, held out with great obstinancy, not shrinking from any danger, although they were ready to be carried away in streams of their own blood. Thus with great obstinancy continued they fighting, until the sable night parted their fury, when each side retired to their camp.

Next morning, no sooner had Aurora ushered in the day, but both armies met again in the field ; and as if their stock of valour were fresh renewed, with more eagerness and earnestness than before they fell to their work of mankind's destruction. The thundering drums beat alarums of death, and the shrill trumpets sounded forth that day the knell of many thousands. Horror, death, and destruction surrounded the Pagans on every side ; yet still their fresh numbers made more work for the Christians' valour. In the heat of this fight it was Sir Guy's chance to meet with the horse-faced Tartar, whom he resolved to encounter ; but the sight of him so affrighted the other horses, that not one of them could endure to come near him : whereupon Sir Guy alighted from his steed, and with his battle-axe approached the monster, whose very looks would have affrighted any but such an one, whose heart was fraught with true magnanimity. The monster was readier to assail than to be assailed ; so that between the two began a most fierce and terrible combat. The monster was so nimble, and laid on blows so strangely, that Sir Guy was never so put to it in all his life. At last, espying his advantage, he gave the monster such a wound on his head that, sending forth a hideous yell, he ran from him with nimble pace, to the rear of his army. And now the Pagans began to shrink, and the Christians to gain ground; when the wizards and enchanters, which the Egyptian king had brought with him, began to show their skill; so that on a sudden there was such a fear and consternation throughout all the hosts of the Christians, as put a stop to their full career of victory; for immediately such a darkness overspread them, that they could hardly discern one from the other ; and withal they received divers blows, yet could not perceive who it was that gave them. This continued for the space of three hours, which much daunted the Christians' courage ;

but making their hearty supplications to God, they were not only delivered from their unseen blows, but also the darkness turned upon the Pagan army; from whence was heard such hideous shrieks and howlings, with such other dreadful noise, as if hell were broke loose. Upon this the Christians, not daring to pursue them any further, retreated to their camp; and having set a strong watch, they reposed themselves for that night.

The next morning, preparing themselves to fight, they heard behind them a sound of trumpets, as it were of an army upon a march; whereupon Sir Guy sent out a party to discover what they were; who found them to be the thrice renowned Champions of Christendom, that after their departure from Thessaly, having a prosperous wind, by the report of Fame's loud-sounding trumpet, where these sons of Mars were assembled together, they with a speedy march made up unto them. But now to express the great joy, mixed with wonder and amazement, between these noble heroes, at this their meeting, it would require the skill of Homer, and the aid of Calliope, that sweet-tongued sister of the Muses, to express: to see such near and dear relations, who were supposed to be dead, and to see them at such a time when their help was so needful, it far surpassed the joy of that Grecian father when his three sons returned home victors from the Olympic games.

Whilst they were thus congratulating the happy sight of each other, they had an alarm from the camp of the Pagans, who being conducted by the three giants, with an assured confidence of victory, came marching up to the Christians' army, thinking them so shattered and dismayed as not able to endure another fight, and therefore came rather for spoil, than to be encountered: but they found the Christians ready to entertain them with a bloody banquet; for coming in disorder, they were received with such a lusty charge as sent many of their souls to the infernal regions. St. George perceived the three giants, the only stop of the Christians' victory, he singled out one of the chief of them; the valiant champion St. Denis encountered with another; and the courteous St. Anthony with the third. Whilst they were thus engaged against each other, dealing such blows as if Alcides were again living and fighting with the giant Anteus, it was Sir Guy's fortune to meet with the Egyptian king, accompanied with his magicians and soothsayers, who began afresh to use their enchantments; and first they raised up the likeness of a mighty black bear, which running hither and thither in the Christian's army, put them in great disorder. At last she ran violently against Sir Guy, who laying manfully about him, he thought he had cut off one of her legs, but when she had vanished away, it proved only a leg of a stool. Next came running among them a mighty wild boar, with tusks as large as an ordinary cow's horn. This boar so frighted the soldiers, that wheresoever he came they tumbled over one another in heaps. And having thus displayed his freaks among the English, he next ran into the army of the Spaniards, snorting and tearing the ground with his tusks. The valiant knight Predo, hearing the shout of the soldiers, and wondering what was the matter, came riding in haste to the place; and seeing the boar, he ran against him with all his might; but notwithstanding his sword was made of the purest Lydian steel, yet it made no impression on the sides of the boar: wherefore Sir Predo, seeing that way would not do, the boar coming towards him with open mouth he ran his sword down his throat, thinking thereby to cleave his heart in twain; but the boar therewith vanished in a flame of fire, which singed the mane of Sir Predo's horse and made such a smoke that they hardly could discern one another.

Whilst these necromancers were thus practising their devilish enchantments, the three renowned champions had by their magnanimous prowess conquered the giants; with whose fall fell also the courage of the whole Pagan army, so that in great disorder they began to run. And now all hands were bathed in blood, and the thirsty soil ran with a purple stream. In one place lay severed heads, dispossessed of their natural seignories; there lay arms whose fingers yet moved, as if they would feel for those that made them feel; and legs, which, contrary to common reason, was made heavier by being discharged of their burdens.

And now the Christians, over-wearied with killing, had, with the day, brought many thousand Pagans to their ends, when the sable Night, drawing her black curtain over the hemisphere, put a period to the pursuit. The next morning the soldiers arose betimes to pillage the field, which they found very rich. Most of the Pagan commanders were slain, and the whole army shattered, that scarce a hundred of them were left together in one company. The horse-faced monster, with some others, made their escape, being so swift that no horse could overtake him. Amongst the rest of the prisoners that were taken, was one of the chief Egyptian magicians, who being stripped of his uppermost robe, there was found about him a number of spells, charms, and other necromantic characters: amongst others were the picture of a fiend, this label proceeding out of his mouth:

"Thou, by our help, to pass shall bring
Many a great and direful thing."

Which label being by one of the soldiers pulled off from the picture, underneath it was thus written:

> "When in ten years thou com'st to tell,
> Then bid thy skill in charms farewell,
> For thou must then descend to hell."

And now it seemed the time was come when his charms were at an end, as also were those of several of his companions, whom satan had by that label deluded; but by the writing on the other side deceived: for these sorcerers, thinking, notwithstanding their army was routed, to raise up such a company of infernal spirits as should be able to deal with the whole Christian army, they therefore began to use their invocations, and to call for help unto satan as they used to do; but now, instead of the spirits obeying their commands, loud noises were heard in the air, and the artillery of heaven began to roar; the amazed firmament seemed to rend in twain, and the affrighted rafters of the sky to shake: black pitchy clouds obscured the horizon, and all the light which was to be seen was only the dreadful flashes of lightning. This dreadful tempest continued near the space of an hour, when all on a sudden it began to be calm, and the winds to retire, and sink into their seat; Phœbus sent forth his lightsome rays which dispelled the darkness of the pitchy clouds: when the Christians, looking upon them, saw the most rueful spectacle that ever mortal eyes beheld: the field was strewed with mangled carcasses, and those as black as pitch, stinking of sulphur and brimstone; for, the term of years being expired wherein they had convenanted with the devil, he now sent his spirits to fetch their souls, who had mangled their bodies in that awful manner we have related; a just reward for all such as devote themselves to the service of the devil.

The Christians having obtained this signal victory, gave thanks to God throughout all their army. And now, victuals growing scarce, by reason of the great number of soldiers, they resolved to break up the camp, and discharge those who wished to depart home to their own countries. Sickness and disease also increased daily among them, by reason of the hotness of the climate: whereupon Sir Turpin, with his Frenchmen, took their leave, and departed homewards; soon after Sir Predo, with his army of Spaniards; and quickly after, most of the rest; so that at last there were none left but the English with Sir Pandrasus and his warlike Danes. The Seven Champions of Christendom, who for their former acts had been enternized all the world over, were resolved to depart away in a ship by themselves. And now, being thus scattered, we shall (sweet Clio, the sacred sister of the nine Muses, assisting us) relate the several adventures which happened to each of them in their several perambulations.

CHAPTER VIII.

How Sir Turpin of France, Sir Predo of Spain, Sir Phelim of Ireland, and Sir Owen of the Mountains, arrived in Cyprus; how they put down the Tyrant Isakius, and restored the rightful Prince Amadeus to the Throne.

AND now shall our pen first attend the actions of Sir Turpin and his warlike Frenchmen; who having marched by land for many miles together, then took shipping, and after a tedious passage at sea arrived on the island of Cyprus; to whose king they sent a friendly message, desiring provision for their present necessity, and wherewithal to victual their ships, promising to pay him for the same to the uttermost farthing. But this king, named Isakius, being a tyrant, and having wrongfully attained the crown, not only denied their reasonable request, but also prepared to make war against them, and by force, to drive them out of his country; which he was the more confident to do, having then in his court a giant named Guylon, whom with great rewards he had hired to side with him in his tyranny. This Guylon was a giant of wonderful stature, having been bred up in the deserts of Hyrcania. He would eat up a fat sheep at a meal, and afterwards drink up four gallons of wine; which made him of such a vast proportion, that it was most terrible to behold. The usual weapon wherewith he fought, was a square bat of iron, having a knob at the end of it of thirty pounds weight, and on his body he wore a coat of mail of a wonderful strength. This proud giant was so conceited of his own strength, that he thought himself able to encounter singly with an host of men; and therefore taking with him only the guard which belonged to the king, he marched against the French, promising to bring them bound unto Isakius. But promises without performance signify nothing. In this high resolution, with fury he fell upon the French, dealing as many wounds as blows, and as many deaths almost as wounds: and now his iron bat was all imbrued with blood, and heaps of slaughtered carcasses lay on each side of him; the common soldiers ran from his reach with as much fear as the partridge from the pursuing hawk. Sir Turpin, seeing such havoc made amongst the soldiers, thought it high time to show his valour, and to put a stop to such proceedings; wherefore with much force, guided by prudence, he set upon him: but the giant's armour was of such proof that he nothing prevailed; for notwithstanding Sir Turpin was as gallant a knight as ever buckled on armour, and that he used his utmost endeavour, for the honour of his country and glory of his nation, to overcome him, as well as for their own safeguard; yet, all his force and valour, it availed nothing, but he was forced to give way to the fury of the giant. Sir

Turpin, seeing himself thus overmatched by strength, thought to use policy; and therefore, counterfeiting a flight, retreated to a place where, advantaged by the ground and his chiefest captains, he might the better deal with him: but Providence had ordained a better remedy, for at that very instant it so happened that Sir Predo, with his army of Spaniards, having been sorely weather-beaten at sea, were by stress of weather, forced to that island for succour; where they were no sooner landed, but they had information of this battle; and therefore, after a short refreshment, they made up to them. And now slaughter and destruction fell heavy on both sides, the devouring sword making dreadful havoc amongst the combatants. Much courage was shown on both parts, each striving to gain honour by the other's ruin; and now, notwithstanding the giant's brag of bringing the Frenchmen bound to the king, he was forced to go without his errand, and for safeguard of his men make a retreat towards the city. But there he found but cold entertainment, for the citizens, hearing how the Frenchmen were landed, and that the giant with the king's guard were gone to fight with them, they took the opportunity of the time, and making a general insurrection, seized upon the king, secured the gates of the city, and stood upon their own defence; and immediately dispatched a messenger to the French and Spaniards, to inform them what they had done: who, upon the hearing of the news, sent forth such a shout that the earth rang with the noise thereof. The giant, with his company, hearing the loud shout of the French and Spaniards, were in a wonderful amaze: and seeing themselves surrounded with danger before and behind, they saw there was no other way but to secure themselves by flight; which proved the more advantageous to them, by reason the French were so enfeebled, through lack of sustenance and long fighting, that they were not able to pursue them. Wherefore, leaving the chase, they marched directly into the city, being of the citizens entertained with much joy; who presently sent forth fresh men after the giant, whom Sir Predo would needs head, whilst the rest refreshed themselves in the city. These fresh men, by the intelligence of the country people, had soon notice whither the giant with the greatest part of his men were gone: whereupon Sir Predo, taking along with him a choice party of the swiftest horsemen, pursued him so fast, that in a short space they had a view of him; but the envious Destinies had so ordered it, that near thereunto there was a strong castle, into which he had entered before he could be overtaken; wherefore they resolved to besiege it, and either force him by famine to submit himself, or to gain his freedom by hazard of battle.

Whilst they were thus busied in besieging the giant, and

the army refreshing themselves in the city, it happened that the captain of the guard, with a party of such as fled with him, being joined to some others, whose despicable fortunes made them desperate, having intelligence that the French and Spanish ships were but weakly guarded, he with incredible celerity seized on them, forcing those seamen that were in them to weigh anchor, hoist sail, and proceed to sea, intending to go into the island of Zeylon, near thereunto adjoining, to raise forces to withstand the enemy ; or if that failed, to seek an habitation in some other remote country. Whilst they were thus hovering at sea, it chanced that Sir Owen of the Mountains, with a band of his valiant Welshmen, came sailing that way, being severed from Sir Phelim with his Irish, by a storm at sea. Sir Owen, seeing these ships, imagined them to be his faithful friends the French and Spaniards, and therefore made up to them ; but the mistake being soon perceived, they instantly fell to fighting pell mell. And now Death showed himself with much horror, and blood filled the wrinkles of the sea's visage, which the water would not wash away, that it might be witness it was not always his fault when we condemn his cruelty.

Sir Owen with great valour defended himself, notwithstanding he was oppressed with the multitude of his enemies, which were so many in number above his men, that he was in some danger of being worsted, had not, in the very nick of opportunity, Sir Phelim with his Irish, come timely to his rescue ; but now being strengthened with this recruit, they so resolutely charged on the Cypriots, that first they began to retreat, and afterwards sought to shift away the best they could by flight. But these soldiers were so unskilful in sea affairs, and the seamen whom they had forced to go along with them, being joyful to be relieved by the Welsh and Irish, they ordered the business, that the ships were all taken, and the soldiers in them carried back to the port from whence they had been forced away.

Sir Turpin and Sir Predo, hearing of this gallant enterprise of the Welsh and Irish, in all haste went unto them. But now to recount the great joy at their happy meeting, it is beyond my art to express ; but after congratulations had passed between them, they took order for the better safeguard of their ships, and then with the prisoners marched to the city ; where they were entertained with exceeding great joy, being magnificently feasted by the citizens, and complimented with shows and representations, performed with great cost and art. Whilst they were thus revelling in delights, there came to them a messenger from the giant Guylon, with a letter directed to the officers of the Christians' army, which had invaded the island of Cyprus. This letter or challenge being opened, contained these words :

"Think not, proud Christians, although by stealth and fraud you have invaded our country, that you shall ever subdue our hearts, although you may hap to subjugate our bodies. Now if your arms be answerable to your artifices, you will maintain with your sword what you have compassed by craft; I challenge the best of you all to fight with me, upon this condition, that if you overcome me, we will submit ourselves and country to your disposal; but if you be overcome by me, then to pass away quietly out of our land, and restore what unjustly you have taken away from us. This you cannot refuse, if you have any spark of valour in you.
"GUYLON."

This bold challenge being read before the four heroic captains, they each of them desired to have the combat, and that with such earnestness as it almost bred a quarrel amongst them; but to avoid all controversies, it was agreed to cast lots amongst them, to whose honour it should befal; which being done accordingly, the lot fell on the renowned knight Sir Owen of the Mountains, who returned the count this answer to his challenge:

"Proud Giant,

"Whose valour consisteth in boasting, and who triumphest before conquest, know that thy challenge shall be answered in justification of what we have done; prepare, therefore, thyself against to-morrow, when I will not fail to meet thee. Till then farewell.
"OWEN of the Mountains."

Accordingly the next day, being richly mounted on a grey Barbary steed, armed in a coat of mail, with a sword by his side, and a strong keen falchion in his hand, he rode towards the castle, accompanied with the French, Spanish, and Irish captains, and a band of lusty soldiers, lest there should be any treachery shown by the other side. Soon after came the giant forth of the castle, attended only by a dwarf: he was on foot, for he was too heavy for any horse to bear. He was likewise armed in a coat of mail, and came with his great bat of iron in his hand, which he flourished over his head with great pride and ostentation. Drawing near unto Sir Owen, with a haughty voice, stuffed with arrogancy, he thus spake unto him:

"Proud knight, now shall thy life pay for thy presumption, and thy ruin be the effect of thy overdaring; who thinkest to encounter with me in single combat, from whose presence whole troops have run, as dreading to come within the compass of my invincible arms: therefore before thou urgest me too far, let me advise thee to dismount, and humble thyself at my feet, which may be a means to obtain the more favour at my hands."

Sir Owen, smiling at the words of the giant, returned the braggadocia this answer:

"Giant, leave thy proud boasting; for now it will behove thee to use thy hands more than thy tongue. When thou hast me in thy power, use me as thou wilt; and since thou wert so courteous as to advise me, I shall also be so kind as to warn thee to have a care of thyself, lest with my sword I so belabour thy jacket, as shall make thee promise less, except thou couldest perform more."

And now Sir Owen, seeing the giant on foot, alighted from his horse, that it should not be said advantage added any thing to his victory: then drawing their swords, they laid on blows with great courage, dealing such strokes as to the beholder's sight the least of them would leave death behind it, and those laid on so thick as if that every blow would have been foremost. Thus continued they for some time; their swords, like cannons, battering down their armour, making breaches almost in every place for troops of wounds to enter. At last the giant began to faint; the weightiness of his great iron club, together with the heat of the sun, which then shined forth in its brightest lustre, made him so sweat as if he had been working at the Cylops' forge, or hammering at the sooty god Vulcan's anvil: yet, like the dying taper, willing to give one flash of valour before his fall, taking his iron club in both his hands, struck at Sir Owen with all his might; but his eyes being blinded with the sweat, he missed his blow, and with the force thereof tumbled down upon his face, giving Sir Owen thereby a fit opportunity to finish his victory; which he soon did, by cutting off his head from his body.

The Cyprians, seeing their champion slain, presently yielded up the castle; and the news being bruited abroad in the country, they came from all places, and submitted themselves unto these valiant captains' mercy, who received their submissions with much gentleness and courtesy. Soon after, they caused an assembly to be made of the chief persons of all the realm, before whom the usuper Isakius was brought; where the council being set, one of the chief advocates of the land spake as follows:

"Right honourable, you may please to understand that this Isakius, here before you, the pretended king of Cyprus, was brother to Amadeus our lawful king, whose ancestors have for many years enjoyed this crown. This Amadeus, when he died, left behind him one only son, a child of two years old, named also Amadeus, to whom he bequeathed his crown; making his brother Isakius a guardian and protector to him during his minority. But he, instead of a guardian to defend, proved a wolf to destroy; instead of a protector to nourish, became a tiger to devour: for he, having risen in authority, and secured the chiefest strength of the realm in his hands, he soon picked a quarrel with the nobility whom he thought in any way favoured Amadeus, and by surmised faults bereft them of their lives, and seized on their estates. And that he might not be brought to an account for these lawless actions, he gained to his support the assistance of the giant Guylon, which by your matchless force hath been brought to this end. And now being secure, as he thought, in his tyranny, he soon disposed of young Amadeus ; but how, or which way, is to us unknown. Our request therefore is, most noble captains, that he may by force be made to confess what he hath done with him ; that if alive, he may be restored unto us ; but if otherwise (which the gods forbid), he may be punished for the same according to his deserts.

Then was Isakius called to answer for himself ; who, trembling for fear, having a load of guilt upon his conscience, with a pale countenance and faltering speech made this reply :

"If a fair acknowledgment may mitigate my crime, I shall hereby give it freely to you, confessing to the uttermost of my knowledge ; that by imparting the same I may in some measure unburden my conscience, which now doth grievously oppress me. Know, then, that an ambitious desire of sitting on the throne, made me a ladder of mischief to ascend thereunto ; in order hereof, having levelled my way by destroying all those whom I thought would oppose my designs, yet thought I not myself sure until I had so disposed of the heir that he might not be heard of, knowing that people have always great affection to the lawful successor; yet I resolved not to murder him, that, if afterwards I should be called to an account, by preserving his life I might the better secure my own. Therefore, by the help of a trusty servant, I placed him with a shepherd of this country, he not knowing him to be the prince, but the illegitimate son of some gentlewoman who was not willing to have her shame known ; yet with this caution, that he should bring him up as his own son ; and for so doing, he was liberally rewarded with a considerable sum of money. Thus, gentlemen, have I given you a true relation of what I have done with the prince ; and if you please to send to the shepherd, you will have the truth confirmed by eyesight, he being at this time in good health, as I am informed by the same servant which placed him there, and who (if you please) shall conduct those whom you send unto the place where he now resides."

Isakius having ended his speech, it was concluded that the prince should be immediately sent for ; whereupon two gentlemen of quality were deputed to be the messengers ; who being attended with different servants, and guided by Isakius's confidant, in a short time came unto the shepherd's house, who seeing such a company before the door, was in bodily fear; but at last spying Beno (for so was Isakius's servant named) his heart waxed more cheerful. But when he heard them demand where the young prince then was, mistrusting, by Beno's presence, young Ornus (such had they named Amadeus) to be the party they inquired for, he had almost fallen into a swoon, expecting no other but that he should be hanged up: but being a little come to himself, he informed them that the prince was at the present time keeping sheep, not half a mile distant from that place; whereupon two of the chief of them, being guided by the shepherd, went to seek him. Now as they came near him, being entered into a little thicket, they heard a voice which with great harmony uttered forth this sonnet:

> The little lark that in the ground is hatch'd,
> And there bred up till feathers make her fly,
> No sooner she a flight or two hath catch'd,
> But up she mounts unto the lofty sky;
> Where if she sees sun shine and weather fair,
> How then for joy she twitters in the air!
>
> But if she see the wind begin to blow,
> Or pour down rain, and tempests do arise,
> Within a bush she keeps herself full low,
> Where, pretty wretch, close to the ground she lies,
> Until such time as all the storm be past,
> And then again she mounteth up in haste.
>
> Which plainly shows the nature in the lark
> Is still to seek to mount the lofty sky;
> And though perhaps you know and then may mark
> A kistrel kite to make a flight so high,
> Yet, all things weigh'd, if each thing have his right,
> A lark will far be lik'd above a kite.

The prince having ended this sonnet, they went up to him, doing him reverence, which put him into a fear and amazement, wondering at what was done unto him; yet was not his fears so great as was the old shepherd's, seeing him with them, whom he reputed to be his father. At last the old shepherd acquainted him with their message, which could not at first enter his heart, although he had always entertained noble thoughts under a vulgar habit; yet this so sudden a message made him doubt whether that he were awake, or that he had seen some vision or apparition; at last a little recollecting himself, he spoke in this manner:

"Think it not strange, gentlemen, if your words on the sudden surprise me; nor blame not if I am slow to believe wonders, for such your speeches do import. 'Tis true indeed, I have heard of several persons who have left their commands, and riches to enjoy the quiet of a retired life; but for the servant of a shepherd to be the son of a king, and he ignorant of it, appears no less than a miracle to me."

But the messengers seconding the old shepherd's speeches,

and with many asseverations confirming the truth of their
words, at last, he believed what they said; and, committing
his sheep to the guidance of another, he returned with them
to the shepherd's cottage, to refresh himself before his journey.
But when the old shepherd's wife understood their servant
was a prince, she was herself in conceit no less than a queen;
saying, "Ornus (for so, as I told you, they called the prince),
when thou comest to thy kingdom I hope thou wilt bestow on
me a new gown." The gentlemen laughed heartily at her
request, promising in the prince's name, she should have a
good one. This so overjoyed the old woman's heart, that she
brought forth unto them the choicest cakes she had in the
house, whereon they fed very heartily: and so taking leave
of the shepherd and his wife, who could scarcely speak for
weeping, they prepared for their journey. The princely
shepherd comforted the aged couple with great promises of
love and friendship which he should bear unto them, for the
care they had of him in his childhood; so taking horse, in a
short time they came to the city, where they were very joyfully received by the four Christian champions. But when
the citizens understood how their rightful prince was returned
to rule over them, it is not to be imagined the joy they received, which they expressed by ringing bells, making of
bonfires, and other demonstrations of great shoutings and
laughter. Then, by the general consent of the states, the
prince Amadeus was crowned king, and the usurper Isakius
committed to prison; which being done, the four Christian
captains, having victualled their ships, and having a prosperous wind, put forth to sea, where we will leave them, to show
what befel to the other Christian champions during the mean
time.

CHAPTER IX.

The famous Adventures of the two renowned Captains, Sir Orlando of Italy, and Sir Ewin of Scotland; how they redeemed the Duke of Candy's daughter from her enchantment, with other things that happened.

Now shall our pen attend the valiant exploits of those two
famous captains, Sir Orlando, who conducted the bold Italians,
and Sir Ewin, the captain of the warlike Scots; who having
taken their leave of the Seven Champions, as also of St.
George's three warlike sons, marched from thence with the
remainder of their army, the greatest part of them being
consumed by the pestilence and for want of victuals. Having
in their march passed the confines of Asia, and gone through
the fruitful countries of Greece, they at last took shipping in
a haven town of Peloponnesus, when, after three days' sailing, they saw before them a goodly island, from whence they

heard most terrible shrieks, as it were of tortured persons and
people in great distress; whereupon Sir Orlando and Sir
Ewin commanded the mariners to make up to it, which they
endeavoured to do; but coming near to it, it moved so from
them, that, notwithstanding all their endeavours, they could
not reach it. Whilst thus they stood amazed at this strange
adventure, there appeared to them out of the sea a certain
triton, or sea-god, in the likeness of those which they call
mer-men, who shaking his locks, spake to them in the ship in
this manner:

"I know you much wonder at the strange moving of this
island, and at the cries and shrieks which you hear from
thence: to satisfy you then, know that this island belongeth
to the famous necromancer Bandito, whose great skill in the
art of magic hath made his name known through most of the
countries of Africa and Asia. This Bandito, before such
time as he practised the Black Art, fell in love with the duke's
daughter of Candia, and by reason of his extraordinary riches,
and high parentage, was well entertained by the duke her
father; but her affections were wholly settled on a young
gentleman named Dyon, one whose virtues were above his
wealth, and his comely personage above his patrimony. To
him her love was so firmly linked, that she resolved that
nothing but death should part their affections; and therefore,
to prevent their father's importunity, who each hour endeavoured to prevail upon her to match with Bandito, she agreed
with her lover Dyon to forsake her father's house, and accompany him to any other country, where they might freely enjoy
each other's affections. Accordingly the next night, dame
Cynthia favouring their designs, she packed up the choicest
of her jewels, and, attended only with one servant, whom she
could trust, stole out of her father's house; and meeting with
her beloved Dyon, at a place where they had appointed, having a bark, they entered therein, and the next morning,
before she was missed, were gotten out of the pursuit of her
father; who having intelligence thereof, like a madman,
exclaimed against the heavens in a prodigious manner, and
threatened severe punishment on his daughter. But when
it came to the ears of Bandito, he, in great fury at being
disappointed, vowed revenge on all her relations; but wanting means to effect his desires, because the duke was very
strong and potent, he betook himself to the assistance of a
fiend, and entering into a solitary wilderness, having with
him a store of magical books, he fell unto his conjurations,
and in a short space raised up the fiend, with whom he agreed,
That having by his means revenged himself upon his enemies,
and to live the remainder of his life in all delight and pleasure, at the expiration thereof his body and soul to be at the

fiend's disposing. Having thus agreed in this wicked contract his desire of revenge was so urgent that he rested not until, by his magical arts, he learned where these two unfortunate lovers were landed; of which he presently informed the duke, who hasted thither with all speed in order to surprise these deplorable innocents; but this Bandito, having them now together, wrought so by his wicked enchantments, that the island wherein they were removed from the place of its proper station, and wafted upon the face of the ocean whither he pleased to direct it. And having thus done, he raised up four infernal hags, who with burning whips continually tormented these three persons; which by the Fates is ordered to endure until such time as two worthy Christians, from the confines of Christendom, shall put an end unto the enchantment; which two worthy persons ordained by the Fates to put a period to their torments, shall have, the one of them a cross, the other a star, depicted on their left shoulder, by which they may know themselves ordained to be those for whom this adventure was allotted."

And having uttered these words, the triton again sunk into the sea, leaving all the people in the two ships in great wonder and admiration.

The triton being thus vanished, the two noble captains, Sir Orlando and Sir Ewin, for the better encouragement of their soldiers, stripped off their doublets, and showing them their shoulders, there was visible thereon the two signs of the assured conquest, which was promised unto them; whereupon the soldiers gave such a shout as sounded like to the cataracts of the Nile, and seemed to rend the clouds asunder.

The noise being ceased, the island, which before seemed to move, now became fixed, so that with ease they approached near unto it; but attempting to land, they were often opposed by spirits in the likeness of dragons and fiery serpents, which so frightened the soldiers, that no words could induce them in battle; whereupon Sir Orlando and Sir Ewin, in whose breasts were sown the seeds of true magnanimity, to show them an example of undaunted resolution, leaped on shore, and with their strong battle-axes, made of the purest Lydian steel, they laid about them with as great strength and courage as did Alcides when he encountered with the Cyclops, or the magnanimous Hector fighting against the Greeks in the plains of Ilium.

Whilst they were thus occupied in these martial adventures, the magician Bandito, knowing by his spells that he must quickly render up his body a loathed carcase to the disposal of infernal Furies, was resolved in the mean time to do what mischief he could: and first he raised up a spirit in the likeness of a flaming fire, which encompassing the two knights, so heated their bodies, that they felt as if they had been fighting in the scorching deserts of Africa. Next appeared a terrible monster in the shape of a lion, having eyes as large as saucers, and teeth longer than the tusks of a boar bred up in the Caledonian woods, who assaulted the two knights with great fury. In the mean time the soldiers landed themselves, and in a warlike posture came to the rescue of the two champions, who by this time, through the scorching heat of the fire, and the strength of the monster, began to faint. Whereupon a selected party of the chiefest of them, being armed with coats of mail, and having in their hands steel javelins, which would penetrate and strike through any armour, although as strong as that Vulcan by the request of Venus made for Achilles; these with a valiant resolution ran towards the monster; but coming at him, he vanished away, leaving behind him such a horrible stench, as if it had proceeded from the lake Avernus, one of the poisoned rivers of hell. In the mean time the destructive artillery sent forth such loud noises as rent the air, and made the ground whereon they stood to shake, attended with dreadful flashes of lightning; when presently followed a serene sky; and a seeming castle, which stood before them, immediately vanished; whither approaching, they found the dead carcass of the magician, his joints dislocated, and the trunk of his body as black as the sooty Moor, or Cimmerian darkness. The duke and the two lovers were eased from their torments, whom they congratulated upon their happy deliverance. These three persons though much amazed at what had happened, yet could hardly believe themselves delivered from their persecuting torments; but being made sensible of their preservation by the two noble captains, their joy was inexpressible; the king returning them his grateful thanks in these words:

"Most magnanimous heroes, to whom I am indebted for the remainder of my unfortunate life, you have so far obliged me by this favour, and that so perfectly, that I must be your debtor all the days of my life. All that I can offer unto you is, that you would employ me in your service, that I might testify unto you in some part a requital of your favours; which I acknowledge you have so undeservedly conferred upon us."

"Most courteous prince," replied Sir Orlando, "all the requital we shall desire at your hands is, that you will pardon what is past, and freely bestow your daughter on this gentleman, whose deserts did far transcend Bandito's wealth; for know, we have heard the story of their loves; and in so doing we shall think ourselves sufficiently requited for what we have undertaken and performed for your freedom."

"Sir," said the prince, "your words, like music, please me

so well, that it shall be the greatest joy of my heart to have it so ;" and thereupon embracing Sir Dyon, as also his daughter, who humbly kneeled at his feet desiring forgiveness for what she had done ; "Dear daughter," said he, "may thy joys with him hereafter be as comfortable, and more during, than thy troubles and afflictions have been hitherto ; and know, it repenteth me for my unkindness to thee, which hath forced thee to do what thou hast done."

After these words were spoken, with many other expressions of love and forgetfulness of what was past, they all went to view the body of the magician, which they found so fearfully dismembered as cannot without horror be expressed. Here lay his brains in one place ; in another an eye ; there a piece of his jaw-bone ; here an arm ; there a leg ; in another place a piece of his trunk, wrapped up with some of his entrails, and all smelling so abominably, that the stench thereof was not able to be endured.

And now, there being no entertainment in that island for so many people as they had with them, they resolved upon their departure ; but before they went, they erected up a high pillar near to the place where the magician was rent in pieces ; on which pillar these verses were inscribed :

> "Wicked Bandito, bent unto all evil,
> Did for revenge his soul sell to the Devil.
> His whole delight was blood and cruelty;
> And as he liv'd in blood, so he in blood did die.
> Whoe'er thou be, that doet this writing read,
> Of magic arts and wicked acts take heed ;
> Lest like Bandito, that same bloody wretch,
> The Devil for thy deeds thy soul do fetch."

And just underneath was written :

> "Wretched Bandito, near unto this place,
> Was by the Devil all in pieces torn ;
> Thou that read'st this, learn to have more grace,
> Or better far it were thou ne'er wert born."

The pillar being erected, the two valiant captains, Sir Orlando and sir Ewin, with the duke of Candia, the princess, and Sir Dyon, took ship ; and having a prosperous wind, in a few days arrived on the fruitful coast of Candia, and with speed marched to Cidonia, the chief city thereof, where they were entertained most joyfully ; the bells rang, the bonfires blazed ; the walls, windows, roofs, towers, steeples, and battlements, all beset with people to behold the sight : the windows were hung with rich arras and curious tapestry, and the conduits ran with Greek wine. Thus in great triumph did they march through the streets, until they came to the duke's palace, which for stately bravery and magnificence was erected according to what the height of fancy could express. The fluted pillars, the strange Colossuses, the ascents, and the statues, were wonderful to behold. Here were they entertained by the duke with all honour imaginable. Each day there was a sumptuous banquet, where nothing was wanting to crown the appetite with content: the boards were served with princely dishes; and the juice of the grape flowed in cups of burnished gold. But these two valiant captains, in whose breasts were sown the seeds of true magnanimity, soon grew weary of these carpet delights, and therefore informed the duke of their intention to depart; who, though very loth, as persons to whom he owed whatever he was, yet he condescended thereunto. But before their departure, in a grateful acknowledgment of the great kindness he had received from them, he presented sir Orlando with a rich sword, the pummel of which was enchased with diamonds, rubies, and other stones of rich price: upon the blade was this motto engraven:

"The benefit receiv'd shall not
By me for ever be forgot."

To Sir Ewin he presented a rich silver target, beset on the sides with emeralds, sapphires, and other stones of great value, of such a refulgent lustre as gave a light in the night like unto so many wax candles. In the middle thereof was pourtrayed Hector and Achilles in a single tournament, the one breathing these words out of his mouth:

"In a just cause, who would refuse to fight?"

The other answering,

"But then you must be sure your cause be right."

To the other captains and soldiers were also given gifts of great value; so that they departed away, all of them, very well satisfied.

In their way homewards they met with certain pirates, who, roving along the coasts of Italy, took many of the inhabitants prisoners; among others was the beautiful Ciropa, sister unto Sir Orlando. With these pirates they engaged with much resolution; who made a very stout resistance; so that the air was made dark with their flying darts, and the sea colonred with blood issuing from the scoop-holes. Many were slain, and more wounded, before the pirates would hearken to yielding; but at last, seeing themselves not able to hold out, they cried for mercy, which the generous captains Sir Orlando and Sir Ewin freely granted them. And so, the pirates delivering up their weapons into the conquerors' hands, they entered their ships. But when Sir Orlando beheld his sister amongst the captives, he was entranced with wonder, and stood as if his soul had been gone upon some serious errand, and left the corpse in pawn till it came back. She, on the other side, was as much surprised to behold her brother and deliverer, whom she ran unto and kindly embraced. But if

Sir Orlando was surprised with admiration, Sir Ewin was stricken into an ecstasy on beholding her divine perfections, esteeming her to be nature's chief master-piece, whose rare composure modellized forth the height of all beauty: so transcendently did she show in this low estate, that he esteemed her to be the magazine or common-wealth of all perfections, and the very true elixir of all beauty.

These excellencies shot a thousand darts of Cupid into the heart of Sir Ewin; so that being emboldened by love, he accosted her in this manner:

"Most divine lady, who art inspired with all the excellencies that the world can bestow upon your sex, I shall account it an honour to me to become your servant; my resolution herein being so magnanimous, that I suppose no ill fortune can attend upon it. Deign, then, madam, to accept me for such, which may prove a spur to my courage, in fighting under so divine a beauty."

To whom the lady Ciropa with a smiling countenance replied in this manner:

"Sir, I acknowledge myself doubly engaged to you, as for your love, so also for my liberty, for which I cannot in the least make you a requital; but since you do establish your content upon my acceptance of your service, your hopes cannot deceive you much, if an acknowledgment of my affections to you may be any ways the means of making you happy."

These loving passages between Sir Ewin and the lady Ciropa were very pleasing unto Sir Orlando, who desired nothing more than the alliance of so valiant and good a knight as Sir Ewin. And now was Sir Orlando moved to inflict severe punishment on the captain of the pirates for stealing away his sister, but he remembered his promise, which he would not violate for all the wealth in Asia: he therefore took the chiefest riches of their ships from them, which he distributed amongst his soldiers; and having released all the prisoners, he put the privates into one of their empty ships, and sent them away; whilst their own fleet with a merry gale of wind set forwards for Italy: whither in a short time they safely arrived; and to complete their joy, not long after Sir Ewin was married unto the lady Ciropa, upon whom Sir Orlando bestowed many rich gifts, and sent them away to the country of Scotland; where for a while we will leave them, and return to speak of the strange travels and adventures of the Seven Champions of Christendom.

CHAPTER X.

How the Seven Champions came to a land where the men for their sins were changed into the shape of beasts; and how by finishing the Adventure of the Golden Cave, they returned to their shapes again.

Now come we to speak of the Seven Champions of Christendom; who, not long after the departure of Sir Orlando and Sir Ewin, being desirous to return to their native countries, to repose their bodies where they had their births, taking their leave of St. George's three sons, they also took shipping in a single ship, and cutting the briny face of Neptune for three or four days, were favoured with a gentle gale of wind, which made the sailors' hearts full merry; but on the fifth day, notwithstanding that Phœbus sent forth his beams with much radiancy, until such time as he became an equal arbiter of the forepast and coming part of the day, there fell a mist upon the face of the ocean, which in an instant grew to such darkness that neither men nor masts on the deck were discernible; so that the pilot was at a loss which way to steer: yet could they perceive that their ship moved with a swift motion, although there was then so great a calm; and such a gentle air, as not to stir one hair of their heads. This continued for the space of seven days; so that the whole company were given over to silence and sadness; when, to comfort their hearts, the renowned champion of England, St. George, calling them together, made to them this following oration:

"Renowned champions, and fellow-soldiers in arms, be not dismayed at this which hath happened unto you, since nothing comes by chance, but what is before pre-appointed of the gods, and must inevitably come to pass; which things, though seeming to us strange and wonderful, yet many times are the forerunners and causes of good both to us and others: let us therefore be armed with patience, and not think to fight against Heaven, as they do who murmur and repine at any mischance which befals them; for know assuredly, whom the gods love they will protect, and to a valiant mind no peril comes unlooked for; and if we perish in this extremity, let it be our comfort that we die unconquered of our enemies."

This oration of St. George much comforted the hearts of all that heard him; but soon after greater comforts appeared, for on a sudden the sky began to clear, and the sun, which they had not seen for many days, began to appear, and to shoot forth his enlightening rays. Their ship now did not move of itself, nor knew the mariners off what coast they were; yet was their joy exceeding great to behold the lightsome beams of the sun, and to converse with their companions as well with their eyes as with their ears. Soon after they espied land, unto which they made with all the speed they could; and having landed, found it a very fruitful country, stored abundantly with all sorts of beasts, birds, and other living creatures; but neither men, women, nor houses, nor any signs of any that had ever been there. This struck them all into wonder and amazement; but that which most of all amazed them, was to see these beasts and birds flock about them, and with bellowing, bleating, chirping, crying, and other signs, seemed to make their moan unto them. Whilst they were thus wondering, there appeared unto them an ancient palmer, clad in a russet gown down to the ground; his hair as white as Venus's doves, or snow upon the Scythian mountains; his aged limbs supported with an ebony staff tipped with silver; his look seemed to have formerly carried majesty with it, though now Time's plough had printed deep furrows in his aged face. He, seeing this company, made up to them, and addressing himself to St. George, as to the chiefest of them, spake as followeth:

"Renowned English champion, for of your country I am not ignorant, having in my youth travelled through most parts thereof; know that by the Destinies I was informed of your coming hither, and therefore came to this place on purpose to meet you: come then along with me, and I will show you things transcending the power of a strong belief; and with that he led them through a spacious plain, unto an intricate thicket or labyrinth, having in the midst thereof a most stately building, which overlooked all the plain round about. Hither, through unknown ways, did the palmer bring them; where he caused his servants (having about twenty of them) to provide for the champions and their retinue such a costly dinner, as was not imagined to be gotten in such a desert place. After dinner, having refreshed themselves with some bowls of Leatic wine, he led them up to the top of his palace, which had a gallery round it to overlook the plains. Here, having placed the champions so that they might have a full prospect of the whole country, sitting down in a chair by them he thus began:

"Know, worthy knights at arms, that this country wherein you now are is called Scobellum, of such a fruitful soil, that it may well be styled the garden of Ceres and vintage of Bacchus; such is the plenty of all things therein; nor was it less populous of inhabitants than fruitful of necessaries for to maintain them; but this their plenty caused pride, and abundance of all things caused abundance of all manner of vices amongst them; so that, if they had engrossed the corruptions of all nations to themselves, they could not have been a more defiled people than they were, exceeding the Cannibals for cruelty, the Persians for pride, the Egyptians for luxury, the Cretans for lying, the Germans for drunkenness, and all nations together for generality of vices. Such a mass of evils

x

called for a mass of punishments which the gods inflicted upon them, and that according to the nature of their deserts and the quality of their crimes; for those great plenty of beasts and fowls which here you view, were once men and women, as in other places, but now changed to the likeness of what you see. Drunkards were changed into swine, who still retain the same nature, there being no difference between a drunkard and a swine. Lecherous persons were changed into goats. Proud people were turned to peacocks. Scolds were metamorphosed to magpies and chattering jays. Such as lost their estates at cards and dice, were transformed to asses. Those whose delight was only in music and singing, were changed to thrushes and nightingales. Envious persons were metamorphosed to dogs, who lying on hay will eat none themselves, nor suffer the hunger-starved ox to feed thereon. Those women who would work hard, but were troubled with other bad qualities, were transformed to milch-cows, who would give pails full of milk, but as soon as they had so done kick them down with their heels. Jesters, buffoons, and jack-puddings, were transformed to monkeys, baboons, and apes. Dancers on the ropes were turned to squirrels. Usurers, misers, and such like covetous persons were changed to moles. In brief, worthy champions, (for I would not trouble your patience too long) there was a general metamorphosis made of them all, each one according to the degree wherein he had formerly lived; and this their punishment, destined by the Fates to endure until such time as some hardy knight should be so bold as to attempt the conquest of the Golden Cave; which if he overcome, then shall their transformations cease, and they return again to their proper places.

"Now, worthy knights, the adventure of the Golden Cave is this. About six miles from this place lieth a cave, the entrance whereinto is through divers windings and turnings, like unto a labyrinth; in which cave is kept a continual fire, made by such art as nothing shall quench it, but only the water of a cistern at the entrance of the said cave, which is guarded by two giants and two centaurs, with whom they must combat before they can attain to the cistern. Now, worthy chieftains, if there be any amongst you so adventurous, as for the sake of these poor transformed people will adventure your lives, the enterprise will not only be honourable to yourselves, but you will also oblige thousands in thankful gratitude to your memories for so inestimable a benefit."

"Now, by the honour of my country England," said St. George, "never let me buckle on armour, if I make not one in this enterprize;" so likewise said the other six champions, each striving which should have the honour to accompany St. George in so noble an enterprise; wherefore, that emulation might not cause any strife, they agreed to cast lots amongst the six, which of the three should accompany him: so accordingly they did, and the lots fell upon the three famous champions, St. Anthony of Italy, St. James of Spain, and St. Patrick of Ireland; who, glad of their good fortunes, prepared themselves against the next day to try the adventure; and in the morning, no sooner did Aurora usher in the day, and from the glowing east display her purple doors, but the four champions mounted on their warlike steeds, who, glad of such a burden, pranced under them in as great state as did the famous Bucephalus when he was bestridden by the warlike Alexander, so taking a guide with them from the palmer, they proceeded to the Golden Cave, where they alighted and gave their guide their horses to lead. Here they were met by a dwarf who spake to them in these words:

"Proud knights, presume not to come within the compass of these gates, lest you repent your folly, and with the loss of your lives pay for your presumption." To whom St. George answered: "Dwarf, go tell your masters we come to try our skill with them, to prove which of our swords cuts sharpest." "That shall you soon see," said the dwarf; and returning to the cave, told the giants what St. George had said to him; who presently came marching out to them, with each an oak upon his shoulder, which, when they came near unto the champions, they brandished over their heads, as if they had been hazel twigs.

"Audacious villians," said the giants, "do you desire to feel the strength of our arms? You shall soon try to your cost what we can do;" and therewithal struck at the champions with such fury, that the earth shook with the force of their blows. Who would have seen the picture of Alecto, or with what manner of countenance Medea killed her own children, needed but take their faces for the full satisfaction of their knowledge in that point. The champions nimbly avoided their blows, and getting within the compass of their oaks, made up to the giants, whose sides they so thwacked, and were so liberal of their blows, that the giants, feeling the weight of them, betook them to their heels, and left their knotty clubs behind them, to be viewed by the champions with wonder and admiration at the strength of those that could wield such massy weapons. But determining to prosecute the adventure, they followed the giants; who, however, were by this time gotten out of sight, and the champions found themselves at a loss in finding them, the multiplicity of paths leading each way made them doubtful which to choose. At last they resolved each of them to take a several path, and if they met not together at the cave, then to return each to the same place again. Now, it so chanced that, as they were going in those paths, each of them met with an opposer; and first St. George met with one of the centaurs, being of a terrible shape and incredible strength; betwixt whom began a most fierce combat with great courage and magnanimity, insomuch that St. George was never so put to it in all the battles he had ever fought before; for the centaur was both nimble and strong, and fought with great skill and courage; but St. George having with a side-blow given him a deep wound on the ribs, he sent forth such a hideous yell, as was like the loud rattle of the boisterous wind, or cannons when they disgorge their fiery vomits; and, nimbly turning him about, fled amain towards the cave.

The renowned champion St. Anthony of Italy had not gone far in his path but he met with one of the giants, who came now armed in a coat of mail, with a great bar of iron on his shoulders; with whom St. Anthony encountered with great courage; nor was the giant backward in his endeavours of obtaining the conquest, dealing such blows each to the other, that whoso should have beheld them would have thought each blow had death attendant on it. This giant was twelve feet high; so that St. Anthony with the point of his sword could hardly reach his crown; which advantage he supplied with nimbleness, so that the giant spent his blows in vain; and being now wearied with the weight of his armour, the sun also shining in his greatest glory, he sweat so exceedingly, that it entering into his eyes, he was almost blinded therewith, and endeavouring to wipe it off with his hand, St. Anthony, taking the advantage, with a sudden blow cut his hand off by the wrist; whereupon the giant yielded himself and craved mercy.

In like manner St. James, the noble Spanish champion, as he walked along in his path met with the other giant; betwixt whom was fought a most terrible battle, striking so thick and fast at each other, as if every blow would strive to be foremost: the noble champion behaving himself so gallantly with his Bilboa blade, made of the purest Spanish steel, that he cut deep furrows in the giant's flesh, from whence issued such abundance of blood as changed the grass from a verdant green to a crimson red; so that the giant, through the loss of such abundance of blood, began to faint; which St. James perceiving, renewing himself with all his strength, gave him such a blow as brought him headlong to the ground; when, smiting off his head, he left his dismembered carcass, and proceeded further in his path towards the Golden Cave.

Lastly, the renowned champion St. Patrick of Ireland, whose breast still thirsted after honourable adventures, proceeding forwards in his path, met with the other centaur; betwixt whom began so fierce a combat, that to describe the same

The centaurs being archers and armed with pole-axe struck S! [...] with great fury

CHAP V PART

to the life would wear my pen to the stump, although it were made of refined brass or the purest Lydian steel. Here on each side was strength matched with skill, fury with fortitude, and true valour with matchless magnanimity. The centaur being nimble, and armed with a pole-axe, struck at St. Patrick with great fury, which he avoided with the greatest skill he could, and with his keen falchion returned the centaur his blows with interest. The fight, as it was sharp, so it endured long; when, being both willing to take breath, they paused from fighting for some time, when St. Patrick spake to the centaur in these words:

"Monster of nature, let me advise thee to yield thyself, and not to oppose us any further in the conquest of the Golden Cave, since it is resolved by the Destinies that I and my fellows should be the persons that, by finishing the adventure, should restore the people to their human shapes."

The centaur, finding himself deeply wounded, was ready to yield, when St. Patrick commanded him to deliver up his pole-axe, which the centaur accordingly did: so they both marched towards the Golden Cave, where they met St. George, St. Anthony, and St. James, and, relating to each other their several successes, they presently proceeded to the finishing of the adventure; and approaching the cistern, they each of them filled their helmets with water, and being guided by the dwarf, who now was obedient to the champions, they came to the fire, into which they threw the water, and never left off until such time as they had quenched it; which being done, the cave and all about it vanished out of sight, and the thick grove or wilderness about it was all level and even. So returning to the messenger, whom they left walking their horses, they mounted on them to return back to the aged palmer's, meeting by the way with multitudes of people, who by the finishing of the adventure were now restored to their former shapes.

In this manner they marched along to the aged palmer's, who entertained them with great joy, by whom likewise they were congratulated on their happy return and noble achievement, as also they were by the three other champions, St. Denis, St. Andrew, and St. David; and after they had refreshed themselves with some victuals, they were conducted to a spacious room, where they had their wounds bathed with wine, milk, and other precious ointments. The next morning the people were assembled together, to whom St. George made a pithy oration, exhorting them hereafter to lead a better life, and not to have their natures addicted to such beastly vices, as made them, though not in shape, yet to differ not from beasts in their actions; with many other words to the like effect; all which they promised to perform. And afterwards taking leave of their host the aged palmer, they returned to their ship, and having a gentle gale of wind, set sail towards Christendom.

CHAPTER XL.

How St. George's three Sons were separated by a tempest; and how Sir Alexander met with the ship wherein the Seven Champions were. How he was married to the Princess Mariana, and crowned king of Thessaly. The tragical Story of the Duke Ursini, and death of the Seven Champions.

NOT long after the departure of the Seven champions, St. George's sons, resolving also to see their native country, in order thereunto embarked themselves with their companies in three several ships, and for the space of eight or ten days sailed with a prosperous gale of wind; the courteous sea all that time smoothing his wrinkled brow, but about the eleventh day the wind and sea contended in a robust manner; the beaten ships were tossed like a forceless feather; now riding up on the mountain waves, as if their top-masts tilted at the moon; anon falling again with such a precipitate low descent as if they were sinking into hell's low abyss. In this furious storm they were separated one from the other; where we will leave two of them, and speak only of Sir Alexander, and his party, who, after the storm was over, directed their course as near as they could towards the coasts of Christendom; and having sailed the space of three days, they saw before them a ship in fight with two galleys, or men of war; to whom they made up with all the speed they could, and coming near to them, they perceived by the streamers (wherein was woven the red cross of England) that it was the same ship wherein the Seven Champions were embarked; which when they knew, they sent forth such a loud and lengthened shout and holloa, as reverberated upon the waves, or as the sea makes when it trembles underneath its banks, to hear the replication of its sounds. They in the other ship answered them with the like holloa, and then, jointly setting upon the two galleys, they with pikes, bills, and darts plied Death's fatal task, sending numbers of the Turkish souls to be transported on Charon's ferry; so that the two galleys, which at first were assailants, could no longer hold out defendants, but yielding themselves, craved for mercy; which the Christian champions were the more willing to grant them, in regard that many of their company had been sorely wounded before Sir Alexander came to their rescue.

So entering the two galleys, they took from them such things as they needed; amongst which they found some hogsheads of Greek wines, which very much refreshed the fainting soldiers. They also took from them their armour, that they might not be able to offend others; and setting free those few prisoners they had taken, they let them go; and having stayed a while in mending the tattered cordage of their ships, which was much shattered in the fight, with a prosperous wind they set sail, and in a few days arrived on the pleasant banks of Thessaly; on sending a messenger to the court, to give notice of their arrival, the message was so welcome to the princess Mariana (who now was become queen of that country, her father being lately dead) that she caused the bells to be rung, and bonfires to be made, as at a public rejoicing. She sent some of the chiefest of her nobles to invite them to the court, with such accommodations as she judged most needful for them at present; in the meantime she prepared to entertain them in the best manner she could; which at their coming they found to be so costly and splendid, as it raised great wonder in them to behold it; the streets all the way they passed to her palace being railed in, and guarded on both sides with companies of foot soldiers; the conduits ran with wine; and from the balconies was heard all manner of music that could be imagined. First before them marched a complete troop of horse, having between each four ranks a trumpeter sounding with a silver trumpet: the troops were all in their buff coats, with silver belts, and the pummels of their swords inlaid with glittering stones, which sparkled like diamonds. Next followed four heralds, in four distinct coats of arms. After them, the nobility of the land, in rich robes, with coronets on their heads. Then came the Seven Champions, and St. George's valiant son, in four rich chariots, lined with cloth of gold, and studded with studs of massy silver. After them followed the colonels, majors, and captains, with silken streamers waving before them, being ranged two by two, each English officer with a Thessalian, and mounted on prancing Barbary steeds. And lastly, the under officers, with the army in goodly arms, and accoutred most richly. In this order they marched to the palace, where they were met by the queen, attired in a rich robe of ermine, with the crown imperial upon her head, who with a smiling countenance entertained them in these words:

"Thrice welcome hither, most renowned champions, whom the gods have appointed for the relief of the distressed and chastisement of the vicious. Fame's golden trumpet hath sounded the renown of your honourable actions; and by quelling the force of the Pagan armies, giving us great hopes hereafter to enjoy halcyon days of peace." And applying herself more particuarly to the princely knight Sir Alexander; "Sir," said she, "how much I am bound to the immortal Powers for your preservation, my heart is not able to conceive, much less my tongue to express. Now, as Heaven has been kind to me, in hearing my prayers for your safe return, so shall I account it my future happiness, that, leaving off arms, you now come to enjoy the fruits of our amours; and instead of following the camp of Mars, we solace ourselves in the tents of Cupid. Mistake me not, dear sir: 1 mean not, by spending our time in wanton dalliance, but in the honourable state of matrimony, that, being joined in Hymen's bands, we may have our joys crowned with the issues of an unfeigned love."

"Most gracious princess," replied Sir Alexander, "your speeches are the sole effects of my thoughts, and your desires to me absolute commands, being such as tend only to my profit and welfare; wonder not then, most peerless madam, if I willingly embrace, what I so earnestly covet." And so sealing his love on the red wax of her lips, they hand in hand paced it into her palace, accompanied with the Seven champions, as also with many of the chief lords and ladies of the land; where was provided for them a sumptuous dinner of of such costly viands, as might teach the feeblest palate how to eat; and those placed so thick and plentiful, as if the table would crack with the pile of such weighty dishes. All the while they were at dinner, melodious harps and songs saluted their ears, which were breathed forth in such a curious harmony, as charmed their very souls to an ecstasy. After dinner they fell to dancing, tripping it so nimbly, as if they had been all air, or some lighter element. In these delights they wasted eight or nine days. But the Seven Champions soon grew weary of such pastimes, and, desirous to go home to their native countries, were minded to take their leaves of the queen Mariana; but Sir Alexander and she, having concluded their nuptials should be celebrated very suddenly, they were with much entreaty persuaded to stay until they were over.

The appointed day being come, early that morning, by such time as Aurora, the blushing goddess which doth sway the downy confines of the day and night, began to appear, both bridegroom and bride were saluted with most sweet-sounding music; which being ended, their ears were accosted with this epithalamium:

"Sol, thy beams no longer hide;
Call the bridegroom to the bride;
Let each one rejoice and sing,
Make the air with Hymen ring.
May all pleasure and delight
Crown your day and bless your night;
And the warm embrace of love
Be soft as down on Venus' dove:
May your oft-repeated kisses,
Bring with them as many blisses;
And these joys remain in state
Till your end, and that come late."

These solemnities being over, and the bridegroom and bride risen from their beds, they prepared themselves to go to church: the bridegroom was apparelled in a suit of flame-coloured tabby, to signify how he burnt in the flames of chaste love; the bride was attired all in white, to denote her unspotted virginity and maidenly modesty. Sir Alexander was led by two duke's daughters, and the princess Mariana by two of the chiefest barons of the realm; having her train borne up by four ladies of honour. Thus did they walk in great state unto the temple, where the priest joined them together in Hymen's rites; which being done they returned again in the same order to the palace, all the way the people showing such great demonstrations of joy as were wonderful to behold. To rehearse the great cheer prepared for this royal dinner, the maskings, revellings, and other costly shows, which were solemnized by the lords and ladies, and other courtiers, would tire the pen of an industrious writer.

The next day was appointed for the coronation of the prince Alexander and the princess Mariana, which was performed in great splendour; the multitude of spectators that came to behold it being so many, that notwithstanding great store of money were thrown about in other streets, to divert the people from thronging so thick at the coronation, yet the people regarded not the money at all, for the great desire they had to behold their new king.

After the usual ceremonies were ended, which appertain to such solemnities, the trumpets sounded, and the people with a very loud shout cried, "Long live Alexander and Mariana, king and queen of Thessaly." The knights and barons, to honour the solemnity the more, appointed the whole afternoon to be spent in jousting and tourneying, wherein was shown very much skill and valour; but above them all, duke Orsin, a near kinsman to the queen Mariana, carried the chief credit, having unhorsed fifteen knights that day; for which king Alexander presented him with a rich chain of gold, and St George, in reward of his valour gave him a costly diamond ring. And now, king Alexander being thus solemnly crowned, was fulfilled that prophecy, which was by the fairy queen predicted of him, as you may read in the Fourteenth Chapter of the First part of this honourable history, which contained these words:

> "This child shall live likewise to be a king,
> Time's wonder for device and courtly sport:
> His tilts and tournaments abroad shall ring,
> To every coast where nobles do resort.
> Queens shall attend, and humble at his feet;
> Thus love and beauty shall together meet."

After some few days spent in royal triumph, the Seven

Champions resolved to stay no longer, but to hasten to their own countries. In pursuance of this their resolution, they acquainted king Alexander and queen Mariana of their intentions, who were very loth to part from their company; but the Seven Champions were so resolute in their determination, that no persuasions could induce them to stay any longer. The king and queen, seeing them so fully bent upon going. with a great train of lords and ladies attended them to their ships, where they had caused a stately banquet to be provided for them; and so, after many rich presents and mutual embracings had passed between them, the Seven Champions took ship, and having a gentle gale of wind, soon lost the sight of the Thessalian shore. So sailing along on Neptune's watery front, the wanton mermaids sporting by the sides of their ship, and scarce a wrinkle seen on Thetis's face, but the sea as calm as when the halcyon hatched on the sand; they saw before them a ship, all whose sails and streamers were black, having black flags and pendants stuck round the sides of the ship. The sight of this ship, so strangely attired in black, made them have a longing desire to know what it should mean: so making up to it, they hailed them, according to the sea phrase, when a gentleman on the deck, gave them to understand that they were of Italy, and were come from Scandia, bringing with them the dead body of the duke Ursini, lord of the fruitful land of Campania; which when St. Anthony understood (the duke Ursini having formerly been his loving friend) he declared unto them who he was, and what were his companions, and also how they were bound for Italy; whereupon there was great rejoicing on both sides; and the gentleman, and captain, and master of the Italian ship, were invited into the other; where, after some compliments passed on both sides, and a short collation, the sea being calm, and like a standing pool, no waves nor billows to arise, they entreated the gentleman, now that their ships lay thus at hull, to declare unto them the manner of the duke Ursini's death, and how he came to die in so remote a country. To which the gentleman willingly condescended, and spake as follows:

"It is now full two years since the renowned prince Oswy, duke of Ferrara, at the celebration of his marriage with the famous lady Lucinda of Mantua, kept solemn jousts and tournaments, with royal entertainments for all comers; which invited thither not only the prime nobility and gallants of the Italians, but also, the news being spread abroad into foreign countries, several persons of great quality resorted thither: amongst others was Julian, the daughter of Lampasco, prince of Scandia; a lady of such glorious eye-surprising rays, that in her face Love seemed to sit enthroned in full majesty; nor wanted she therewith the helps of art, to set forth her natural perfections; so that she seemed rather a divine goddess, than a human creature. These her admirable endowments were looked on by duke Ursini through a magnifying glass, which rendered her to him the most admirable of all creatures; capturing his heart in such a thrall to her beauty, that he vowed himself a servant to her virtues; and to endear himself the more in her respect, by some achievements of honour, he entered the lists, as chief challenger against all comers, being mounted on a milk-white Barbary courser, trapped with caparisons of silver, and on his burgonet a plume of goodly feathers: his armour was blue, resembling the azure firmament, spangled with stars of gold; with these words for his device, "Virtue, like the clear heaven, is without clouds." He encountered with sundry knights of great worth, against all which he had much the better, which gained him both great applause and envy.

"Nor was he less skilful in the intrigues of love than in the management of arms, and could court a lady as well as encounter with an enemy; which he, with much artificial eloquence, demonstrated in an address to the lady Jilian, who seemed much affected with his person; and so far the matter went, that there seemed nothing wanting to the consummation of their marriage, but only the consent of her parents; which to obtain, he sailed with her unto Scandia, where he was most nobly entertained, and his suit very well liked.

"Now it was so, that a young baron of that country, named Lamprido, had formerly borne a great affection unto the princess Jilian, and had so far prevailed with her that he was in great hopes of obtaining her love; but his means not being answerable to her high dignity, it was kept very close from prince Lampasco's ear; yet he hoped in time, either by the death of Lampasco, or some secret stratagem, he should compass his ends. But now seeing prince Ursini in so great favour, he began utterly to despair in his suit, unless by some means he could find a way to deprive him of his life. It happened, not long after, that prince Lampasco proclaimed a general hunting of the wild boar; to which princely exercise all the flower of the nobility, and every one whose breast was fired with a desire of glory and renown: amongst others, none was more forward to this royal sport than prince Ursini, who at the appointed time came into the field, armed with his boarspear, and mounted on a Spanish jennet, who for their swiftness are said to be engendered of the wind. Being come within view of the place where they were to hunt, each man was ordered according to his stand; when a brace of lusty beagles were let loose to rouse the boar: in the mean time every man prepared himself for the handling of his weapons, and with a nimble eye to watch all advantages that might be taken. It was not long before the beagles had roused the boar out of his den; who seemed to regard no danger, nimbly turning round about, with a kind of wallowing running pace, ran where he could see any company. The first that struck at him was an Italian knight, who accompanied prince Ursini in his voyage to Scandia, who broke his spear, but wounded him not, for his skin was scarcely penetrable, being as hard as a bull's hide when it is tanned. Leaving this Italian, he ran against a valiant knight, named Piaster, who encountered with him very courageously; yet could not his courage, strength, nor skill, all which he was in a full measure master of, prevail any thing. Yet was his performance so much that, giving him a small wound on the leg, feeling the smart, he ran towards baron Lamprido; who used his utmost strength and skill to withstand him; but the smart of the wound in the boar's leg so exasperated him, that he ran with such fury against Lamprido as turned him, horse and man, to the ground, and undoubtedly had slain him, had not duke Ursini come to his rescue; who with undaunted courage set upon the boar, and with great strength, guided by skill, so followed his blows, that he made the boar begin to stagger; who yet with open mouth came towards him: which advantage duke Ursini spying, thrust his boar-spear down his throat, and therewith tore his heart asunder, yielding unto him the absolute victory.

"By this time divers knights were come in to him: amongst others Lamprido, having recovered his fall, came in with the thickest; but when he saw that the boar was killed, and by the hands of Ursini, his blood boiled within him for anger, out of envy that he had done it; which he knew would more endear him in the love and affections of the lady Jilian, as also that his own overthrow would much lessen her opinion of him. Hereupon a desire of revenge entering into his heart, his study was how to effect it with privacy; not only for fear of the law, but dread of duke Ursini's valour, whom he knew he could not match in single combat: he therefore concluded to do it by treachery, which not long after he brought to pass in this manner:—

"Amongst other exercises which duke Ursini much delighted in, one was the art of angling, in which he would oftentimes spend many hours, and that with as much privacy as he could, because a multitude of persons was a hindrance to his sport. It so chanced one day, that he, accompanied only with one servant, and having no armour but his sword, went in a boat unto a spacious river a fishing. This being known unto Lamprido, he thought it now a convenient time to accomplish his purposed ends; and therefore, having engaged seven or eight other stout persons to his side, they armed themselves, and in two boats, to prevent suspicion, betook themselves also to the water, taking two different ways, the better to surround him in the middle. Duke Ursini was all this while so busy at his exercise, that he took no notice of their intentions; and at last, not perceiving that they had any armour (it being hid under their linen frocks), he permitted them to come so near his boat, that one or two of them, leaping in, began to lay hold of him; when, snatching up his sword, he defended himself so gallantly, that he had well near sent them to attend at Charon's ferry, the biting steel being pursued by such streams of blood, that his boat was well bestained with a crimson dye. In the mean time the other villains leaped in, and so surrounded him on every side, that he had no room to wield his weapon. However, as if he had been a man made all of fire, having a courage that knew not how to fear, he resisted them all, and in a while, though over-matched, had sent four of their souls to the Stygian bay, whereof Lamprido was the third. Thus for a short space did the goddess Victoria seem favourable to him. And now his man who all this while had done his utmost in defence of his master, having grasped one of the villains, they chanced both to fall overboard into the water; when duke Ursini, endeavouring to help his man, the other villain gave him a mortal wound on the head; yet before he fell, he tumbled the villain also into the water, to accompany his fellow; which was no sooner done, but, through the loss of so much blood which issued from his wounds, he fell down in a swoon, when at the very instant there came thither a boat with some citizens in it, intending also to have fished there; but seeing the latter part of this skirmish, they made up to them; where they found, in duke Ursini, Death's pale visage pourtrayed in his cheeks, and he ready to take his oath to be Death's true liegeman. The citizens did what they could in staying his soul, which was now making a separation from his body; but all their endeavours were in vain; for Death, Nature's bold pursuivant, had taken an absolute possession of him.

"Whilst they were thus busied in seeking to recal life unto him again, they heard one of the two parties, which he had encountered withal at first, to give a great groan; whereupon using their helping hands for to revive him, they at last brought him to his speech: of whom they asked who were the persons, and what was their difference; which he declared unto them in manner as we have before described; and having made an end of his relation, he presently therewith expired.

"Hereupon the citizens, taking along with them the boat wherein were the dead bodies, returned to the city, and declaring the news, there was great sorrow and lamentation for duke Ursini; especially by the lady Jilian, who from her tearful eyes shed many vain offerings to the dead. Nor can you think, most noble champions, but that the grief which then seized upon us who accompanied him in this his voyage, was any thing less than what possessed the hearts of the chiefs for hearing the news we sat in such a given-over posture, as if any one had beheld us would have thought Silence, Solitariness, and Melancholy were come, under the ensign of Mishap, to conquer Delight, and plunge us into the deep abyss of Misery.

"After some little time, being raised as it were out of this trance of sorrow, we craved leave to depart home, with the corpse of our dead master; which the prince Lampasco freely granted, and furnished us with all things fitting, as here you see."

At which words grief so stopped the passage of his speech that he could proceed no further.

The Seven Champions heartily condoled with the gentleman in this mishap, that so worthy a knight should fall so treacherously. And now with all the speed they could they sailed to Italy; where having arrived, duke Ursini was interred with all the funeral pomp that could be devised. Where the other six champions leaving St. Anthony behind them, they posted each one to his own country; where they had not long remained, but that they died, and were buried in their former sepulchres.

CHAPTER XII

What happened to St. George's eldest Son, Sir Guy, after he was parted from his two Brothers. The woful Story of Selindus; how he was deprived of his Barony by Euphemius, and restored again by the Valour of Sir Guy and Captain Bolus.

Now shall our pen endeavour to describe the valiant acts of St. George's eldest son, Sir Guy, whose honourable achievements were so many and great, that to declare them in full I might as well attempt to empty the sea with a spoon, or to scale Olympus with a ladder of sand. This valiant knight, being with his ship separated from his two brothers, as you read in a former chapter, they sailed through many dangerous straits and passages; and as they sailed thus along, they came to a broad sea, in the middle of which they thought they saw a small island, to which they made up, and landed some of their men, who made a fire thereon to dress some meat. Now when the fire grew hot, and that the meat was nigh sodden, the island began to move, which made them all sore afraid, and they ran with all the speed they could again to their ship. Now this which they thought to be an island, was only a great fish named lupus, which laboureth day and night to put his tail in his mouth, but by reason of his greatness could not ; which when they understood, they fetched their kettle and meat from off the fish's back, and so sailed forwards till they came to a very fair island, named Miconicum, in which lived the famous enchantress the wise Medea, who gave out prophecies concerning future events; which being understood by Sir Guy, he, with his chief captain, named Bolus, went to her habitation, being in a dark valley beset all with myrtle trees: the building was fair and sumptuous, having a brazen gate for entrance thereunto, on which was pencilled these verses :

> "You, who would with wise Medea speak,
> Blow with the trumpet which doth hang hereby ;
> And ere you can a question to her break,
> She will your doubts resolve assuredly.
> Such pow'r the Fates did unto her bestow,
> For benefit of those which live below."

Whereupon sir Guy set the trumpet to his mouth, and with a strong breath blew such a blast as echoed in the air like a peal of ordnance ; when immediately the gate of its own accord flew open, where stood a dwarf ready to entertain them ; who conducted them into a spacious hall, which was adorned with many statues of antique work, and wherein in a huge frame hung the picture of Medea, how she, by letting out Æson's old blood and by infusing new in the room, was made young again. In another table was pourtrayed king Midas, who for preferring Pan's pipe before Apollo's harp was for his pains rewarded with a pair of ass's ears. Whilst they were viewing these pictures with delight, the enchantress Medea came down from her chamber ; who beholding Sir Guy with a fixed look, thus said unto him :

> "Sir knight, return unto thy ship ;
> Let not advantage from thee slip ;
> For now the time is nigh at hand
> Thou must be joined in Hymen's band :
> Thy constancy to her is known,
> Who seeks to have thee for her own :
> But ere these things to thee betide,
> Thou many troubles must abide."

Having thus said, she vanished out of their sight, leaving behind them much wondering at what they had heard. Then taking their leave of the dwarf, they returned again towards their ship ; but in their way, as they passed along by a river's side, which gently running made sweet music, with the enamelled stones, and seemed to give a gentle kiss to every surge he overtook in his watery pilgrimage ; there came, crossing a meadow towards them, an ancient shepherd, who by the downfall of mellow years seemed as if nature had brought him near to the door of Death ; yet were not his hairs so grey by years as by sorrow, of which his blubbered countenance gave a doleful token. Suppressing his sighs, he thus expressed himself:

"Sir knights," said he, "if ever compassion harboured in noble breasts, let my aged years and extreme misfortunes crave your pity; who from a contented, and not despicable estate, am now become Fortune's tennis-ball, by the inconstancy of that blind goddess."

Here he waited for a reply; and Sir Guy desiring him to relate the story of his misfortunes, he thus proceeded:—

"Know then, worthy knights, my name is Selindus; once possessed of the wealthy barony of Monpeliar, situated in this island of Miconicum; a place which, for the richness of the soil and pleasantness of the situation, is scarcely paralleled in all the country. These fair possessions of mine, left unto me when I was young, soon procured me a wife, of which yet I had no cause to repent, being a lady replenished with all the ornaments and endowments of nature, which might make her in every way complete. Happily we lived together for some short space of time, when the fruits of her womb gave us great hopes of more future joys: but the Fates had decreed otherwise; for upon her delivery, the birth of the infant proved the death of the parent, and she, to bestow a gem on the earth, became herself a pearl in the starry firmament. What shall I say more? I lost a wife and gained a daughter; and indeed a daughter of such super-excellence as might put a cessation to sorrow for the mother. This daughter, whose name was Praxida, did I bring up in all virtuous education; who in a short time became the wonder of her sex, having in her such perfections as made her the object of universal admiration; and as she grew more in years, so did she add more to her perfections; which admirable endowments attracted to her many adorers, who sued for her favour; amongst them was one whom she most fancied, whose name was Euphemius, a knight of Placida, being an island not far off, under the queen Artemia, who had made him sole governor thereof.

"Betwixt this Euphemius and my daughter, unknown to me, had passed a solemn contract; she fearing to disclose it to me, as doubting my consent, his estate not being answerable to my revenues; wherefore they got privately married together. Now it happened not long after, upon some offence against the queen, Euphemius was committed to prison: and having lain there some few days, was brought before the queen to be examined, who beheld him with great wonder and astonishment, for indeed he was a person of a lovely countenance, and in whom dame Nature had done her utmost to the making of him in all parts complete; which so wounded her heart with an affection towards him, that, instead of his being her captive, she became his; and in part to manifest the same unto him, she frankly gave him his freedom, and with many kind words entertained him very graciously in her favour. Yet could not all this kindness endear her unto him; but the more she showed love to him on the one side, the more was his hatred to her on the other; and that not so much in respect of my daughter, as the mortal spite he bare to her for his imprisonment; so that seeing a fit opportunity offered him, he fled from the court, and, confederating with some friends, intended to levy war against the queen.

"The queen, hearing of his departure, acted like a distracted woman: wringing her hands, and beating on her ivory breasts, she cast herself upon the ground, tearing the lovely tresses from her head. Her ladies comforted her in the best way they could; but that cherished fire, which blindly crept through every vein of her fluent blood, would suffer her to take no rest; but being at last informed in what place he was, she sent him this following letter:

"'Could I in the least imagine what should cause your so sudden departure, if it lay in my power, the cause thereof should be removed; but the sore not being known, how can the remedy be administered? If you think upon your restraint, think also upon free-given liberty, and not write the one in marble the other in sand. That I seek for love to you, impute it not to lightness, but to a real affection; and let your return again to me demonstrate that your heart is not inexorable; when perhaps my presence may plead more in my excuse than can this paper messenger: so wishing you, what she wants herself, health, she remains ever yours,

"'ARTEMIA.'

"This letter she sent by a trusty messenger; but his mind was so fully bent against her, that instead of liking, it caused loathing. Wherefore taking his pen in his hand, he sent her again this bitter return:

"'What should cause you to dote, where you are hated? I cannot imagine love, but lust; therefore I shall not esteem your syren's tongue, knowing that bees have stings as well as honey. Nor think not to entrap me any more by your sugared baits; but know, that none so much hates the memory of you, as doth you sworn enemy,

"'EUPHEMIUS.'

"This answer was to Artemia as a dagger piercing her heart, so that she immediately fell into such a deadly swoon, that her ladies about her could hardly recover her.

"'Unhappy Artemia,' then said the queen: 'and must I live to be despised, and he triumph in my overthow! Ungrateful man, can all my courtesies reap no other profit but only disdain? Is it possible that I can continue to love thee, that deservest rather to live in my hatred! But why do I thus exclaim against him, who perhaps doth this only to try me?—No, no, Artemia, he slights thy love!—Then die, fond queen; defer not to live any longer, Yet, dear Euphemius, in my death shall I make it known how near thy love was to my heart, and how highly thou wert prized in my affections.'

"In this manner did the woful queen spend her days, until sickness coming on, put the harmony of nature out of tune in her body, which by little and little languished away in such sort, that she became a mere skeleton or anatomy: and now finding that death by degrees began to seize on her vital parts she called her nobles unto her, and spake to them these words:

"'My lords, I am now taking my last leave of you; the spent hour-glass of my life is near at hand; and now at my parting I do adjure you, as you will answer it before the Higher Powers, whither I am now going to appear, that ye invest Euphemius king when I am dead and gone. And though I doubt not of your performance herein, yet for more assurance, and that my soul may quietly rest hereafter, I shall desire you to take an oath to do it; which if you should fail in the performance of, know assuredly you will both wrong yourselves and him, in depriving him of his crown and yourselves of a good king; he being a prince kind, wise, just, and merciful, and only unkind to me.'

"The nobles, to satisfy her request, freely took their oaths to be true to Euphemius. And now, the queen being fully satisfied with what was done, willingly yielded up the ghost; whom the nobles buried in a most sumptuous manner; which being done, they sent an honourable messenger to Euphemius to certify him of the queen's death, and how she had bequeathed her crown to him: which messenger set forth Artemia's love in such pathetical words, as wrought in him a strange alteration; for when he thought upon her unalterable affection towards him, the constancy of her love, her matchless beauty, rare endowments, and super-excellent parts, he began to reflect upon himself, his unkindness to her, his vile ingratitude, that could wrong her which died for love of him. These considerations made him to like where before he loathed, and to loathe where before he loved; for whereas before he used to give many private visits to my daughter, protesting all constancy and loyalty towards her, now the poison of hatred entered into his heart against her, as taking her to be the chief obstacle which hindered him from the enjoyment of the queen, and might be also the same of the kingdom, if it should be known he were married unto her; wherefore he departed along with the messenger, never so much as bidding her farewell, or sending any messenger unto her.

"The nobles entertained him very splendidly, and with great solemnity crowned him king. In the mean time the poor Praxida was well nigh distracted with discontent, finding herself to be with child, fearing to discover it to me, and finding such an alteration of love from him. Her case being thus desperate, knowing it impossible to be long concealed, she sent to him this following letter:

"'My dear Euphemius,

"'Men do tax our sex for being inconstant, but now I must apply that fault to you; I say to you, whose oaths did give so great a testimony of your fidelity, that I durst not doubt them for fear of injuring myself. Ah, Euphemius, doth honours change manners? Can you so soon forget Praxida, whom you swore so firmly to love? Now if thou hast no pity for me, take some compassion on the fruit of my womb, the seal of our loves, wherein thy lovely image is implanted; and if thou hast any thing of nature in thee, thou canst not but deplore its condition, and provide a remedy for the same. Still hoping thou wilt remain constant, I rest thine own
"'Praxida.'

"Euphemius received this letter with great indignation, vowing revenge; the Rhamnusian Nemesis possessing his vengeful breast in all her blackest form, and now his enraged blood being tickled with the thoughts of pleasing himself: for as he thought it his disgrace in her claiming him as her husband, he intended the destruction not only of her but of all her kindred, and that to be performed as soon as he could find any pretended cause of a quarrel with her. In the mean time, to deter her from any further prosecution of her claim, he returned to her this invective answer:

"'Hath your impudence no other person to father your bastard brat upon, but me, whose known reputation is such as will free me, in the consciences of all honest persons, from the known calamities of such a vile strumpet? Was it not my virtue preferred me by a general consent to a kingdom; and do you think by detraction to bespatter my good name? Cease then, perverse monster of woman-kind, to prosecute any further claim unto me, lest it prove the deserved destruction of thee and thine.

"'Thy deserved enemy,
"'Euphemius.'

"But before she received this letter, feeling the burden of her womb to grow great, she desired leave to go visit an aunt of hers, named Milesia, pretending indisposition of health; to which I readily acquiesced, knowing my sister very careful over her for her good. To this her aunt she discovered all what had passed betwixt Euphemius and herself, desiring her aid and secresy therein: and indeed it was but high time, for within three days after her coming thither, she was delivered of a goodly boy, whom her aunt named Infortunio, and put him out to nurse to one of her tenants.

"Soon after she received the letter from Euphemius; which when she had read, her grief and sorrow were so great, that she deemed herself in the very height of misery; and falling into a swoon, it was long ere her aunt and the other attendants could recover her to life: but coming a little to herself, she thus began to exclaim:

"'And is it possible such perjury can remain in men! Do they think oaths are not binding, or that divine vengeance doth not follow upon breach of promise? Ah, Euphemius, can thy heart prove so disloyal! were all the protestations thou so often didst reiterate unto me, only feigned baits to entrap me to my destruction! then glory in thy triumph!' and saying these words, she stabbed herself to the heart with a bodkin, which she had hid within the trammels of her hair.

"Praxida having acted this woful tragedy on herself, put all the household in a great uproar, especially my sister Milesia. At last, the extremity of her passion being over, she sent me word of what had happened; which into what a distracted grief it put me, let them be the judge who are the parents of an only child. My greatest comfort in this distressing condition was, to study revenge against Euphemius; but how to accomplish it, there was the difficulty, as knowing myself too weak to oppose him by open force. Whereupon I sent a letter to the chiefest of the nobles, declaring how unworthily he had done by my daughter, and imploring their aid to revenge his disloyalty: who greatly pitying my misfortune, and remembering how he had been the death of their good queen Artemia, they by a joint consent banished him from their kingdom; who by this means being implacably incensed against me, accompanied with a crew of fellows of as desperate fortunes as himself, he warred against me, and quickly ousted me from my barony. Wherefore, being destitute of friends, and hopeless of ever attaining my pristine glory, I betook myself to a shepherd's life, the better to be shrouded in obscurity; yet I live in hope, being assured by the wise Medea, that there should one day come a knight out of a far country, who should again restore me to my barony."

Sir Guy having heard the shepherd's discourse, it wrought in him great pity and compassion; and turning himself to captain Bolus, he thus said, "Now by the honour of knighthood, and by the love I bear to my country England, I will not enter into my ship until I have reseated him again in his barony." And to make good his promise, he took with him a hundred of his choicest soldiers; and being guided by the old shepherd Selindus, they marched to Monpelior; where they heard how Euphemius was lodged in a strong castle, and guarded with five hundred soldiers, having also in pay a certain Marisco, of a wonderful stature and strength, armed in a coat of mail, and using a bar of iron of forty pounds' weight for his club. Having approached within half a mile of the castle, Sir Guy sent a messenger to Euphemius, demanding to restore the castle, with all that belonged to it, to Selindus, or else to expect the worst that should happen upon such refusal. But Euphemius was so far from granting his request, that he bid the messenger to charge his master forthwith to depart from his territories, or else his life should pay for his presumption, in seeking to meddle with what he had nothing to do with. Hereupon both sides prepared themselves for fighting; Euphemius himself with the giant, Marisco, accompanied with three hundred of his choicest soldiers, setting upon Sir Guy with such fury, that had he not been of undaunted courage, and always watchful against such desperate onsets, he had undoubtedly overthrown him; but Sir Guy, having with great valour stood the shock of their fury, fell upon Euphemius and his men with such undaunted resolution, that notwithstanding he made a notable resistance, yet his soldiers began to give back: which the Marisco perceiving, he singly set upon Sir Guy, and with manly courage dealt about such blows, that whoso should have beheld him would have thought the great Alcides had descended again upon the earth to teach mortals the way of mankind's destruction: but Sir Guy so nimbly avoided his blows, and with such dexterous skill set upon the giant with his never-failing sword, that he made many wounds in his flesh, where death might enter in at: which Euphemius perceiving, he made up to Sir Guy to succour the Marisco: but before he could get up to him, he was set upon by captain Bolus, with so great courage, that he found he had enough to do to defend himself. At last, Sir Guy, enforcing himself with all his might, gave such a blow on the giant's helmet, as, piercing the same, it came forth all embrued with his brains, who, without speaking any word, fell down dead to the ground.

Euphemius, seeing his friend the Marisco fall, would have fled away; but he was so environed by soldiers that all means were taken from him to escape: whereupon he was forced to yield himself a prisoner, and was, both by Sir Guy and captain Bolus, entertained with great civility.

In the mean time Sir Guy's soldiers had pursued their enemies with such vigour, that those who were in the castle opening their gates to entertain their flying friends, before they could shut them again Sir Guy's soldiers also entered with them. And now within the castle began a most desperate conflict, neither defendants nor assailants expecting any mercy if overcome; wherefore each were busy in plying death's fatal task; their swords making such sad work, that every place was filled with slaughter, and their mingled blood made a purple flood that overflowed in each place they fought.

Whilst thus death was reaping his plenteous harvest, and the soldiers so thronged as they could scarcely wield their slaying hands, Sir Guy and captain Bolus coming amongst them, soon turned the scales on the assailants' side; so that the defendants, being overcome more by valour than number, yielded themselves and the castle to the mercy of the conquerors; the possession whereof Sir Guy freely surrendered into the hands of Silendus, together with the disposal of all the prisoners: but Euphemius, remembering how discourteously he had dealt by Selindus, falling on his knees, desired of Sir Guy that he might remain still with him, promising him faithfully to be his true prisoner; but his crimes were so notorious, that Sir Guy would in no wise consent thereunto: whereupon captain Bolus begged him of him, which was granted, he having before presented the captain with a jewel of an inestimable price.

And now did the friends of Selindus come flocking unto him, whereby he was in a capacity to maintain his barony against all opposers. Whereupon Sir Guy took his leave of him, and returned to his ship; his soldiers, according to their merits, having been before richly rewarded by Selindus.

CHAPTER XIII.

How Sir Guy arrived in Sicily, where he overcame the Rebels, which, after the King of Sicily's Death, had rebelled against the Queen Urania; how he was married to her, and was afterwards crowned King of Sicily.

SIR GUY, after having restored Selindus to his barony, took ship, together with captain Bolus, and his prisoner Euphemius, and having a prosperous wind, they in a few days arrived on the coasts of fruitful Sicily, to the great joy of Sir Guy, it being the happy port whereto his desires were directed; but it happened contrary to his expectations, that the scene of action was quite altered there; for soon after his departure from thence, on his expedition against the infidels, the king of Sicily died, whereby the crown came to the princess Urania; but one Nefario, a potent nobleman of that country, and who had many dependants belonging to him, of great worth and quality, raised a strong rebellion against her, pretending the ill management of the affairs of the kingdom; and so well had Fortune hitherto favoured his endeavours, that he had gained from the queen several strong places; insomuch that many of her captains, seeing his success, revolted from her, and sided with him. Sir Guy, understanding the badness of her affairs, repaired all he could for her speedy relief; and taking with him three hundred of his stoutest soldiers, he marched with them towards the city of Syracuse, wherein he was informed she was besieged by a great many of her enemies. Willingly he would have given her notice of his arrival, but all places were so stopped that he could not possibly do it: whereupon, dividing his men into two companies he gave the one of them to the command of the captain Bolus, and the other he led himself; and so in the dead of the night set upon his enemies; who not in the least dreaded any danger. And now was nothing but cutting, hacking, and slashing throughout the camp; so that in every place you might see a throng of carcasses, whose lifeless eyes were closed with dust and death. Sir Guy, remembering that he was now rescuing his dear lady out of the hands of rebels, did wonders. And now had the cries and shrieks of the soldiers alarmed Nefario, who put himself forward to withstand this inundation, which he perceived was ready to overwhelm his former successes. In the mean time captain Bolus had taken an eminent commander prisoner, by whom he understood the state of the army; whereupon, joining with Sir Guy, they with united courage set upon Nefario, with such fury, that he, not able to withstand them, was forced to give ground; whom Sir Guy did not eagerly pursue, but sent a messenger to the city to inform them of what was done; who thereupon presently issued out, killing many, and bringing in more prisoners. But when the queen Urania understood how Sir Guy was come to her aid, she sent the chief of her nobles presently unto him, to conduct him to her presence; to whom she said, "Thrice welcome to me, most honoured knight, who wert born for the good of our country. O how are we bound to the Immortal Powers for thy preservation, and sending thee to do us good."—"Most gracious princess," replied Sir Guy, "I account it my greatest happiness that I can in anywise serve you, though I wish it had not been upon this occasion, but since it is so, let not this opportunity be slipped, but, whilst the enemy is in a maze, let us fall upon him with a resolution worthy the justness of our cause."

This proposition being with great reason applauded, the soldiers were ordered to have refreshment, having been wearied in the late fight. But whilst they were thus at their repast, they heard from afar the sound of trumpets: at which, much marvelling, they sent a messenger to know what was the matter; who returned with this answer, "That there were six thousand Thessalians come to the queen's aid:" for king Alexander, soon after his coronation, hearing how the queen Urania was oppressed by her rebellious subjects, sent these six thousand soldiers, resolving, if they would not do, to follow himself with a sufficient army.

Sir Guy, hearing this welcome news, sent word to them instantly to refresh themselves, and he would join his forces with them, and set upon the rebels, whilst this general fear and consternation was upon them. And having joined to him four thousand of the choicest Sicilians, he was marching to them; but, behold a sudden change put a stop to his proceedings; for in their way they met with about a hundred of the adverse party, who hearing that Sir Guy was come to the queen's rescue, knowing his manhood, not only by former exploits, but also by dear-bought experience in the last battle, to secure their lives and fortunes at the queen's hands they seized on Nefario, and, as a peace-offering, intended to present him a prisoner to the queen. Sir Guy understanding what they had done, sent a herald to the residue, promising them the queen's pardon if they would lay down their arms and submit to her; and undoubtedly they would have done, but at the very instant of time, Grimaldo, brother to Nefario, came to recruit his army with ten thousand soldiers more, which he had gotten up out of the adjoining countries thereabout. But when he heard how his brother was carried away by his own army, and of the defeat they had received the last night, he was very much troubled in mind; but that his army might not take any notice of it, he encouraged them in the best way he could, telling them such defeats were but the chance of war; and for his brother's imprisonment, it might be made good by taking some of the choicest of the other side prisoners;—that now they had so far drawn their swords, there was no other course to take but to throw away their scabbards; all hope of reconcilement with the queen being clean taken away, and therefore no other means but to use their utmost manhood, either to conquer or die honourably. With these and the like speeches did he so encourage the rebels, that when the messenger came to them with the queen's pardon, it was rejected with scorn. Which being made known unto Sir Guy, he presently joined with the Thessalians; and having complimented the chief commanders, he encouraged the soldiers in such a pithy oration, that, throwing up their caps, they gave such a hallo, as made the earth reverberate with the sound of the same.

And now both armies faced each other; when presently began a terrible fight, that Mars himself might have been a spectator of. In one place stood a well ordered body of erected pikes, like a young leafless wood, to oppose the invading horse: in another place were bands of archers, whose feathered arrows out-run the piercing eye, and cut a passage through the fleeting air, repelling the brains of the insulting foe. Here stood horses prancing with their feet, raising such clouds of dust as covered the face of the darkened sky; when presently pikes, bills, and darts, like a moving wood, rushed against each other. Their horses, angry in their masters' anger, with love and obedience brought forth the effects of hate and resistance, and with signs of servitude did as if they affected glory. And now all hands were busied in killing. The poor soldiers stood in fear of death, as if dead-struck; the thirsty earth drank up whole streams of blood; and mounds were made of slaughtered carcasses. Sir Guy did wonders that day with his sword, sending thousands of souls to the infernal regions. And thus he made lanes of his enemies' dead bodies, he came at last to meet with Grimaldo, with whom he entered into combat, and, notwithstanding his body was enclosed about with glittering walls of steel, yet made he such breaches therein, as Death had many ways to enter, and Life as many holes whereby to creep out. And now Grimaldo craved for mercy, which Sir Guy refused, saying, "No, varlet; thou mightest have taken it when it was offered thee; but now nothing but death can satisfy for disloyalty:" And therewithal gave him such a blow, as brought him headlong to the ground.

Grimaldo being killed, the whole army betook themselves to flight; whom Sir Guy and his company pursued eagerly, killing and destroying whomsoever they overtook, without any remorse or pity.

Having obtained this signal victory, Sir Guy ordered a part of the army to pursue the residue of the rebels, whilst he with the rest marched back unto the city. And now was such universal joy amongst the citizens, as was not to be credited; all the way as Sir Guy passed along the streets the people sent forth loud acclamations. When they came to the palace gate, they were met by the queen, accompanied with a great train of ladies and nobles that attended on her; before all whom the queen, taking Sir Guy about the neck, gave him a kiss: "My dearest love," said she, "what recompense can our country afford in return for such inestimable benefits as the Divine Powers, by your victorious arms, have bestowed upon us?" And so hand in hand they marched up to the palace, where he was entertained with a stately banquet; Sir Guy behaved himself so affably and courteously to the nobles and ladies, that he won their applause.

And now all things being thus quieted, and the two princely lovers assured of their affection towards each other, their hearts and minds were very well satisfied. The Thessalian army, being richly rewarded, went home, and with them an honourable messenger to king Alexander, to return him thanks for his aid, as also to invite him to the wedding of Sir Guy and the queen Urania, the day whereof was appointed near at hand.

The marriage day being now approached, the nobles and

knights prepared a solemn joust to be holden against all comers, and many costly pageants and delightful shows were prepared by the citizens : the ladies got many costly jewels, and other rich ornaments to adorn themselves against that day : and, to complete the solemnity, king Alexander, with a splended train of followers, came to Sicily : and were most magnificently entertained by Sir Guy and the queen Urania. On the marriage morning, the bride and bridegroom were saluted with most sweet-sounding music ; the palace was hung round about with garlands ; and rich perfumes cast into fires, which gave a most odoriferous smell ; melodious harps and songs tickled the ears with delight. In short every thing was so well ordered as befitted such a royal solemnity. All the way as they went to the temple, the roads were strewed with flowers of Flora's chiefest pride ; and the priest having joined them in Hymen's nuptial bands, as they returned there was a great store of money thrown amongst the poorest sort of people, that they also might participate in the gladness of the day ; the bells rang, trumpets sounded, cornets flourished, and the acclamations of the people were so great, as would have silenced the falls of the Nile, or thunder shot from a divided cloud. The afternoon was spent in dancing, masking, revelling, and other delightful sports, until such time as Morpheus, the drowsy god of the night, summoned them to bed, there to take their repose.

Next morning the knights and nobles prepared themselves to joust ; Sir Guy, king Alexander, and the queen Urania, with divers ladies and peers, seating themselves on scaffolds to behold the same.

The first that entered the lists was a Sicilian knight named Sir Albert, mounted on a horse of a fiery sorrel colour, with black feet, and a black list on his back. His armour was green like to the earth when it begins to put on its summer livery. On his shield was pourtrayed the resemblance of a garden, with divers springing flowers, and this motto, "Still increasing." Against him entered a Corinthian knight named Agelastus, mounted on a milk-white horse, but that upon his shoulders and whithers he was freckled with red stains, as when a few strawberries are scattered into a dish of cream. His armour was blood-red, denoting terror to his enemies ; and on his shield was pencilled a hawk seized by a pigeon, yet hurting it not : the word was, "True glory the only prize." They ran fiercely against each other, breaking their staves with much gallantry ; but at the second course Agelastus was driven quite from out of the saddle ; which disgrace he would have revenged with his sword, but that the judges forbad it, it being quite contrary to the order set down.

To revenge this disgrace, there entered the list a Laconian

knight, named Lysander, riding on a Barbary horse of a coal-black colour; his armour answerable to the same. On his shield was portrayed the goddess Fortune, who, Janus-like, looked two ways, to denote that nothing in this world is so certain, but that, if good went before, ill might come behind: the word was, "The end crowns all." These two encountered each other with equal courage for a long time; Sir Albert's horse leaning hard upon the other, and winning ground. The other horse, feeling himself pressed, began to rise a little before, as he was wont to do in his curvet, which advantage Sir Albert taking, set forward his own horse with the further spur; so that Lysander's horse came over, with his master under him, giving to Sir Albert the honour of the victory.

Many other knights and great personages were by him worsted, as Sir Egre of Sparta, Don Zaras of Argos, Wildamore of Crete, and many others: but as we have seen the sun in a serene day disperse his beams with great splendour, enlightening the world, to the content of all the beholders, and towards the evening his radiant lustre set in a darkened cloud; even so the glories gained by Sir Albert were darkened by his last enterprise, in an encounter against an Arcadian knight named Sir Selvador, who, at the ebb of day, when Phœbus's bright chariot had run past the proud pillars of Alcmena's son, and with his earth-born shades began to clothe the earth with night, entered the lists, in an armour representing only confusion; no piece answerable to the other, yet all so well compacted, as if art had made order in confusion. At the signal of the trumpet's sounding, they set spurs to their horses, encountering each other with such well-guided courage and valour as showed them each to be a master of martial prowess; but at the third course it was Sir Albert's ill fortune to miss his rest, which he could not recover, before Sir Selvador had met him, and by main strength cast him to the ground.

The honour of the day remaining thus to Sir Selvador, the approach of night put a period to those martial exercises for that day, which yet were continued with manly courage and resolution for several days after. And now, before king Alexander's return home to Thessaly, the coronation of Sir Guy with his queen Urania was appointed; which was performed with all the art and splendour imaginable; which also made good the prophesy that the fairy queen had predicted of him, as we mentioned before in the Fourteenth Chapter of the First Part of this history.

> A soldier bold, a man of wonderous might.
> A king likewise this royal babe shall die:
> Three golden diadems in bloody fight
> By this brave prince shall also conquered be,
> The towers of fair Jerusalem and Rome
> Shall yield to him in happy time to come."

The coronation being thus over, king Alexander with his retinue returned to Thessaly, being accompanied part of the way by king Guy and his queen Urania. Captain Bolus also, with the English soldiers, departed to their own country, being highly rewarded by the king and queen. And now here must we leave these worthy captains, to relate what befel to the heroic knight Sir David, after he was separated from his two brothers in the storm, as you heard before.

CHAPTER XIV.

How Sir David and his company were almost famished with hunger; how they came to the Isle of Fortuna, where Sir David slew a dragon, and delivered the Island of Ancona from enchantment.

AFTER the angry seas had, by the fury of the tempest, separated the three brothers, as related before, the magnanimous knight Sir David was with his ship by the force of the storm, driven upon unknown seas; where they sailed for several days, in great want both of victuals and fresh water, having nothing to quench their thirst, and ready to eat one another to satisfy their hunger. The sailors were growing so feeble that they were not able to handle their sails, and the soldiers, instead of encountering their enemies, were ready to embrue their hands in their fellow's blood, and like cannibals to devour those whom they slew. The disconsolate Sir David, seeing his soldiers thus with weakened limbs and empty stomachs, thus complained to himself:

"O you Immortal Powers, why did you preserve us thus from the hands of our enemies, to perish by a more lingering and ignoble death! Oh why was I born to see this day! Far better it had been for us to have been slain by the swords of the infidels, then had we died in the bed of honour; and not thus miserably to end our lives, by that which valour cannot encounter, nor the stoutest courage be able to resist."

In this manner did the noble knight Sir David make his inward grief. He comforted them in the best way he could, although his own hopeless misery could present no comfort to himself. But now at last, when all hope seemed desperate, and every woe that could by despair be brought presented itself to his troubled thoughts, it chanced that one of the company, as he thought, spied land; which he imparting to his fellows, they upon view imagined the same; whereupon some sparks of comfort began to enter their disconsolate breasts: and making towards it, as well as their weak bodies were able to guide the ship, with much ado they got on land; which to their great comfort they found plentifully stored with sheep, conies, and divers sorts of fowls, with which they refreshed their almost famished bodies. Then searching up further into the country, they found divers trees laden with fruit, very delightful to the eye, and seemed as delicious to the taste; but no sooner had they eaten of it, but they presently fell down into a dead swoon or trance, bereaved both of sense and motion; which put Sir David and the rest, who had not tasted of it, into great grief, thinking themselves only reserved from famine to die by the strange and unknown operation of some poisonous fruit.

As they were thus deploring their miserable condition, there presented himself to them an aged hermit, clothed in a long gown of grey, his head covered with an hoary fleece, and his silver hairs speaking experience. By the hand he led two pretty children, a boy and a girl, whose tender looks pleaded innocence. The old gentleman, without any fear, came boldly up to them, demanding what chance brought them thither, whither not any of mankind had come before in threescore years, save only that boy he led in his hand, together with the girl, who were brought thither by the working of the sea in a little boat, and by him miraculously preserved.

Sir David, with tears standing in his eyes, thus answered the hermit:

"Most reverend father, we may well be said to come from the land of sorrow, our excess of grief scarcely giving way to the relief of words, such has been our pinching want of victuals at sea; and death here on land has deprived me of most of my followers: for coming for succour unto this island, the greatest part of my men, by eating of some deadly fruit unknown unto them, were soon arrested by nature's bold pursuivant, grim ghastly Death, under whose dominion they lie, if no other remedy can be procured than what we have knowledge of."

"Most courteous knight," replied the hermit, "both cause and cure are well known unto me, and which I will show to you presently." So desiring some part of them to accompany him, we went unto a little grove hard by, where grew great quantities of an herb whose leaves were much like our English sassafras. This herb he pressed between two stones, and straining the juice of it into their mouths, who thus lay for dead, they presently revived, to the great joy and admiration of Sir David and the rest of his followers. After congratulations for their happy revival, the aged hermit conducted them to his cell, which was pleasantly seated by a river's side, that ran upon such fine and delicate ground, as one could not easily judge whether the river did more wash the gravel, or the gravel purify the river; the banks on either side were fringed with most beautiful trees, that resisted the sun's darts from over-much piercing the natural coldness of the river; which ran not forth straight, but continually winding as if it had a delight to play with itself.

Here the old hermit fetched out what victuals he had; but that not sufficing, they killed some sheep, goats, and other beasts, which they dressed in the old man's cell. After they had sufficiently refreshed themselves, Sir David requested the old man to inform them where they were, and of the condition of the place; to which he readily condescended and began after this manner:

"Know, worthy gentlemen, that this island wherein you now are, is called Fortunia, not large for circuit, but plentiful for sustenance, supplying with her abundance the country of Ancona, not far distant from this island, and of which once I was the unhappy governor; being blessed with a beautiful wife, and more beautiful daughter, whom we named Estrilda: living for a long time together in great love, and abundance of all earthly blessings, until the Fates, envying our happiness, sent thither a famous necromancer, named Orpin, who rode in a burning chariot, drawn by flying dragons; and who was so expert in his devilish art, that all the infernal furies were at his command, and the subterranean spirits obeyed his charms and spells. This wicked magician, tempted by the evil spirit Asmodeus, burned with a base passion for my wife; and the better to accomplish his desires, having ingratiated himself in great favour at my court (for such then it was), he thought nothing possible to hinder his designs; but my wife being as virtuous as she was beautiful, not only resisted his temptations, but also acquainted me with his base intentions; whereupon I was resolved to seize him, and by severe justice to bring him to condign punishment; but knowing the great power he had in the Black Art, I was fearful in what manner to accomplish my design. At last I resolved to invite him to a banquet, and, after he had been fully inebriated with the juice of Bacchus, to have an armed guard to set upon him; but vain were all the attempts which I devised against him: for no sooner did they lay hands on him, but he was rescued by spirits, which presently appeared in a full army, overspreading the places thereabouts, and sending forth such horror and amazement amongst all my people, as happy were they who could get farthest off from their sight. In these hellish shapes did they pursue my men all the island over, not leaving till such time as there was not one man left but only my wretched self, whom they detained prisoner. Then these infernal spirits conveyed all the male children away; but all the females, guarded by divine protection, they had not the least power to hurt or touch. Next did he, by his magical arts, upon a rock adjoining to the island, erect a citadel or small castle, which is kept by a dragon, that each morning out of his mouth sendeth forth such a poisonous breath, as killeth all the males which are upon the island, but over the females his breath hath no power. Just over against the castle standeth a pillar, whereon are inscribed these lines :

"' What man soe'er sets foot within this isle,
He by our charms immediately shall die ;
Which shall remain in force until the while
A knight shall overcome the enemy,
For then great Orpin's charms and spells shall cease,
And then the land shall peopled be in peace.'

"Having proceeded thus far in his devilish arts, he next by his spirits brought me into this island, where I have now remained the space of ten years, not having the company of any, either man, woman, or child, save only of these two, which were sent in a most miraculous manner.

"For walking by the sea-side one morning, at such time when the sun begins his golden progress from the east, and gilds the horizon with his radiance, as I cast my eye upon the briny face of Neptune, I beheld something floating on that glassy deep ; and staying to take better notice of it, I perceived it to be a boat, which without the help of either man or oars made towards the shore ; and being come near, I drew it to land ; wherein were laid these two children fast asleep, and between them a table written in letters of gold, which contained these words :

"' Left to queen Chance, two babes of knightly birth
Are to the rage of wind and seas expos'd ;
If that they gain a habitable earth,
By this their parents dear may be disclos'd ;
Fonteious' children, whom Death prisoner keeps,
Their mother in th' enchanted castle sleeps.

"' Their step-father, Sir Vuylon, who did owe
A grudge unto them for their mother's sake,
To end their lives his malice did bestow,
On whom the queen of Chance did pity take :
Declaring they shall by an English knight
Restored be unto their father's right.

"' Thus Fate decreed ; and those do strive in vain ;
Whoe'er they be, to alter Fate's decree ;
By unknown means our ends we oft attain,
And farthest ways to thought may nearest be,
Learn then for to be just, without offence,
Heavn's punish evil, protect innocence.'

"Now from what place these children came, I am as ignorant as they themselves, whose tender age was such as made them incapable of any knowledge, either of parents or country ; yet was I much revived by the writing, which promised their restoration by an English knight, in which I also hoped my own was included ; wherefore ever since I have carefully brought them up, and fostered them in the best manner I could ; and now I hope the time is come about, wherein what was promised by the queen of Chance will be performed ; not doubting but that such magnanimous resolutions as

I see seated in your noble breast, joined with a just cause, will make you courageous to perform the adventure and to free me from this tedious trouble and thraldom."

Sir David hearing the story with much admiration, remembered how he and his brothers had freed their mother from the enchanted castle, as also of the knight, which told how Sir Vuylon had exposed these two children to the mercy of the sea; all which he related to the ancient gentleman, and withal promised him his utmost effort to finish the enchantment, and restore him again to the island of Ancona.

And now was much mirth and joy on all sides: Sir David was entertained in the hermit's cell, together with as many of the first commanders as it would conveniently contain; the rest of the soldiers cut down boughs from trees, and therewith made themselves huts to shelter from the heat of the sun, when his bright rays fell directly on the parched earth; sheep and goats they killed in abundance, so that there were stores of boiling, broiling, frying, roasting, stewing, and other ways of dressing dishes, to refresh their bodies, after their sore and bitter hunger sustained at sea. This continued for a week's time; but then Sir David, remembering his promise made to the aged hermit, he buckled on his armour, and putting himself into his ship-boat, rowed with two mariners, and, guided by the old hermit, he undauntedly landed before the enchanted castle, and marched directly towards the gate thereof, whither he was no sooner come, but the dragon most fiercely issued out, when presently began between them the most fierce encounter that ever was heard of; so that to describe it to the full, I want the skill of Orpheus, that sweet Thracian singer, or the invention of Homer, in describing the battles of the Greeks and Trojans. The dragon most furiously assailed Sir David, seeking to catch him in her paws, which he nimbly avoided, and gave the dragon many blows, who lifting up her head sought to throw the whole weight of her body upon Sir David; which he perceiving, slipped aside, and gave her a wound on the belly, wherein she was only penetrable, which made her give forth a hideous yell; this advantage Sir David espying, he thrust his sword into her mouth, which she so strongly bit with her teeth, that had it not been made of the purest Lydian steel, it would have been in great danger of being bitten in two; so that Sir David, to draw it out, was forced to use great strength; but withal it so cut her tongue, that the poisonous blood came pouring out of her mouth, which so enraged the dragon, that, turning her about, she gave him such a blow with her tail as made him stagger, as if stunned; the sword was ready to drop out of his hand; so that the aged hermit and the two mariners, who all this while sat in the boat to behold the combat, began to doubt of the success thereof. But Sir David, recovering himself against she came to assail him again with her tail, taking his sword with both his hands, he struck such a stroke as cut off two yards in length of her tail. And now the dragon, being thus wounded, began to use her first play, and sought to seize upon Sir David with her paws; but her strength was so feeble through the loss of so much blood, that her force availed her not. On the other side, Sir David, gathering strength at the sight of her weakness, ran against her with all his might; and by main force tumbled her all along; and before she could recover, thrust his sword into divers parts of her belly, which was as big as any tun, and in colour like to burnished gold; whereout issued such abundance of poisonous filth, and withal smelt so abominably, as, not able to endure it, he retreated to his companions in the boat, who were ready to receive him; where they beheld how the ugly monster rolled about, and beat the earth with the remainder of her tail, until at last she died; when was heard a mighty clap of thunder, and immediately the castle vanished away.

No sooner had they beheld the castle vanish away, but they put forth to land, where Sir David on his knees gave thanks to the Immortal Powers for this victory; and then going up higher into the land, they came to a little village, the inhabitants whereof were greatly astonished, some of the younger sort having never seen a man before in their lives, and those that were older, in not many years before. By them they understood that the queen, wife of the aged hermit, was dead, and that her daughter, the beautiful Rosetta, did govern the island; whereupon they determined to go to the young queen, and sent the two mariners back for the chiefest of their company to go along with them. Now whilst they staid there, many of the people came to see them; some of the eldest of which remembering their king, fell down at the aged hermit's feet, rejoicing to have seen the day that they might behold again their sovereign. Then was great inquiry made for the rest of the men; some for their husbands, some for their brothers, and other relations; to whom the aged king Antenor, for such was his name, and by which title we shall now call him, could give no intelligence; for he knew nothing about them at all. In the mean time some of them had posted to the court, and acquainted the young queen where her father was; who at first could not believe their reports, such unlikelihood did the truth of the story carry with it: but being confirmed by so many, at last she believed what she most desired to be true; and taking with her some of the choicest of her maids, she hastened to him with all the speed she could. But it was a strange sight to behold into what wonder and admiration they were both stricken at the first sight of each other; for she, having never seen a man before that she could remember, thought his long beard and other attire were most strange to behold; and he on the other side having not seen her for so many years, the remembrance of her was quite out of his memory. However, she having been instructed in the honour that children should do to their parents, humbled herself to him on her knees, whom he most lovingly embraced.

Much talk had they concerning the death of the queen, and what occurrences had passed in the mean time; during their discourse Sir David beheld the princess Rosetta with admiration; so that love through his eyes stole into his heart, and there took full possession: but having not an opportunity now to disclose it, and the queen inviting them to her palace, whilst they were preparing to set forwards, the rest of the ship's company came up to them, together with the two Thracian children, destined to destruction by Sir Vuylon, and who were preserved by Antenor, as before related.

All the way as they went to the palace, they were entertained with great joy; a troop of maidens, clothed all in white, going before them with timbrels in their hands, with which they played very melodiously, singing songs, and answering one another in pleasant roundelays. The people, all the way as they passed, came flocking about them, the younger sort wondering at the men, as if they were monsters; and the men wondering as much to behold in every place nothing but women. The queen Rosetta entertained Sir David with very high respect, who returned her kindness with obliging civility. The chiefest commanders were accommodated with tents peculiar to themselves, and stored with delicious viands and wines. Nay, the very meanest soldiers were so well gratified and entertained, that they thought themselves very much obliged both by the queen and the rest of her subjects. In this condition we will leave them for a while, to tell you what happened soon after in the island.

CHAPTER XV.

Sir David is married to Queen Rosetta, and overcomes the remains of the Pagan Army. Sir Pandræus, with his Men, land in Ancona.

CONQUERING love had so possessed the heart of Sir David, that all sports and pastimes seemed tedious to him, and he gave himself over to melancholy, till such time as finding a fit opportunity, when Rosetta was alone, he brake his mind to her in this manner:

"Madam, I see so many perfections residing in you, that not to love you would argue a stupidity of knowledge, and obliges me to honour your excellent endowments to the utmost of my power ; for, believe me, maiden, my desires flow from a sincere affection towards you; that if you please to yield me your love, you shall find me both constant in affection towards you, and loyal, not to do any thing disagreeable to your will."

"Most courteous knight," replied the queen, "to whose valour we are much indebted, for your suit in love I cannot promise you any thing in it, as not being at my own disposal, my father and country claiming a knowledge thereof before I give consent to a thing of such consequence ; yet as I would not have you hope too much, so I would not have you despair, since you shall not find me, who am most concerned in it, displeased at your suit. Account me not, dear sir, over fond in my expressions, since such high deservings cannot but attract a willing acceptance of that which is so virtuously offered."

Whilst they were thus discoursing, there came towards them a woman on horseback, who, by the haste she made, proclaimed that her errand was of great importance ; and so it proved ; for coming near to them, she cried out. "Arm, arm, with all the speed you can ; for enemies are upon our coast, who have already done much mischief, and if not prevented, are like to do much more." These enemies which thus molested this island, were the residue of the Pagan army, which had escaped from the battle fought against them by the Christians, and were conducted by the horse-faced Tartar, who had escaped from the sword of Sir Guy, as we told you before in the Seventh Chapter. These vagabond fugitives, being headed by this monster, as also by a sagittary, who came with the prince of Tripoli, having gotten some ships, intended to escape to Persia, but by a storm at sea were driven they knew not whither, amongst several islands, where they maintained themselves by robbing, killing, and other inhuman ways towards the inhabitants ; who, joining together, set upon them, and by the slaughter of some of them, forced the rest to put forth to sea again. After several turmoils, they chanced to land on this island ; upon which they no sooner had set foot, but they fell to their old trade of robbing and killing ; so that the affrighted inhabitants ran from their presence, as the fearful sheep from before the devouring wolves.

Sir David, understanding what had passed, commanded his men presently to arm ; and taking a gentle farewell of Rosetta and Antenor, he marched directly against the Pagans, being guided by the woman who brought the news. As he marched along, he was met by divers women, who all fled from the merciless hands of their enemies, praying for the good success of the English, on whose victorious arms depended all the hopes of their safety.

The Pagans, seeing none but women to oppose them, thought themselves secure, and therefore heeded not their arms, but fell to eating, defiling, ravishing of women, and all manner of outrages that a barbarous nation could act: when Sir David with his men set upon them, killing and destroying them at their pleasure. The horse-faced Tartar and the sagittary seeing this, betook them to their swift-paced heels, thinking to get away in their ship; but there was none to help them to put forth to sea; so that, being pursued by a party of soldiers, they were both taken prisoners, and carried in triumph back to Sir David, who, with the rest of the soldiers, had by this time wearied their arms and blunted their swords with the slaughter of those infidels, so that few or none of them were left.

But now, the amazement of each person was to behold the strange shapes of these monsters, resembling as much beasts as men : and therefore, the better to secure them, and that they might freely be beheld by the people, the soldiers made them a great wooden cage, which, running on wheels, they drew about with them whithersoever they went; and in this manner they led them along until they came to the queen's court, where Sir David and his men were entertained with unspeakable joy. And now did the queen Rosetta manifest her love by the kind reception she made Sir David, which she expressed so openly, that not only her father, but many of the ladies that attended on her, took notice of it; love being of the nature of fire, which cannot be hid, unless it be deeply covered over with the ashes of dissimulation. Yet this was the comfort of it, there was not any that thought but wished it so, which they outwardly declared by the great pleasure they received at the mere report thereof: but when it was made known to king Antenor, he was overjoyed at the news, desiring it might be consummated as soon as possible.

And now all hands were preparing to do something worthy such a solemnity; some in making tents to feast in, some preparing choice viands to feast upon, others tuning their instruments against the day came: and because there was no men for the exercise of arms, either for jousts or tournaments, as upon such occasions commonly used to be, it was concluded, for the divertisement of the spectators, that there should be a battle fought between the horse-faced Tartar and the sagittary; in order to which, a square place was railed in with ropes, with seats of curious workmanship for the gentlemen and ladies to sit and behold it.

All things being thus prepared, upon the prefixed day the bridegroom and bride were led in great state unto the temple, he attended by a choice band of English soldiers, and she waited on by a troop of beautiful ladies. After the priest had joined their hands in holy wedlock, they were conducted back in the same state as they went, all the people sending forth loud acclamations of joy. At their return to the palace, they feasted in most sumptuous manner, all the afternoon being spent in dancing, masking, and such-like revellings.

Next morning was designed for the combat between the Tartar and sagittary; to behold which, Antenor, Rosetta, Sir David, and all the chief of the English commanders, and the Ancona ladies, took their places on the stages provided for them. About nine o'clock the two combatants were brought forth; the Tartar had on a quilted jacket, wrought full of eyelet-holes, at each of which hung a needle, fastened by thread; on his head, for a helmet, he wore a cap made of tortoise-shells, and so interwoven with steel wire, that it was not penetrable; he was armed with an ebony javelin, headed with steel, yet something blunted, as designed more for sport than hurt. The sagittary had on a garment made of a panther's skin, so hard and tough that no sword could pierce it: his javelin was of Laconian ash, studded with ivory, with a head of burnished silver. Great was the expectations of the spectators concerning this combat; but they, knowing that their own ruin was only intended for the mirth of others, resolved rather to sell their lives to the destruction of their enemies; and therefore nimbly leaping over the rails, in despite of all opposition that could be made, they hasted away as swift as if their veins ran with quicksilver, turning about as doth a swallow, being here and there, and yonder, all at once.

Sir David and the other men of war, seeing the agility of the monsters, thought it high time to bestir themselves, and thereupon getting on horseback, made what speed they could after them; but their flight was as swift as if they had been freed from the dregs of the earth, and they were as nimble as fairy elves, so that in an instant they had lost sight of them. And now being at liberty, and armed, they made each place they came at a place of slaughter; so that they might be followed by the tracks of mischief, which everywhere they did; and though Sir David and the other pursuers were oftentimes very near them, yet could they not fasten on them, nor hinder them from doing an extraordinary deal of mischief.

It happened at that very time that Sir Pandrasus, with his warlike Danes, having been a long time tossed about on the sea, and relieved at some of the islands where those Pagans had been plundering before, they, in requital of such courtesies, promised to pursue the infidels, and to revenge the outrages they had done them; and hearing they made towards the island, they followed after; not knowing that Sir David, or any Englishman was upon the coast. Great was the wonder both of the English and Danes to see one another so unexpectedly; but the English informing the Danes of their chase after the two monsters, they resolved to join with them in the pursuit. The Danes had at that time in their ship a Scythian dog, much stouter of courage than the English mastiff, and far swifter than an Irish greyhound. This dog being brought from the ship, they led him in a string, till they came within view of the monsters, who were still practising their old trade of mischief. The dog being let loose, ran with as nimble speed as the shafts fly from a Parthian bow, or as if his flight were supplied by wings. And now the monsters were foiled in their shifts; for the dog, soon overtaking them, seized on the sagittary, who roared like a bull, striving (but in vain) to disentangle himself from the dog.

In the mean time the horse-faced Tartar scudded away as swiftly as a well-driven javelin flies, or as a hawk pursues the fearful dove. Sir David, with some others, seizing on the sagittary, he commanded him to be hanged upon the next tree; and then, with Sir Pandrasus, and those others who were nimblest mounted, pursued after the Tartar; who now, more wary by his fellow's harms, staid not in any place, that they should not suddenly overtake him, never ceasing till he came to a rock near to the sea-side, in which espying a hollow vault or cave, he crept therein, and so sheltered himself for a time.

Escaping thus their hands, after much search made in vain for him, Sir David making order for a watch to be laid all about the island, that he might do no further mischief, he invited Pandrasus to the court, who went along with him, accompanied with several Danes of great rank and quality, and were most courteously received by queen Rosetta, who thought herself the happiest woman, and most favoured of Fortune, who had sent her such a noble hero for her husband, and had doubly rescued her country from destruction.

After two or three days spent in feasting, and no news heard of the Tartar, it was judged by all that he had drowned himself in the sea, and therefore they began to cease watching more after him. And as Sir Pandrasus, with the flower of the Danish commanders, were there, it was concluded to crown Sir David king of Ancona, and all those islands which belonged to it; which Antenor was the most forward to do, seeing in Sir David such excellent accomplishments.

The day prefixed for the solemnity being come, before the palace gate a stately show was presented, performed by three English knights, three Danish, and six Ancona ladies; who in a kind of warlike dance seemed to contend; the knights amongst themselves, which of their ladies was most beautiful; and the ladies, which of their knights was most valorous. This was done in a kind of a double matachin dance, for every single one had two enemies. At last there issued to them a shepherd and a nymph, who were to decide all the controversy; which they did in a dialogue song, of which this was the conclusion of every verse;

> "Valour doth beauty honour and regard,
> And beauty is to valour a reward."

Many other devices they had, with other stately pageants and shows, as they went to be crowned, where, ascending a scaffold prepared for that purpose, and Sir David and Rosetta placed on two rich thrones, after some set speeches and ceremonies used, two boys in the shape of angels descended from the battlement, with each a crown in his hand, which they placed on the heads of Sir David and Rosetta; which was no sooner done, but the people gave a shout, crying, "Long live David and Rosetta, king and queen of Ancona, with all the islands belonging thereto." Then did the trumpets sound, and several sorts of instruments play: which being finished they marched back again in great state unto the palace, where was provided a most sumptuous banquet, in which neither art nor cost was wanting to please the appetite of each several guest. In the afternoon was a joust held between an English knight and a Dane, which was performed with such valour and resolution, as gave great satisfaction to the beholders, and gained great honour to themselves.

And thus Sir David being crowned king, was fulfilled the third prophecy, which the fairy queen had predicted of him, being this which follows:

> "The Muses' darling for true sapience,
> In princes' courts this babe shall spend his days;
> Kings shall admire his learned eloquence,
> And write in brazen books his endless praise;
> By Pallas' gift he shall achieve a crown,
> Advance his fame, and lift him to renown."

The rest of the afternoon of this coronation day was spent in a variety of pastimes, each one studying some quaint device to set forth the glory of so magnificent a triumph.

CHAPTER XVI.

The taking of the Horse-faced Tartar, as also of the Necromancer Orpin. The Relation of Sir Pandrasus, concerning his strange Adventures after his departure from the Seven Champions of Christendom.

NEXT morning they were alarmed with the dreadful outcries and shriekings of several women, who in great multitudes came running towards the palace; for the Tartar, constrained by hunger to come out of his hole, ranged up and down for sustenance; and finding none to resist him but feeble women, he fell again to his occupation of rapine and mischief. This being made known to those noble commanders, they presently armed themselves for the encounter, but only with defensive weapons, as knowing their enterprize to consist more in pursuing than fighting. They took also with them the Scythian dog, to whose swiftness they trusted more than any thing else, knowing that catching him was half the victory. Marching in this equipage, more like hunters than soldiers, they spread themselves; but the chiefest of them kept together, going into that road they were directed by the affrighted women; when at last they espied him upon a hillock, whose barking stomach was gormandizing upon a sheep which he had newly seized on. But having a sight of his pursuers, he left his prey, and ran away as swift as a stag, who scorning the earth with his heels, runs from the shrill cries of the full-mouthed hound: but the Scythian dog having gotten a sight of him, scowered after as swift as the flight of lightning through the air, so that in an instant he had nigh overtaken him; which the Tartar perceiving, turned about; and seeing he must die, resolved yet to give one breath of valour before his expiring; and with his ebony javelin ran against the dog with all his might, and gave him a wound upon the shoulder; whereupon the dog, nimbly turning about, flew upon his face, and catching hold of his ear, made him bellow most hideously: then rising upon their hind feet, they tumbled over one another; in which fall the Tartar got his ear loose from the dog, and withal gave him a wound on the back; but then the dog caught him by the leg, and there held him till the company came up who seized on him, and sending for the wooden cage wherein he was before, put him into the same again, and carrying him back to the palace, hung it upon one of the arms of a stately oak, where he remained a spectacle for the people to gaze upon.

Whilst they were thus busied about the Tartar, another party, who had been out in search of him, returned, bringing with them the necromancer Orpin, whose charms and spells, upon Sir David's conquering his enchanted castle, became of no effect; so that now, instead of riding in his burning chariot drawn by dragons, he, vagabond like, wandered about upon his feet; being almost starved for want of sustenance, dreading to come near any habitation, his wicked life being so notorious as to deserve no pity or compassion. Antenor, seeing him, could hardly forbear running him through with his sword, such a deep impression had the wrongs he had received imprinted on him. Nor would the necromancer have been unwilling to die, had not the fear of going to a worse place made him willing to enjoy the privilege of breath a little longer: but that they might make his life as uncomfortable to him as he had made others' to them, they clogged him with irons, and cast him into a dungeon, there sustaining him with bran and water.

And now that the monster and necromancer were both secured, for joy thereof Antenor prepared a costly banquet, to which were invited king David and queen Rosetta, with Sir Pandrasus, and the English and Danish captains. After the banquet was ended, king David desired Sir Pandrasus to give him a relation of his travels after they had parted from the Christian army: to which he readily condescended, and began as follows:—

"Know then, most worthy audience, that after we had taken our final leave of those magnanimous heroes, the Seven Champions of Christendom, whose names shall live for ever enrolled in the books of Fame, we intended to steer our course directly for Denmark, whose fruitful banks we greatly longed to behold; but Fate had otherwise decreed, for our pilot being unskilful in those seas, after many wanderings to and fro, we at last arrived in an island named Barcona the Warlike, for that both king and people of the same inure themselves continually to the exercise of arms, and thither people from all places resort as unto a school of war. Here were we courteously entertained. The next day was held a solemn joust, wherein the king and twelve others were challengers, against a prince of a bordering island and twelve of his partners. In these conflicts were broken between the parties five hundred and eight spears. On the next day was kept a tournament for all persons to try their valour, which was done with great courage and magnanimity on both sides. This being done, they fought with much eagerness and courage at the barriers. And in these exercises they did commonly spend their time.

"After some communication with the king, of our travels and adventures, he, knowing us to be soldiers, and that I was commander-in-chief, challenged me to joust with him, and to that purpose furnished me with horse and arms. At these jousts it chanced, by the shivering of a spear, that one of the splinters entering the king's helmet, pierced his brain, so that he fell down presently dead. The nobles, seeing their king thus killed, were in a marvellous rage, and, vowing revenge, sought to lay hands upon me; but I, perceiving their intentions, defended myself as well as I could: so that some blows began to be dealt amongst us; when my men, seeing what danger I was in, armed themselves, and stoutly stood in my defence. And now much mischief might have ensued, had not one of the ancient noblemen stepped in between them and us, and desiring us to forbear until such time as he had spoken a few words, he then delivered himself in this manner:

"'Let not, dear friends, sudden passion so prevail over reason, as without causes thoroughly weighed, and mature deliberation taken, to engage in such a quarrel wherein the victor must needs suffer. Here is nothing of premeditated malice; and shall we go about to murder those for doing that which they themselves wish had never been done? Therefore, in seeking to do justice to the dead, let us not go about to do injury to the living; but that, without any more mischief, we may discuss the case by argument, rather than arms, since it is a well known approved maxim, "That where the sword bears sway, justice for that time hath no place."'

"This proposition was well received on both parts, and the next day was the time appointed wherein all controversy should be decided; which being come, and the matter argued, I was acquitted by the most of those who were then present, as a thing only accidental to the exercise of arms. But whilst these things were arguing, in a large plain before the king's palace gate, which was the place were the accustomed jousts used to be held, there came a trumpeter, attended with two other persons clad in armour, one of them being of a gigantic stature, who declared that, hearing of the martial prowess of this king Belphegar (for so was he named), they came on purpose to try their manhood with him. The nobles with a sad countenance declared unto them the mischance which had befallen their king: however they told them their challenge should be answered; and I requested I might have the honour to joust with him in the biggest armour; and one of the nobles, who was most eager in prosecuting me, undertook the other; and so we prepared for the encounter.

"I was mounted on the same horse, and in the same armour, wherewith I had jousted against the king; with which I entered the lists; wherein I had not been long, but my antagonist came, riding on an iron-grey horse, of a marvellous great strength and bigness. His furniture was made into the fashion of the branches of a tree from which the leaves were falling, and so artificially were the leaves made, that, as the horse moved, it seemed indeed that the leaves wagged, as you may behold, when Zephyrus with a gentle breath plays with them. His armour was black, and in his shield he had for his device a phœnix rising out of her spicy nest, with these words; 'Virtue ever lives.'

"At some distance from us did the nobleman and other champion also enter the list, well prepared to encounter each other. At the trumpet's sounding we set spurs to our horses, and with eager fury each one assailed his adversary. And here I must confess did I use my best endeavour for obtaining the victory, not only out of desire of glory to encounter with so potent an adversary, as also to regain the good opinion of the natives, which now I seemed to have lost. Whilst each of us strove for the palm of victory, and to purchase fame by our well-deservings, we more wearied ourselves than got any advantage of each other: and in this equal fight did we continue, until such time as the parted day held an equal balance, between the foregoing and ensuing light, and that bright Phœbus had half-way mounted to the highest storey of his Olympic palace. And in this equal condition of fight we both parted; when I, greatly desiring to know who it was that had so valiantly encountered with me, he pulling off his helmet, to my great wonder I found him to be the giant Wonder, who came with us out of the land of Denmark; and his second a captain who came likewise along with us. Hereupon we most lovingly embraced each other.

"Now you must understand, that when we parted from the Seven Champions, as I told you before, we embarked in two ships; but it chanced that that ship wherein he was, in the night time running upon a rock, was split in pieces, most of them perishing in the sea; only he, with some few others, getting astride upon the main-mast, by the favourable working of the sea, were driven on shore to a small island near adjoining. The inhabitants thereof received them kindly, and furnished them with such necessaries as they wanted. Long had he not been there, but, hearing of the renown of king Belphegor aforesaid, he sold some jewels which he had preserved from the wreck, and with his champion, putting themselves into armour, came to try their fortunes at the island of Barcona, and where it was my chance to encounter with him, as I have declared unto you.

"Here did we stay until the obsequies of the king were over, whose funeral was solemnized with all the rites that belong to martial discipline. Afterwards we were feasted by several of the nobles. At one of which feasts a gentleman, there present, was declaring that in an island not far off was a fountain of pure wine, both delicious to the taste and extraordinarily wholesome to the body; about whose banks grew trees that bore fruit which healed all manner of sores and diseases whatsoever. This fountain was guarded by a giant, and a lion of a monstrous proportion; and for the more defence thereof, surrounded with a wall of such stupendous height, that it was impossible to climb over it: having no entrance but only a narrow wicket, which was so ordered by necromancy, that only two at a time should enter therein; for so it was declared by a tablet, which hung over the wicket, to this effect:

> 'Two for to try their valour here may venture,
> But a third person is forbid to enter.'

"Sir Wonder and I, having heard this relation, resolved to

undertake this enterprise; and declaring our minds unto the company, they applauded us for our heroic resolutions. So the next day, being furnished with armour according to what we desired, guided by the gentleman who had given us the relation, we came before the enchanted fountain; and having read the writing, we espied by the side of the wicket a silver horn, for them to blow which would have entrance; which Sir Wonder putting to his mouth, it gave forth a sound as loud as when cannons disgorge their fiery vomits, or that which the Nile maketh when the water falls from the precipitous cataracts; when immediately the wicket opened of itself; and no sooner were we entered, but it shut again of its own accord. Being thus entered, we heard the lion send forth such a hideous yell, as the noise thereof might have been heard at the Antipodes. Whereupon we prepared ourselves for the encounter; and high time it was, for immediately we perceived both the giant and lion come marching against us. The giant had on a coat of mail of wonderful strength and goodness, with an oak-tree in his hand for a club: the lion had on his neck a collar of brass, wherein the necromancer had written these lines:

'Who me doth overcome, he for his pain
The conquest of the fountain shall obtain."

"The lion came directly towards me, and the giant marched against Sir Wonder; and then began a most terrible conflict on both sides; for knowing our lives depended on the success we obtained, there needed no spur to whet on our courage. The lion, being most nimble, came first up to me, thinking with his paws to have fastened upon me; but I nimbly avoiding his grasp, stepping aside, gave a side blow against his ribs, which being as hard as brass, wrought no effect upon him, only made him a little to stagger. The giant, on the other side, came flourishing with his oak against Sir Wonder, intending with one stroke to have made a separation between his soul and body; but ere he could strike, Sir Wonder gave him such a blow on the elbow, as he had well near dropped the club out of his hand. The lion having missed his aim at me, with a short turn whisking his tail about, gave me such a blow on my waist, that I was almost persuaded I was cut in two by the middle; but recovering myself, I thrust at him with my javelin, which, notwithstanding it was made of the strongest ash, yet shivered into a thousand splinters: whereupon drawing my sword, and the lion coming fiercely at me, I gave him such a blow on the fore-leg, as cut it well near halfway off. But in the meantime the giant had so wounded Sir Wonder, that he began to faint; which I perceiving, thought it high time to use my utmost endeavour; and striking at the lion with all my might, it was my chance to cut him a deep gash on the eye; whereupon he roared most horribly, and retreating back, gave me opportunity to succour Sir Wonder, who now was upon the point of falling, being deeply wounded, and having lost abundance of blood. The giant, seeing the lion retreating towards the fountain, desired a parley; but I would hear of no conditions, but only an absolute submission of himself to my mercy; which at first he refused to do; whereupon we entered into a fresh combat, giving and receiving many blows on each side; so that, being almost wearied, I resolved to make quick dispatch; and getting within compass of his club, closing with him, we both tumbled down together, I falling uppermost, for should he have tumbled down upon me, he would have well near crushed me to pieces.

"The great weight of the giant bruised him much in his fall, so that he was scarcely able to rise, when I, getting upon my feet, presented my sword unto his throat: but then did he bellow out to spare his life, and he would reveal all the secrets of the fountain unto me, and deliver to me the possession thereof; which I was the more willing to do, because I saw the giant Wonder lying at that time upon the ground like a lifeless corpse; yet doubting of his truth, I could hardly believe him; wherupon he swore by Mahomet, Termagant, and Apollo, that he would be true to me; upon which I promised him his life, which easily I might have taken away, he being scarcely able to stand on his feet: but my care for Sir Wonder made me apply myself wholly to him, who was now ready to cast off the robes of clay, and to be raked up in Death's cold embers; but I now, to try the faithfulness of my new servant, commanded him to fetch me some wine from the fountain, which immediately he did, together with some of the fruit which was growing on the banks thereof; which he had no sooner poured down Sir Wonder's throat, but he presently revived, such was the sovereign virtue thereof; and in a little space got upon his feet; and by the direction of the giant we went towards the fountain, where by the way we met with the lion, who seeing the giant without harm in our company, he also fawned upon us. Now, when we were come to the fountain, and had tasted of the fruit, it seemed unto us that we were as whole and sound as ever we were before the fight.

All this while did the giant with great seeming submission wait upon us, showing us all the varieties that belong to the place; but under these ashes of dissimulation lay harboured a cankered heart, which burned with the fire of revenge. It now was the ebb of day, wherefore we resolved to repose that night; and were conducted by the giant to a spacious chamber, wherein stood a stately bed; but, dreading the giant's prefidiousness, we slept not both of us together, but one always stood upon his guard; which no doubt prevented him from further mischief at that time, and therefore what he could not do one way, he sought to act another; and knowing of a poisonous fruit, which grew within six miles of the fountain, the nature of which was, that being no sooner eaten but it cast them into a deadly sleep for the space of eight hours after; he therefore, to accomplish his devilish design, travelled thither at night, and early next morning he came unto us with a smiling look, and presented to us some of the fruit to eat: but at the same time from my nose there fell three drops of blood, and a diamond ring, which I had on my finger, sweat, and looked as pale as ashes; whereupon, foreboding some treason, I commanded him to taste first thereof himself; which with an obstinate denial, he refused to do; and his treachery being discovered, he thought there was no way but to conquer by arms or die, and thereupon struck at me with all his might which I warded off as well as I could; however, he gave me a slight wound on my arm; hereupon, snatching up my sword, 'False villain,' said I, ' now shall thy life pay for thy treachery; not all the wealth of the Indies shall redeem thee out of my hands.' And now, he being out of his coat of mail, I could the better deal with him, laying upon him with all the strength and skill I had, making such deep furrows in his flesh, that the blood sluiced from him as from a crack in a strait pipe of lead.

"Whilst we were thus fighting, the lion with like fierceness assailed Sir Wonder, who was newly awaked from his sleep, hearing the clattering which the giant and I made with fighting. But the giant did not long endure my blows, but made towards the fountain, to taste some of the fruit, the virtue whereof he knew to be such, that it would have cured him of all his wounds in an instant. But ere he had gotten half way thither, I run him in at the back with my sword; whereupon, turning himself towards me, he gave me such a blow on my wrist, which so numbed my hand, as my sword was ready to drop out of it; but I, having the use of one hand as well as the other, quickly recovering my sword, gave him such a deep gash on the ham, that he came tumbling down like a great timber log, enough to shake the ground and make an earthquake; when running my sword into his bowels, I left him, as I thought, for dead, and returned to the succour of Sir Wonder; who by this time had overcome the lion, and laid him for dead, and was coming towards me; at our meeting we kindly embraced each other, thanking divine Powers for this so notable a victory.

"Returning back towards the giant, we found he was not quite dead, who, before his expiring, confessed unto us his treason, that if we had eaten of the poisonous fruit, as soon as we had fallen asleep, he would have digged a deep pit, and therein have buried us alive, so near were we to the jaws of destruction.

"By this time the gentleman that conducted us to this island, attended with some few resolute soldiers, came (but not without much doubting) to see what was become of us, intending with their best aid to help us to the obtaining of the victory; but finding the work done to their hands, they rejoiced exceedingly at our good fortune.

"And now being thus happily met together, we resolved to try an experiment of the poisonous fruit upon three dogs which our gentleman conductor had brought with him; and in order thereunto, we gave to one dog two apples, to the second three apples, and to the third four; when in an instant they all presently fell asleep: but we resolving to find whether the effects were answerable to what the giant had told us, staid to see what would be the event. Now it so happened that the first dog, which had eaten two apples, in six hours' time awaked, and as if suddenly raised from a trance, like to one frantic, ran away from us, and we could never see him after. The second dog, having lain about the space of seven hours, giving great groans, began to stir and tumble about, but came not to himself till about an hour after, still continuing very sick; but we, giving him one of the precious apples, he presently revived and became well; but the third dog, who had taken four apples, never came to himself again: by which we experimented the nature of that poisonous fruit, thanking the Immortal Powers for our escaping so imminent a danger.

"This being done, we went all of us to the fountain, where we caroused of the wine very freely; and soon after came to us divers of the nobles and knights from Barcona; who beholding the bodies of the giant and lion, highly applauded our courage in the attempt, and with a general consent proffered us the government of the fountain, with all the island thereunto; which Sir Wonder freely accepted of; but I, being desirous to return home, as I had faithfully promised to those of my followers which remained, having furnished myself with what necessaries I wanted, took ship, and, after many difficulties, arrived in this island."

CHAPTER XVII.

How Sir Pandrusus, in his return homewards, came to an Island where Sir Phelim and Sir Owen had killed a great Giant, and taken his Castle, and what torments the Giant inflicted on his prisoners.

SIR Pandrasus having finished his story, they all very much marvelled at the virtues of that rare fountain, king David resolving after some time to go and see it, with a desire also to visit his old friend Sir Wonder; but Sir Pandrasus being desirous to return home, furnished himself with all necessaries which were freely given him by king David and his queen Rosetta; and so taking his solemn leave of them both, he with the rest of the Danes, took ship, and with a prosperous gale cut the briny face of Neptune, and not meeting with any adventures remarkable, they came to an island called Micomicum, where they landed; and leaving some of the company to guard the ship, Sir Pandrasus with the rest marched up into the country, and came to a high hill, which was beautified with many stately trees, whose curled tops seemed to brave the skies; at the foot of this mountain lay the body of a giant newly killed, of a marvellous size, his eyes being as big as foot-balls, his mouth six feet wide, his skull so large, that, being emptied, it would hold five pecks of wheat, his shin-bones six feet in length, his whole body full eight-and-twenty feet long. They very much marvelled at the vast proportion of this giant, but more at the matchless strength of him that killed him; and being desirous to be further informed, they saw a plain beaten path leading up to the top of the hill, by which they ascended, and found on the top thereof a castle of a curious structure beautified with all the cost and cunning that the height of fancy could express; and upon the front whereof was a large tablet of brass, wherein these lines were written:

> "Within this castle lives the scourge of kings,
> The giant Briomart, of wond'rous might;
> That to his pow'r he doth subdue all things,
> Whoever dares encounter him in fight:
> As hundreds by their deaths have plain made known,
> Who by his martial might have been o'erthrown,
> Let none then dare to enter in this gate,
> Lest for his folly he repent too late."

Sir Pandrasus, having read the writing, notwithstanding he saw the giant slain, yet not knowing what danger might ensue, commanded all his company to arm themselves before they entered into the castle; which being done, he himself went foremost with his sword drawn, when from the battlements a knight called to him to know what he was, and for what business he came thither. To whom Pandrasus made this answer: That he was of the country of Denmark, and being necessitated for provisions at sea, was come thither for succour. "And that shall you have freely," said the knight, "please you to stay whilst we come down to you;" when presently they were met by several persons unarmed, who with a smiling countenance came unto them; two of which company chanced to be Sir Phelim of Ireland, son of St. Patrick, and the valiant Welsh knight, Sir Owen of the Mountains, son of St. David who after their return from Cyprus, separated from Sir Turpin of France, and Sir Predo of Spain, chanced to arrive in this island ; and coming to the castle, having read the writing aforesaid, they resolved to encounter the giant, where, after a long tedious fight, valiantly performed on both sides, he was at last overcome and slain by them.

This giant was of a nature as cruel as those tigers who are nourished in the Hyrcanian wood, to whose heart nature had set a lock to shut out all pity, delighting to bathe and paddle in the blood of men ; so that the dread of him ran all the country round about, for whomsoever he took, he so tormented, that death was to them the least punishment. He kept only one old woman for his domestic servant, as cruel as deformed ; and so deformed, that I want art to describe the same. This deformed hag, whose face was enough to proclaim her a witch, all the time the fight was between the giant, Sir Owen, and Sir Phelim, was mumbling Satan's Pater-Noster for the good success of her master; but when she saw that he was slain, she exclaimed against heaven, and cursed all the infernal powers, wishing the ground might open and swallow them up, although she herself were enveloped in their destruction ; nay, her desperation was such, that she would have cast herself from the walls, and given her soul a cursed sacrifice to Satan, had she not been prevented by Sir Phelim ; who, as soon as he saw the giant fall, ran in at the gates, for fear they should have been shut against them ; and ascending the castle, found this old witch ready to have executed vengeance upon herself ; but he seizing upon her, found in her custody a great bunch of keys. And now Sir Owen, seeing the giant quite dead, was also come up to the castle, where, partly by threats, and partly by force, they compelled her to show them the several rooms, that they might not only release such as were prisoners therein ; but to see what variety of tortures this tyrant inflicted on those poor creatures, it would make any one almost distracted to behold them. In the first room she opened, there lay four knights bound neck and heels together ; they were four brothers, sons to a certain baron, named Clemander, who coming to revenge themselves upon the giant, who had defiled their sister, were by him taken prisoners ; having unbound them, and told them how the giant was killed, they were transported with an ecstasy of joy. In the next room they entered, there lay a young man loaded with irons of so vast a weight that he was not able to stand upright, and seemed to be only a living corpse ; with much ado they knocked the irons off his legs, who, whilst they were doing it, oftentimes swooned away, but being revived by some cordial spirits of rare waters which they had brought with them, they at last brought him to himself ; and demanding what he was, and what misfor-

2 A

tunes brought him thither, after two or three deep-fetched sighs, he thus said:

"I am," said he, "one born a native of this country, my father a count thereof; who in a quarrel having killed a peer of the realm, sought to fly into another land, but in his passage thither was drowned at sea; which my mother hearing of, fell distracted: and, to add to our miseries, the king seized upon his whole estate. But this was not all: for, as if Fate were resolved to use her utmost spite against me, my only sister, who was then upon her marriage, being thereby disappointed of her portion desperately stabbed herself; so that now all the happiness which remained to me was a security that I was so miserable that Fortune could not make me worse.

"Yet the king, commiserating my condition, took me to be one of the gentlemen of his bed-chamber, and withal allowed me a competent estate for my maintenance, so that my sorrows seemed in part to be mitigated; but as if my heart was a stage for nought but tragedies, this serene sky did not last long, for I and the king being out hunting, he was on a sudden surprised by this giant, none but I standing by him, although followed by a great company; the ugliness of his proportion so affrighted them, that they depended upon the protection of their lives to their feet. And now the king and I, thus left to his mercy, nothing would redeem our lives but the delivering up of this castle to him, which then was the royal mansion of his majesty; and though this was done according to his desire, yet this perfidious lump of flesh retained us both prisoners; and how he used the king is to me unknown; but for myself, my miseries under him were so great, that Death would have been very welcome to have arrested my body, and laid me in the cold prison of the grave."

This sorrowful relation wrought great compassion in the hearts of Sir Owen and Sir Phelim, who with wrathful countenances commanded the old hag to show them presently where the king was; but she denying there was any such one there, they threatened her with words, and that not prevailing, they cut off one of her fingers, telling her they would cut her in pieces joint by joint, if she did not perform it; whereupon she promised them that she would; and leading them up to the top of the castle, as if he had been imprisoned in one of the garrets, she cast herself from the top of the battlements to the ground, dashing her brains out against the pavement, and so made an end of her unworthy life. Sir Phelim and Sir Owen taking the keys from this wretched corpse, opened many doors, and in every room they went beheld sad spectacles of the giant's cruelty; and at last they came to the place where the king lay, whom they found making his moan in this manner:

"O ye Immortal Powers, what have I done to deserve the punishment inflicted on me? How is it that Death seizes on those who would willingly live, and flies from him who would court his embraces? O that Atropos would cut in twain the thread of life, to put a period to my miseries! But they are as inexorable as this monster of mankind, whose adamantine heart will not hearken to my request. Come, gentle Death! O come, come, for it is thou alone who canst ease my misery."

When they opened the door, he, seeing the keys in Sir Owen's hand, thinking they were come to torment him afresh, with a wrathful countenance thus spake unto them :

"Monsters of nature! whose wanton cruelty knows no end and who please yourselves in making others feel the effects of your tyranny, now satiate yourselves in cruelty : for you shall not be readier to afflict than I to suffer what the utmost of your malice can lay upon me."

Whilst thus he was proceeding in his exclamation, the young man who was taken prisoner with him came towards him as fast as his trembling legs would carry him, and falling on his knees, he said; "Most gracious sovereign, blame not these matchless heroes, whose invincible manhood hath gained our freedom, and whose peerless prowess hath overcome our insulting enemy."

The king, seeing young Clodius (for so was the gentleman named), was in a strange kind of amaze, not thinking any power possible able to overcome the giant; but being by them assured that he was slain, to confirm their words, they carried him to a window out of which he might behold his dead carcass : and at that time it was when Sir Pandrasus came unto them. Great was the joy amongst these valiant knights for their so happily meeting together ; but being informed by the king that there were many more prisoners behind, they resolved not to take any repast until they had set them all at liberty ; and so entering into several rooms, and setting free divers prisoners, they came at last to a room, wherein was enclosed a beautiful virgin, whom grief had almost distracted; who at their entrance into the room took no notice of them, but like to an entranced soul stood as one with ghosts affrighted.

"The miseries," said the king, "that this virgin hath endured, might move a heart of stone to pity, and cause the most obdurate soul to lament. She is the only daughter of a wealthy knight, endued as you see with Nature's chiefest ornaments ; so that, before grief had made a transfiguration of her, the queen of love might have served as a foil unto her. It was her chance, a fatal chance, to fall in love with a young gentleman that waited on her father, one answerable to her in all respects, had his estate been equal with his parts ; and he answering her love with like reciprocal affection. But as it is incident to lovers to meet with crosses, so did these at the very beginning thereof ; for her father coming to know it, this young gentleman, whose name was Matheo, was soon turned away, and forbid ever after from coming near unto the house, and she confined to a chamber without any other liberty ; but as love will creep where it cannot go, so did he find means to pursue his suit in love unto her, and as he thought in a safe way, and that in this manner :

"There was growing just by the chamber window where she lay, a stately tree, upon which in the dead of the night he used to ascend, and there had parley with his love. This they continued for some time, to their great content and satisfaction ; but it so chanced upon a night he was espied by one of the servants, who immediately informed his master thereof ; which when he heard he was so transported with rage, that taking a cross-bow, and aided with a glimmering light by Madam Cynthia, the pale-faced lady of the night, he sent a bullet into his belly, which wrought such effect, that tumbling from off the tree, he only said, 'My dearest, I die for love of thee ;' and presently expired.

"But when the lady saw what had happened, she fared like unto mad Orestes ; impatience lowering in her face : so that had she not been prevented, by a maid that came into the chamber at that moment, she had by a knife put a period to the race of her loathed life ; but being hindered of her design, she fell into a swoon, as if her soul had made a total separation from her body. Lying in this trance, the maid who came to her, ran and cried out for more help, but notwithstanding all the means they could use, it was long before her sullen soul would re-enter her body, or that any hopes of life were perceived ; yet could not all this mitigate the rage of her incensed father, who commanded she should be confined still to her chamber, and not any one suffered to remain with her ; wherefore in the night she uncorded the bed, and tying the line to a pillar of the window, by the help thereof she slid down to the ground, and wandering, she cared not whither, so she was out of the reach of her father's cruelty, she chanced to come near this castle, whom the giant espying, caught her flying from his loathed sight, and brought her into the castle, where, ever since she hath remained in the condition which you see."

CHAPTER XVIII.

How Sir Phelim and Sir Owen, with Sir Pandrasus, fought with the Giant Curio, who came to be revenged for the death of his brother Briomart.

THE king having ended his discourse, it wrought great compassion in all them that heard it, especially Sir Pandrasus, who much pitied her sad condition; and therefore, to comfort her, he having brought a bottle of the healing wine from that precious fountain whereof Sir Wonder was now governor, he gave her some part thereof to drink; which she no sooner had received, but her spirits revived, and her colour came to her as if fresh roses budded in her cheeks: and then telling her that now all danger was past, that the giant was killed, and she was freed, joy began by little and little to enter in at her heart. And now all parties being surrounded with joy, messengers were sent to all parts of the kingdom, to declare to them the joyful news of their king's delivery; whereupon, soon after a great number of lords, knights, and gentlemen came to congratulate their prince's freedom, and to express their joy for the death of the giant, whose dead body they beheld with great wonder and admiration. But in a few days it began to smell so abominably that they were forced to bury it.

But should I go about to express the great joy of the people for this wonderful victory, had I as many tongues as Argus had eyes, yet were I not able to express the same; the heavens were struck with the sound of the trembling bells. Mirth digged her pits in every cheek, Grief and Sorrow were buried, Care was cashiered, and every soul was cheered with gladness.

Amongst other news that came to the castle, one was, that the knight, father to the distressed lady, was dead, whereby she became heiress to his whole estate; who, having notice thereof, notwithstanding his great unkindness to her, yet did she make great lamentation for him, showing therein the true nature of a dutiful child. After some few days passed, through the earnest solicitations of the king, Sir Phelim, Sir Owen of the Mountains, and Sir Pandrasus, she was persuaded to cast her affections upon the young count that was her fellow-prisoner; in consideration whereof the king restored him to all his father's estate, and made him an earl.

The marriage was solemnized with great splendour; when on a sudden there was a great uproar, and cry of the people, who came running towards the castle, as swiftly whirling as the whisking wind; for this giant Briomart had a brother named Curlo, who lived in an island hard by, where he used as much cruelty as his brother did in this: he, hearing of the slaughter of his brother Briomart, raised what force he could, and landing in the island, killed all that he could catch, sparing neither men, women, nor children. This being made known to these valiant knights, they armed themselves with all the speed they could, mustered what forces they could raise at present; and being prepared, they staid near unto the castle, expecting the coming of the enemy, who with great pride and confidence came marching towards the castle; the giant Curlo at the head of them. Sir Phelim seeing the giant marching in this manner, with a strong pole-axe came up to him; between whom began a most fierce encounter. In the mean time the two armies joined together, with as much rage and fury as was possible, each striving to exceed the other who should cloy Death's jaws the soonest, so that the field was strewn with dead carcasses, and mounds of slain bodies surrounded with moats of blood: Sir Owen and Sir Pandrasus making lanes to pass wheresoever they went, as if they together minded mankind's destruction. None were spared but every one sacrificed to the sword.

Whilst they were thus in the heat of the fight, the king, with the new bridegroom-earl, came, with those whom desire of liberty and allegiance to their sovereign had brought to take up arms with him, and giving a furious onset to the adverse party, they were forced a little to retire: but the giant Curlo had so far prevailed against Sir Phelim, that he was forced to recoil; whereupon our new earl, to add to his honour, entered in combat with the giant; but alas! his strength was not answerable to his heart, having been so much enfeebled by his long imprisonment: so that, notwithstanding Sir Phelim did all he could in his rescue, yet was he slain by him; which Sir Owen of the Mountains perceiving, with great rage, guided by courage, and governed by discretion, joined with a manly resolution, opposed himself against the giant, and so lustily laid about him, that in the end he brought him down headlong; who in his fall made such a horrid loud noise as filled the people with terror, like the roar of a whole herd of lions, enough almost to make an earthquake. But Sir Owen knowing the success of the battle depended upon the giant's life, nimbly leaped on him, and with his keen falchion cut off his head; which when the rest of his soldiers perceived, they thought to save themselves by flight: but these valiant knights were so exasperated by the death of this new earl, that, banishing all pity from their breasts, like enraged lions they fell upon them, and without remorse never ceased till they left not one of them alive.

And now having obtained such an absolute victory, they returned again in triumph, carrying the dead body of the earl to his newly married lady, and now disconsolate widow. When she beheld the corpse she was like one quite bereft of reason. "And am I," said she, "capable of more sorrow! Can all the compass of the light show a more unhappy creature than I? Did I no sooner receive a glimpse of comfort, but on a sudden to be thrown down again into a dungeon of misery? Ah, my dear lord, since I could not live with thee, I will not live without thee!" and with that she would have struck a knife to her heart, had she not been prevented by those that stood by her, "And will you also," said she, "become my enemies? What injury have I done you, that ye deprive me of the only benefit I desire to enjoy!" And now again she would have killed herself, but was the second time prevented. But the king, Sir Phelim, Sir Owen, and Sir Pandrasus, with much entreaty persuaded her, that she engaged to them not to lay violent hands upon herself; and the better to divert her from any such thoughts, and to cheer up her heart, overladen with grief, the king made a most sumptuous banquet, to which were invited all the lords, knights, and chief captains then present; against which time divers pastimes were devised, and costly shows performed, with most excellent music, rare dancing, and other delights, to provoke her to mirth; but all was as water spilt on the ground: it made no impression upon her soul; such indelible characters of sorrow had grief engraven on her heart.

And now these warlike knights, wishing to go into their own countries, took their solemn leave of the king, who rewarded them with many rich gifts and presents, giving them many thanks for the valour shown in his defence: so taking ship, they launched from shore; when soon the sails grew big-bellied with the wanton wind, and the ship glided safely on Neptune's briny face, capering for joy upon the silver waves, until such time as they each of them arrived in their own countries; where they were received with much joy, and where we will leave them for the present, to relate what befel Sir David in going to see Sir Wonder at the Fountain of Health.

CHAPTER XIX.

How Sir David sailed to the precious Fountain, and rescued Sir Wonder. How he put to death the tyrant Almantor, and settled again Pandion to his estate.

THE valorous and renowned champion Sir David, being now well settled in his kingdom of Ancona, as related in the Fifteenth Chapter, was very desirous to see Sir Wonder, and to experience the effects of the precious fountain, as Sir Pandrasus had declared unto him: wherefore, selecting out a choice number of approved soldiers, he took ship, and having a prosperous wind, he in a few days arrived in that fertile island: but, contrary to his expectation, instead of being received with great friendship, no sooner was he landed but a number of armed soldiers came marching against him, bidding him either leave the country or yield up his arms into their hands, or else to abide what their force could compel him to. For so it was, that soon after the departure of Sir Pandrasus, those of the Warlike Island, understanding the rare virtues of the fountain, and the fruit that grew on the banks of it, resolved to become masters thereof; and to that purpose in friendly manner visited Sir Wonder, seeming to applaud his happy fortune in being possessed of so rare and precious a jewel as that fountain; and so far did they insinuate into his favour, that he trusted them with all his secrets, which they wrought to his ruin; for after a while they locked him in an inner room, and seized on his servants by a party which they secured in a private place: and from that time while Sir David landed, had kept them close prisoners.

But now was the time of their deliverance come about; for Sir David, understanding there was no way to be used but force, setting his men in order, gave such a charge as put them to the rout, the greatest part of them being slain in the chase. The residue of them that escaped, flying to the fountain, raised all their whole force; who having armed themselves, speedily marched against Sir David. And now began a most terrible fight between them, and such a cruel slaughter of men, that the earth was covered with dead bodies. Sir David with his keen falchion hewed his way through his enemies, until he came unto their general, with whom he encountered hand to hand; and after many blows exchanged between them, slew him outright; whereupon the residue sought to save themselves by flight, but were so eagerly pursued, that very few of them escaped; not above three persons returned alive. And then giving thanks to the Immortal Powers for this great victory, they went the next day to the fountain, and released Sir Wonder and the rest of his men from their captivity.

Great was the joy at this their meeting; for Sir Wonder, notwithstanding his vast strength, yet was so strongly imprisoned, that he despaired of ever regaining his former liberty, which being so unexpected, made him prize it the greater. Then did Sir David with his soldiers drink of the wine of the fountain; when presently they felt the powerful virtue thereof, being in an instant as fresh and lively as when they first began the fight. Afterwards Sir Wonder banquetted them with the fruits of the trees that grew upon the banks thereof, which were of such various tastes, and yet all of them so delicious, as gave great satisfaction to the most fastidious palate. But they were not only delightful to the taste, and pleasant to the appetite, but also of that super-excellent virtue, that whosoever tasted of them was immediately cured of all the hurts and wounds he had about him, were they ever so deep and deadly.

That night they slept soundly, and the next morning went forth to behold the rarities of the country. In every place they came to they heard the birds, the air's winged choristers, warbling forth their ditties most harmoniously, as if with their chirping they sung carols to the rosy morn, and with their music courted the sullen wood, and invited mortals to walk abroad.

Besides the singing-birds named before, there was an infinite number of partridges, pheasants, quails; and phœnixes, which are not to be found in other countries, but were here very plentiful; all which were so tame that you might take them up in your hands, and being killed, and held up against the sun, would be instantly roasted, needing no basting but their own fat; but in the eating they were so delicious, that the choicest viands, which your curious cooks with much art prepare, came far short of their goodness.

Being thus extraordinarily well satisfied in beholding the curiosities of this incomparable island, they drew down to the sea-side, where they sat beholding how the ocean's fry were playing on the briny face of Neptune; and casting their eyes a little farther, they beheld a boat come rowing towards them, wherein sat an old man, whose hair did wear the sober hue of grey, and whose wrinkled countenance seemed to cast the account of many cares. They came rowing directly towards them; and being landed, the old gentleman desired to speak with the chiefest of their company; and being brought unto Sir David, he spake to him in this manner:

"Most worthy knight, whose valiant acts are immortalized all the world over; let melting pity creep into your heart to give some comfort to my calamity. Know then, most worthy chieftain, that in my native country, being an island hard by, there liveth a cruel tyrant, one whose will is his law, and who seldom sleeps soundly unless he hath blood for his bolster, thinking nothing unlawful that makes for his advantage; and to that intent keeping a constant kennel of blood-hounds to accuse whom he pleaseth, and who are so desperately wicked for his purpose, that they will depose whatsoever he would have them. By these men was I accused of having conspired against his life, and though there were neither plain evidence, nor any circumstances conducible thereunto, yet being judge in his own cause, I was condemned and presently had my estate seized on; which indeed was the main cause of my accusation.

"I was then blest with a lovely daughter, named Tremelia, for whom this tyrant had base desires, and took her from me, pretending to keep her as a pledge of my fidelity; but having her in his keeping, sought to violate her; but she resisting his impure desires, and having given him some opprobrious words, he in a great rage struck her to the heart with his dagger. I having notice of what was passing, thought it high time to provide for myself; and daring to trust no-

warbling forth their ditties most harmoniously, as if with
their chirping they sung carols to the rosy morn, and with
their music courted the sullen wood, and invited mortals to
walk abroad.

Besides the singing birds, indeed there was an
infinite number of partridges, pheasants, quails, and phœ-
nixes, which are not to be found in other countries, but here very plentiful; all which were so tame that one might take them up in your hands, and being killed and held up against the sun, would be instantly roasted, needing nothing but their own fat; but in the eating they were so delicious, that the choicest viands, which your cooks with never so much art prepare, came far short of their goodness.

Being thus extraordinarily well satisfied in beholding the
curiosities of this incomparable island, they drew near to the
sea-side, where they sat beholding how the waves they went playing on the briny face of Neptune; and coming some-what a little farther, they beheld a boat some rowing towards them, wherein sat an old man, whose hair did wear the silver livery of grey, and whose wrinkled countenance seemed like the ruins on account of many cares. They came rowing directly towards them; and being landed, the old gentleman stepped up to them with the chiefest of their company; and looking wistfully on Sir David, he spake to him in this manner:

"Most worthy knight, whose valiant actions resoundeth all the world over; let melting pity assuage your noble breast, and give some comfort to my miseries. Know that I am a great chieftain, that in my native country _____ there liveth a cruel tyrant, _____ seldom _____ soundly _____ thin_____ to t_____ acc_____ for_____ hav_____ aga_____

cc, we (and om it

body, I lay hid for two or three days and nights among bushes, thorns, and brakes, when, disguising myself, I went to a village hard by, where I heard of your noble achievements in conquering this island; hoping, according to your former favours to others in distress, that you would afford me some succour in redressing my wrongs."

Sir David hearing this sad relation of the ancient gentleman, was moved with great pity towards him, so that he vowed, by the honour of knighthood, either to revenge him of the tyrant, or lose his life in the attempt: and so giving the ancient gentleman some of the water of the fountain to drink, and some of the apples to eat, he was so refreshed, that he seemed to forget his former sorrows, and to have new life and vigour inspired in him. They therefore agreed to send for more succour from Sir David's country, intending to stay there until their return; but in the mean time this ambitious tyrant, whose name was Almantor, having heard how this island was conquered by a few persons, and of the rare qualities belonging thereunto, he thought in an instant to surprise it; and to that purpose manned out what force he could make, and with great bravery sailed toward this fruitful island, having conquered it in conceit before he came thither. Sir David, seeing this fleet of ships, laid an ambush to surprise them, and upon their first landing seemed to fly, until he had brought them into the net prepared for them, when, turning head, he gave them such a brisk charge, as put them to a fatal rout. Almantor himself fought most valiantly, doing what in him lay to obtain the victory; and as if he had a spirit that dare war against the Fates, seemed to dread no danger; but all his valour would not bear him out against Sir David, who coming up to him with hardy blows, after a smart fight, took him prisoner. Few were saved alive besides; for the soldiers were so enraged against them, that all compassion was for the present banished their breasts.

The victory being thus obtained, they led Almantor towards the fountain, where first they refreshed themselves with some of those healing fruits, and afterwards sat in judgment upon him; where was laid to his charge all the tyrannies, murders, and rapines which he had committed; all which he could not excuse, nor very well deny, and therefore he was adjudged for his crimes to be put to death. His crimes were of too sanguine a dye to be forgiven, and all his sorrow only feigned: they therefore concluded he should be put to death, and gave him choice of eight sorts of ways whereby to die: viz. 1. to be hanged on a gibbet; 2. to be put into a sack, and thrown into the sea; 3. to have his head smitten off; 4. to be poisoned; 5. to be burned to death; 6. to be stung to death with snakes; 7. to be cast down head-long from a high tower; or, 8. to be shot to death with arrows.

"Sad is the choice," said the wretched Almantor, "choose which I will : for, 1. to hanged on a gibbet, is to die the death of a dog ; 2. to be put into a sack and drowned, is to be devoured by fishes, and want decent burial ; 3. to have my head smitten off, is indeed the death of a nobleman, but which no nobleman would willingly have ; 4. to be poisoned, is to be a stinking carcass before I am cold in my grave ; 5. to be burned, is of all deaths the most cruel ; 6. to be stung to death of snakes, is a painful lingering death ; 7. to be cast from a high tower, uncertain death. What then remains, but the last kind of death, to be killed with arrows? and that is the death of a soldier, which I shall sooner choose. Come then, seeing you think me not fitting to live, quickly dispatch me out of the world."

Then rending open his doublet, he tied a handkerchief before his eyes, and leaning his back against a tree, he cried out, "Now do your worst;" whereupon immediately some soldiers, who were planted on purpose, sent a flight of arrows into his breast, so that in an instant he fell down and died.

Whilst this was doing, the soldiers which Sir David had sent for arrived in the island ; whereupon Sir David, leaving some few for the guarding of the island under the conduct of the giant Wonder, he with the residue sailed towards the island where Almantor lived, taking along with him the ancient gentleman for his guide, and sailing thither in the same ships wherein Almantor came ; which they of the island espying, seeing their own ships afar off, began to rejoice ; but when they perceived strangers in them, they began to arm themselves with all the speed they could, and put themselves in a posture to resist their landing. But Sir David, nothing daunted at their appearance, landed in despite of all the resistance they could make, and with his sword quickly made way for his soldiers to follow him, who, encouraged by his example, soon made lanes of their slaughtered enemies. But now the fury of their rage being over, Sir David, scorning to insult over a vanquished party, caused a retreat to be sounded, and sent messengers after them, that he would parley with them ; to which they willingly condescended, and to that purpose sent three or four of the chiefest of them, to whom Sir David spake as followeth :

"The cause of my sending to you is, to offer you peace and liberty : liberty from the thraldom of an insulting tyrant, to whose insatiable avarice you were in thrall ; one who not only delighted in cruelty, but took delight in executing the same ; who hath now paid his just deserts by the stroke of justice, being shot to death for his cruel tyranny : instead of whom we shall present you for your governor one well known" (and here he presented to them the ancient gentleman,) " whom if you refuse to accept, then expect no other than what the sword and a conquering arm will enforce you to do."

The messengers having heard these words, with a loud voice cried out, "Long live our lord Pandion" (for so was the ancient gentleman called); and thereupon they desired leave to acquaint the rest with their determination; which when they had done, there was a general acclamation and shout of the people. And thereupon coming all to Sir David, they submitted themselves, promising faithful obedience to the aged Pandion. And having settled him in the tyrant Almantor's place, he returned to the island of the precious fountain; where leaving a sufficient guard with Sir Wonder, he returned back to his own country, where he was very welcome to queen Rosetta, and joyfully entertained by the rest of his subjects.

CHAPTER XX.

How Sir Guy, Sir Alexander, Sir David, as also Sir Turpin of France, Sir Predo of Spain, Sir Orlando of Italy, Sir Ewin of Scotland, Sir Phelim of Ireland, and Sir Owen of Wales, met at great Jousts at Constantinople.

SIR David had not been long in the kingdom of Ancona, but there arrived an herald, who proclaimed solemn jousts, to be held by the emperor of Constantinople, in honour of his son's nuptials, who was contracted to the king of Trebizond's daughter, the beauteous Lucinda. These jousts were proclaimed in all the kingdoms of the earth; so that at the time appointed there arrived at his court the most approved knights that were then living: amongst others were St. George's three renowned sons, Sir Guy, Sir Alexander, and Sir David; the valiant Sir Turpin from France, Sir Predo from Spain, Sir Orlando from Italy, Sir Ewin from Scotland, Sir Phelim from Ireland, and Sir Owen from Wales. Being come to the emperor's palace, they were by him most kindly entertained: and because the jousts only lasted nine days, he appointed each of them to be champion on his particular day.

But before the jousts began, the prince Rosinda, son to the emperor, was with great magnificence married to the beauteous Lucinda. Great were the triumphs performed that day by pageants, fireworks, and other costly devices; all which we shall pass over, and speak of the warlike acts performed by our nine renowned heroes.

On the first day of the jousts entered Sir Guy, king of Sicily, mounted on a Barbary steed. His armour, like the colour of his horse, was a dark brown; and for his device on his shield was an anchor, with these words, "Anchora spe." Against him entered a Phrygian knight named Dorosus, upon a sorrel horse of an Epiran breed and flaming nostrils. His armour was green; and the device on his shield a laurel tree, with these words, "Ever flourishing." At the trumpet's sound they encountered each other with such great skill and violence, that, breaking their staves, the splinters flew into the air. But at the third course Sir Guy ran against him with such might, that both horse and man fell to the ground. With like valour did he overcome twenty-five knights, and was with great triumph conducted home unto his lodging.

The next day Sir Alexander entered the lists, as chief challenger against all comers. His armour was red : and for his device in his shield was an ox bleeding, with these words, "Such to opposers." The first that ran against him was a Macedonian lord, named Lentulus, of gigantic stature, and approved manhood ; but by the valour of Sir Alexander he was overthrown, as also nineteen other knights of prowess and fortitude.

The third day Sir David appeared in the lists, chief champions against all opposers. His horse was a chestnut colour ; his armour azure ; and on his shield was painted a serene sky, with these words, "Without clouds." This valiant knight behaved himself so well that day, that he brought to the ground thirty-four knights, to his great commendation and honour.

On the fourth day appeared for chief champion against all comers the renowned Sir Turpin of France, mounted on an Arabian courser. His armour was of a tawny colour ; and on his shield was painted an orange tree, with these words, "Fruitfully comforting." This valiant knight behaved himself so gallantly that day, that the emperor threw unto him a gold chain, at the end whereof hung a rich medal beset with pearls and diamonds.

On the fifth day the heroic knight Sir Predo of Spain entered the lists, mounted on a Spanish jennet. His armour was of a flame colour ; his device in his shield was a salamander living in the fire, with these words. "Not so consumed." This renowned knight by his martial prowess overthrew no less than thirty-four champions that encountered with him ; insomuch that the princess Lucinda gave him her glove to wear, and called him her knight.

Upon the sixth day, as Sir Orlando of Italy entered the lists, there met him a squire, who spake to him in these words ; " Sir knight, my master by me advises you to make the best defence you can, that by your stout resistance he may obtain the greater honour in your overthrow." To whom Sir Orlando replied ; " Go tell thy master I am prepared for him : and that it is not good to sell the lion's skin until he be dead." Accordingly hereunto encountering each other, they fought with so much skill and valour, that Mars might have been a spectator of their worthy achievements, being men of such prowess as not to know fear themselves, and yet to teach it to others that had to deal with them. Long time did Victory equally play upon their dancing banners; but at last Conquest displayed her silver wings on Sir Orlando's head, and his antagonist's brags vanished in smoke, his body with his honour being laid in the dust. With the like success did he overcome eighteen knights that day, whereby he won the reputation of a most valiant knight.

On the seventh day the renowned knight Sir Ewin of Scotland was chief champion, who entered the lists, on a Scottish galloway. His armour was black; as also his shield, with these letters in white, "Hoping for day." His success was such that he foiled no less than sixty knights, gaining to himself immortal fame by their overthrow.

The eighth day was managed by Sir Phelim of Ireland, as brave a knight as ever trod the field of Mars. He was mounted on an Irish hobby, decked with a plume of peacock's feathers: his armour so contrived as if it had been made up of several pieces, yet all joined together in a loving confusedness. On his shield was pourtrayed a robin-red-breast, with these words, "Innocently harmless." He encountered that day with twenty-five knights, all of whom he overcame.

On the ninth and last day there entered the lists that heroic undaunted knight Sir Owen of the Mountains, mounted on a stately English palfrey. His armour was milk-white; his attiring else all cut in stars, which made the cloth of silver spangles each way seem to cast many aspects. In his shield was a sheep feeding in a pleasant field, with these words, "Without fear or envy." This valiant knight Sir Owen behaved himself so gallantly, and dismounted so many knights that day, that the prince Rosinda entitled him, "The Mirror of Chivalry, and Pattern of true Magnanimity."

After the jousts were finished, the emperor entertained these nine worthy knights in a most sumptuous manner, spending several days in their company, and, in reward of their martial performances, gave unto them nine most rich and precious stones, each of them valued at a king's ransom, besides other rich presents from the prince and princess; and so taking their solemn leave of the emperor and other high estates, with great honour and applause, they returned each to his own country.

MILNER AND SOWERBY, PRINTERS, HALIFAX.

www.ingramcontent.com/pod-product-compliance
Lightning Source LLC
Chambersburg PA
CBHW020741020526
44115CB00030B/724